Theology of the New Testament

THEOLOGY

OF THE

NEW TESTAMENT

by

RUDOLF BULTMANN

Professor Emeritus of New Testament,
University of Marburg

VOLUME II

TRANSLATED BY

KENDRICK GROBEL

CHARLES SCRIBNER'S SONS

This translation was supported in part by funds
made available jointly by the Carnegie Foundation
and Vanderbilt University. The author and the
translator are solely responsible for the statements
made in this book.

Contents

PART III

The Theology of the Gospel of John and the Johannine Epistles

PART IV

The Development toward the Ancient Church

[v]

CONTENTS

PART THREE

THE THEOLOGY
OF THE GOSPEL OF JOHN
AND THE JOHANNINE EPISTLES

CHAPTER I

Orientation

§ 41. The Historical Position of John

1. To determine the historical locus of the Gospel of John (with which the Epistles of John are closely connected*) a *comparison with the synoptics*, which for the time being must confine itself to form and characteristic themes, is of service. The distance which separates John both from the proclamation of Jesus and from that of the oldest Church is straightway apparent. Whether John was acquainted with one or more of our synoptics is debated; at any rate, it cannot be proved with certainty that he was. Nevertheless, he is familiar with the tradition which is worked into shape in them, as is clear from certain sayings of Jesus, from certain miracle stories, and especially from the account of the passion. The miracle stories, which the evangelist presumably took from a written source, indicate by their very style a more advanced stage of development than that of the synoptic tradition.† Originally, their point lay in the miracle they report, but for the evangelist they take on a symbolic or allegorical

---

* Whether the Epistles were written by the author of the Gospel himself or simply came out of his "school," can here be disregarded. In the following discussion, references to the Gospel are given simply by chapter and verse; references to the Epistles have I Jn., etc., prefixed.

Quotations from the Bible are given according to the Revised Standard Version, copyrighted 1946 and 1952, with the kind permission of the copyright owner, Division of Christian Education, National Council of the Churches of Christ in the U.S.A., unless there is an indication to the contrary. "Blt." (=Bultmann's version) means that the author himself translated the passage into German, for which an English equivalent is here offered; "tr." (=translator's version) means that the author quoted only the Greek text, which the translator of this book felt compelled to translate anew in the sense implied by the author's context. Rarely King James or a modern private translation is quoted, and always by name.

† For this assertion and all that follows I refer to my commentary "Das Evangelium des Johannes" in Meyer's *Kommentar*, 2nd ed., 1950.

meaning, and throughout the Gospel he uses them as points of departure for discourses or discussions, which, throughout his presentation, are the form of Jesus' activity. The result is a stylistically and historically completely different picture from that depicted by the synoptics. The latter offer short dialogues with disciples or opponents in which Jesus answers the honestly inquiring or his opponents with a short, striking saying (often formulated as a counter-question or a figurative saying). Instead of this, we find in John an extended discourse of Jesus or a dialogue occasioned by the miracles or by ambiguous statements or concepts like being born ἄνωθεν, 3:3f. ("again" or "from above") or ὕδωρ ζῶν, 4:10ff. ("running water" or "living water"). While the speeches of Jesus in the synoptics are mostly sayings strung on a string, in John they are coherent discussions on a definite theme. Into such discourses and dialogues are woven the few sayings which John adopted out of the synoptic tradition (2:19; 4:44; 12:25f.; 13:16, 20; 15:20). The themes taken up are not those found in the synoptics. In John, Jesus appears neither as the rabbi arguing about questions of the Law nor as the prophet proclaiming the breaking in of the Reign of God. Rather, he speaks only of his own person as the Revealer whom God has sent. He does not argue about the Sabbath and fasting or purity and divorce but speaks of his coming and his going, of what he is and what he brings the world. He strives not against self-righteousness and untruthfulness but against disbelief toward himself. And precisely where a theme of Jesus' synoptic preaching seems to lie before us—the accusation of breaking the Sabbath, ch. 5 and ch. 9—the difference is apparent. For here attention is not focused upon the question how far the Sabbath-commandment has validity for *man* (as in Mk. 2:23–3:6); rather, the authority of Jesus as Son of God is being demonstrated. The parables so characteristic of the synoptic Jesus are completely lacking; in their place appear the great symbolic discourses of the good shepherd (ch. 10) and the true vine (ch. 15) which by a symbolic figure represent Jesus as the Revealer. They belong to a cycle of words and discourses whose distinguishing characteristic is the "I am . . ." of the Revealer, and are without analogy in the synoptics. Even the passion narrative, in whose outline John is, relatively speaking, nearest to the synoptics, is completely transformed. Jesus' last meal with his disciples is no longer the Passover meal, nor does it institute the Lord's Supper; it is the point of departure for long farewell discourses which are without parallel in the synoptics. The dialogues in the hearings before the Sanhedrin and Pilate are completely transformed, as is the account of the crucifixion, which closes with the Revealer's utterance, "It is accomplished" (tr.)—just as in the beginning of the Gospel the Baptist is no longer the preacher of repentance but the witness to Jesus as the Son of God.

While in the synoptics the vicissitudes, the problems, and the faith of the earliest Church are reflected, scarcely anything of the sort can any longer be discovered in John. The questions that were characteristic for the earliest Church—the validity of the Law, the coming or the delay of the Reign of God—have died out. The problem of the mission to the Gentiles is no longer actual, as a comparison of Mt. 8:5–13; Lk. 7:1–10 with Jn. 4:46–54 indicates: a story which once told about the faith of a Gentile now serves to answer the question about the relation between faith and miracle. Proof from prophecy plays a scanty role: only in 2:17; 12:14f., 38, 40; 13:18; 15:25; 19:24, 36f. and perhaps in 6:31 and 45 does it occur. The single problem that has retained its old importance is that of the relationship of Jesus and the Church to the Baptist and his followers (*cf.* Mk. 2:18 and parallels, Mt. 11:2–19, par., Lk. 11:1), indeed it has gained in importance (1:6–8, 15, 19–36; 3:23–30; 5:33–35; 10:40–42), and Acts 18:25 and 19:1–7 also show that this problem was occupying the Hellenistic Church. So far as the situation of the Church is reflected in the Gospel of John, its problem is the conflict with Judaism, and its theme is faith in Jesus as the Son of God. The Christian congregation is already excluded from the synagogue association (9:22; 16:1–3)—in fact, the evangelist feels the Church's estrangement from Judaism to be so great that in his account Jesus already appears as no longer a member of the Jewish people or its religion but speaks to the Jews of their Law as "your Law" as if he were a non-Jew (8:17; 10:34; *cf.* 7·19, 22). In John, "the Jews" no longer appear in their concrete differentiation as "pious" and "sinners," tax-collectors and harlots, scholars in the Law or fishermen, but simply as "the Jews," differentiated only into "the multitude" and the leaders, who are called "the rulers" or the "high-priests" or "the Pharisees," the last of whom are often conceived as a sort of official board (7:45, 47f.; 11:47, 57). Furthermore, for John "the Jews" are representatives of "the world" in general which refuses to respond to Jesus with faith.

[5]

2. The observation that in John the Pauline discussion about the Law plays no role has often led to the false deduction that John must be regarded as the culmination of the development that leads out beyond Paul, a culmination in which the debates about the Law are a thing of the past. But the *relation of John to Paul* cannot be understood on a linear scheme of development from the theology of the earliest Church; the two lie in quite different directions. Since John is somewhat remote from the earliest Church, he is likely younger than Paul; but he does not presuppose Paul as a link between himself and the earliest Church. The later development of Paulinism is shown by the deutero-Pauline literature (Col., Eph., II Thess., the pastorals, I Pet.)—it is a different world from that of John.

It is true, however, that in regard to the *current religious atmosphere* Paul and John have certain things in common. Both come within the sphere of a Hellenism that is saturated with the Gnostic stream, so that a certain agreement between them in dualistic terminology is not surprising. Both use the term "world" (κόσμος) in the dualistic depreciatory sense and also agree in understanding "world" as basically the world of men (3:16f., etc.; for Paul see § 26). The antitheses typical of John—"truth-falsehood" (8:44; I Jn. 2:21, 27), "light-darkness" (1:5, 8:12; I Jn. 1:5, etc.)—also occur, at least occasionally, in Paul (Rom. 1:25; II Cor. 4:6).* The antithesis "earthly-heavenly" is found in both (3:12; I Cor. 15:40; *cf.* Phil. 2:10). Above all, in both John and Paul christology is formed after the pattern of the Gnostic Redeemer-myth (§ 15, 4c, I, pp. 174–6): the sending of the pre-existent Son of God in the disguise of a man (Phil. 2:6–11; Jn. 1:14, etc.). The parallel Adam-Christ, it is true, is not drawn in John as it is in Paul (Rom. 5:12ff.; I Cor. 15:21f., 45f.). Yet for John, too, the sending of the Redeemer is the eschatological event; it is the turning-point of the ages (3:19; 9:39, etc.; Gal. 4:4). However, the Johannine terminology of the Redeemer's "coming" and "going" (8:14, etc.) and John's ambiguous "be exalted" (ὑψωθῆναι, 3:14, etc.) are lacking in Paul. John, for his part, avoids expressions that stem from Jewish apocalyptic and are frequent in Paul ("this age," I Cor. 1:20, etc.; "the fulness of time," Gal. 4:4; a "new creation," II Cor. 5:17; Gal. 6:15 and the like).

* II Cor. 6:14 is not cited because it is non-Pauline; see I, p. 202, note 1. For "darkness" Paul says not σκοτία but σκότος, a word which occurs in John only at 3:19 and I Jn. 1:3.

Nor is it surprising that Paul and John agree to a certain extent in the use of *common-Christian terminology*. Like Paul and the rest of the New Testament John, too, naturally speaks of "life (eternal)" as that which salvation gives, though he scarcely speaks of the Reign of God any more (3:3, 5; I, p. 76). The terms "joy" (17:13, etc.; Rom. 14:17, etc.) and "peace" (14:27, etc.; Rom. 14:17, etc.) serve to describe the gift of salvation, though they are used by John in a peculiar way: as gifts of the departing Jesus to the Congregation remaining behind in the world. Agreement in the use of "send" (ἀποστέλλω and πέμπειν) for the sending of Jesus (Gal. 4:4; Rom. 8:3, Jn. *passim*), or of "give" (διδόναι 3:16, for which the common-Christian expression is παραδιδόναι, "give up" Rom. 8:32, etc.) for God's bestowal of him, are of course no indication of any special relation between John and Paul. Neither is their agreement on Jesus' exaltation to lordship in "glory" (17:5, etc.; Phil. 2:9; 3:21, etc.). The sending of the Spirit (15:26) to the Church after Jesus' exaltation is a common-Christian view (§ 14), not specifically Pauline, and there is no parallel in Paul for the name Paraclete which the Spirit bears in John. Though Is. 53:1 is quoted in defensive argument both in Jn. 12:38 and Rom. 10:16, that, of course, does not prove John's dependence upon Paul. If in the tradition utilized by John the saying of Jesus about following him quoted in 12:26 was already formulated with the word "servant" rather than "disciple" (Lk. 14:27), that may well be due to the influence of Pauline or of deutero-Pauline usage (II Cor. 3:6; Eph. 3:7, etc.).

Since there is such contact with common-Christian terminology in both John and Paul, it is all the more significant that *the specifically Pauline terminology is missing in John*. Though Paul and John both use the term "world" and in the same sense (see II, p. 6), Paul's dominant contrast "flesh-spirit" retreats far into the background in John, occurring only at 3:6 and 6:63. In fact, "flesh" only rarely occurs (1:13f.; I Jn. 2:16—except in the passages that speak of Jesus' coming "in flesh": I Jn. 4:2; II Jn. 7). The characteristic Pauline expression "according to flesh" (κατὰ σάρκα, see § 22, 3) has an analogy, if at all, only in κατὰ τὴν σάρκα, 8:15. "Desire" (ἐπιθυμία, § 23, 2) occurs only in 8:44, I Jn. 2:16; the verb "desire" (ἐπιθυμεῖν) never does. Paul's characteristic anthropological terminology derived from the Old Testament is not found in John: *soma* and *psyche* in the Pauline sense do not occur, "heart" is relatively rare (13:2; 14:1, 27;

[7]

16:6, 22 in addition to the quotation 12:40, with which *cf.* I Jn. 3:19–21), "mind" (νοῦς or νόημα) is completely missing. Also missing are "boast" and its cognates (καυχᾶσθαι, καύχημα, καύχησις) and "care," noun and verb (μέριμνα and μεριμνᾶν). Likewise missing are the terms that Paul took over from the Stoic-Cynic *diatribe*: "conscience," "virtue," "nature."

Still more important is the fact that *Paul's terminology relating specifically to the history of salvation is not encountered in John.* He does not know "God's righteousness" (δικαιοσύνη θεοῦ) as a designation for salvation itself; δικαιοσύνη occurs only in 16:8, 10 (where it means Jesus' "vindication"; i.e. his victory in the suit with the world in which he is involved) and in I Jn. 2:29; 3:7, 10 in the Old Testament phrase "to do righteousness." Naturally, then, rightwising (δικαιοῦσθαι, "to be justified") and the antithesis "by works of the Law—by faith" are lacking; in fact the noun "faith" is found only at I Jn. 5:4. For while πιστεύειν (believing) is demanded, it is demanded not in the specifically Pauline but in the common-Christian sense (I, pp. 88f.). Faith as the right way to salvation is not contrasted with false "zeal for God" (Rom. 10:3); in John the way to salvation as a problem actual for the Jew is not under discussion. The antithesis "law-grace" occurs only at 1:17, and here we evidently do have an echoing of Pauline terminology; but even in this case the Pauline antithesis is altered by the fact that the "grace" which is set up against "law" is combined with "truth." Otherwise, "grace" occurs only in 1:14, 16 and in the salutation-formula II Jn. 3; χάρισμα (an act of grace) and χαρίζεσθαι (to be graciously treated) are completely missing. The passion-narrative, Jn. 19, naturally mentions "the cross" and "crucify"; but it is not as terms of the history of salvation that these words are used. Hence, they occur neither among the words of Jesus nor in the Johannine epistles.

The history-of-salvation perspective as a whole is lacking in John. True, the Johannine Jesus appeals to Abraham against the Jews and denies their descent from Abraham (8:33–58); and in conflict with the Jews he knows Moses to be on his side (5:45f.; *cf.* 1:45). But the idea of God's covenant with Israel or of the new covenant, God's election of Israel and His guidance of the People play no role. Hence, it is quite understandable that the proof from prophecy scarcely plays any role (see above) and that the history-of-salvation term for the Congregation, *viz.* Church (ἐκκλησία, § 6, 2; § 10, 1) does not occur in John. The word is found only in III Jn. 6 and 9f., where it denotes the individual congregation. Of "calling" in the history-of-salvation sense, the "call," and "the called" (§10, 3) there is no mention. The verb "choose" (ἐκλέγεσθαι, 6:70; 13:18; 15:16, 19) may be an echoing of Paul's technical term, though in John it says of Jesus what otherwise is ascribed to God (I Cor. 1:27, etc.). But the nouns "choice" or "election" (ἐκλογή) and "the chosen" (ἐκγεκτοί, § 10, 3) are missing.* The designation of Christians as "saints" (ἅγιοι) or "sanctified ones" (ἡγιασμένοι, § 10, 3) is also missing, though Jn. 17:17 and 19 may be echoes of it. The Hellenistic ecclesiological terminology is also lacking —at least in the original text of the Gospel—and so is any reference to the Kyrios-cult and the sacraments. Kyrios occurs in redactional glosses in 4:1; 6:23; 11:2; otherwise only in ch. 20, the Easter story, as a designation of the risen Jesus. The sacraments were subsequently introduced into the text by editorial process (3:5; 6:51b–58).† The evangelist avoids speaking of them, evidently having misgivings about sacramental piety, even going so far as to omit narrating the institution of the Lord's Supper, for which he substitutes Jesus' farewell prayer, ch. 17.

Clearly, then, John is not of the Pauline school and is not influenced by Paul; he is, instead, a figure with his own originality and stands in an atmosphere of theological thinking different from that of Paul. As far as that goes, even in such a different atmosphere the influence of Paul could take effect, as Ignatius shows—a writer who is related to John by belonging with him to a certain world of thought, but who was nevertheless strongly influenced by Paul. Comparison with Ignatius well shows how much John stands by himself; and this independence of John emerges all the more clearly as one perceives *the deep relatedness in substance that exists between John and Paul* in spite of all their differences in mode of thought and terminology. This does not mean, of course, relatedness in such details as the fact that John like Paul can sum up the plural "works" into its singular "work" (6:28f.)—in which, moreover, the difference is greater than the resemblance because in John the "work" is faith and not that working which springs from faith, as it is in I Cor. 15:58, I Thess. 1:3. The real relatedness lies in the fact that in both of them the

---

* "Elect lady" II Jn. 1 and "elect sister" II Jn. 13, it seems, are designations of individual Christian congregations.
    † See below, § 47, 4.

eschatological occurrence is understood as already taking place in the present, though John was the first to carry the idea radically through. In both writers the idea of Jesus' "glory" is made historical occurrence (1:14; II Cor. 3:7ff.; I, p. 334), and for both the new life appears under the mask of death (11:25f.; 16:33; II Cor. 4:7ff.; I, pp. 345–7). Both John and Paul de-mythologize Gnostic cosmological dualism in the fact that by both the world continues to be understood as God's creation and in the fact that the God-concept of both contains the paradoxical union of judgment and grace. But all this must await the detailed presentation of Johannine theology for its clarification.

3. *Who the author of the Gospel and Epistles of John was* and where they were written is unknown. As to the time of writing only this much can be said: the Gospel must have originated some interval of time after the first literary fixation of the synoptic tradition but very probably still within the first century, since its existence is testified by quotations in papyri that come from the beginning of the second century.* At any rate, the thought-atmosphere out of which it (and the Epistles) grew is that of *oriental Christianity.* The Gospel as a whole was not originally written in a Semitic language (Aramaic or Syriac) and then translated into Greek, but was undoubtedly written in Greek. But its *language* is a semitizing Greek both as to grammar and to style, though in a different way from the Greek of the synoptics, of which the same is true. Furthermore, it is at least probable that the evangelist used an originally Aramaic (or Syriac) source in certain places: namely, for the prologue and the sayings and discourses of Jesus wherever they are not derived from the synoptic tradition or from the already mentioned (II, p. 3) collection of miracle-stories which also served him as a source. Whether it be that the source of Jesus' sayings and discourses—let us call it the "Revelation-discourses" after its chief content—was translated from the Semitic or was conceived in Greek, in any case its style is that of Semitic speech; more accurately, of Semitic poetry such as is known to us from the Odes of Solomon and other Gnostic texts. A definite plan, open, of course, to variation and frequently reworked into dialogues by the evangelist, underlies such revelation-discourses.

---

* The "Unknown Gospel," the fragments of which were edited in 1935 by H. Idris Bell and T. C. Skeat and especially the fragment of John edited by C. H. Roberts in 1935 indicate that John was known in Egypt about 100 A.D.

This plan includes the motif of the self-presentation of the Revealer introduced by the characteristic formula "I am . . ."; it also includes the call of invitation and promise and a threat for him who will not believe. The discourse unfolds in the parallelism of members that is characteristic of Semitic poetry. Here it displays the peculiarity that in cases of antithetic parallelism the antithesis is often not simply the opposite of the thesis (as it is, e.g. in Sir. 3:9; Mt. 8:20; Mk. 10:42–44), but a negation of the opposite made either by repeating the thesis with a negative or by some very slight alteration of its wording (e.g. 3:18a, 36a; 4:13f.; 8:23).

The stylistic form of the Revelation-discourses expresses the *basic dualistic view* which they presuppose. Also in keeping with this dualistic view are the antithetical terms which run through these discourses: light and darkness, truth and falsehood, above and below (or heavenly and earthly), freedom and bondage. We are led into the same sphere of dualistic-Gnostic thinking by the *symbols* which characterize the Revealer in his contrast to the "world" and in his meaning for salvation or which describe the gift he brings: he is the light of the world, the good shepherd, the true vine; he dispenses the water of life, the true bread from heaven. What he is and what he gives is "true" ($\dot{\alpha}\lambda\eta\theta\iota\nu\acute{o}s$, 1:9; 6:32; 15:1; I Jn. 2:8); in fact, he can simply be called "the truth" (14:6)—which is just the mode of expression of that dualism to which everything earthly is falsehood and seeming. All that man seeks in this world and all that he thinks he finds is, in the Revealer, "truth"—i.e. reality. In all that man seeks he is seeking "life"—in the Revealer it is present. As he is "the truth," he is also "life" (14:6; I Jn. 1:2). Of course, for Paul also and for primitive Christianity as a whole, as indeed for the Old Testament and Judaism, "life" is the redemptive good that is striven for. But it came to be the dominant designation of salvation only in those circles of the Hellenistic religions, and especially Gnosticism, in which the life of this world lost its lustre and worth to such a degree that it was regarded as a mere semblance of life which in truth is death. It is from within such an atmosphere that John writes, and in his writing the terms "truth" and "life" take the place of "Reign of God" and "righteousness of God."

Terminologically, this complex of views is also expressed by the fact that Jesus as the Revealer is called he whom the Father has "sent" or "commissioned." This mode of expression, too, ($\pi\acute{e}\mu\pi\epsilon\iota\nu$, "send," or ἀποστέλλειν "commission") took on a special meaning in Gnosticism.* It is characteristic for this dualistic view because it denotes the irruption of the beyond into the here in the person of a Revealer— the Ambassador. In him the world of "truth" and "life" appears within the realm of this world; the eschatological event becomes present reality in his word which as the Ambassador he speaks in his Father's commission. If, then, for John, as for Paul, the eschatological salvation-event is already taking place in the present, it nevertheless does so with a difference suggested by their very terminology.

Paul may also say, it is true, that God "sent" His Son (Gal. 4:4; Rom. 8:3); but in Paul this term plays no such role as his expression that God "gave up" His Son. This expression was traditional before Paul and familiar to him (παραδιδόναι Rom. 4:25; 8:32; I Cor. 11:23); he evidently recast it in speaking of the Son's self-surrender (διδόναι, giving, or παρα διδόναι, surrendering ἑαυτόν, of himself; Gal. 1:4; 2:20; the expression subsequently occurs in the school of Paul at Eph. 5:2, 25; I Tim. 2:6; Tit. 2:14). In John this "giving" (διδόναι) occurs only at 3:16 (παραδιδόναι occurs rather often, but means "betray") and denotes simply the sending of the Son in common-Christian terminology. For the idea of the (self-) surrender of the Son *as sacrifice* is not present here, since the preposition "for" (ὑπέρ Gal. 1:4; 2:20; Eph. 5:2, 25; I Tim. 2:6; Tit. 2:14) or "for the sake of" (διά Rom. 4:25), which is characteristic of this sacrificial terminology, is missing.

While for Paul the earthly Jesus, as the pre-existent one appearing in the form of a servant, is empty of any divine glory (Phil. 2:6ff.; II Cor. 8:9; Rom. 8:3), in John the incarnate Logos reveals his "glory" in his work on earth—though admittedly in a paradoxical fashion visible only to the eyes of the believing (1:14; 2:11). Therefore, the words which the heavenly voice speaks to Jesus (Jn. 12:28) at the turning-point of his fate can scarcely be imagined as occurring in Paul: "I have glorified (i.e. in the Revealer's earthly activity) and I will glorify again (i.e. through the exaltation which will take place on the cross)."

In short, then, the figure of Jesus in John is portrayed in the forms offered by the Gnostic Redeemer-myth (§ 15, 1, I, p. 166) which had already influenced the christological thinking of Hellenistic

---

* On which see especially: Geo. Widengren, *The Great Vohu Manah and the Apostle of God,* 1945; and *Mesopotamian Elements in Manichaeism,* 1946. Cf. also Hans Jonas, *Gnosis und spätantiker Geist* I, 1934, 120ff.

Christianity before Paul and then influenced him (§ 15, 4c). It is true that the cosmological motifs of the myth are missing in John, especially the idea that the redemption which the "Ambassador" brings is the release of the pre-existent sparks of light which are held captive in this world below by demonic powers (§ 15, 1, I, pp. 165f.). But otherwise Jesus appears as in the Gnostic myth as the pre-existent Son of God whom the Father clothed with authority and sent into the world. Here, appearing as a man, he speaks the words the Father gave him and accomplishes the works which the Father commissioned him to do. In so doing, he is not "cut off" from the Father but stands in solid and abiding unity with Him as an ambassador without fault or falsehood. He comes as the "light," the "truth," the "life" by bringing through his words and works light, truth, and life and calling "his own" to himself. In his discourses with their "I am . . ." he reveals himself as the Ambassador; but only "his own" understand him. So his coming accomplishes the separation between those who hear his voice, who become "seeing," and those who do not understand his speech, who suppose themselves seeing and remain imprisoned in their blindness. In the world out of which he calls his own to himself he is despised and hated. But he leaves the world; as he "came" so he "departs" and takes leave of his own, whom in his prayer he commits to the Father's care. But his departure also belongs to his work of redemption, for by his elevation he has prepared the way for his own to the heavenly dwelling-places into which he will fetch his own. Out of Gnostic language, finally, and not, as some maintain, out of the Greek philosophical tradition comes the pre-existent Revealer's name: Logos. How John interprets this myth, and how it can serve him to express his theological thoughts will have to become clear in the exposition of the latter.

Gnostic terminology places its stamp mainly on the words and discourses of Jesus, but it is by no means confined to the Revelation-discourse source which presumably underlies them; rather, it runs through the whole Gospel and the Epistles. If the author's background was Judaism, as rather frequently occurring rabbinical turns of speech perhaps prove, it was, at any rate, not out of an orthodox but out of a gnosticizing Judaism that he came.* Especially the

---

* While a pre-Christian gnosticizing Judaism could hitherto only be deduced out of later sources, the existence of such is now testified by the manuscripts recently discovered in Palestine.

[13]

literary devices with which he builds the discussions—the use of ambiguous concepts and statements to elicit misunderstandings—are indicative that he lives within the sphere of Gnostic-dualistic thinking. For those ambiguities and misunderstandings are far from being merely formal technical devices. Rather, they are the expression of his underlying dualistic view: the Revealer and the "world" cannot understand each other; they do not speak the same language (8:43); the world confuses truth with appearance, the real with the unreal and cannot but drag down into the realm of the unreal what the Revealer says of the real and thus cannot but misunderstand it.

CHAPTER II

Johannine Dualism

§ 42. World and Man

1. John's proclamation consists of the message that God so loved the world that He sent His "only-begotten" Son—not to judge it, but to save it (3:16; I Jn. 4:9, 14). Judgment would be what it deserves, for "the whole world lieth in wickedness" (I Jn. 5:19, KJ); it stands in need of being saved.

As for Paul (§ 26), so for John the *kosmos* means primarily the world of men; on it the judgment falls that it is evil and would be lost were it not for the coming of the "Son." In its radical opposition to God it is characterized as in Paul by the term "this world" (ὁ κόσμος οὗτος 8:23; 9:39; 11:9; 12:25, 31, 13:1; 16:11; 18:36; I Jn. 4:17), which comes from apocalyptic eschatology. In this term, the point is the contrast between the nature of the world and God, not a contrast between two ages (except in the quotation at 12:25). Accordingly, John speaks neither of "this age" or "the present (ἐνεστῶς) age" nor of the "future" (μέλλων) or "coming (ἐρχόμενος) age."

But what is *the essence* of the *kosmos*?

The sentence: "It (the light) was in the world, and the world came into being through it, yet the world did not recognize it (the Logos)" (1:10 tr.) corresponds to the sentence: "The light is shining in the darkness, and the darkness has not grasped it" (1:5 tr.). The essence of the *kosmos*, therefore, is *darkness* (*cf.* 8:12; 12:35, 46; I Jn. 1:5f.; 2:8f., 11)—darkness not as a shadow lying upon the world, an affliction imposed upon it (as in Is. 9:1, for example), but as its own peculiar nature in which it is at ease and at home, for: "the light has come into the world, and men loved darkness rather than light" (3:19 RSV). Just this—that the world appropriates to itself its darkness—can come to expression in the judgment that men are

[15]

blind, blind without knowing it and without wanting to acknowledge it (9:39–41; *cf.* 12:40; I Jn. 2:11). Hence, it means the same thing when the world's nature is designated as *falsehood,* which indirectly takes place by Jesus' assertion that he came into the world to bear witness to the truth (18:37). It occurs again when he promises knowledge of the truth to him who is loyal in faith (8:32) or when it is said of him that through him came grace and truth (1:17), that the word he brings is truth (17:17), that he himself is the truth (14:6, *cf.* also I Jn. 2:21; 3:19). But the world's nature is directly designated as falsehood when Jesus accuses "the Jews" of not being able to hear his word because they are of the devil, i.e. sprung from falsehood, and therefore do not believe when Jesus says the truth (8:43–45; *cf.* I Jn. 2:21, 27). Whoever does not acknowledge Jesus as the Messiah is a "liar" (I Jn. 2:22). Furthermore, this compound of darkness and falsehood that is characteristic of the world, which it, itself, has appropriated as its own, is a power to which the world has fallen into bondage—an idea that is expressed by the promise of freedom to those who know the truth (8:32). *Kosmos,* then, is in essence *existence in bondage.* The "ruler of the (or this) world" is the devil (12:31; 14:40; 16:11). Because he is their father, the "Jews" are his offspring (8:44); so are the "sinners" (I Jn. 3:8, 10). For bondage to the devil is synonymous with *bondage to sin,* which is the very thing from which the knowledge of the truth emancipates men (8:32–34). To love darkness more than light means to do evil (3:19f.). To be blind means to be left stuck in one's sin (9:41)—which in turn means to be *under the sway of death.* In their sins the "Jews" will die (8:21, 24). In fact, the world is really already dead; for of him who believes in Jesus it is said that he has already gone over into life from death (5:24). Whenever Jesus' word sounds forth, the hour of the resurrection of the dead has arrived (5:25), and it is just because the world lies in death that Jesus brings the water of life and the bread of life (4:10, 6:27ff.), that he is the light of life (8:12), the resurrection, and life itself (11:25; 14:6). But the most ghastly thing of all about its bondage to death is the world's enmity to life. As the devil is by nature (ἀπ᾽ ἀρχῆς 8:44) a murderer, so likewise are they murderers who spring from him like Cain (I Jn. 3:12) or the "Jews" (8:40). Hatred of one's brother is nothing less than such will to murder (I Jn. 3:15; *cf.* 2:9, 11). Hence, Jesus' "new commandment" is that of brotherly love (13:34f.; I Jn. 2:7ff., etc.), and as he who believes

is said to have gone over from death into life, the same is said of
him who loves his brother (I Jn. 3:14).

Is the devil a reality for John in the mythical sense? That is
very doubtful, to say the least. But be that as it may, he represents
in any case the power to whose domination the world has surrendered
itself: the power of darkness and falsehood, the power of sin and
death. The devil is God's antagonist; i.e. darkness and falsehood, sin
and death are the enemies of light and truth, freedom and life. But
the devilish power of all evil is not gnostically conceived as a cosmic
power under whose domination men have come by a curse inflicted
upon them. The world does not have its origin in a tragic event of
primeval time (see I, pp. 165f.). Rather, *the world is the creation of
God.* For everything was created by the Word (1:3) which was with
God in the beginning and, indeed, was God. And that means that
God revealed Himself in His creating; the same implication lies in
the fact that the Word, insofar as it was "life" for that which was
created, was also the "light" for men.*

2. John's concepts, light and darkness, truth and falsehood,
freedom and bondage, life and death, come from Gnostic dualism,
but they take on their specific Johannine meaning only in their
relation to the idea of creation. For what does *light* mean? Naturally
it means in John, as in religious language everywhere, that which is
salutary. But how can we more exactly determine its meaning? The
way is indicated by those sentences that speak of "walking" or
"working" in the light (or, by day) or of the opposite, "walking" in
darkness (or in the night). Only in the light is it possible to walk and
work sure of one's way; in the dark a man is blind and cannot find
his way (9:4; 11:9f.; 12:35; I Jn. 2:11). Light, that means, is understood in its original sense: the daylight in which man is able not only
to orient himself about objects but also to understand himself in his
world and find his way in it. But the "true light" (1:9; I Jn. 2:8) is
not the light of literal day, which makes orientation in the external

---

* This somewhat ambiguous sentence of John (1:3–4; ὃ γέγονεν, ἐν αὐτῷ ζωὴ
ἦν) means either "That which came into being—(for it) there was life in it (*sc.*
the Word)" (in more tolerable English: "In the Word there was life for that
which was created") or it means "That which came into being—in it (the Word)
was the life" (in better English: "In that which was created the Word was the
life").

But the ultimate meaning is the same in either case; see my *Kommentar,*
pp. 20–22.

world possible, but the state of having one's existence illumined, an illumination in and by which a man understands himself, achieves a self-understanding which opens up his "way" to him, guides all his conduct, and gives him clarity and assurance. Since creation is a revelation of God and the "Word" is at work as the "light" in that which was created, then man is given the possibility of a genuine self-understanding in the possibility of understanding himself as God's creature. *Darkness*, then, means that a man does not seize this possibility—that he shuts himself up against the God revealed in the creation. It means that instead of understanding himself as creature he arrogates to himself a self-sovereignty that belongs to the Creator alone. To the question whence darkness comes, John gives no mythical answer. For the possibility of darkness—illusory self-understanding—is provided by the possibility of light—genuine self-understanding. Only because there is revelation of God, is there enmity toward God. Only because there is light, is there darkness. Darkness is nothing other than shutting one's self up against the light. It is the turning away from the origin of one's existence, away from that which alone offers the possibility of illumining one's existence. When the world shuts itself up against the light it thereby rebels against God, making itself independent of the Creator—i.e. it attempts to do so, vainly imagines it can do so. So, being in darkness, the world is simultaneously *in falsehood*. For it is this illusion about itself, not some immoral conduct, that is the lie—an illusion, however, which is no mere error in thought, but the illusion of a false self-understanding out of which any immoral conduct that may develop proceeds to grow—a self-understanding which is revolt against God, against the "truth."

For just as "falsehood" has no merely formal meaning in John, neither does "*truth*" (ἀλήθεια), as if it meant the nakedness of that-which-is in general or reality in the purely formal sense in which that can be predicated of any object (in contrast to a mistaken notion about it). Rather, the basic meaning of "truth" in John is God's reality, which, since God is the Creator, is the only true reality. The emancipating knowledge of the truth (8:32) is not the rational knowledge of the reality of that-which-is in general; such a knowledge would at best free one from the prejudices and errors occasioned by tradition and convention. No, this knowledge of the truth is the knowledge, granted to men of faith, of God's reality; it frees one of

sin (8:32–34). True, ἀλήθεια does have the formal meaning "truth"
when it is said that Jesus tells the truth (8:45), or that the Spirit
guides us into all the truth (16:13). But the truth into which the
Spirit guides is factually the reality of God; and Jesus does not
merely *tell* the truth but also *is* the truth (14:6; § 48). So truth is not
the teaching about God transmitted by Jesus but is God's very reality
revealing itself—occurring!—in Jesus. For whoever has seen him has
seen the Father (14:9); in him the Father is and works (14:10f.); and as
he is the "truth," for that very reason he is also "the life" (14:6). If,
as the incarnate Word, he is full of "grace" and "truth" (1:14), that
says in a hendiadys that in him God's reality encounters men as a
gracious gift. If God's word is the "truth" (17:17), that is because it
is in his word that God's reality becomes manifest. And if believers
are to be "consecrated" (17:17=set apart) by the truth, that will
occur in this way: that the reality of God, manifesting itself in the
Word, takes them, though still in the world, out of the world's sphere
of power (17:14–16). If God demands such worshipers as worship
him "in spirit and in truth" (4:23), here again we have a hendiadys
which means that true worship of God is solely such worship as is
brought about by God's power and His own revealing of Himself.
But the world has become indifferent to the reality of God with an
indifference expressed by the question with which Pilate shrugs it
off: "What is truth?" Nevertheless, as "to be of the truth" (18:37;
I Jn. 2:21; 3:19) is synonymous with "to be of God" (7:17; 8:47; I Jn.
3:10; 4:1ff.; 5:19), so "to be of the world" (8:23; 15:19; 17:14, 16;
18:36; I Jn. 2:16; 4:5) or "of the earth" (3:31) is synonymous
with "to be from below" (8:23) and "to be of the devil" (8:44;
I Jn. 3:8).

Now if truth is the reality of God as the only true reality, then
the lie which denies this reality is not merely a false assertion. Rather,
the "liar" withdraws from reality and falls into the unreal, *death*.
For if God is the sole reality, then *life* is simply openness to God and
to him who makes God manifest: "And this is eternal life, that they
know thee the only true God, and Jesus Christ whom thou hast sent"
(17:3 RSV—"eternal life" is equivalent to "life"; the terms are used
interchangeably by John with no difference in meaning). In turning
its back to the "truth," the world simultaneously turns away from
"life" and thereby turns itself into a specious reality, which, being a
lie, is simultaneously death. This specious reality is the Nothing

which professes to be something, and which cheats of his life him who takes it for truth; it is a murderer (8:44).

In its rebellion against God, the world remains God's creation; i.e. man can produce only a specious reality which actually is a lie, a nothing. For, being a creature, he does not, like God, live out of his own resources, but ever lives only out of an uncontrollable origin which has power over him. He always comes from a Whence, and for him there is only the possibility to be from God or from the world, which means: from God or from falsehood, from God or from Nothing. If he repudiates his origin from God, then his origin is Nothing, to which he has given power over himself. In John "to be from" and "to be born from," the expressions which serve to characterize men and their conduct, have lost the cosmological sense that they have in the Gnostic myth and denote the individual's essence which asserts itself in all his speaking and doing and determines the Whither of his way. Face to face stand the opposing possibilities: "to be of (=from) God," etc., or "to be of the world," etc. (see above); or "to be born of (=from) God" (1:13; I Jn. 3:9; 4:7; 5:1, 4, 18—or "from above" 3:3, 7—or "of the Sprit" 3:6) or "to be born of the flesh" (3:6). This means a man is determined by his origin and in each present moment does not have himself in hand; he has only one alternative: to exist either from God (reality) or from the world (unreality). By man's Whence, his Whither is also determined; they who are "from below," "of the world," will die in their sins (8:21–23); "the world" and its "lust" pass away (I Jn. 2:17). The *bondage*, therefore, to which the world has surrendered itself, consists in this: that by disavowing God the creator as its origin it falls into the hands of Nothing. And *freedom* is this: that, by acknowledging the truth the world opens itself to the reality from which alone it can live.

The concepts light, truth, life, and freedom explain each other: so do the concepts darkness, falsehood, death, and bondage in the contrasting group. They all derive their meaning from the search for human existence—for "life" as "life eternal"—and denote the double possibility of human existence: to exist either from God or from man himself. They all imply that only in the knowledge of his creaturehood can man achieve true understanding of himself; this is the *light* that illumines his way. Only in such knowledge does he perceive the *truth*—the true reality which makes itself available to him in the revelation of God; and only so does he escape the delusion that he himself can establish a reality of his own by forming a world in rebellion to God. Only in such knowledge does he achieve *freedom* from specious reality, which actually is darkness, falsehood, bondage, and death. And only in such freedom does he have *life*, for in that freedom he is living out of and by his true origin. Each man is, or once was, confronted with deciding for or against God; and he is confronted anew with this decision by the revelation of God in Jesus. The cosmological dualism of Gnosticism has become in John a *dualism of decision*.

§ 43. Johannine Determinism

1. The language of this "dualism" is that of Gnosticism. In particular *the division of mankind into two groups*—those who are "of God" or "of the devil," "of the truth" or "of the world," "from above" or "from below"—makes it seem as if mankind falls into two classes each of which is from the outset determined as to its essence and its fate by its specific nature. Is not each man stamped by his origin? Does not his origin determine the direction of his way?—even his decision in regard to Jesus, in whom God-made-manifest encounters him? Is it not true that only he whom the Father "draws" comes to Jesus (6:44), only he to whom it is "given" by the Father (6:65; *cf.* 6:37, 39; 17:2, 6, 9, *1*2, 24)? Is it not said that only he can "hear his voice" who is "of the truth," who is "of God" (18:37; 8:47)—that only he can believe who belongs to his "sheep" (10:26)? And is it not solely "his own" whom he calls to himself (10:3f.), whom he knows and who know him (10:14, 27)? And does not the prophet's word (Is. 6:10) confirm the opinion that unbelief rests upon the hardening imposed by God (12:39f.)?

But how can that be?—for Jesus' demand for faith goes forth to all! And the assertion that they are stuck in darkness and blindness and stand under the wrath of God applies to all men. And men are asked, one and all, whether they want to *remain* in this situation (3:36; 9:41; 12:46). But—Jesus' words are not didactic propositions but an invitation and a call to decision.

Typical are the utterances which contain a promise in the main clause. By having a prefatory participle which states the condition for receiving what is promised, they are also calls to decision. (The italicized words represent participles in the Greek text.)

5:24: "Truly, truly, I say to you,
he who hears my word and *believes* him who sent me,
has eternal life; he does not come into judgment,
but has passed from death to life."

Or 6:35: "I am the bread of life.
He who comes to me shall not hunger;
and *he who believes* in me shall never thirst."

Or 8:12: "I am the light of the world.
He who follows me will not walk in darkness,
but will have the light of life."

(*Cf.* further 3:18, 33, 36; 6:47; 11:25f.; 12:44f.).
No less typical are the utterances in which the invitation
(which may be paralleled by a threat) is preceded by an if-clause
in place of a participle:

6:51: "I am the living bread . . .
if anyone eats this bread,
he will live for ever."

Or 7:16f.: "My teaching is not mine,
but his who sent me;
if any man's will is to do his will,
he shall know whether the teaching is from God. . . ."

Or 8:51: "Truly, truly, I say to you,
if any one keeps my word,
he will never see death."

(*Cf.* further 10:9; 12:26; 14:23 and the clauses containing
"unless"—ἐὰν μή τις—3:3, 5; 15:16)
All forms of this cry of invitation and decision are combined
in 12:46–48:

"I have come as light into the world,
that whoever believes in me may not remain in darkness.
If any one hears my sayings and does not keep them,
I do not judge him. . . .
He who rejects me and does not receive my sayings,
has a judge. . . ."

[22]

In 7:37 the invitation is formulated in the imperative, and the following participle, though it does not formulate the condition as a demand, nevertheless in substance has the same implication:

"If any one thirst, let him come to me,
and let him drink *who believes in me*" (tr.).

Inasmuch as the assertion that no one can come to Jesus whom the Father does not "draw" (6:44) is followed by the statement, "Every one who has heard and learned from the Father comes to me," the πᾶς by itself ("every one") indicates that everyone has the possibility of letting himself be drawn by the Father (and also the possibility of resisting). The Father's "drawing" does not precede the believer's "coming" to Jesus—in other words, does not take place before the decision of faith—but, as the surrendering of one's own certainty and self-assertion, occurs in that coming, in that decision of faith, just as Paul's "being led by the Spirit" does not mean being carried along willy-nilly by the Spirit, but is the decision of faith, the decision to surrender to God's demand and gift (§ 38, 3; I, p. 336). As in Paul (§ 37) John's predestinatory formulations mean that the decision of faith is not a choice between possibilities within this world that arise from inner-worldly impulses, and also mean that the believer in the presence of God cannot rely on his own faith. He never has his security in himself, but always in God alone. So if faith is such a surrender of one's own self-assertion, then the believer can understand his faith not as the accomplishment of his own purposeful act, but only as God's working upon him. This and nothing else is the meaning of the statements that only he comes to Jesus to whom it is "granted" (6:65) by the Father, only those whom the Father "gives him" (6:37, 39; 17:2ff.).

2. The expression "to be (or be born) of . . .," which makes it seem as if John attributed a man's conduct to his "nature" (φύσις— a Gnostic term which John significantly avoids), in reality intends to attribute all specific conduct to a man's *being*, in which his conduct is founded. Since man never exists by his own power, but can only commit himself to a power that controls him, reality or unreality, God or Nothing—and since factually "the world" exists from Nothing (§ 42, 2)—the encounter with the Revealer calls into question whether this existence-from-Nothing is existence at all. And the decision in

[23]

response to the Revealer's word, unlike decisions within this world, does not take place out of man's still unquestioned existence, as if the decider, having chosen this or that, could remain what he was. On the contrary, here he is asked just this: whether or not he wills to remain what he was—i.e. to remain in his old existence or not. This is clearly said by the sayings that speak of "remaining" in the old situation:

3:36: "He who believes in the Son has eternal life;
he who does not obey the Son shall not see life,
but the wrath of God *rests* (KJ: abides=remains)
upon him."

12:46: "I have come as light into the world,
that whoever believes in me may not *remain* in darkness."

9:39, 41: "For judgment I came into this world,
that those who do not see may see,
and that those who see may become blind. . . .
If you were blind, you would have no guilt;
but now that you say, 'We see,' your guilt *remains*."

It is clear: before the light's coming all were blind. "Those who see" are only such as imagine they can see. "The blind" are such as knew of their blindness or know of it now that the light encounters them. The "blind" and the "seeing," accordingly, are not two groups that were already present and demonstrable before the light's coming. Now, and not before, the separation between them takes place in that each one is asked whether he chooses to belong to the one group or the other—whether he is willing to acknowledge his blindness and be freed from it or whether he wants to deny it and persist in it.

The conduct of every man, therefore, corresponds to his origin, i.e. to what he is, his essence. But, unlike Paul, John does not attribute the fact that all men in their essence are evil, or that "the whole world lieth in wickedness" (I Jn. 5:19 KJ), to Adam's fall (§ 25, 3). Does he attribute that fact to the *devil*? Not necessarily. Admittedly, John's "of the devil" (synonymous with "of the world," "from below") applies to all men; and the statement that God sent His Son into the world to save the world (3:17) means the same thing as I Jn. 3:8: "The reason the Son of God appeared was to destroy the works of the devil." But his conception is not that men, because of a trespass committed by the devil in primeval time, are enmeshed in sin as a sinister heritage. Rather, his conception is that the devil lurks behind every particular sin; for "he was a murderer"— not "in the beginning," but "from the beginning" onward (8:44), or still more clearly in the present tense: "the devil sins from the beginning on" (I Jn. 3:8 tr.). It is in this sense, therefore, that "he who commits sin stems from the devil" (I Jn. 3:8 Blt.). That is, having the devil as one's father is a term to describe the sinner's existence. Or, said in another way, sin is not an occasional evil occurrence; rather, in sin it comes to light that man in his essence is a sinner, that he is determined by unreality, Nothing.

The *universality of sin*, i.e. the determination of men by unreality, is therefore not attributed to a mythical cause but simply shows itself to be *a fact*—a fact by virtue of the light's coming: "The light shines in the darkness, and the darkness did not grasp it. . . . It was in the world and through it the world had come into being, yet the world did not recognize it. It came into its own (*viz.* the world), and its own (=men) did not receive it " (1:5, 10f. tr.). "And this is the judgment, that the light has come into the world, and men loved darkness rather than light" (3:19). Not only because men (by and large) refuse to believe does the universality of sin show itself to be a fact but equally by the circumstance that there are those who come to faith ("but as many as received him" 1:12 KJ, 3:21). For faith, as we have seen, is the admission that one has hitherto languished in blindness, has been enmeshed in the "works" of the devil, and has now come over from death into life (9:39; I Jn. 3:8; Jn. 5:24; I Jn. 3:14).

In short: before the light's coming the whole "world" is in darkness, in death. But by the light's coming the question is put to man whether he chooses to remain in darkness, in death. By sending His Son into the world God put the world, so to say, in the balance (*in suspenso*): "If I had not come and spoken to them, they would not have sin; but now they have no excuse for their sin" (15:22). Man cannot act otherwise than as what he is, but in the Revealer's call there opens up to him the possibility of *being* otherwise than he was. He can exchange his Whence, his origin, his essence, for another; he can "be born again" (3:1ff.) and thus attain to his true being. In his decision between faith and un-faith a man's being definitively constitutes itself, and from then on his Whence becomes clear. The

"Jews," who are asserted to be "from below" (8:23) and are reviled as children of the devil, are those who by refusing to believe have anchored themselves to their sins (8:44). The children of God and the children of the devil are henceforth recognizable by whether one "does right" and "loves his brother" (I Jn. 3:10)—for brother-love is the fulfilment of the "new" commandment (13:34; I Jn. 2:7ff.), which has now become possible to those who "have passed out of death into life" (I Jn. 3:14; 2:8). By its opposition to the Revealer the "world" definitively constitutes itself as "world"; thereby the "world" and its ruler are "judged" (12:31; 16:11).

§ 44. The Perversion of the Creation into "the World"

1. The fact that God holds His judgment in the balance, so to speak, until men, in view of the sending of His Son, have either anchored themselves by un-faith to their old existence or have appropriated by faith the new possibility of existing, indicates that in spite of its rebellion against God, human life before the encounter with the Revealer has no unambiguous meaning. For even in its rebellion the world does not escape being God's creation (II, p. 20). This comes to light in the fact that *man's life is pervaded by the quest for reality* (ἀλήθεια), the quest for life. John gives expression to this quest in his sayings that deal with that which is "true" (ἀληθινόν).

When Jesus is called the "true light" (1:9; I Jn. 2:9)—the real, genuine, authentic light—it is presupposed that man does know of light (in general) and is in quest of it. For he must walk his way through the world; to do so he needs an understanding of himself in his world. He can, of course, go astray and follow a false light; but even though he factually does so and is a blind man supposing himself to have sight and a slave imagining himself free, he nevertheless shows himself consciously or unconsciously concerned with a quest for light. When Jesus calls himself the light of the world (8:12), he is presenting himself as that which the world is seeking. Human existence knows, overtly or covertly, of its dependence upon that from which it can live. It hungers and thirsts, for it has a will to live. And though this will is directly concerned with mere food and drink, the imaginative mythical notions of miraculous food (6:31) and life-giving water (4:15) indicate in themselves that its longing is ultimately for life itself. When Jesus calls himself the bread and the water of life (6:27ff.; 4:10ff.; *cf.* 7:37), he assumes such a preliminary understanding as is expressed in mythology. He is the fabled tree of life told about in myth (15:1ff.). The "I-am" pronouncements are the answer to this quest for life. For the "I" in them is a predicate nominative, not the subject (§ 48, 2), and they mean: in him that for which man seeks is here. In him it is very reality in contrast to all seeming. The "true bread from heaven" (6:32) is he; the "true vine" (15:1) is he. The same is meant when he calls himself the "good shepherd" (10:11; 10:14); here "good" (καλός), instead of the usual "true" (ἀληθινός), denotes the real shepherd in contrast to the "hireling." His "I am" offers the answer to man's quest for life, his quest for "abundance" (περισσόν, 10:10, the more-than-enough which definitively stills all longing); it presupposes man's overt or covert knowledge of being dependent upon Him who bestows life.

2. The delusion that arises from the will to exist of and by one's self *perverts truth into a lie, perverts the creation into the "world."* For in their delusion men do not let their quest for life become a question about themselves so as to become aware of their creaturehood, but instead they give themselves the answer so as to have a security of their own. They take the temporary for the ultimate, the spurious for the genuine, death for life. They give themselves the answer *in their religion*, in which, it must be conceded, they show that they have a knowledge of something beyond man and his world. But by supposing themselves made secure by their religion they pervert this knowledge. The various religions debate against each other, and each disclaims the validity of the other's worship. But neither in Jerusalem nor on Mount Gerizim is God legitimately worshiped; the "true worshipers" are they who worship Him "in Spirit and in reality." Right worship of God, that is, is an eschatological occurrence which God Himself brings about by His Spirit, and it becomes a reality by the coming of the Revealer (4:19–24).

Taking the *Jewish religion* as an example, John makes clear through it how the human will to self-security distorts knowledge of God, makes God's demand and promise into a possession and thereby shuts itself up against God. In so doing, John takes as his starting-point not the Jewish striving after "righteousness" but the will-toward-life (§ 41, 3; II, p. 11) which is active in every religion. The sin of "the Jews" is not their "boasting" on the basis of works, as in Paul (§ 23, 2; I, pp. 242f.), but their imperviousness to the Revelation which throws into question their self-security—which in substance, of course, is the very same sin. One might almost say: the sin of "the Jews" lies not in their ethics, as in Paul, but in their dogmatics. They search the Scriptures because in them they suppose themselves to "have eternal life," and therefore reject Jesus, who otherwise could bestow life upon them (5:39f.). They pervert the meaning of Scripture; for they do not see that it is just of Jesus that it bears witness—Jesus, who as God's Revelation shatters all self-security. The very Moses they appeal to, on whom they have "set their hope," becomes their accuser (5:45). Their religion, which ought to cast them into unrest and keep them open for the encounter with God, is to them a means of rest and shuts them up against God. Actually they do not know God at all (5:37b.; 7:28; 8:19, 55; 15:21; 16:3). For knowing Him does not mean having thoughts about Him, even right ones perhaps, but acknowledging Him as Creator and being open for the encounter with Him.

Hence, all that is right becomes false in their mouths. They appeal to *their Law* in order to set aside the disturbance which Jesus is for their self-security (ch. 5). The argument of 7:19–24, which accuses "the Jews" of not keeping their Law (v. 19) and of breaking the sabbath-law in order to be true to the Law (v. 23), indicates that the Law is not an unambiguous entity capable of granting security. They ought to recognize that by the conflict of the circumcision-law with the sabbath-law Moses is directing them to inquire into the true meaning of the Law. The way "the Jews" use the Law only as a means of security for themselves is shown by 7:49f.: Nicodemus accuses the Jewish councillors of having condemned Jesus without giving him a hearing, thus violating the Law. But they have their reply ready: according to Scripture no prophet is to arise out of Galilee. Their search of Scripture stands in the service of a dogmatics which gives them self-security by furnishing them criteria for judging the Revelation, but this makes them deaf to the living word of the Revealer. Chapter 9 also shows that with them misuse of the Law for their own purposes is compatible with complete correctness toward the Law. The verses 8:17f., finally, pour ridicule on appeal to the Law; here Jesus applies the principle that a matter is to be regarded as proved by the testimony of two witnesses (Deut. 17:6; 19:15) to his own testimony and that of the Father. For reflection on this ordinance of the Law ought to indicate that it is only applicable to men, and that God's Revelation does not have to present its credentials to men. God's word cannot be subjected to the human demand for substantiating testimony; for if it could, then that statute would have to be applied—which would be absurd!

"The Jews" play off *the revelation in their history*, documented in Scripture, against Jesus. How can he raise a claim that would make him one greater than Abraham (8:25)! But Abraham did not suppose that in himself God's gift to Israel was once for all accomplished, but looked forward to the eschatological day of fulfilment (8:56). As in their appeal to Moses "the Jews" do not understand the meaning of the Law, neither do they understand in their appeal to Abraham that his meaning for them is not that of a possession but that of a promise. They consider themselves Abraham's children (8:33) and therefore free, not recognizing that freedom cannot be a possession but can only be an eschatological gift. They would have the right to appeal to their descent from Abraham if they understood its meaning to be that of a promise which points into the future and puts them under obligation to the future. Looking back into their history ought not to make them feel secure, but ought to obligate them to faithfulness toward God's dealing, which points man away from himself toward God's future, for which it is man's duty to keep himself open. Whether they understand Abraham—whether faithfulness to their past will turn out to be openness for God's future—that necessarily shows up at their encounter with Jesus. By closing themselves up against him and wanting to kill him they show that they are not Abraham's children.

Certainly, "the Jews" have *a hope of their own* and to that extent are oriented toward the future. But they have converted their hope into a theology of the Messiah, by which they have robbed themselves of freedom for the future. They know that the Messiah's place of origin will be mysterious—and protest that Jesus' home town and his parents are known (6:41f.; 7:27; *cf.* 1:46)! And even in this protest there is still correct knowledge embedded: what encounters man in the Revelation is not something human but something divine. But this knowledge is perverted! For in their theology they conceive the divine as a phenomenon whose divineness man can verify by means of his own criteria rather than as an occurrence which destroys the man who here tries to verify. Their resisting protest fails to understand that the divine cannot be contrasted with the human in *such*

[29]

a manner as they in the security of their judgment suppose: "How can a mere man claim to be the Revealer?" Just this—for human thinking an absurdity—is the mystery of the Revelation, which is understood only when a man lets go of his self-security, in which he supposes he can distinguish the divine and the human as verifiable phenomena. What "the Jews" call mystery is no genuine mystery at all; for in their mythologizing theology they make the other-worldly— Jesus' mysterious origin in God—into a this-worldly thing that is subject to their approval or disapproval. There is no longer any mystery at all for him who professes to be able by criteria at his disposal to establish whether and when God's mystery stands before him; for what the recognition and acknowledgment of God's mystery presupposes is exactly that the acknowledger shall have been cast into doubt as to the validity of the prevailing standards. That is why the "world" remains blind when faced with the Revelation, and just because it "knows," it knows nothing. The true mystery is comprised in "The word became flesh" (1:14), and John either does not know or refuses to know anything of an attempt to draw this mystery down into terms of this world by a story of a mythological birth (*cf.* 1:45; 6:42; 7:27f.); "the Jews" are in error not because they are misinformed about Jesus' origin but because they apply the wrong standard to him.

Others play off another messianic dogma against Jesus: the Messiah must be a son of David born in Bethlehem, but Jesus comes from Nazareth (7:42)!—and by their wrong question they block up the door by which they might enter into faith. They know that the Messiah when he comes will remain forever (12:34)! They await the Messiah, that is, as one who will realize human air-castles, one who will make the salvation he brings into a lasting earthly condition— so the attempt was made to make Jesus king because he miraculously filled the hungry (6:15). They do not know that the salvation which the Messiah brings is the calling-into-question and the negating of the world, nor that to accept him means to surrender all air-castles. However, the Revealer will remain with his own if they faithfully remain with him (15:4f.)—but not in such a way that he will become a this-worldly figure! No, his earthly presence will come to an end, and not until he has departed from the earth will he come again to his own and along with the Father make his home with them (14:23) in a manner that will be hidden from the world (14:22).

The world in general knows the right concepts and the right quests. It speaks of *"honor"* (δόξα; also = "glory"), and in its craving for honor (mutual approval) the correct knowledge comes to light that man, just by being man, is insecure and must seek for approval from outside himself. But the world perverts this proper quest by providing itself with its own answer. The world fails to realize that man's existence as a whole, being that of a creature, is in question and that the court of which it should seek approval or standing is God. But the "honor" that God gives is not sought by the world. For to seek it would mean to recognize the utter insecurity of all human existence and to relinquish one's self-created security. Instead of doing that, men in their need for standing take honor from each other, each conceding the other his "honor" in order that the other in turn may let him have standing (5:44). And thereby they are shutting themselves up against God's Revelation.

The world is acquainted with *love* of course! But it loves only its ἴδιον, what is "its own" and familiar to it (15:19). Ultimately, then, it loves only itself and hates him who exposes its own problematical character. The world is acquainted with joy and proves thereby that human existence, if it were in accord with its own character, would find fulfilment in the joy in which all seeking ceases, the joy which the Revealer bestows (15:11; 16:24; 17:13). But the world knows no true, and therefore eternal, joy, but only joy over its own (seeming) success. The world speaks of freedom and is unaware that it is in bondage; that is to say, in sin (8:32–36).

The world speaks of *sin, righteousness, and judgment,* but understands these terms in its own sense, and the judgment which the Revelation brings consists in disclosing the true meaning of these terms (16:8–11). What is sin? It is the unbelief in which the world anchors itself to itself, as becomes apparent in its attitude to Jesus. What is righteousness (or vindication)? To the world it means to turn out to be in the right, to be crowned with visible success; in reality it means to prevail over the world, as Jesus does at his departure from the world (Jesus' "vindication" is his "victory" in 16:33; *cf.* νικήσεις, "prevail" [RSV] or "overcome" [KJ], in the context of Rom. 3:4). What is judgment? The judgment (the context indicates that God's judgment is meant), in the world's opinion, takes place in that which is visible, either as a cosmic catastrophe (the apocalyptic view) or in catastrophes within world history (the expectation of the Old Testament prophets and, in part, of Judaism). In reality the judgment takes place in the decision of men toward Jesus as the Revealer of God, so that he who does not believe is already condemned (3:18; 12:48), as the "ruler of this world" is also condemned when Jesus by his death is "lifted up" (12:31).

Thus the world creates for itself a *security* of its own and operates within it as that which is *familiar and to be taken for granted*. It shrugs off the disturbance which is created for it by the appearing of Jesus with its incredulous question: 'How can this be?" (3:9), or with similar "how's" (6:42; 7:15; 8:33; 12:34). No, it does not reject everything new without discussion, but it tests it by the standard of the old that it knows and is certain of: "Search and you will see that no prophet is to rise from Galilee" (7:52). The world asks for Jesus' credentials (5:31ff.); it has its experts whose opinions it follows: "Can it be that the authorities really know that this is the Christ?" (7:26). The world has its ideals, too; instead of being extravagant one ought to aid the poor (12:5). That which is tangibly present (σάρξ, "the flesh") is regarded as the real. Jesus' saying about rebirth is unintelligible to the world because it reckons only with the possibilities of the natural, not with God's wonder-working power the Spirit (3:3–8). It judges "according to the flesh" (8:15) or, synonymously, "by appearance" (7:24).

The world also knows an institution which takes care of justice on earth: the *state*. To it the world flees in order to be rid of the disturber of its peace, Jesus. But not only does the state turn out to be too weak to accomplish its task when it shuts itself up against the Revealer's word, but, above all, the world itself perverts the meaning of the state by misusing it to fulfill its own wishes and in doing so resorts to lies and defamation (19:12).

CHAPTER III

The "Krisis" of the World

§ 45. The Sending of the Son

1. *Within this world of death life appeared* (I Jn. 1:2), into the world of darkness came the light (1:5; 3:19)—it came by *the coming of the Son of God* into the world. Jesus is he. Though he came after the Baptist in time, he nevertheless was prior to him (1:15, 30). He even claims that he was before Abraham (8:58); yes, even more: that he was before the foundation of the world (17:5, 24). It is he in whom the Christian Congregation believes as the one "who is from the beginning" (I Jn. 2:13f.). In him the "Word" which in the beginning was with God became flesh (1:1f., 14) and came into its (his) own property—i.e. into the world, which belongs to it, and hence to him, as the one through whom it came into being (1:9–11).

To what extent are such statements, which speak of Jesus in mythological form as the pre-existent Son of God who became man, to be understood in the actual mythological sense? That can only be answered in the course of more detailed interpretation. At any rate, the beginning of the first Epistle, intending to say the same thing as the prologue to the Gospel, significantly speaks of the *life* that in the beginning was with the Father, and has audibly, visibly, and tangibly appeared (in Jesus, of course—that goes without saying). It speaks of this *life* as "*that which*" was in the beginning," as a thing and not as a person (I Jn. 1:1f.). At any rate, it is clear that in the person of Jesus the transcendent divine reality became audible, visible, and tangible in the realm of the earthly world. Jesus is "the Christ, the Son of God, he who is coming into the world" (11:27).

In all that he is, says, and does, he is not to be understood as a figure of this world, but his appearing in the world is to be conceived as an *embassage from without, an arrival from elsewhere.* Jesus is he "whom the Father consecrated and sent into the world" (10:36).

[33]

That the Father sent him is testified by his works (5:16); this (his sending) is what is to be believed (6:29; 11:42; 17:8) or acknowledged (17:25); for eternal life is this: to "know thee the only true God, and Jesus Christ whom thou hast sent" (17:3). So God's name accordingly is: "the Father who sent me" (six times) or simply: "(he) who sent me" (nineteen times). (Both expressions, as crystallized participial phrases, might better be translated with nouns: "my Commissioner, the Father," and "my Commissioner.") And so the congregation confesses: "And we have seen and testify that the Father has sent his Son as the Savior of the world" (I Jn. 4:14). The counterpart of his sending is his "coming" or his "having come." The sending and the coming may, of course, be combined in the same statement. Being the envoy, he did not come on his own initiative: "for I went forth from God and have come (hither). For I am not here (ἐλήλυθα, perfect) of my own accord, but he sent me" (8:42, tr.; cf. 7:28f.; 17:8). Repeated time and again are statements that he "came into the world" (3:19; 9:39; 11:27; 12:46; 16:28; 18:37), or that he "came from the Father (or God)"—(8:42; 13:3; 16:27f., 30; 17:8), or simply that he "has come" (5:43; 7:28; 8:14; 10:10; 12;47; 15:22).* This is just the thing that his own have come to know and to acknowledge (17:8) and is what faith confesses (11:27), while "the Jews" know not whence he comes (8:14) or have a false notion about his origin (7:28f.), and the false teachers deny that Jesus Christ has come "in the flesh" (I Jn. 4:2; II Jn. 7). In more vividly mythological formulation it is also possible to say that he came down from heaven (3:13; 6:33, 38, 41f.).

His coming is the Revelation of the divine reality in the world; this aspect of his coming is emphasized by *the correspondence of his departure to his coming*. By his coming, that is, he does not become a phenomenon of the world, a figure within world-history. He is here, so to speak, only as a guest; the hour is coming when he must depart (13:1; cf. 1:14 "he tented among us" tr.). He came and will go again (8:14):

"I came from the Father and have come into the world;
Again, I am leaving the world and going to the Father."

(16:28; cf. 13:3; 14:12, 28; 16:5, 10, 17). The time of his sojourn on

* Many of the references in all three groups contain the Greek perfect tense. Its full translation would be cumbersome: "being come, I am here," but frequently the overtone "I am here" is at least as strongly sounding as the fundamental tone, "I have come" (Tr.).

earth is but short, and when he is gone he will be sought in vain (7:33; 8:21; *cf.* 13:33). As he came down from heaven—mythological language again—he will ascend again thither where he previously was (6:62; *cf.* 3:13). He will be "elevated" (3:14; 12:32, 34; *cf.* 8:28); he will be "glorified" (12:23; 13:31f.; 17:1; *cf.* 7:39; 12:16), glorified with the "glory" that he had had in pre-existence with the Father (17:5, 24). His coming and his going belong together as a unit, the unity of his activity as Revealer; this is indicated by the fact that both his coming and his going (3:19 and 12:31) can be termed the judgment and by the fact that both his exaltation and his sending can be regarded as the basis for the gift of eternal life (3:14 and 3:16).

2. The sending of the Son is *the deed of God's love*: "In this the love of God was made manifest among us, that God sent his only Son into the world, so that we might live through him" (I Jn. 4:9). "For God so loved the world that he gave his only Son, that whoever believes in him should not perish but have eternal life" (3:16).

That it is God's love that is manifested in the sending, is expressed both by the content of the sentence and by its formulation. The latter uses not only the word "gave" (ἔδωκεν), which suggests the common-Christian term παρ-έδωκεν ("delivered up to death"; see I, pp. 82f. and II, p. 12 and Rom. 4:25, I Cor. 11:23), but also the characterization of the Son as μονογενής ("only," "unique"). Only in Jn. 3:16, 18; I Jn. 4:9 (and probably also in Jn. 1:18, though the wording of the text is not certain here) does "only Son" occur in the New Testament as a characterization of Jesus. This designation will probably have to be understood on the basis of its use in the Septuagint as an epithet of value, meaning "beloved above all," and synonymous with ἀγαπητός. In Jn. 1:14, however, where it is used without any noun, it is probably to be regarded as stemming from Gnostic mythology—on which see my *Johanneskommentar*, p. 47.

The intent of this sending is therefore fulfilled in those who believe in Jesus as the Son sent from God: they receive the love of God—"we have come to know and to believe the love God has for us" (I Jn. 4:16 tr; *cf.* Jn. 17:26; I Jn. 2:5; 3:17; 4:7–12), while he who loves the world is not embraced by the love of God (I Jn. 2:15, understanding the genitive, with KJ, as subjective, not objective).

The fact that the love of God is the basis for the sending of the Son is expressed by the way in which *the purpose of his sending or coming* is given. He came into the world only "to bear witness to the 'truth' " (18:37), or, meaning the same thing, he came into the world as "light," in order "that whoever believes in me may not remain in 'darkness' " (12:46). Again, it means the same when Jesus says he came "that they may have life and have abundance" (10:10 tr.), or when the author says God "gave" him in order that "whoever believes in him might not perish but have eternal life" (3:16), or that God sent him into the world "so that we might live through him" (I Jn. 4:9), or that he sent him as "the expiation for our sins" (I Jn. 4:10, if this sentence is not a redactional gloss). In altogether general formulation it is also said that God sent him "that the world might be saved by him" (3:17).

Jesus, accordingly, can be called "*the savior of the world*" (4:42; I Jn. 4:14). While in this term he is accorded the specifically Hellenistic title of the salvation-bringer (see I, pp. 79f.), the meaning of his sending is more frequently expressed by the title that comes out of the Jewish and earliest Christian tradition: Messiah; whereas the Kyrios-title is completely missing.

Not until ch. 20 (and the added chapter, 21) does the *Kyrios-title* appear in John. That is, it is not used previous to the Easter accounts, for the occurrences of it in 4:1; 6:23; 11:2; are due to a glossator. Various manuscripts also insert it in II Jn. 3. Did the evangelist wish to avoid the application of the cultic title (§ 12, 2) to the earthly Jesus in order to reserve it for the risen Jesus? If so, why is it missing in the Epistles of John? Was it too strong a reminder of the "many lords" (I Cor. 8:5) of the Hellenistic religions (F. C. Grant, *The Growth of the Gospels*, 1933, p. 207)? Was it incompatible with the view that Jesus' disciples were not "slaves" (δοῦλοι) but "friends" of Jesus (15:14f.; W. Bousset, *Kyrios Christos*, 2nd ed., 1921, p. 155)? Or was the title avoided, or at least greatly repressed because John took so reserved an attitude toward the whole realm of the cultic and the sacramental, and because this title was not adapted to expressing just that which was the essential thing to John: Jesus as an eschatological figure?

Jesus is the *Messiah* (1:41; 4:25) or "the Christ" (which in both passages is explicitly pointed out to be the translation of "Messiah," see I, p. 80). Whether he is to be accorded this title, is a question that again and again comes up for discussion among "the Jews" (7:26f,

31, 41f.; 9:22; 10:24; 12:34; *cf.* 1:20) and is answered in the negative by the false teachers (I Jn. 2:22), but the believers' confession of faith is that he is the Messiah (11:27; 20:31; I Jn. 5:1). The old royal meaning of the messiah-title is retained, for *"King of Israel"* occurs as an alternate for it (1:49) and when it is explained by the term *"Son of God,"* then the latter, too, evidently has as its immediate meaning the old messianic one (§ 7, 5), even though in the intent of the evangelist something more is expressed by it in keeping with the differentiated Hellenistic understanding of the term (§ 12, 3). Likewise out of Jewish and earliest Christian tradition comes, finally, the title *"Son of Man"* (§ 5, 1; § 9, 4). Though John mostly understands it in the sense of the Gnostic myth as a designation for the pre-existent one who became man and must be exalted again (1:51; 3:13f.; 12:23, 34; 13:31 and elsewhere), he nevertheless is referring to the Jewish and earliest Christian meaning in letting Jesus' office as judge of the world be founded upon his being Son of Man (5:27, unless this sentence is a redactional gloss).

3. What is expressed by all these titles is that Jesus is the eschatological salvation-bringer, that *his coming is the eschatological event.* By his coming the predictions of Moses and the prophets are fulfilled (1:45; *cf.* 5:39, 46). To the Samaritan woman who expects enlightenment from the Messiah, Jesus answers, "I who speak to you am he" (4:25f.). The Jewish expectation that the Messiah, as the "second redeemer," will bestow bread from heaven as Moses, the "first redeemer," did of yore is fulfilled by Jesus who bestows the true bread of heaven (6:31f.). When he calls his coming "my day" which Abraham rejoiced to see (8:56), that means that his coming is "the Messiah's day" which was part of the Jewish and earliest Christian expectation (see I, pp. 75f.).

But the assertion that his coming-and-going, which constitute a unity as we have seen (see 1 in this §), is the eschatological event is primarily made in those sentences where his coming or going is termed *the judgment of the world:*

"And this is the judgment, that the light has come into the world,
    and men loved darkness rather than light" (3:19).

"For judgment I came into this world,
    that those who do not see may see,
    and that those who see may become blind" (9:39).

The historizing of eschatology already introduced by Paul is radically carried through by John in his understanding of κρίσις and κρίμα as both having the double sense "judgment" and "sunderance." The judgment takes place in just the fact that upon the encounter with Jesus the sunderance between faith and unfaith, between the sighted and the blind, is accomplished (3:19; 9:39). He who believes is not judged (i.e. not condemned), but he who does not believe remains in darkness, remains under the wrath of God, and is thereby judged (i.e. condemned):

"He who believes in him is not condemned,
he who does not believe is condemned already" (3:18).

Right now, while Jesus' word is sounding forth, the "sunderance" which is also "judgment" is taking place:

"He who hears my word and believes him who sent me,
has eternal life; he does not come into judgment (=condemnation),
but has passed from death to life."

". . . the hour is coming, and now is,
when the dead will hear the voice of the Son of God,
and those who hear will live" (5:24f.).

In sending Jesus into the world the Father gave him authority to raise the dead and hold judgment (5:21f., 26f.). Therefore, he who believes in him already has life:

"He who believes in the Son has eternal life;
he who does not obey the Son shall not see life,
but the wrath of God rests (i.e. remains) upon him" (3:36; cf. 6:47; I Jn. 5:12).

Jesus declares:

"I am the resurrection and the life;
he who believes in me, though he die, yet shall he live,
and whoever lives and believes in me shall never die" (11:25f.; cf. 8:51).

The judgment, then, is no dramatic cosmic event, but takes place in the response of men to the word of Jesus. As it accordingly may be said that Jesus came into the world for judgment (9:39), so it can also be said that God sent him not to judge but to save (3:17). He can say that he judges no one (8:15), and again can say that he judges nevertheless (8:16; 5:30). It is not he who is the actual judge, but the word that he speaks:

"If any one hears my sayings and does not keep them,
I do not judge him
For I did not come to judge the world
but to save the world.
He who rejects me and does not receive my sayings
has a judge;
the word that I have spoken will be his judge" (12:47f.).

A later ecclesiastical redaction has here added "on the last day," "correcting" the text by introducing the traditional futuristic eschatology, just as it did in 6:39, 40, 44 by inserting the refrain "but (or "and") I will raise him up at the last day." This is a sentence which has an organic place in 6:54 within the passage 6:51b–58, which likewise was inserted by ecclesiastical redaction; in this passage the bread of life, which in the preceding discourse is Jesus himself, is equated with the Sacrament of the Lord's Supper and the latter is understood (in Ignatius' sense) as the "medicine of immortality." Even more jarring than these additions, if that be possible, is the insertion of 5:28f., where in direct contradiction of v. 25 the "hour" of the resurrection is transferred from the present to the future. On I Jn. 2:28; 3:2 see below (§ 50, 6).

The theme of whole sections is that Jesus' coming-and-going is the "judgment" of the world (3:1–21, 31–36; 4:43–46; 7:15–24; 8:13–20). A concrete scene, 6:60–71, depicts the "sundering" which takes place through his word: at his "hard saying" true and false disciples are put asunder, they separate themselves. Moreover, the sundering accomplished by Jesus' ministry is underscored by the author's dividing his portrayal of this ministry into two parts: chs. 2–12 portray Jesus' revealing-activity to the world, and chs. 13–17 (or 13–20) his revealing-activity to the community of believers.

The historizing of eschatology* also finds expression in the fact that the world is oblivious to what is happening. In its sight there is only a disturbance, a commotion that leads to "divisions" (7:43; 9:16; 10:19). It has no inkling that in these "divisions" a decision

---

* A specific example of John's de-mythologizing of eschatology in his interpretation of the mythical figure, Antichrist. In I Jn. 2:18, 4:3 the appearing of false teachers is interpreted as the coming of the Antichrist. It is even said: "now many antichrists have come!"

and a sunderance are being reflected. This obliviousness grimly demonstrates that the world is judged—condemned. While for it the hour of the passion is the hour of triumph and joy (16:20) because in it the "ruler of the world" seems to be in command (14:30), in reality this hour is just the opposite: the judgment of the world and judgment over its "ruler" (12:31; 16:11).

§ 46. The Offense of the Incarnation of the Word

1. How does God's Son come into the world? As a human being. The theme of the whole Gospel of John is the statement: "The word became flesh" (1:14). This statement is defended by I and II John against the false teachers. These are evidently Christian Gnostics who deny the identity of the Son of God with the human Jesus either by asserting that their union was only temporary or by flatly rejecting the reality of the human Jesus and docetically regarding the human form of the Son of God as only a seeming body. John's answer to them is: every spirit that does not confess that Jesus Christ came in the flesh, that does not confess Jesus (the man as the Son of God) is not "from God"; indeed, such false doctrine is nothing less than the work of Antichrist (I Jn. 4:2f.; II Jn. 7). Just because John makes use of the Gnostic Redeemer-myth (§ 41, 3) for his picture of the figure and activity of Jesus, a demarcation of his own position from that of Gnosticism is particularly incumbent upon him.

It is clear to begin with that for him *the incarnation of the Son of God is not*, as it is in Gnosticism, *a cosmic event* which sets into motion the eschatological occurrence (the unfolding of redemption) as a process of nature by which the union of the essentially opposite natures, light and darkness, is dissolved. The Gnostic Redeemer releases the pre-existent human selves, who by virtue of their light-nature are related to him, out of the matter (body and "soul") that trammels them, and then leads them to the world of light above. John eliminated both the Gnostic concept of φύσις ("nature") and the Gnostic notion of the pre-existence of human selves and their unnatural imprisonment in the material world. He does not accept the Gnostic trichotomy of man, according to which man's true *self* is imprisoned in a *body* and a *soul* (I, pp. 165, 168). Neither is the incarnation of the Son of God for John a device for transmitting "Gnosis" to men in the form of teachings about cosmogony and

[40]

anthropology or for bringing them secret formulas and sacraments, on the strength of which their selves can safely make the journey to heaven (§ 48,3).

The Revealer appears not as *man-in-general*, i.e. not simply as a bearer of human *nature*, but as a *definite human being in history*: Jesus of Nazareth. His humanity is genuine humanity: "the word became flesh." Hence, John has no theory about the pre-existent one's miraculous manner of entry into the world nor about the manner of his union with the man Jesus. He knows neither the legend of the virgin birth* nor that of Jesus' birth in Bethlehem—or if he knows of them, he will have nothing to do with them. Jesus comes from Nazareth, and this fact, offensive to "the Jews," is emphasized (1:45; 7:52) rather than deprecated. "The Jews," knowing Jesus' place of origin and his parents (7:27f.; 6:42), are not in error as to the facts, but err in denying the claim of this Jesus of Nazareth to be the Revealer of God. They err not in the matter upon which they judge but in making a judgment at all κατὰ σάρκα (according to the "flesh" —according to external appearances).

Neither does the Revealer appear as a mystagogue communicating teachings, formulas, and rites as if he himself were only a means to an end who could sink into unimportance to any who had received his "Gnosis." Though Jesus says in departing from the earth, "I have manifested thy name to the men whom thou gavest me out of the world" (17:6; *cf.* v. 26), still he has imparted no information about God at all, any more than he has brought instruction about the origin of the world or the fate of the self. He does not *communicate anything*, but *calls men to himself*. Or when he promises a gift, he is, himself, that gift: he himself is the bread of life that he bestows (6:35); he himself is the light (8:12); he himself is life (11:25; 14:6).

Jesus, the Son of God who has become man, is a genuine man— which again does not mean that in his personality the divine became visible so as to fill men with enthusiasm and touch their feelings or to fascinate and overwhelm them. If that were the case, the divine would then be conceived of simply as the human exalted and intensified. But according to John, the divine is the very counter-pole to the human, with the result that it is a paradox, an offense, that the Word

* In some Latin witnesses to the text of Jn. 1:13 "*qui . . . natus est*" (who . . . was born) is found instead of "who . . . were born"; this is certainly a "correcting" of the original text.

became flesh. As a matter of fact, the divinity of the figure of Jesus in John is completely lacking in visibility, and the disciples' relation to him as "friends" (15:14f.) is by no means conceived of as a personal relation of human friendship. It is the farewell discourses especially that strive to teach this distinction by making clear that the disciples will not achieve the right relation to him until he has departed from them—indeed, that he is not in the full sense the Revealer until he has been lifted up and glorified (see especially 14:28; 16:7; § 50, 6).

2. In what sense, then, can it be said of the incarnate Word, "We have beheld his glory" (1:14)? Is his human figure, so to speak, a translucent picture through which his divinity gleams? On first thought it might seem so, for many passages of the evangelist represent *Jesus as the* "*divine man*" (θεῖος ἀνήρ) in the Hellenistic sense (I, pp. 130f.)—a man who has miraculous knowledge at his command, does miracles, and is immune to the plottings of his enemies.

It is as a "divine man" that *Jesus sees through the people he meets* (Peter, 1:42; Nathanael, 1:47f.) and knows the past of the Samaritan woman (4:17f.). But to the evangelist these stories taken from tradition are symbolic pictures which indicate that the believer feels himself searched and known by God and that his own existence is exposed by the encounter with the Revealer. When 2:24f., generalizing, says that Jesus sees through men, the author is not thinking of a supranatural ability but of the knowledge about man which arises from knowing God, and therefore knows what a stumbling-block God is to men. The same motif underlies the words, "But I know that you have not the love of God within you" (5:42)—Jesus deduces this from the unbelief of the "Jews"; he knows that face to face with the divine Revelation human resistance to God comes to light. Thus he knows that men mutter when they hear the Revealer's "hard saying" (6:60f.) and knows what oppresses believers and limits their comprehension, so long as they have not freed themselves from the notion that the Revelation ought to cause an alteration within this world (16:19).

Jesus' omniscience is confirmed by the disciples: "Now we know that you know all things" (16:30)—but not because he has demonstrated it by miraculous knowledge, but because now at his farewell he has spoken "plainly" (παρρησίᾳ) without any "figure" (παροιμία, "riddle," 16:29). But in reality it is not some progress in Jesus' conduct that is characterized in the transition from "riddles" to "openness" but a change in the disciples' situation. For in the end Jesus has not said anything materially different from what he had always been saying, but what he had previously said now is seen in a new light; for in the light of Jesus' departure it now appears as something provisional for which only the future can bring a definitive unveiling—that is to say, a genuine understanding (16:12–28, especially vv. 25f.). The disciples' confession therefore anticipates this future and simply means that in Jesus' work as Revealer, which has now reached its end, all knowledge is contained. In keeping with this the confession continues not, "and you need to question no one," but: "And no one needs to question you." The "omniscience" of Jesus is therefore not understood to be his super-human ability, but his knowledge which is transmitted to the believer: whoever has recognized him as the Revealer by knowing that one thing knows everything, and Jesus' promise is fulfilled: "On that day you will ask me no questions" (16:23).

The mention of *Jesus' miraculous knowledge* in the story of Lazarus is the result of unconsidered adoption of tradition (11:4, 11–14). Naturally, Jesus knows of his coming betrayal by Judas before the event (6:64, 70; 13:18). Perhaps this is due to an apologetic motif (if it is allowable even to look for such in this Gospel). But in addition to this possible motif, it is probably another idea that is dominant here: the idea that in the very nature of the Revelation— because it arouses man's resistance—there lies the possibility for the apostasy even of a disciple. Faith has no guarantee, and the Church must surmount the stumbling-block created by the fact that the devil finds his tool even in her own midst. Jesus' prediction of the disciples' flight and of persecution for the Church (16:32; 15:18–16:4a.) is to be interpreted in a similar fashion: it is a foreknowledge which results from insight into the nature of the Revelation. That is also the way in which Jesus' knowledge of the fate that awaits him is to be understood. He is both the bringer of the Revelation and is himself the Revelation. Therefore he knows what is to befall him (2:19, 21); he knows "the hour" (13:1; 18:4; 19:28). For him, the perfect "Gnostic" (i.e. knower), fate is no riddle.

Several times *Jesus eludes harm* or is snatched out of his enemies' hands until his hour is come (7:30, 44; 8:20, 59; 10:39). This motif has the purpose of demonstrating the fact that the Revealer's fate is not determined by human will but is in the hands of God.

[43]

3. Jesus *performs miracles*, a fact that is sometimes mentioned in general terms (2:23; 3:2; 4:45; 7:3, 31; 10:41, 11:47; 12:37; 20:30) and sometimes is depicted in accounts of specific miracles (2:1–12; 4:46–54; 5:1–9; 6:1–25; 9:1–7; 11:1–44). The term used for these miracles is σημεῖα ("signs" and, secondarily, "miracles"), and in John this word retains its true meaning of "sign." The "signs" reveal Jesus' glory (2:11; *cf.* 9:3; 11:4), and the disbelief that refuses to be convinced by so many miracles is reproved (12:37). On the other hand, however, Jesus says in rebuke: "Unless you see signs and wonders you will not believe" (4:48). And the risen Jesus addresses to Thomas the reproving word: "Do you believe now because you have seen me? Blessed are those who see (me) not and yet believe" (20:29 tr.). It is an indication of disbelief when "the Jews" ask: "Then what sign do you do, that we may see, and believe you? What work do you perform?" (6:30; *cf.* 2:18). They ask for a miracle analagous to the manna-miracle of Moses, and have no understanding of the work Jesus is performing. The fact that their question chronologically follows the sign of the bread-miracle makes it clear that the meaning of the sign does not lie in the miraculous occurrence. In fact, this had already been said in v. 26: "You seek me, not because you saw signs, but because you ate some of the loaves and were filled" (6:26 tr.).

As "signs" the miracles of Jesus are ambiguous. Like Jesus' words, they are misunderstandable. Of course, they are remarkable occurrences, but that only makes them indicators that the activity of the Revealer is a disturbance of what is familiar to the world. They point to the fact that the Revelation is no worldly occurrence, but an other-worldly one. They are pictures, symbols. The wine-miracle, an epiphany (2:1–12) symbolizes what occurs in all Jesus' work: the revelation of his "glory"—not the glory of a miracle-worker, but that of him by whom the gift of "grace and truth" is made. The cure of the official's son (4:46–54) and the healing of the lame man at the pool (5:1–9), both miraculous, are "signs" only in the general sense that they point to the Revealer's work as of life-promoting kind. But the bread-miracle (6:1–15), the cure of the blind man (9:1–7), and the raising of Lazarus (11:1–44) have specific symbolic meaning: they represent the Revelation as food, light, and life, respectively. It can hardly be decided whether the walking on the water is appended to the multiplication of the loaves only by the force of tradition or whether it is meant to convey that the Revealer and the Revelation are not subject to the laws of natural life.

We have already seen how 6:26 and 30 indicate that the "signs," though they are miraculous occurrences, do not furnish Jesus with legitimating credentials. The remark that the faith of the many, which rests upon the miracles, is no trustworthy faith (2:23–25) indicates the same thing. John's whole presentation shows, rather, that if the miracles are not understood as signs, they are an offense! The healing of the lame man and the cure of the blind man both elicit enmity and persecution, and the raising of Lazarus brings Jesus to the cross. The miracles may be for many the first shock that leads them to pay heed to Jesus and so begin to have faith—for this purpose, miracles are, so to speak, conceded; nevertheless, for the leaders of the people, the representatives of "the world," the miracles are the offense that leads them to condemn him to death (11:47; *cf.* 12:18f.).

4. Just because the miracles are "signs" which require understanding, they also provide the possibility of *misunderstanding*. After the bread-miracle which raises the question whether he is "the prophet who is to come into the world" (6:14), the crowd wants to make him king (6:15) because it expects material benefits of him (6:26). His brothers want to take him to Jerusalem to the Feast of Tabernacles so that he may make himself conspicuous there, saying: "For no man works in secret if he seeks to be known openly. If you do these things, show yourself to the world" (7:4). They do not understand the way in which the Revelation works. They do not understand that from the world's standpoint the Revelation must always be a "hidden thing" (*cf.* "in secret" 7:4) and that it nevertheless occurs "openly"—not, however, with demonstrative obtrusiveness but with the unobtrusiveness of everyday events. What is true of the miracles is true of all that Jesus does: it is not understood. Even the disciples understand the cleansing of the temple no more than "the Jews" do. Not until after the resurrection does its meaning dawn upon them (2:17); likewise with the entry into Jerusalem (12:16). Peter does not grasp the meaning of the foot-washing (13:4ff.).

As Jesus' actions are *misunderstood*, so are *his words* so long as they are conceived in the categories of worldly thought. "The Jews" cannot but grossly misunderstand the saying about the destruction and rebuilding of the temple (2:20). As Nicodemus is able to understand re-birth only in the external natural sense (3:4), so the woman of Samaria misunderstands the saying about "living water" first to mean running water and then to mean miraculous water (4:11, 15). The disciples cannot conceive what food Jesus means as his secret nourishment (4:33), nor can "the Jews" guess what the bread from heaven is that Jesus bestows (6:34). Jesus' saying about his departure is misunderstood as an intention to go to the Dispersion (7:35f.) or even to kill himself (8:22). The disciples misunderstand the sentence addressed to Judas: "What you are going to do, do quickly" (13:27f.). And Thomas cannot cope with the statement that the disciples know the way which Jesus will take (14:4). The disciples do not understand the "little while" used by Jesus of his approaching departure and return (16:17f.). They do not see why Jesus does not wish to manifest himself to the world (14:22). The incomprehension of the crowd is symbolically illustrated by the fact that some misunderstand the heavenly voice in answer to Jesus' prayer as thunder and others understand it as the angel voice which it is, but without perceiving that it is really speaking not to Jesus but to them (12:28–38).

In all these misunderstandings the offense of the assertion, "the word became flesh" finds expression. This offense lies in the fact that the Revealer appears as a man whose claim to be the Son of God is one which he cannot, indeed, must not, prove to the world. For the Revelation is judgment upon the world and is necessarily felt as an attack upon it and an offense to it, so long as the world refuses to give up its norms. Until it does so, the world inevitably misunderstands the words and deeds of the Revealer, or they remain a riddle for it (10:6; 16:25, 29), even though Jesus has said everything openly all along (18:20). The world's inner incapacity to understand comes most crassly to expression in the demand, "If you are the Christ, tell us plainly." Jesus, of course, had been telling them for a long time, so he can only answer, "I told you, and you do not believe" (10:24f.). Evidently he is to the world a foreigner whose language it does not understand. Why not? Not because he is not a real man, but because he, a mere man, demands credence for his claim to be the Revealer: "Why do you not understand what I say? Because you cannot hear my word" (8:43 tr.). Why do "the Jews," who know him and his home town, nevertheless not know who he is nor where he comes from? Because they do not know God (7:28)! So, on the one hand, Jesus can say that he does not bear witness for himself; if he did, his testimony would not be true (5:31f.). On the other hand, he is constantly bearing witness for himself by claiming to be the Revealer, and can assert that his testimony is true when he does so (8:14). Each statement is true, according to which point of view is adopted: such a testimony as the world demands, a legitimation, he cannot and must not give. But there is a testimony which consists of his claim to be the Revealer, a claim which denies the world's competence to judge; in the world's opinion this cannot be considered true testimony (8:13). But this testimony he must bear.

The offense of the assertion, "the word became flesh," comes most clearly to light in the *direct contradiction of Jesus' claim* (see II, pp. 29f.). It can only appear as an insane blasphemy that he, a man, makes himself equal to God, and the authorities seek to kill him (5:17f.). His claim calls forth the accusation that he is demon-possessed and a "Samaritan" (8:51f.). So does his assertion that whoever keeps his word will not see death (8:51f.). And when he claims that he is older than Abraham (8:57), they want to stone him 8:59). His assertion that he and the Father are one fills them with such indignation that once more they want to stone him (10:30f.). In short, his "hard word" is intolerable to hear. And his persistence in his claim results in the apostasy of all but a few of his very disciples (6:66). What a scandal (σκάνδαλον) his cross will one day be to men, he hints in the words: "Does this (his "hard word") scandalize you? What, then, if you see the Son of Man ascending where he was at first?" (6:61f., tr.)—a saying of remarkably double meaning, for the world will, of course, perceive only the outward form of his "ascending": his crucifixion. John at the end brings this *skandalon* drastically into view when he has Pilate present the scourged and thorn-crowned Jesus to the crowd with the words, "Behold the man!" (19:5 KJ) and, "Behold your king!" (19:14 KJ). Here and in the inscription over the cross (19:19) the paradoxical stumbling-block of Jesus' claim is presented in a symbol of tremendous irony.

5. By his presentation of Jesus' work as the incarnate Son of God John has singularly developed and deepened Mark's theory of the *Messiah-secret* (§ 4, 4). Over the figure of Jesus there hangs a mystery, even though—or rather just because—he quite openly says who he is and what claim he makes. For to the world he is still in spite of all publicity the hidden Messiah, not because he conceals

anything or commands anything to be kept secret, but because the world does not see with seeing eyes (12:40). His hiddenness is the very *consequence* of his self-revelation; his revealing of himself is the very thing that makes "those who see" become "blind" (9:39).

His work as a whole, which forms a unity framed by his coming and his departure (see 2 in this §), is both revelation and offense. His departure or "exaltation" (i.e. upon the cross) not only belongs to the whole as its culmination but is that which makes the whole what it is: both revelation and offense. The possibility considered by Jesus in the meditation which is John's substitute for the Gethsemane scene of the synoptic tradition, "What shall I say? 'Father, save me from this hour'?" Jesus immediately rejects: "No, for this purpose I have come to this hour" (12:27). In his passion the meaning of the sending of Jesus is fulfilled. And by his conceiving and accepting it as the fulfilment of the mission enjoined upon him by the Father (14:31), it becomes the hour of exaltation, the hour of glorification. Seen from the vantage-point of this fulfilment the whole work of the man Jesus is a revelation of the divine glory. Whereas in the Gospel of Mark we can recognize the historical process by which the un-messianic life of Jesus was retrospectively made messianic, in John the inner appropriateness of that process is made clear. This is expressed by the evangelist by means of the petition of Jesus which follows the deliberation mentioned above: "Father, glorify thy name" (12:28) and by the heavenly voice which answers this prayer, "I have glorified it, and I will glorify it again" (12:28). Hence, the glorification of God's name which begins with Jesus' exaltation by crucifixion and the glorification of God's name by the ministry of the earthly Jesus (17:4) are a unity. Neither exists without the other; each exists only through the other. But the glorification of the name of God is also the glorification of Jesus himself, and Jesus' other prayer, "Father, the hour has come; glorify thy Son" (17:1), corresponds to this one ("Father, glorify thy name"). And the motive for this prayer—"that the Son may glorify thee"—makes the unity of God's glory and Jesus' glory evident. And when the motive is further developed in the words "since thou has given him power over all flesh" (17:2), the unity of his glory after the exaltation with that before it is once again made clear. Both unities are once more expressed in the words which pronounce the granting of this prayer:

"Now is the Son of man glorified,
and in him God is glorified;
if God is glorified in him,
God will also glorify him in himself
and glorify him at once" (13:31f.).*

In the "now" of the "hour" when the Son of God departs from the world the past and the future are bound together, as it were. And since not until the future will the past be made into what it really is (*viz.*, the revelation of the "glory"), the disciples can only be glad that Jesus is going away (14:28; 16:7).

Faith in Jesus, then, is faith in the exalted Jesus, but not as if he were a heavenly being who had stripped off the garment of earthly-human existence as the Gnostic Redeemer was conceived to do. Rather, the exalted Jesus is at the same time the earthly man Jesus; the "glorified one" is still always he who "became flesh." In other words, Jesus' life on earth does not become an item of the historical past, but constantly remains present reality. The historical figure of Jesus, i.e. his human history, retains its significance of being the revelation of his "glory" and thereby of God's. It is the eschatological occurrence. Of course, this is not visible to the world, for the exalted Jesus does not reveal himself to it (14:22)—indeed he cannot, for it cannot receive the Spirit of truth which gives knowledge to those who believe (14:17; 16:13f.). But those who believe can now look back upon Jesus' earthly life and say, "We have beheld his glory" (1:14). What, then, is the picture of that life at which faith arrives?

§ 47. The Revelation of the Glory

1. In the hour of Jesus' departure Philip asks him: "Lord, show us the Father, and we shall be satisfied." The answer he gets is: "Have I been with you so long, and yet you do not know me, Philip? He who has seen me has seen the Father . . . Do you not believe that I am in the Father and the Father in me?" (14:8–10). In the person of the man Jesus—and only in him—is God Himself to be met, for: "no one comes to the Father, but by me" (14:6). In constantly varying expressions *this unity of Jesus the Son with God the Father* is insisted

* In the text of John as we now have it this passage precedes the prayer by some chapters. But the original arrangement has been disturbed. This section, 13:31f., must be the sequel to ch. 17; see my *Kommentar*, pp. 350f.

[49]

upon: "I and the Father are one" (10:30). With a formulation from
the Gnostic myth it is said: he is not alone, but the Father who sent
him is with him (8:16, 29; 16:32). Formulations from mysticism are
pressed into service to describe this unity: the mutual knowledge of
Father and Son (10:14, 38) and the mutual immanence of each in the
other (10:38; 14:10f., 20; 17:21–23). Or, in mythological language
once more, we read that the Father "loves" the Son (3:35; 5:20; 10:17;
15:9; 17:23f., 26) and that the Son "abides in his love" (15:10). The
continuation of the answer to Philip nevertheless indicates that in
none of these expressions is either mythology or mysticism really
present, nor is a metaphysic in the sense of the later two-nature
doctrine. This continuation is an exegesis of "I in the Father and the
Father in me": "The words that I say to you I do not speak on my
own authority; but the Father who dwells in me is doing his works"
(14:10 tr.). In the work of Jesus, therefore, God appears, but God is
not perceptible, as Philip's request implies, to the gaze of an observer.
He is perceptible only to that man who has the openness to let himself be reached by the work of Jesus, the man who can "hear" his
word (8:43). Yes, God in Jesus encounters even him who shuts
himself up against his word—encounters him to judge him. In I Jn.
the unity of Father and Son often has the peculiar result that it is
impossible to decide whether the author is talking of God or of
Jesus (e.g. 5:14f.).

God Himself encounters men in Jesus, a Jesus moreover who is
a man in whom nothing unusual is perceptible except his bold
assertion that in him God encounters men. In that fact lies the
paradoxical nature of the *concept of Revelation*, a paradox which John
was the first to see with any distinctness. It never occurs to Paul to
reflect about the revelation which took place in the human figure of
Jesus and his work and fate. For him the earthly Jesus is only the
"emptied" one (Phil. 2:7), the "impoverished" one (II Cor. 8:9), not
one who in his earthly interlude bears heavenly glory and riches.
But John emphatically expresses this paradox. He accordingly
presents the fact that in Jesus God encounters man in a seemingly
contradictory manner: in one direction by statements that declare
that Jesus has equal dignity and rights with God, or even that God
has abdicated His rights to Jesus, so to speak. In the other direction,
John declares that Jesus speaks and acts only in obedience to the will
of the Father and does nothing on his own authority. Returning to

the former direction, we read that God gave Jesus His (God's) name (17:11)*, gave "all things" into his hand (3:35; 13:3), gave him "power over all flesh" (17:2), granted him "to have life in himself," as God Himself has life (5:26), and correspondingly gave him "authority to execute judgment" (5:22, 27). Consequently, he wakes the dead as the Father does and makes alive whom he will (5:21); he works as the Father does (5:17), and is entitled to claim the same veneration as He (5:23). But in the other direction, we find Jesus declaring: "I have come down from heaven, not to do my own will, but the will of him who sent me" (6:38). He acts in obedience to the "charge" which he received from the Father (10:18; 12:49f.; 14:31; 15:10). Only in that charge does he have his existence: "My food is to do the will of him who sent me, and to accomplish his work" (4:34). In keeping with this saying, the last word uttered by the crucified Jesus is: "It is accomplished" (19:30 tr.). His work is to accomplish the task enjoined upon him by the Father (5:36; 9:4; 10:32, 37; 17:4), which he does, not to his own glory but for the sake of the Father's glory (7:18; 8:49f.; *cf.* 11:4). As for Jesus' own glory, the Father sees to that (8:50, 54; *cf.* 16:14).

The negative formulations of this theme are repeated again and again: Jesus did not come of his own accord or on his own authority (7:28f.; 8:42; *cf.* 5:43). Of himself he can do nothing; he acts only according to the Father's instruction (5:19f., 30; 8:28). He speaks and teaches not of his own accord, but only speaks the words which the Father has bidden him speak (7:17f.; 12:49; 14:10, 24; 17:8, 14). Of course, the intent of such statements is not to diminish the authority of Jesus and his words, but just the opposite: to establish it. Just because he does not speak of his own accord it can be said that he speaks the words of God (3:34), or that whoever hears him hears the words of God unless his mind is hardened (8:47), or that whoever hears his word has life insofar as he believes (5:24). These negative formulations are not in the least meant as descriptions of Jesus' humility; the high priest does not speak "of his own accord," either (11:51), any more than long ago Balaam did (Num. 24:13). The notion that it is Jesus' humility that is being described by them is refuted by 5:17f.; for "the Jews" are quite right in being enraged at Jesus' words; regarded from the human standpoint they would be

---

* The text of 17:11 should be read with ᾧ "which," not οὕς "those whom." The latter is a correction, attempting to approximate this verse to v. 6.

blasphemous presumption. But it is just this standpoint, from which Jesus' character would be measured by ethical standards, which is the wrong one; and what the author is trying to make clear is not Jesus' humility but his authority: the paradoxical authority of a human being speaking the word of God. In other words, it is the idea of the Revelation that the author is setting forth.

2. But now let us inquire what *the works* are that Jesus accomplishes in his Father's commission. Or what is his one *work*? For the "works" which Jesus does at his Father's behest (5:20, 36; 9:4; 10:25, 32, 37; 14:12; 15:24) are ultimately one single work. At the beginning of his ministry we read: "My food is to do the will of him who sent me, and to accomplish his work" (4:34) and in retrospect we are told a very similar thing at the end of it: "I glorified thee on earth, having accomplished the work which thou gavest me to do" (17:4).

In the *kerygma* of the Hellenistic Church Jesus' death and resurrection are the *facts of salvation* (§ 9, 4, I, pp. 80ff.). Being a unity, they might have been called "the work" of Jesus, though this terminology does not occur. Neither does Paul speak of "the work" of Christ, even though he, too, might very appropriately have so spoken of Jesus' death and resurrection.* Though for Paul the incarnation of Christ is a part of the total salvation-occurrence, for John it is the decisive salvation-event. While for Paul the incarnation is secondary to his death in importance (§ 33, 1), one might say that the reverse is true in John: the death is subordinate to the incarnation. But on closer inspection it turns out that incarnation and death constitute a unity as the coming (incarnation) and the going (death) of the Son of God (§ 45, 1). But within that unity the center of gravity is not in the *death*, as it is in Paul. In John, Jesus' death has no preeminent importance for salvation, but is the accomplishment of the "work" which began with the incarnation (§ 46, 5): the last demonstration of the obedience (14:31) which governs the whole life of Jesus. The phrase "obedient unto death" (Phil. 2:8), quoted by Paul from a Christ-hymn (see I, pp. 131, 298), is developed by John in the whole sweep of his representation of Jesus. Thus Jesus' death takes on a double aspect in John: it is the completion of his obedience, but it is also Jesus' release from his commission, and he can return to the

---

* "The work of Christ" in Phil. 2:30 is not what the earthly Jesus accomplished but the *work* of Christian missions carried on in the service *of Christ*.

glory he previously had in pre-existence (6:62; 17:5). Therefore the crucifixion, which John, of course, narrates, is regarded from the outset as Jesus' "elevation" (ὑψωθῆναι), a peculiarly ambiguous word (3:14; 8:28; 12:32, 34), or as his "glorification" (7:39; 12:16, 23; 13:31f.; 17:1, 5). But the Pauline vocabulary, the "cross" and "the crucified" (§ 41, 2, II, p. 8), is not found in John; and in Jesus' predictive words about his death the terms "be exalted" (or elevated) and "be glorified" have supplanted the terms "be killed" and "be crucified" known to us from the synoptic predictions of the passion. Of course the way to exaltation leads through death (12:24), in which the sending of Jesus finds its meaning fulfilled (12:27; § 46, 5). But his death is not an event whose catastrophic nature could be removed only by his subsequent resurrection. On the contrary, his death itself is already his exaltation. And that means: John has subsumed the death of Jesus under his idea of the Revelation—in his death Jesus himself is acting as the Revealer and is not the passive object of a divine process of salvation. John does not use the term "suffer" (πάσχειν) of Jesus, nor speak of his "sufferings" (παθήματα). The synoptists said that Jesus "must suffer" (Mk. 8: 31, etc.). A similar unfathomable "must" (see I, pp. 46f.) occurs once in John, but its complementary infinitive is not "suffer" but "be exalted" (3:14). And 14:31 does not say "so it must be" (*cf.* Mt. 26:54) or the like, but simply "so I do." John's passion-narrative shows us Jesus as not really *suffering* death but *choosing* it—not as the passive victim but as the active conqueror.

The common Christian *interpretation of Jesus' death as an atonement for sins* (I, pp. 46f., 84f.) is not, therefore, what determines John's view of it. At the most, one may wonder whether in using certain expressions John was adapting himself to this common theology of the Church. When John the Baptist points out Jesus with the words: "Behold the Lamb of God who takes away the sin of the world" (1:29), "take away" is the literal translation of what Jesus does;* I Jn. 3:5 is parallel: "he appeared to take away sins." The figure of the Lamb, probably taken from Christian tradition by John, compels us to think of sacrifice. But nothing compels us to conclude that the evangelist sees this sacrifice only in Jesus' death rather than

---

* Αἴρειν means "remove," "carry away" in John, agreeing with the basic meaning of the verb; it does not here mean "take upon himself"—*cf.* I Jn. 3:5 with I Jn. 1:9.

in his whole ministry. The latter view would correspond to John's total view of Jesus. I Jn. 1:7, I admit, is a different matter: "the blood of Jesus . . . cleanses us from all sin"—certainly the common Christian conception of Jesus' death as an atoning sacrifice is present here. But the clause lies under suspicion of being redactional gloss. It competes with v. 9, just below, "If we confess our sins, he [God] is faithful and just, and will forgive our sins and cleanse us from all unrighteousness." The two sentences which refer to Jesus as "the expiation for our sins" (I Jn. 2:2; 4:10) are probably likewise redactional glosses.

Outside of I Jn. 1:7, Jesus' blood is mentioned a few other times. In the Gospel we find it in 6:53–56—i.e. within the passage (6:51b–58) inserted by an ecclesiastical editor, which reinterprets the preceding discourse or discussion (in which Jesus had revealed himself as the bread of life) as referring to the sacrament of the Lord's Supper (§ 47, 4). It occurs again in 19:34b, where the ecclesiastical editor has given the spear-wound a deeper significance by adding: "and at once there came out blood and water." This deeper meaning can only be that both sacraments, Lord's Supper (blood) and baptism (water) are founded upon Jesus' death. The case of I Jn. 5:6 is different: "This is he who came by water and blood, Jesus Christ." For here "water" and "blood" denote not the sacraments but the points of time at which his ministry began and ended: his baptism by John and his death. The purpose of the remark is to assert the reality of the Redeemer's human life against the views of the docetic Gnostics. That is why the sentence continues: "not with the water only but with the water and the blood"—i.e. let no one think that the Redeemer united with the human Jesus only at his baptism and then departed from him before his death; no, the Redeemer also suffered death. There is no allusion at this point to the death or blood of Jesus as having significance for salvation.

Whatever may be the origin of these passages, the thought of Jesus' death as an atonement for sin has no place in John, and if it should turn out that he took it over from the tradition of the Church, it would still be a foreign element in his work. It is significant that John does not narrate the founding of the Lord's Supper, in the liturgy of which (I, p. 146) the atonement idea occurs in the words "for you" (or "for many"). He substituted for it the farewell prayer of Jesus, in which the words, "And for their sake I consecrate myself" (17:19), are a clear allusion to those words of the Lord's Supper. These words do characterize Jesus' death as a sacrifice, it is true, but here, as everywhere else in John, his death is to be understood in connection with his life as the completion of his work. His life-work as a whole is sacrifice—an idea well expressed in the description of Jesus as he "whom the Father consecrated and sent into the world" (10:36).* Neither does "he gave his only Son" (3:16) specific-ally mean God's giving him up to death, but His sending Jesus to men. Neither is it said that his sacrifice is an atoning sacrifice for sins. Neither Jn. 17 nor the other farewell discourses deal with for-giveness of sin. In the whole Gospel, in fact, forgiveness of sin is mentioned only once—20:23—where the authority of the disciples to forgive sins is attributed to a saying of the risen Jesus. This passage alludes to ecclesiastical practice; so does I Jn., which takes ecclesi-astical terminology into account more than the Gospel does. Twice forgiveness of sin is mentioned in I Jn.: it is conferred by God upon him who confesses his sins (1:9 see above, II, p. 53) and it is a characteristic of members of the Church that their sins are forgiven (2:12). In the Gospel, however, it is promised that release from sin will come through Jesus' word, or through the "truth" mediated by his word: "If you continue in my word, you are my disciples, and you will know the truth and the truth will make you free"—free from sin, as the sequel says (8:31–34). A parallel to this is the statement that whoever accepts Jesus' ministration is "clean" (13:10); for this service of his consists in his having revealed to his own the name of the Father, and given them the words that the Father had given him (17:6, 8). And 15:3 says: "You are already made clean by the word which I have spoken to you." So now at last the full meaning of 17:17 ("for their sake I consecrate myself") becomes evident, for it continues: "that they also may be consecrated in truth." This clause, however, only says how a fulfilment of the prayer, "Consecrate them in truth," is to come about (the explanation in 17:17b explicitly identifies "truth" with "thy word": "thy word is truth"). Jesus' death, therefore, is not a special work, but is conceived as of one piece with the whole life-work of Jesus, being its completion.

---

* However, the possibility must be left open that 10:34–36 with the apologetic scripture proof may be a later interpolation. Even so, v. 36 is a formulation quite in John's manner and thought.

3. If Jesus' death on the cross is already his exaltation and glorification, *his resurrection* cannot be an event of special significance. No resurrection is needed to destroy the triumph which death might be supposed to have gained in the crucifixion. For the cross itself was already triumph over the world and its ruler. The hour of the passion is κρίσις (of the world) and means the fall of the "ruler of this world" and his condemnation (12:31; 16:11). As a conqueror over whom the "ruler of the world" has no power, Jesus strides on to meet his passion (14:30 and see above, II, p. 53). There is not a word in John of the idea that not until the resurrection and exaltation after his death was Jesus made lord of all cosmic and demonic powers (*cf.*, for example, Phil. 2:11; Eph. 1:20f.; I Pet. 3:21f.; Pol. Phil. 2:1). For the Father did not delay the gift of life-creating power to him until the resurrection but gave it to him from the outset: "he has granted the Son also to have life in himself" (5:26). It is as he who is the resurrection and the life, or the way, the truth and the life (11:25; 14:6) that he encounters men and calls the believer into life now (5:24f.; 11:25f.), as the raising of Lazarus demonstrates (ch. 11). That is why we also fail to find in Jesus' words in John the prediction of his "rising" or "being raised" as we know it from the synoptics. The evangelist himself mentions it only in an aside (2:22): "When therefore he was raised from the dead, his disciples remembered. . . . " But as a substitute for it we find in 12:16: "but when Jesus had been glorified, then they remembered" . . . (tr.). "To rise" (ἀναστῆναι) occurs only in a redactional gloss at 20:9 and "to be raised" (ἐγερθῆναι) only in the redactional epilogue (21:4). Both terms are completely lacking in the Epistles of John.

It is not surprising that the evangelist, following the tradition, narrates some *Easter-stories.* The question is, what do they mean to him? The original close of the Gospel (20:31) just after the Easter-stories says, "Now Jesus also did many other signs." Evidently, then, the resurrection appearances just like the miracles of Jesus (§ 46, 3) are reckoned among his "signs." They symbolize the fulfilment of the prediction of 16:22: "So you have sorrow now, but I will see you again and your hearts will rejoice" (*cf.* 16:16). So far as they are actual occurrences—and the evangelist need not have doubted their reality—they resemble the miracles in that ultimately they are not indispensable; in fact, there ought to be no need for them, but they were granted as a concession to man's weakness. The Thomas-story is used to make this idea clear: his wish to see the risen Jesus in the body, even to touch him, is granted. But in the same moment he is reprimanded: "Because you have seen me have you come to faith? Blessed are those who though they do not see me yet believe" (20:29 tr.). It is hard to believe that the evangelist closes his representation of Jesus with this as his last word without a deep intention behind it. In it lies a criticism of the small faith which asks for tangible demonstrations of the Revealer. It also contains a warning against taking the Easter-stories for more than they are able to be: signs and pictures of the Easter faith—or, perhaps still better, confessions of faith in it.

The same conclusion can be drawn from the promises made in the farewell discourses. Parallel to the Easter-promise ("but I will see you again," 16:22, already mentioned above, within the whole passage 16:16–24) is another, 14:18; "I will not leave you desolate; I will come to you." This is the promise of his "coming," i.e. his parousia. But when it continues: "Yet a little while, and the world will see me no more, but you will see me; because I live, you will live also," the promise of the parousia is merging into the Easter-promise. What this means is that Jesus' resurrection and parousia are identical to John. Not only that, but parallel to these parallel promises stands a third, the promise of the Spirit (the Paraclete 14:15; 16:33), i.e. the promise of Pentecost. Hence, for John Easter, Pentecost, and the parousia are not three separate events, but one and the same. Consequently, the terminology appropriate to Easter again and again mingles with that appropriate to the parousia—reunion with him is mentioned in 14:19; 16:16, 19, 20; the fact that he lives, 14:9; his appearing to the disciples, 14:21f. But out of the traditional parousia-expectation these themes occur: his coming, 14:3, 18, 23, 28; and the phrases characteristic of eschatology, "in that day" 14:20; 16:23, 26 and "the hour is coming," 16:25. And into the midst of these the promise of the Spirit is thrust: 14:15–17, 26; 15:26; 16:7–11, 13–15. But the one event that is meant by all these is not an external occurrence, but an inner one: the victory which Jesus wins when faith arises in man by the overcoming of the offense that Jesus is to him. The victory over the "ruler of the world" which Jesus has won, is the fact that now there exists a faith which recognizes in Jesus the Revelation of God. The declaration, "I have overcome the world" (16:33), has its parallel in the believer's confession: "this is the victory that overcomes the world: our faith. Who is it that overcomes the world but he who believes that Jesus is the Son of God?" (I Jn. 5:4f.). In the short dialogue between Judas and Jesus it is explicitly stated that this is a matter of inward occurrence: "Lord, how is it that you will manifest yourself to us, and not to the world?" Jesus answers, "If a man loves me, he will keep my word, and my Father will love him, and we will come to him and make our home with him" (14:22f.). The same is said of the sending of the Spirit—"the Spirit of truth, whom the world cannot receive, because it neither sees him nor knows him; you know him, for he dwells with you, and will be in you" (14:17).

If, as John maintains, Jesus' original coming is already the κρίσις (judgment), then it is evident that for him the parousia is not an impending cosmic drama (see § 42, 1). Accordingly, John contains none of the synoptic parousia-predictions of the coming of the Son of Man in the glory of his Father, on the clouds of heaven, or the like (Mk. 8:38; 13:26f., etc.; see I, p. 29).

4. As we have seen, the "facts of salvation" in the traditional sense play no important role in John. The entire salvation-drama— incarnation, death, resurrection, Pentecost, the parousia—is concentrated into a single event: the Revelation of God's "reality" (ἀλήθεια) in the earthly activity of the man Jesus combined with the overcoming of the "offense" in it by man's accepting it in faith. It is only consistent with this concentration that *the sacraments* also play no role in John. It is true that he clearly presupposes that baptism is a practice of the Church when he reports in 3:22 that Jesus is winning and baptizing disciples. (The reader is assured by way of correction in 4:2 that not he himself but his disciples did the baptizing. Is this an ancient gloss?) But in the text that has come down to us in 3:5 ("unless one is born of water and the Spirit, he cannot enter the kingdom of God") the two words "water and" are clearly an interpolation made by an ecclesiastical editor, for what follows deals only with rebirth by the Spirit with no mention of baptism. Besides, it would contradict the untrammeled blowing of the Spirit (v. 8) if the Spirit were bound to the baptismal water. The foot-washing (13:4ff.) has often been taken to represent baptism, but this is an error. It depicts, rather, the service of Jesus in general which makes his disciples clean; according to 15:3, it is the word Jesus has spoken to them that has made them clean. The ecclesiastical redaction

of the account of the spear-wound (19:34a) made a gloss (34b, 35), and saw in the blood and water flowing from the wound symbols of both sacraments (II, p. 54). The knowledge-bestowing ointment (χρῖσμα) which I Jn. 2:20, 27 says the Church has received (it "abides in you, . . . and teaches you about everything, and is true . . ." v. 27) is the "Spirit of truth," of which the same statement is made (14:17: "it dwells with you and will be in you" [tr.]; 14:26 "it will teach you all things [tr.] *cf.* 16:13). Whether the author thinks of this Spirit as mediated by baptism—the term "ointment" would make it a natural assumption—is a question one may properly ask. But since the Spirit of truth in the Gospel (14:17, 26: 16:13) is the power of the word at work in the Church (§ 50, 7), the epistle's "ointment," too, is probably the word filled with power.

The Lord's Supper is introduced by the ecclesiastical redaction not only at 19:34b but also in 6:51b–58 (II, p. 54). For in the latter passage the "bread of life" of Jesus' preceding words surely does not mean the sacramental meal, but (like "water of life" and "light") means Jesus himself as the one who brings life in that he is life (11:25; 14:6). Again the notion of a "medicine of immortality" contained in 6:51b–58 does not agree with John's eschatology (§ 45, 3, II, p. 39). Finally, the offense which the "Jews" take at Jesus' offer of his own flesh as food is of a quite different sort from the Johannine *skandala* that arise from the peculiar Johannine dualism which is missing here. In John's account of Jesus' last meal there is no mention of the institution of the Lord's Supper, and for it the farewell prayer of Jesus is substituted (II, p. 54). John also substitutes the "new commandment" (13:34) for the "new covenant," of which the traditional eucharistic sayings speak (I Cor. 11:25). But the editorial appendix, ch. 21, reports in v. 13 a mysterious meal which the risen Jesus grants the disciples, and this evidently does mean the Lord's Supper.

It is therefore permissible to say that though in John there is no direct polemic against the sacraments, his attitude toward them is nevertheless critical or at least reserved.

§ 48. The Revelation as the Word

1. We have still to ask what the works are that Jesus accomplishes and that "bear witness" to him (5:36; 10:25). Are they *the "signs,"* the

miracles which Mt. 11:2 calls the "works of the Christ" (tr.)? No, at least not in the sense of being an unambiguous legitimation. For, as we have seen (§ 46, 3), they are ambiguous signs whose meaning can only be found in faith. In that respect they resemble Jesus' words. which are just as ambiguous and open to misunderstanding (§ 46, 4). In fact the miracles in John are neither more nor less than words, *verba visibilia*. Otherwise, it would be incomprehensible how Jesus' ministry could be called in retrospect a "doing of signs" (12:37; 20:30), whereas in the actual account of his ministry the "signs" are secondary in importance to the "words"—and the farewell prayer, looking back, describes Jesus' ministry as the passing on of the *words* God gave him.

That is the fact—the *works of Jesus* (or, seen collectively as a whole: his work) *are his words*. When Jesus says, "The works which the Father has given me to accomplish, these very works which I am doing, bear me witness that the Father has sent me" (5:36 tr.), the words of the preceding discussion (5:19ff.) indicate what the true works of Jesus are: "judging" and "making alive." They also indicate how these works are accomplished: by Jesus' word. Numerous formulations indicate that to John deed and word are identical.

8:28: "then you will know that I am he and that on my own authority I *do* nothing; but as the Father taught me, that I *speak*."

14:10: "The *words* that I *say* to you I do not speak on my own authority; but the Father who dwells in me *is doing* his *works*" (tr.).

15:22, 24: "If I had not come and *spoken* to them, they would not have sin . . . If I had not done among them the *works* . . . they would not have sin."

In addition *cf.* in 8:38 the interchange between "speak" and "do"; in 17:4, 8, 14 the equivalence of "work," "words" ($\dot{\rho}\dot{\eta}\mu\alpha\tau\alpha$) and "word" ($\lambda\acute{o}\gamma os$). There is a corresponding interchange between "see" and "hear" in 8:38, etc.; on which see below. 10:38 and 14:11 seem to contradict our assertion that the works are not added to the words to substantiate them but are nothing but the words themselves. Both times we read: "even though you do not believe *me*, believe the *works*" (in one case "for the sake of the works"). Does not "me" mean "my works"? But 14:11 is the continuation of 14:10, and together they indicate

that the "works" of v. 11 are neither more nor less than the
"words" of v. 10. When Jesus thus points away from himself to
his working, that can only mean that he is rejecting an
authoritarian faith which will meekly accept what is said *about*
Jesus. In its place he is demanding a faith that understands
Jesus' words as *personal address* aimed at the believer—i.e. as
Jesus' "working" upon him. This is the sense in which Jesus
refuses the demand of "the Jews" that he openly say whether or
not he is the Messiah (10:24f.). The answer to that they ought to
gather from his works—or workings—which bear witness for him.

The identity of work and word can be further seen in what is said
of the effect of the word. "The words that I have spoken to you are
spirit and life," (6:68). This is followed by Peter's confession: "You
have the words of eternal life." Whoever believes the word of Jesus
and Him who sent him, has eternal life, has stepped over from death
into life (5:24). Whoever keeps his word will never see death (8:51).
His word therefore bestows life. And neither more nor less than that is
meant when it is said that his word leads to knowledge and hence to
freedom (8:31f.). His word cleanses and consecrates (15:3; 17:17),
Therein, of course, the word is *also the judge* over unbelief:

"If any one hears my words and does not keep them,
    I do not judge him . . .
He who rejects me and does not receive my words
    has a judge:
the word that I have spoken judges him" (12:47f. Blt.).

2. Now what of *the content of Jesus' word* or words? *What Jesus
saw or heard with the Father* he speaks. (Or, as a consequence of
identifying word and deed, John may also say that he "shows" it or
"does" it.) This is in accord with the final sentence of the prologue:
"No one has ever seen God; the only Son, who is in the bosom of the
Father, he has made him known" (1:18; *cf.* 6:46).

Jesus testifies or speaks what he saw with his Father (3:11;
8:38) or what he saw and heard (3:32) or simply what he heard
(8:26, 40; 15:15; *cf.* 5:30—the same thing is said of the Spirit in
16:13). He speaks what the Father taught him to speak (8:28,
cf. 7:17), or commanded him to speak (12:49). He speaks the
words that the Father gave him (17:8). He does what he sees the
Father do, what the Father shows him (5:19f.). Expressed also
in a very general way: he reveals the Father's name (17:6, 26).

[61]

It makes no difference whether the present tense is used of what the Son sees and hears (5:19f., 30), or a past tense of what he saw and heard (all the other passages), any more than there is a difference between "all that the Father *gives* me" (6:37) and "my Father who *has given* them to me" (10:29).

But the astonishing thing about it is that Jesus' words never convey anything specific or concrete that he has seen with the Father. Not once does he communicate matters or events to which he had been a witness by either eye or ear. Never is the heavenly world the theme of his words. Nor does he communicate cosmogonic or soteriological mysteries like the Gnostic Redeemer. His theme is always just this one thing: that the Father sent him, that he came as the light, the bread of life, witness for the truth, etc.; that he will go again, and that one must believe in him. So it is clear that the mythological statements have lost their mythological meaning. Jesus is not presented in literal seriousness as a pre-existent divine being who came in human form to earth to reveal unprecedented secrets. Rather, the mythological terminology is intended to express the absolute and decisive significance of his word—the mythological notion of pre-existence is made to serve the idea of the Revelation. His word does not arise from the sphere of human observation and thought, but comes from beyond. It is a word free of all human motivation, a word determined from outside himself, just as men's speech and deeds can only be determined from outside themselves when they oppose themselves to his word as enemies—determined in the latter case, of course, by the devil (8:38, 41). Therefore his word is not subject to men's scrutiny or control. It is an authoritative word which confronts the hearer with a life-and-death decision.

The same thing is meant by the solemn affirmation that Jesus does or says nothing on his own authority (see § 48, 1). Such statements have the purpose of underlining the authority of Jesus, whose words, although spoken by a man, still are not human words: "No man ever spoke like this man" (7:46). To a certain extent, the word of the Old Testament prophets is analogous in that they also do not speak by their own authority but are inspired by God. But the analogy also uncovers the difference: Jesus' words are not *from time to time* inspired, but he speaks and acts *constantly* from within his one-ness with God (§ 48, 1). Unlike the prophets' words, Jesus' words do not thrust the concrete historical situation of the People into the light of

God's demand with its promise or threat; they do not open men's eyes to what some present moment demands. Rather, the encounter with Jesus' words and person casts man into decision in his bare, undifferentiated situation of being human. None of the prophets was of absolute importance; one followed upon another. No new revealer follows Jesus; in him the Revelation of God is once for all given to the world, and this Revelation is inexhaustible. For whatever new knowledge may yet be given the Church by the Spirit, it will all be only a reminder of what Jesus said (14:26)—or, as Jesus says, "he will select from what is mine and declare it to you" (16:14 tr.; § 50, 7).

Thus comes to light the deeper meaning of that peculiar fluctuation of expression between "speak" and "do" and between "word" and "work." Jesus' words communicate no definable content at all except that they are words of life, words of God. That is, they are words of life, words of God, not because of their content, but because of *whose* words they are. They are something special and decisive not in and by their timeless content, but in and by the act of being uttered—and that is why they are just as much "works" as "words": Whatever Jesus does is a speaking, whatever he says is a doing. His actions speak, his words act.

For that very reason practically all the words of Jesus in John are *assertions about himself* and no definite complex of ideas can be stated as their content and claimed to be the "teaching" of Jesus. Hence the radical difference between Jesus' preaching in John and that in the synoptics; John took over only a minimal quantity of the traditional words of Jesus (§ 41, 1). His words are assertions about himself. But that does not mean christological instruction, or teaching about the metaphysical quality of his person. On the contrary, to understand them in that way would be to misunderstand them; for it would be a failure to understand that his "words" are "deeds." Anyone so understanding him would have to let himself be referred to Jesus' deeds, as were "the Jews" who required of him a clear statement whether he were the Messiah or not (10:24f.; see II, p. 16).

His words are utterances about himself; *for his word is identical with himself* (II, p. 19). What is said of his word is also said of himself: his words are "life," they are "truth" (6:63; 17:17); but so is he himself—"I am the way, and the truth, and the life" (14:6). Whoever hears his word and believes Him who sent him has Life (5:24), but that is what he himself is—"I am the resurrection and the life;

he who believes in me, though he die, yet shall he live" (11:25). His words (12:48; 17:8), his "testimony" (3:11, 32f.), must be "accepted" (λαμβάνειν)—so must he (1:12; 5:43; cf. 13:20). To reject him (ἀθετεῖν) is identical with not accepting his words (12:48). That his own "abide" in him and he in them means the same thing as that his words "abide" in them (15:4–7). He is the judge (5:22, 27)—so is his word (12:48). No wonder, then, that the evangelist can confer upon him for his pre-existent period the mythological title: *Word* (Logos)!

Certain though it is that *Logos* (Jn. 1:1ff.) is meant not as a common noun but as a proper noun, it is also certain that the everyday meaning ("Word") behind the name "Logos" is present in the evangelist's mind. For he is hardly likely to have begun his Gospel with the sentence, "In the beginning was the Logos," without thinking of "In the beginning" at Gen. 1:1 and of the recurrent phrase "God said" in the creation story of Gen. 1. And the same conclusion is to be drawn from I Jn. 1:1, where instead of the personal Word the common noun "word," ("of life") is used as a synonym ("That which was from the beginning, which we have heard . . . concerning the word of life"); here its everyday meaning is clear. The title "Logos" is not derived from the Old Testament, for in it—as also in Judaism—we hear of the "word of God" but never find the unmodified expression, "the Word." But "word of God"—like the rabbinic equivalent מֵימְרָא דיי—does not mean a concrete figure (neither a person nor a cosmic power or "hypostasis"), but the manifestation of God's power in a specific instance. Nor is the title "Logos" derived from the Greek philosophical tradition in general or from Stoicism in particular and transmitted to the evangelist by Philo of Alexandria, for the philosophical idea of *logos* as the rational orderliness of the divine cosmos is quite foreign to John. The figure of the "Logos" is derived, rather, from a tradition of cosmological mythology which also exercised an influence upon Judaism, especially upon Philo. In the literature of the Old Testament and of Judaism there is a figure "Wisdom," which is a parallel to John's "Word." Both figures, "Word" and "Wisdom," appear side by side in Philo. In Gnosticism, which also influenced Philo, the figure "Logos" has not merely cosmological but also soteriological functions. It is within this sphere that the origin of the Johannine Logos lies.

His words are utterances about himself. Accordingly, all the

Revelation that he brings is concentrated in the great *"I-am" statements.*

"The bread of life—it is I.
  He who comes to me shall not hunger,
    and he who believes in me shall never thirst" (6:35 *cf.* 6:51a Blt.).
"The light of the world—it is I.
  He who follows me shall not walk in darkness
    but shall have the light of life" (8:12 Blt. tr.).
"The door is I" (10:9 Blt.). "The good shepherd is I" (10:11, 14 Blt.).
"The resurrection and the life are I" (11:25 Blt.).
"The way, the truth, and the life are I" (14:6 Blt.).
"The true vine is I" (15:1, 5).

In fact, Jesus can pronounce this "It is I" absolutely, without any real subject: "unless you believe that it is I, you will die in your sins" (8:24 Blt.) and: "when you have lifted up the Son of man, then you will know that it is I" (8:28 Blt.). What is to be supplied as the real subject in place of "it"? Obviously nothing definite or specific, but something of this sort: "all that I say is I"—or perhaps better: "he upon whom life and death, being and non-being depend"—"he for whom all the world is waiting as the bringer of salvation." For let it be observed that in these "I"-statements the "I" is a predicate nominative and not the subject.* The meaning is always: "in *me* the thing mentioned (bread of life, light, etc.) is present; it is I" (II, pp. 26 f.).

All these figures of speech—that of the bread and the light, the door and the way, the shepherd and the vine—mean what John, without using a figure, calls life and truth. That is, they all mean that which man must have and longs to have in order to be able truly to exist. With his "It is I" Jesus therefore presents himself as the one for whom the world is waiting, the one who satisfies all longing. This is symbolically represented in the scene at the well in Samaria. The woman of Samaria says, "I know that Messiah is coming . . . when he comes he will show us all things." To which

---

* In Greek there is no change in the person of the verb between "I *am* he" and "it *is* I"—both are ἐγώ εἰμι (contrast, for instance, in both KJ and RSV Jn. 4:26 with Mk. 6:50—both translate ἐγώ εἰμι). The context must determine which is meant. See Bultmann's *Kommentar* p. 167, note 2, on these and two other meanings of the Greek formula "I am." (Tr.).

Jesus replies: "I who speak to you am he" (4:25f.). He similarly answers the healed blind man's question who the Son of Man is: "You have both seen him and it is he who is speaking to you" (9:37 tr.). The world's longing takes form in the concept of the *salvation-bringer* in his various forms, with his various titles. So the titles of the salvation-bringer from both the Jewish and the Hellenistic tradition (§ 45, 2) are conferred in John upon Jesus. Jesus is he in whom the old hope is fulfilled; his coming is the eschatological event (§ 45, 3). But all the traditional titles are insufficient, as is suggested by the title which occurs in Peter's confession: "and we have come to believe and to know that you are the Holy One of God" (6:69 tr.). Only one other time does this title occur in the New Testament: in the demon's confession at Mk. 1:24; it has no tradition (at least no recognizable one), for though Jesus is called "the holy one" at I Jn. 2:20 and Rev. 3:7, in these passages it is not a title but means simply "he who is holy." The title designates Jesus as the absolutely transcendent one whose place is at the side of God and who stands over against the world as the representative of God. At the same time, however, the reader is probably expected to hear in it the etymological overtone: holy—hallow ($\mathring{\alpha}\gamma\iota o\varsigma$—$\mathring{\alpha}\gamma\iota\acute{\alpha}\zeta\epsilon\iota\nu$) and to remember that Jesus is he "whom the father hallowed and sent into the world" (10:36) and he who hallows himself for his own (17:19; II, p. 55).

3. Thus it turns out in the end that Jesus as the Revealer of God *reveals nothing but that he is the Revealer*. And that amounts to saying that it is he for whom the world is waiting, he who brings in his own person that for which all the longing of man yearns: life and truth as the reality out of which man can exist, light as the complete transparence of existence in which questions and riddles are at an end. But how is he that and how does he bring it? In no other way than that he says that he is it and says that he brings it— he, a man with his human word, which, without legitimation, demands faith. John, that is, in his Gospel presents only the fact (*das Dass*) of the Revelation without describing its content (*ihr Was*).

In the Gnostic myth, whose language John uses as his means of expression, it suffices that the Revelation consists of nothing more than the bare fact of it (its *Dass*)—i.e. the proposition that the Revealer has come and gone, has descended and been re-exalted. For even though Gnosticism speaks at length in cosmogonic and soteriological speculations about the content of the Revelation, nevertheless the decisive thing for it is the bare fact of Revelation. The reason for this is that for it the Redeemer is a cosmic figure and that redemption is ultimately a cosmic process by which the light-particles imprisoned in the material world are released and guided to the world of light above (II, pp. 40 f.). Cosmic connection between the Redeemer and the redeemed—that is to say, the identity of their nature (φύσις)—is the presupposition for redemption. By virtue of this identity his fate is theirs, and to know this—i.e. to know one's own nature (φύσις) and its unity with the Redeemer's nature—is the content of the Revelation and is the Gnosis ("knowledge") in which the Revelation is appropriated. But since John eliminates from the myth its cosmological presuppositions, since he does not speak of the "nature" common to the Redeemer and the redeemed or of the fate of human "selves," he appears to retain in his book only the empty fact of the Revelation. He does not give content to the Revelation by filling it with rational or speculative insights, nor by reproducing the message preached by the synoptic Jesus. Consequently, it was natural enough for investigators to declare John a mystic. For the negation of all definable Revelation-content has a counterpart in mysticism: the soul's experience, the content of which goes beyond any possibility of expression. But John is no mystic. The mystic formulas adopted by him he wishes to be understood in the sense of his Revelation-idea (§ 47, 1). Any interest in disciplining the soul or cultivating experiences of the soul ("mystical experiences") is lacking. The negative predications of God characteristic of mysticism are missing. And the negation of the world in John does not have the same meaning that it has in mysticism. That is, it does not have the ontological meaning of describing God's mode of being by the *via negationis*. John's negation of the world does mean the condemnation of man, because John sees the "world" as a historical force—*viz.*, as the world constituted of men in rebellion against God (§§ 42, 44). Therefore, his negating of the world means the rejecting and condemning of man's presumptuous independence and of the norms and evaluations emanating therefrom.

But if the Revelation is to be presented neither as the communication of a definite teaching nor as the kindling of a mystical experience of the soul, then all that can be presented is the bare fact of it. This fact, however, does not remain empty. For the Revelation is represented as the shattering and negating of all human self-assertion and all human norms and evaluations. And, precisely by virtue of being such negation, the Revelation is the affirmation and fulfilment of human longing for life, for true reality. That the Revelation is this positive thing can only be seen by such a faith as overcomes the "offense" and subjects itself to that negation, acknowledging its own blindness in order to receive sight (9:39). Then it becomes clear that the man called to have faith can ask for no credentials, no legitimation, no "testimony" (μαρτυρία) to the validity of the word of the Revelation (II, p. 45).

Jesus cannot legitimate himself, cannot present "testimony" in the sense in which such is demanded by the world. The "Scriptures" do indeed bear witness to Jesus (5:39) but their meaning has been perverted by "the Jews" (II, p. 28). God, too, bears him witness (5:31f.), but this witness is not accepted by the world because it does not know God (5:37; 7:28; 8:19, 55; 16:3). And how does God bear him witness? Through Jesus' own "works" (5:36f.)! But these works, as we have seen, are identical with his word (II, pp. 60 ff.)—identical, that is, with his claim to be the Revealer. The testimony, therefore, is identical with that which is to be substantiated! Hence, contradictory statements can stand in the Gospel, one of which says that Jesus does not bear witness to himself (5:31ff.) and the other that he does (8:14, 18). He bears witness to himself with his "It is I." But only by faith is this testimony understood as testimony: "He who accepts his testimony has affixed his seal that God is true" (3:33 tr.). "He who believes in the Son of God has the testimony in himself. He who does not believe God has made him a liar . . ." (I Jn. 5:10). The paradox is that the word of Jesus does not find its substantiation by a backward movement from the attesting word to the thing attested—as it might if the thing itself were confirmable irrespective of the word—but finds it only in a faith-prompted acceptance of the word. This is also what is meant by the following saying: "if any man's will is to do his will, (i.e. God's) he shall know whether the (*sc.* my) teaching is from God or whether I am speaking on my own authority" (7:17). For "doing the will of God" here is not meant morally, as if the sentence were urging men to begin with ethics and promising that from it an understanding for dogmatics would of itself arise. No, the will of God demands nothing more nor less than faith (6:29). Only in faith is the attested matter seen, only in faith is the witness recognized as legitimate. In other words, the object of faith makes itself accessible to nothing but faith. But whoever, having such faith, "has the testimony in himself," thereby has Life itself: "And this is the confirmation: the fact that God gave us eternal life" (I Jn. 5:11 tr.).

Now it also becomes clear that the Revealer is nothing but a definite historical man, Jesus of Nazareth. Why this specific man? That is a question that must not, may not, be answered—for to do so would destroy the offense which belongs ineradicably to the Revelation. This Jesus had to meet men in a definite form, of course, but John confines himself to letting only that about Jesus become visible which was an "offense." If he presupposes that a traditional picture of Jesus and his proclamation lives on in the congregations for which he is writing, he, at any rate, wishes that picture to be understood in the light of his Revelation-idea. That would mean that he sees the meaning of the synoptic message of Jesus to be that ultimately it is the shattering and negating of the "world's" understanding of itself. In any case, he does not consider the task of the Church's proclamation to be the transmitting of the historical tradition about Jesus. The testimony of the Church is the testimony of the Spirit that was given it. The Spirit, as the "other Counselor," is Jesus' substitute (14:16). And when the Spirit "reminds" believers of all that Jesus said (14:26), this reminding is not an evocation of the past by historical reproduction. Rather, it is that which makes present the eschatological occurrence which with him burst into the world (16:8–11). When it is said that the Spirit "will guide you into the whole truth" (16:13 Blt.), that means that the Spirit teaches the believer by the light of this occurrence to understand each particular present hour (§ 50, 7).

Beyond the mere statement that the Revelation in Jesus took place, is it only by describing it as the "offense," the judgment over the "world," the negation of human self-assertion that anything can be said about that Revelation? There is one way left to try. Since it is to *faith* that it makes itself available as Revelation, the meaning of the Revelation can be further clarified by showing what happens when *faith* takes place.

CHAPTER IV

Faith

§ 49. Faith as the Hearing of the Word

1. The Gospel of John was written "that you may believe that Jesus is the Christ, the Son of God, and that believing you may have life in his name" (20:31). John the Baptist was sent from God to bear witness to Jesus "that all might believe through him." God sent his "only Son"—in order "that whoever believes in him may not perish but have eternal life" (3:16 tr.). To those "who believe in his name" the Incarnate One gave the "power to become children of God" (1:12). "He who believes in the Son has eternal life" (3:36). This demand that one *believe* (or *have faith*) runs through the whole Gospel and the first Epistle (6:29; 12:36; I Jn. 3:23); so does the promise made to him who believes (6:35, 40, 47; 7:37, 38a, 11:25f.; 12:44–46; 14:12; I Jn. 5:1, 10, 13).

Certain figurative expressions mean the same thing. To "come" to Jesus means neither more nor less than to believe in him (5:40; 6:37, 44f., 65), and both are found in synonymous parallelism (6:35; 7:37). Whoever "follows" him as the "light of the world" receives the same promise as he who "believes" in him (8:12). The same is true of him who "enters" through him, "the Door" (10:9) or who "drinks" of the "water" that he bestows (4:13f.; *cf.* 6:35; 7:37). Other expressions also mean believe in him: "accept" or "receive" him (λαμβάνειν, 1:12; 5:43), and "love" him (8:12; 14:15, 21ff.; 16:27).

In his terminology John takes the general Christian usage as his starting-point. In it πιστεύειν (believe) means the acceptance of the Christian message (see I, pp. 89f.; John uses the *verb* throughout, with the sole exception of I Jn. 5:4, which contains the noun πίστις). Hence the object of belief can be specified by a ὅτι-clause ("to believe that. . . ." 6:69; 10:38; 11:27, 42; 17:8; 20:31; I Jn. 5:1, 5, etc.). In place of the foregoing, the

[70]

abbreviated expression "believe in . . ." (πιστεύειν εἰς) may appear (thus *passim* in Jn. and 1 Jn.; alternating with "believe that πιστεύειν ὅτι . . ." in 11:25–27). Equivalent to the last expression is "believe in his name" (1:12; 2:23; 3:18, I Jn. 5:13; *cf.* the alternation in Jn. 3:18). Πιστεύειν by itself has the same sense and can alternate with "believe that . . ." (11:40, 42; 16:30f.) as well as with "believe in . . ." (3:18; 4:39, 41). But it is a specifically Johannine characteristic that in addition to all these expressions πιστεύειν can also be used with the plain dative (in which case it is correctly translated "believe him" not "believe in him": 5:38, 46; 8:45f., etc.; in alternation with "believe in" 8:30f.; πιστεύειν τῷ ὀνόματι ["believe his name"] takes the place of "believe in his name" I Jn. 3:23).

Since Jesus and his word are identical (§ 48, 1), his words can also be named as the object of faith (5:47; *cf.* 2:22)—likewise the "works," which are identical with the words (10:38). Just as he himself is said to be "received" or "accepted" (see above), so are his "words" (12:48; 17:8) or his "testimony" (3:11, 32f.; *cf.* I Jn. 5:9). That explains why "believe him" (simple dative) and "believe in him" are identical for John. It is not as if one first had to believe him, trust him, *in order* that one might believe *in* him, but that one ought to believe him, and in so trusting him is in fact believing *in* him; one can do neither without doing both. Thus it becomes clear that in the proclaimed word the Proclaimer himself is present, acting. This unity is what John is expressing in this usage: "to reject him" and "not to receive his words" are identical (12:48); disbelief (primarily of his words, of course) means "disobeying" the Son (3:36).

A counterpart to the identity of Jesus' word and person is the fact that faith proceeds from *hearing* (5:24), or even directly *is* hearing—provided it is genuine hearing: not mere perception, but a hearkening-and-learning (6:45), or a hearing-and-keeping (12:47). So not all hearing is of the same kind:

> "The hour is coming, and now is,
> when the dead will hear the voice of the Son of God,
> and those who hear will live" (5:25).

"The Jews' " incapacity to "hear" Jesus word (8:43, 47) is synonymous with their incapacity to believe him (8:45f.). Whoever is "of the truth" hears his voice (18:37). Or the same thing is said through a figure: the sheep heed the voice of their shepherd (10:3, 16, 27).

The identity of Jesus' person with his word—or of his "work" with his word—makes it possible for John to speak of "*seeing*" just as he does of "hearing." The two verbs are united in 5:37 and I Jn. 1:1, 3 (*cf.* Jn. 3:32), and in 8:38 one alternates for the other. Just as "hear" and "believe" can be united, so "see" and "believe" can be joined or made parallel to each other (6:40; 12:44f.).

The various Greek verbs for "see" are used by John without distinction: ὁρᾶν (ἰδεῖν, ὄψεσθαι), βλέπειν, θεᾶσθαι and θεωρεῖν. What is seen may be persons, things, or occurrences which are generally perceptible in the visible world of earth (1:38, 47; 9:8, etc.). But beyond that it may be supranatural things or occurrences which can only exceptionally be perceived by certain people (1:32ff.; 20:12, 14, etc.). While in both these cases seeing is a sense-perception, in other cases it denotes the inner perception of matters having no sensory perceptibility; this is the specifically Johannine usage: the "sight" which recognizes the Son of God in the Incarnate One. Paradoxically, this inner sight may coincide with a sensory perceiving of Jesus (1:14; 6:40; 12:45; 14:9 and elsewhere), but the two may also be kept separate as in I Jn. 4:14: "And we have seen and testify that the Father has sent his Son as the savior of the world" (inner sight only). There is no point in dealing here with general figurative usages of "see" (4:19; 7:52, etc.) or with its use in traditional formulas (3:3;, 36; 8:51, etc.).

The parallelism—or rather, identity—of believing, hearing, and seeing indicates by itself that sight to John is not mystical contemplation. Sight, or seeing, is to him faith's perception: faith recognizes in the historical Jesus the "truth" and "life" which only he transmits and which therefore are not perceptible to direct contemplation. This is explicitly pointed out in Jesus' reply to Philip's request: "Lord, show us the Father, and we shall be satisfied." His reply is: "Have I been with you so long, and you have not yet come to know me, Philip? He who has once seen me thenceforth sees the Father" (14:8f. tr.; *cf.* 12:45). Hence "the word became flesh" is also followed by a "seeing": "and we beheld his glory" (1:14). This "beheld" does not mean that "we" were "eye-witnesses" in the sense that is meant in historical inquiry; for in that sense the unbelieving Jews were also eye-witnesses and yet saw nothing of the "glory."

But this "we" includes not merely the believing contemporaries of Jesus (the original disciples), but also the believers of all times. For it was not just once upon a time that the Revealer was incarnate—he remains so forever. Never can faith turn away from him, as if the "glory"—or the "truth" and "life"—could ever become directly visible, or as if the Revelation consisted of a certain thought-content, and the incarnation of the "Word" were only a device, henceforth superfluous, for transmitting that content. Therefore, the role of the believing contemporaries of Jesus is not that they give a certifying guarantee to the faith of following generations by their eye-witness testimony, but that they pass on to them the "offense" of "the Word become flesh."

2. Sight, then, is *the knowing* that is peculiar to faith. Hence "see" and "know" can be combined or be used as alternatives (14:7, 9, 17; I Jn. 3:6; also compare 5:37 with 8:55, or 6:46 with 17:25). *Faith is genuine* only insofar as it is a *knowing* faith. This is expressed by Jesus' promise of knowledge of the truth to believers if they loyally "abide" in his "word" (8:31f.). Genuine faith must not be confused with a seeming faith that is aroused by Jesus' "signs" (2:23f.; 7:31; 10:42; 11:45; 12:11) or may also be evoked by his discourse (8:30). Such faith may be a first tentative step toward him, but it has yet to prove itself as genuine faith. As "hearing" the word must be supplemented by "keeping" it, so genuine faith can be called "keeping" the word (8:51; 14:23; 15:20; 17:6) or as "abiding in the word" (8:31 tr.). Expressions synonymous with both of these are: abiding in the Revealer himself (15:4–7; I Jn. 2:6, 27f.; 3:6, 24; *cf.* abiding in God, I Jn. 4:13, 15f.; abiding in the light I Jn. 2:10; in love Jn. 15:9f., I Jn. 4:16) and the abiding of his words in the believers (15:7; I Jn. 2:24).

The formulation of 8:31f.: "If you continue in my word . . ., you will know the truth," might easily suggest that *knowledge*, instead of being a property already possessed by *any genuine faith*, is some advance beyond faith. But it would be a misconception to take it so. It is immediately apparent that faith and knowledge do not differ as to their substance. That the Father sent Jesus is equally what is believed (11:42; 17:8, 21) and what is known (17:3). That Jesus came from the Father is believed (16:27–30), just as it is known that his teaching derives from the Father (7:17). As "truth" is what knowledge knows (8:32), so faith believes in him who is "truth" (14:6). That

Jesus is the Christ, is believed (11:27; 20:31) but also known (6:69). The unity of the disciples will bring the world both to the belief (17:21) and to the knowledge (17:23) that the Father sent Jesus. A parallel statement is made about believers:

> ". . . they truly recognized that I came from thee
> and believed that thou didst send me" (17:8 tr.).

Since the content of the subordinate clauses is identical, it is clear that "recognizing" and "believing" are not two different acts. Only in cases where "believe" means a first turning toward Jesus, not yet developed into full faith, can "know" be distinguished from "believe" as a distinct act. This distinction is made in 8:30–32 where "the Jews who had come to believe him" are told: "if you abide in my word . . ., you shall know . . ." (tr.). The same distinction is certainly present in 10:38: "Even though you do not believe me, believe the works (the working of my words), that you may begin to know and ever be aware that the Father is in me and I in the Father" (tr.; see II, p. 60). Perhaps this is also meant in 6:69: "we have come to believe and to know that thou art the Holy One of God" (tr.). But believing in the full sense and knowing are not two different acts or stages—this is quite clear from the fact that the order can be reversed as in 17:8 and also in 16:30 and I Jn. 4:16: "And we have come to know and to believe the love which God has for us" (tr.).

Faith and knowledge, we conclude, cannot be distinguished as two stages. In the Christian Church there are not two classes of people, as there were among the Gnostics, who distinguished between "*pistics*" (men of faith) and "*gnostics*" (men of knowledge). Faith is not the acceptance of a dogma upon which there follows a disclosure of items of esoteric knowledge or a mystic vision. No, faith is everything. Knowledge cannot cut loose from faith and soar on out beyond it; faith, however, also contains knowledge—faith itself knows. Since for John all knowing can only be a knowing-in-faith, faith comes to itself, so to say, in knowing. Knowing is a structural aspect of believing.

Accordingly, Jesus' relation to God is never called "believing" but always "knowing" (10:15; 17:25). But all human knowing of God must always be a believing knowledge. This "must" will not cease until earthly existence is over and "believing" is succeeded by a direct "seeing" that is no longer directed toward the "glory" veiled in "flesh" but has "glory" itself for its object (17:24).

§ 50. Faith as Eschatological Existence

1. For John, as for Paul, faith is the way to salvation, the only way. However, "by faith alone" is so taken for granted by John that he does not explicitly emphasize it. The Pauline antithesis "faith— works of the Law" is not found in John; therefore the term "grace" plays no role of importance either (II, p. 8). For John *the central topic for discussion is not what it is for Paul: what is the way to salvation?* For John *the central topic is salvation itself.* He does not address himself to man's longing for "righteousness" nor attack the Jewish error that a man can earn righteousness by his own works. Instead, he addresses himself to man's longing for life and attacks a false understanding of life. The world longs for life, thinks it knows it, finds it, or even has it (5:39). The world is told it is in death (*cf.* 5:25). The world thinks it sees and is told it is blind (9:39). It supposes it knows God, but the "true God" (17:3; I Jn. 5:20) is unknown to it (5:37; 7:28). The true light, the true bread of life, the true tree of life, all are unknown to it (1:9; I Jn. 2:8; Jn. 6:32; 15:1; § 42). But the world is not simply in error; it is a liar. It does not believe Jesus—precisely because he tells the truth. The world does not want to come to the light (3:19).

The demand for faith, therefore, is the demand that the world surrender the understanding it has had of itself hitherto—that it let the whole structure of its security which it has erected in presumptuous independence (§ 42; § 44) of the Creator fall to ruins. The inner unity of this demand with Paul's concept of faith (§ 35) is clear in spite of its orientation against other antitheses than his. Faith is turning away from the world, the act of desecularization, the surrender of all seeming security and every pretense, the willingness to live by the strength of the invisible and uncontrollable. It means accepting completely different standards as to what is to be called death and what life. It means accepting the life that Jesus gives and is (5:19ff.; 11:25f.)—a life that to the world's point of view cannot even be proved to exist.

Faith, then, is *the overcoming of the "offense"*—the offense that life meets man only in the word addressed to him by a mere man— Jesus of Nazareth. It is the offense raised by a man who claims, without being able to make it credible to the world, that God is encountering the world in him. It is the offense of "the word became

[75]

flesh" (§ 45; § 48). As victory over this offense, faith is victory over the world (I Jn. 5:4).

But faith is *not a dualistic world-view*. It does not arise by a man's wavering in his security and getting bewildered at the world and so turning away from it to waft himself up into a world beyond by speculative thought or devout silence. Faith is not an act that can be consummated by man on his own initiative, as if Jesus were only the "impulse" toward it. Rather, it is exactly Jesus toward whom faith is directed: he who is the way, the truth and the life, and without whom no one comes to the Father (14:6; § 46, 1). Faith is not flight from the world nor asceticism, but *desecularization* in the sense of a smashing of all human standards and evaluations.* It is in this sense that the believer is no longer "of the world" (15:19; 17:14, 16); i.e. since the world is no longer his determining origin (§ 43, 2), he no longer belongs to it. That is why the world does not "recognize" the believers just as it did not recognize him (I Jn. 3:1); in fact, it hates them as it hated him (15:18–20; I Jn. 3:13). As Jesus' way led him to death, so the way of those who are his, will lead them to persecution and death (12:24–26; 16:1–4). But their not being "of the world" must not be confused with a retreat out of the world. Jesus prays the Father: "I do not pray that thou shouldst take them out of the world, but that thou shouldst keep them from evil" (17:15). As God sent him into the world, so he sends his own into the world (17:18), not out of it.

In Gnosticism the world is a cosmic power foreign to man's nature (φύσις, which belongs to the world of light), which encompasses man with fateful compulsion. Not so for John. For him the world is a historical power constituted by man who has rebelled against God (§§ 42–44). The membership of a person to the world of darkness or to the world of light is determined not by his fate nor by his "nature" but by his decision. The Gnostic dualism of fate has become a dualism of decision (II, p. 21). And faith is neither more nor less than the *decision*, achieved in the overcoming of the offense, *against the world* for God.

2. This decision does not proceed from motives of this world, but

---

* It would not violate Johannine meaning to add: faith is "conversion" or "repentance." But μετάνοια and the cognate verb, already avoided by Paul (I, p. 287), are entirely lacking in John—evidently because of the possibility of moralistic misunderstanding.

is a decision against the world; it becomes a possibility only through
the fact that God appears to man as He who is revealed in Jesus.
Since this is so, the decision seems to be determined, but it is not
(§ 43, 1). Admittedly, it is wrought by God, but not as if the working
of God took place before faith or, so to speak, behind it; rather,
God's working takes place exactly in it. For when the Revelation
encounters faith, the reply which faith makes to the Revelation's
question feels itself to have been wrought by the question itself. In
making its decision, faith understands itself as a gift. The disciples
did not choose Jesus; he chose them (15:16).

That is where *faith's assurance* rests. The ear of faith hears this
promise: "him who comes to me I will not cast out" (6:37) and this:
"no one shall snatch them (my sheep) out of my hand" (10:28).
Faith knows that it is "protected from evil" in the world, even as the
petition of the departing Revealer had prayed the Father for them
(17:9–19). In the shepherd-discourse faith's assurance is depicted by
the figure of the mutual recognition of the Revealer and the believers:
"I know my own and my own know me . . ." (10:14–18, 27–30).
Indeed John can even venture to say in the mythological language of
Gnosticism: "Every one born of God does not sin; for God's seed
abides in him, and he cannot sin because he is born of God" (I Jn.
3:9 tr.)—a sentence that can be rightly understood only in its dialectic
relation to another: "every one who does right is born of him" (I Jn.
2:29). That is, every one who does right (but no one else) is born of
him. Of this, the former verse is the converse: Every one who is born
of God (as is shown by his deeds) does not sin (see below).

Faith's assurance is both subjective and objective. As subjective
assurance it is described in the shepherd-discourse: the sheep know
the shepherd's voice and with sure instinct refuse to follow a stranger's
call (10:3–5, 8). This assurance belongs to faith because faith is simple
hearing and obeying. If it began to ask reasons for its right to exist
or a guarantee for its own validity, it would have lost its assurance.
As faith that hears, it is to itself the proof of its own assurance; by
accepting the testimony, it confirms God's truth (3:33; I Jn. 5:10;
II, p. 69). But as a faith that hears, it finds its assurance not in
itself, but in that in which it believes. "My own know me" has its
counterpart in "I know my own"—an expression of the objective
side of faith's assurance, which must not be confused with any sort
of guarantee. Faith's overcoming of the world (I Jn. 5:4) means just

[77]

this: the assurance of faith is solely that of hearing. This assurance cannot be reduced to an experience within this world, and for that very reason it cannot be shaken.

3. As an overcoming of the offense and as a decision against the world faith is desecularization, *transition into eschatological existence.* In the midst of the world the believer is lifted out of secular existence —though he is still "in the world," he is no longer "of the world" (17:11, 14, 16). He has already gone through the Judgment and gone over into Life (3:18; 5:24f.). He already has Death *behind* him (8:51; 11:25f.); he already *has* Life (3:36; 6:47; I Jn. 5:12; § 45, 3). To him "the darkness is passing away and the true light is already shining" (1 Jn. 2:8). As Jesus was a foreigner in the world because of his foreign "glory," so the believers who belong to him are also foreigners, and he can say as he departs, "I have glorified myself in them" (17:10 tr.) and "the glory which thou hast given me I have given to them" (17:22).

In what does the "glory" consist which has become the property of believers? The first answer must be: in the *knowledge* which in faith is given to the believer. The statement that Jesus gives his "glory" to his own is synonymous with the other, that he gives them "eternal life" (17:2)—and what is it? "This is eternal life: to *know* thee the only true God, and Jesus Christ whom thou hast sent" (17:3). This double knowledge (of God and of Christ) is really one single knowledge—for God is known only through the Revealer, and the latter is known only when God is recognized in him. Now this double-single knowledge is identical with the "truth" (8:32) which is promised the believer; identical, that is, with the knowledge which grasps the idea that God is the unique Reality and sees through the world's "reality" as sham (§ 42:2). But this knowing is a believing knowledge, not one that stands off in aloof contemplation. Rather, it is such a knowledge that its possessor lets himself be determined by what he knows. It is an existing in what he knows; hence, his relation to what he thus knows can be expressed as a "being in" or a "remaining in" the Revealer of God (15:3f.; 17:21).

Freedom is promised to the possessor of this faith-knowledge. From what? From the world, from sham "reality," from both its seductiveness and its open enmity (§ 42, 2). As Jesus overcame the world (16:33), so faith is victory over the world (I Jn. 5:4). As the "ruler of this world" is defeated and powerless to harm Jesus (12:31;

14:30), neither can he harm the believers, for they "have overcome the evil one" (I Jn. 2:13f.). For that reason, freedom from the world is also *freedom from sin* (8:31–36). He who is born of God can no longer sin (I Jn. 3:9; II, p. 77). He no longer sins, and "the evil one" cannot take hold of him (I Jn. 5:18). Believers, having permitted Jesus' service to them (depicted in the foot-washing), are "clean" (13:10); they have become clean by means of the word which Jesus spoke to them (15:3). He "hallowed" himself in order that they might be "hallowed in truth" (17:19 tr.; II, p. 55), and he prays the Father: "Hallow them in the truth; thy word is truth" (17:17).

The fact that both this prayer and another, "that thou shouldst keep them from evil" (17:15), exist in addition to the declarative statements quoted in the paragraph above is significant. They indicate that freedom from sin is not endowment with a new nature (φύσις) to which sinlessness belongs as a natural quality. Sinlessness, rather, is inherent to faith. But faith itself is not a once-for-all rationally acquired and henceforth possessed conviction, but is the overcoming of the world which must be done over and over again. Declarative statements such as "faith is the victory over the world" and "the believer can no longer sin," have in their context the meaning of imperative sentences. They set before the eyes of those addressed what the faith is, for which, as believers, they have decided—and imply the exhortation: "make it so in you!" "He cannot sin" could, in Gnosticism, describe the empirical condition of its believers. Not so for John. To him it says *what it means* to believe.

Although Paul clearly saw the problem of *indicative and imperative and their relation to each other* (§ 38, 1) and to Christian conduct, he did not treat it in connection with the sinning of believers which factually takes place again and again. He did not so treat it because of his expectation of the rapidly approaching end of the world. With John it is different, for to him eschatology as a time-perspective has dropped out because he has so radically transposed eschatological occurrence into the present. He sees the peculiar *paradoxical tension* that exists between the declaration that the believer does not sin (I Jn. 3:9; 5:18) and the confession: "If we say we have no sin, we deceive ourselves, and the truth is not in us" (I Jn. 1:8). The whole passage (I Jn. 1:5–10) is intended to show that the believer's "walking in the light" and his confession of his sin constitute a paradoxical unity. John's statement, "he cannot sin" does not lead to false security but does the very opposite: it makes radical the consciousness of being a sinner. The believer, knowing his constant need of forgiveness, also knows that he can always be confident of receiving it, if he lets his relationship to God be determined by Jesus Christ. This confidence is expressed in a mythologically formulated statement: "If any one does sin, we have a *paracletos* (intercessor, advocate) with the Father" (I Jn. 2:1; Jn. 16:26 shows that this verse is not to be interpreted mythologically—see below, II, p. 88).

The discourse on the tree of life (the "vine" of 15:1ff.)* depicts *the dialectical relationship between indicative and imperative*. It is doing so when it makes "fruit-bearing" the condition for "abiding" in Jesus, but then (in v. 4) makes the latter the condition for the former. It is also doing so when it represents "cleanness" (v. 2) as bestowed ever anew for each bearing of fruit and yet says, "You are already clean" (v. 3 tr.). And the reason given for this statement, "on account of the word which I have spoken to you" indicates that this cleanness is well described by what Luther called a *"Reinheit extra nos"* (a purity outside ourselves). It is our confession of sin that makes this purity ours, for it is he who confesses his sin who can be confident of being forgiven (I Jn. 1:9; *cf.* I Jn. 2:12; 3:5). Since true faith is a "keeping" of the word (II, p. 73), it is also a keeping of Jesus' "commandments." And keeping his commandments is the condition upon which one may "abide in love" (15:10), which is identical with "abiding in his word" (8:31). "Keeping his commandments" and "keeping his word" constitute an inseparable unity. Consequently, either of two statements can take the other's place: "If a man loves me, he will keep my word" (14:23) and "If you love me, you will keep my commandments" (14:15). Similarly, faith and love can be thrown together as the content of one and the same commandment:

"And this is his commandment,
  that we should *believe* the name of his Son Jesus Christ
  and *love* one another, just as he has commanded us" (I Jn. 3:23).

Hence, "keeping his commandments" is the means of deciding whether we "know" him (I Jn. 2:3–6). The imperative "Keep my commandments," then, reminds the believer what he already is, thanks to the prevenient love of God, encountered in the Revealer (15:9; I Jn. 4:10).

---

* In Greek and German a grapevine is a tree. (Tr.)

4. The content of keeping "his commandments" can first be set down generally. Since the believers remain in the world (17:11), a place full of temptation, this injunction has the initial negative meaning of not "loving" the world (I Jn. 2:15). That is, concretely, to keep one's self free of "worldly desire" (ἐπιθυμία, I Jn. 2:16 tr.). Whoever hopes "to see him as he is," "dedicates himself as he is dedicate" (I Jn. 3:3 tr.)—in accord with the almost identical prayer of the departing Jesus (17:17; II, p. 79). Positively, what this commandment demands can be described as doing "what pleases him" (I Jn. 3:22) or as "walking in the light" (I Jn. 1:6f.).

But "walking in the light" gets a more precise definition in I Jn. 2:9–11; it is to love one's brother. And brotherly love, or "loving one another," is the actual content of Jesus' "commandments," which can also be called collectively his "commandment" (15:12; I Jn. 3:23; 4:21). In this commandment the inner unity of indicative and imperative becomes apparent. Out of the love we have received arises the *obligation to love:* "A new commandment I give you: to love each other as (καθώς) I loved you, in order that you, too, should love each other" (13:34 Blt. tr.)—in which καθώς means both "as" and "because" (i.e. it states both the manner and the cause of this love). "Beloved, if God so loved us, we also ought to love one another" (I Jn. 4:11). "We love, because he first loved us" (I Jn. 4:19). A further indication that a close relationship exists between a believer's receiving the loving service of Jesus and the passing on of that service in mutual love is furnished by the order of the two interpretations the gospel gives of the foot-washing. The first one (13:4–11) sets forth the service which Jesus performs. The second (13:12–20) entitles this service an "example" for the disciples. That faith and love are a unity is shown by the discourse on the tree of life (the true vine, 15:1–17). In it the imperative "abide in my love" (v. 9) which, according to vv. 1–9, is an exhortation to be loyal in faith, is followed by the indicative formulation: "If you keep my commandments, you will be abiding in my love" (15:10 tr.). Furthermore, this unity of faith and love is the chief theme of I Jn.—along with its polemic against false teachings.

The unity of "keeping the word" and "keeping the commandments" signifies that in genuine faith the foundation for all one's future conduct is provided, and also that it is impossible for such conduct to derive its motivation from the world. In faith it is decided in advance, as it were, that all one's conduct is to be conduct in love.

That is why it is in love that faith makes good its freedom from the world—and in this triumph of faith over the world lies the reason why God's "commandments" are not "burdensome" (I Jn. 5:3). It is in this same sense (*viz.*, in relation to its freedom from the world) that the love-commandment is called a "new commandment." For this newness is not its relative historical novelty, for that, of course, would quickly cease to be new. And anyhow from the world's point of view, to which the epistle shifts for a moment, it is not new but old: "I am writing you no new commandment, but an old commandment which you had from the beginning" (I Jn. 2:7). It is "new" because it is the commandment that comes to realization in the new—the eschatological—existence: "Yet I am writing you a new commandment—(a statement) which is true in him and in you—for the darkness is passing away and the true light is already shining" (I Jn. 2:8). Whoever hates his brother is in darkness (I Jn. 2:9, 11), he is a murderer like that fratricide Cain (I Jn. 3:12, 15). Whoever mercilessly shuts the door on a brother in need does not have God's love abiding in him (I Jn. 3:17). Whoever claims to love God while he hates his brother is a liar (I Jn. 4:20). In the act of fulfilling the love-commandment believers will be aware of their eschatological existence: "We know that we have passed over from death into life by the fact that we love our brothers" (I Jn. 3:14 tr.). Consequently, its fulfilment is the criterion by which the world is to know that these are the disciples of Jesus (13:35).

The Christian commandment to love one's neighbor is, of course, neither limited nor annulled by the Johannine commandment to "love one another." Rather, the Johannine demand for brotherly love is the legacy bequeathed by the departing Revealer to the intimate circle of "his own" who have been the recipients of his love: this commandment is to be the rule within the disciples' circle. But this is no closed group. On the contrary, it is the eschatological Congregation whose vocation it is to "bear witness" (15:27). Therefore, the world constantly has the possibility of being drawn into this circle of mutual love. Furthermore, the statements of I John about brother-love seem not at all to be restricted to one's *Christian* brother (e.g. I Jn. 3:17).

5. Two characteristics of eschatological existence are *"peace"* (εἰρήνη) and *"joy"* (χαρά), terms familiar from tradition as descriptions

of eschatological salvation (*cf.* Rom. 14:17, etc.). Εἰρήνη is "well-being" in the full sense of the Semitic word סֹלוֹם (shalom), which includes as one component of its meaning our more restricted term "peace." It is this "well-being" which Jesus gives his own as his farewell gift. "Peace I leave with you," he says; but when he adds "my peace I give to you; not as the world gives, do I give to you" (14:27), that indicates that this "peace" is an eschatological possibility lying beyond all possibilities that are of this world. It is not something that can be realized in the external conditions of life or in some state of mind. On the contrary, since it can be seized as a reality by faith alone, it can no more become a state or condition than can "freedom." In the world believers have not peace, but "trouble" (θλῖψις); it is only "in him" that they have "peace" (16:33). Here again, as in the case of purity (II, p. 80), the "*extra nos*" character of faith's gifts is apparent.

The same is true of "*joy.*" It, too, is conferred upon his own as "his" joy (15:11; 17:13), which makes it different from every joy of this world—it differs also in the fact that what this joy rejoices in is neither said nor can be said. The modifying participle πεπληρωμένη (full, fulfilled, realized, perfect, brought to pass, 16:24; 17:13) also stamps this as eschatological joy. But this joy, although a gift of the Revealer, is never a definitively realized state, but always lies ahead of the believer as something to be realized. This paradox is expressed by the juxtaposition in 15:11: "that my joy may be in you and your joy be brought to pass" (tr.). Joy, being eschatological, can never become a static condition. But it can very well become real in occurring—a kinetic reality, so to speak. It does so in the act of faith which overcomes the "sorrow" (λύπη) that assails the believer in the world (16:20–22). "Joy" also occurs when brother encourages brother; it takes place in both the encourager and the one encouraged: "And we are writing this in order that our joy may come to pass" (I Jn. 1:4 tr.*; *cf.* II Jn. 12). Against the assault of the "world" with its cares and troubles, eschatological joy must be struggled for, but it thereby becomes invincible: "and your joy no one takes from you"

---

* The unexpected and difficult reading ἡμῶν (our), rather than the expected ὑμῶν (your, plural), is probably the right one after all. "Our" joy, then, is the joy of the "you" and the "us" of v. 3 taken together as a larger "us." But even if "your" is the original reading, it is still true in the resulting sentence that joy comes to pass as an event.

(16:22 tr.). Though it has no describable object in which it rejoices, it nevertheless has an existential significance: "On that day (the day of "joy") you will ask me no questions" (16:23). In "joy" all questioning is over, all riddles solved. Once the "offense" is overcome, the Revealer's word seems no longer to be spoken "in riddles" (ἐν παροιμίαις) but in "frankness" (παρρησίᾳ) (16:25 Blt. tr.). In faith the believer has found the understanding of his own existence, because he no longer understands it from the world's standpoint but from God's—and thereby it has lost for him its enigmatic quality. The promise is fulfilled: "While you have the light, believe in the light, that you may become sons of light" (12:36). The "son of light" is in the daylight, the medium in which he understands himself in his world and knows his way (II, p. 17).

6. Another way John uses to describe eschatological existence is to say that the believers *are in the Revealer* or *he in them* in such a way that they are bound together into a unity among themselves and with him. This latter aspect of the unity is simultaneously unity with the Father, in whom the Son is and who is in the Son. So we find it said as both exhortation and promise: "Abide in me, and I (shall abide) in you" (15:4; *cf.* v. 4b, 5) or as sheer promise: "In that day you will know that I am in my Father, and you in me, and I in you" (14:20). In the farewell prayer it is said:

> "The glory which thou hast given me I have given them,
> that they may be one even as we are one,
> I in them and thou in me,
> that they may be perfected into unity" (17:22f. tr.).

The same thing is meant in those passages which formulate the relation between Jesus and his own as a mutual "knowing" (10:2f., 14f., 27). Whereas this manner of speaking comes out of the tradition of mystical language, other sayings that have the same purport use a formulation colored by apocalyptic language: the promise that the Revealer will return and be seen again (14:18f., 28; 16:16f.), particularly 14:23: "If a man loves me, he will keep my word, and my Father will love him, and we will come to him and make our home with him."

It is just as certain that the latter group of sayings is not talking about a realistic parousia of Jesus (II, pp. 57f.) as it is that the former group is not speaking of a mystical relationship (II, p. 50) between

Jesus and his own. All these sayings are describing the believer's eschatological existence withdrawn from the world. But only in faith is this existence a reality—*not in any direct relationship to Jesus or to God.* God is available only through Jesus, which is to say: only through the Incarnate One—and this in turn means: God is never available except when man overcomes that offense (II, p. 48). Neither is there any direct way or direct relationship to the Exalted One—until He Himself fetches the believers to Himself (14:3), whereupon they may behold His glory without a veil between (17:24). So long as they are "in the world" direct sight is withheld. For John the direct personal relationship of the disciples to the historical Jesus was not yet faith-relationship to him as the Son, but only became so "afterward" (13:7): namely, "on that day" (14:20; 16:23, 26), the Day when he was recognized as the Exalted One. In a similar way the faith-relationship of the believer to the Exalted One is no direct one. As Jesus had once said to "the Jews" (7:33f.), so in parting he also says to the disciples: "Yet a little while I am with you. You will seek me; and as I said to the Jews, so now I say to you, 'Where I am going you cannot come' " (13:33). His departure, which dissolves their hitherto direct relationship and interposes a separation between him and them, is necessary, for it is only from across this separation that he can be recognized as he who for them he is. Therefore they ought to be glad that he is going away from them (14:28). His departure is good for them, for if he did not go away he could not send them the Helper, the Spirit (16:7). But this return in the Spirit is the only way in which he will return. John has abandoned the old conception of Jesus' parousia held by the earliest Church. The "world" will see nothing of his coming again (14:21f.; II, p. 57).*

The farewell discourses depict the situation of believers in the world as that of forsakenness—and represent this as the very situation in which the Revelation takes on its real meaning (II, p. 42). Within the world is the very place where believers have the possibility of being detached from the world. This is the possibility that is to become reality by faith's success in penetrating through "trouble,"

---

* I Jn. 2:28; 3:2 mention a future "appearing" of Jesus (φανερωθῆναι) and his "coming" (παρουσία), and 4:17 uses the term "day of judgment." These may be cases of addition by an ecclesiastical editor (like Jn. 5:28f., etc.). If they are not, the only way to interpret them is to follow the guidance of the farewell discourses and regard the coming that is promised in Jn. 14:3 as the "coming" and the "day of judgment" that the epistle means.

"sorrow," and "perturbation" (the noun implied by ταράσσειν, 14:1) to "peace" and "joy." Believers are not removed out of the world but within it have their task (17:15, 18; II, p. 76). Within this world faith does not yet become direct vision. Faith is a desecularization not because its culmination is some world-canceling ecstatic experience. No, faith is itself desecularization—detachment within the world from the world. Or, better: faith as the act of believing constantly brings about this desecularization. It is true faith only when it has this constancy; i.e. when it "abides," when it is faithful (II, p. 73).

The kind of *faithfulness* that is demanded by "abide in me!" (15:4) again indicates that the believer does not stand in direct personal relation to the Revealer. The peculiar thing is not merely that this "abiding" in him is identical with "abiding in his word" (8:31), but particularly that the fidelity between Jesus and the believers is not like that between human friends. The latter are, in principle, equal partners, each both giving and taking, each living both from the other and for the other. But here Jesus alone is the giving one from whom the other lives, as the figure of the vine indicates. And though Jesus does call the believers his "friends" (15:15f.), he immediately forestalls a natural misunderstanding by adding, "You did not choose me, but I chose you" (15:16). So the believer's relation to him always remains that of faith.

Inasmuch as a relationship to God is mediated to the believer by the Revealer, the relationship is that of *prayer*. Both the certainty of the believer that he is united with God and also the separating interval between God and the believer find expression in it. Prayer, too, shows that the believer is still "in the world," but is nevertheless an expression of his eschatological existence which is no more "of the world." For he who prays can be certain that he will be heard: "If you abide in me, and my words abide in you, ask whatever you will, and it shall be done for you" (15:7). In characteristic variations this promise is repeated. In one place it is prayer addressed to the Father "in Jesus' name" that the Father will grant (15:16; 16:24, 26) or that He will grant "in Jesus' name" (16:23). In another place it is Jesus himself who will grant prayer uttered "in Jesus' name" (14:13f.). In all their variations these statements mean just one thing: such prayer is possible only to him for whom a relationship to God has been opened up by Jesus and through him ever remains open. And as he who prays such a prayer makes confession of Jesus in the phrase "in

[86]

Jesus' name," so God also makes confession of Jesus, as it were—acknowledges him as his own—by granting the petition "in Jesus' name." So it amounts to the same thing whether God or Jesus is asked, whether prayer is granted by God or by Jesus. But in order to preclude the mythological notion that the exalted Jesus is conceived as an intercessor standing between God and man, an explicit denial is made, "I do not say to you that I shall pray the Father for you; for the Father himself loves you, because you have loved me . . ." (16:26f.). I Jn. 2:1 is to be interpreted consistently with this. There prayer is also the subject, though a specialized kind: prayer for forgiveness of sin—"if anyone does sin, we have an advocate with the Father, Jesus Christ the righteous" (II, p. 80). "Advocate" (or ("intercessor") is a mythological concept, but here the term means neither more nor less than what the author otherwise means by prayer "in Jesus' name."

Because such prayer flows out of his eschatological existence, the believer can be sure that it will be heard. For he who in faith has gained the upper hand over the world is also master of the world in his praying; i.e. his praying is no longer determined by wishes and fears as to his worldly future. Recall that the granting of prayer is promised to him who "abides in" Jesus and in whom Jesus' words abide (15:7), and also that prayer is explicitly called an "asking according to his (God's) will" (I Jn. 5:14). The author indicates that the answering of prayer does not consist in the fulfilment of whatever worldly wishes one may express in it. That is the inference to be drawn from the following words, "And if we know that, whatever we ask, he hears us, we know that we (therein) have the requests that we made of him" (I Jn. 5:15, tr.)—i.e. no matter what may happen, that which does happen is God's answer to the prayer. Or rather: prayer itself is already its own answer. But this is true only when in praying a believer, eschatologically existing, is making certain of his eschatological existence by asking God "in Jesus' name" to make it a reality.

This attitude in prayer is called "*confidence*" (I Jn. 5:14). This "confidence" is ours "if our hearts do not condemn us" (I Jn. 3:21)—i.e. if we are not obliged to condemn ourselves as sinners. But for the believer there goes hand in hand with this self-condemnation the knowledge that "God is greater than our hearts and he knows everything" (I Jn. 3:20)—the knowledge, that is, that we can be certain of God's forgiveness. And it is just this knowledge which confirms to us that we are "of the truth" (v. 19).* This attitude of "confidence" therefore is a paradoxical one in that it denotes that freedom toward God which springs from self-condemnation before Him; yet this very self-condemnation, if it leads us to "confess our sins" (I Jn. 1:9), is really itself already an evidence of "confidence." This is also the "confidence" that the believer has when Jesus comes (I Jn. 2:28), or that he has "on the day of judgment" (I Jn. 4:17), if these expressions are native to the epistle and not formulations due to an ecclesiastical editor (II, p. 85, footnote).

7. A final criterion of eschatological existence is the *possession of the Spirit*: "We know that he abides in us by this: the Spirit which he has given us" (I Jn. 3:34, tr.). "We know that we abide in him and he in us by this: the fact that he has given us of his Spirit" (I Jn. 4:13 tr.). In the farewell discourses the Spirit is called the Paraclete whom Jesus promises his own (14:16f., 26; 15:26; 16:7–11, 12–15). That the Spirit and the Paraclete are one is made explicit where the latter is identified as "the Spirit of Truth" (14:17; 15:26; 16:13) or the "Holy Spirit" (14:26).† In I Jn. the Spirit is also called the "unction" ($\chi\rho\hat{\iota}\sigma\mu\alpha$, I Jn. 2:20, 27 KJ) possessed by believers.‡ In this evaluation of the Spirit, John takes up the common Christian conception of the Spirit as the eschatological gift (§ 14, 1), which Paul also shared (§ 38, 2). But for John, the Spirit is neither the power that causes miracles and striking mental phenomena, nor the power and norm of Christian conduct (thus Paul; § 38, 3). It is *the power within the Church which brings forth both knowledge and the proclamation of the Word.*

Appropriate to the designation "Spirit of Truth," the Spirit's activity consists in "teaching all things" (14:26), and "guiding into

* Both the text and the interpretation of I Jn. 3:19, 20 are uncertain. I take $\dot{\epsilon}\nu$ $\tauo\dot{\upsilon}\tau\omega$ (v. 19) as referring ahead to the second $\dot{o}\tau\iota$-clause and assume that an $o\dot{\iota}\delta\alpha\mu\epsilon\nu$ has dropped out of the text in v. 20 before $\dot{o}\tau\iota$ $\mu\epsilon\dot{\iota}\zeta\omega\nu$ $\dot{\epsilon}\sigma\tau\dot{\iota}\nu$ $\dot{o}$ $\theta\epsilon\dot{o}s$. (The two verses would then read: "We shall know that we are of the truth and reassure our hearts before him by this: that when our hearts condemn us [we know] that God is greater than our hearts and knows everything." (Tr.)

† The designation "Paraclete" for the Spirit comes out of a tradition—presumably Gnostic—that has not yet been identified with certainty. The meaning of the term here is "helper," not "advocate" as it is at I Jn. 2:1.

‡ In using this designation "unction" John apparently has adopted a term of some Gnostic mystery-cult, against which he turns the barb of his remarks in their own language. Possibly the cult applied the term "chrisma" to baptism; in I John, however, it apparently means the Spirit as the power working behind and in the proclamation of the word (II, p. 59).

all the truth" (16:13). And the consequence, for those who have the Spirit, is that they all "know the truth" (I Jn. 2:20f.) and "have no need that any should teach" them (I Jn. 2:27). However, the knowledge bestowed by the Spirit is not a quantum of information or doctrine supplemental to what Jesus said or surpassing it (II, pp. 62f.). The Spirit will only "remind" believers what Jesus said (14:26). He will not speak "on his own authority" but will only say what he has "heard"; he will take of what is mine" (16:13f.). He will "bear witness" for Jesus (15:26). It is nothing new that the Spirit will teach, but whatever Jesus taught or did will appear in new light under the Spirit's teaching, and thus for the first time become clear in its true meaning (II, pp. 69f.). Jesus' promise, "What I am doing you do not know now, but later you shall know" (13:7), will be fulfilled. In departing Jesus says, "I have yet many things to say to you, but you cannot bear them now" (16:12). This does not refer to any quantitative incompleteness in Jesus' "teaching," but to the non-terminated character of it which is part of its very essence and meaning. For what teaching could still be lacking if it is true, as Jesus says, "all that I have heard from my Father I have made known to you" (15:15)? Or this: "I have manifested thy 'Name' (=Self) to men . . ." (17:6) and also this: "I have made known to them thy Name (=Self)" (17:26)? Furthermore, this last sentence goes on: ". . . and I *shall* make it known" (tr.). This interplay of tenses indicates that the Revelation brought by Jesus is neither a sum of doctrines nor a terminated occurrence but that it is what it is only by constantly occurring anew. And causing this to happen is exactly what constitutes the activity of the Spirit. As a matter of fact, Jesus brought no "doctrine" capable of being summarized in propositions; his word, we have seen, is he himself (§ 48, 2). But what he is, what his coming and his going mean, what it means to be encountered by him—namely: the "sifting" ($\kappa\rho\iota\sigma\iota\varsigma$) of the world which is the judgment of it—all this one must know with ever greater clarity, and must achieve this knowledge anew in ever Now. The Spirit's "testimony" which "calls to mind" Jesus' words consists in the fact that Jesus' word is constantly being understood anew while it remains the same—indeed, it remains the same because of the very fact that it is constantly new. This is the way in which the Spirit "glorifies" Jesus (16:14).

When in relation to Jesus the Spirit is called the "other Paraclete"

(14:16), he appears to be Jesus' substitute, so to speak, after Jesus' departure. Actually, it is Jesus himself who in the Spirit comes to his own, as is indicated by the correspondence between the promise of the Spirit (14:16f.; 16:12–15) and the promise of Jesus' return (14:18–21; 16:16–24; II, p. 57). Thus it is said of the Spirit, just as it is of Jesus, not only that he will be and abide *with* the believers (14:16f.) but that he will be and abide *in* them (14:17; I Jn. 2:27). As the world did not know Jesus (8:19; 17:26), neither has it any means of knowing the Spirit (14:17), and hence the world does not know the believers either (I Jn. 3:1). And as it was said of Jesus that his word is "heard" only by him who is "of God" or "of the truth" (8:47; 18:37), so the same is said of the Church's word (I Jn. 4:6).

Going back to 15:26 with its declaration that the Paraclete "will bear witness to me," we find its continuation to be: "and you also bear witness" (tr.). That means that the knowledge bestowed by the Spirit is to have its activity in the *proclamation*, in *preaching*. It is in and through it that the Revelation time and again becomes event. That occurs particularly in the "convincing" (16:7–11) which the Spirit does: "he will convince the world of sin and of righteousness and of judgment"—i.e. in its proclaiming the Church is to show the world what "sin" is (namely, sheer disbelief, imperviousness to the Revelation), what "righteousness" is (namely, Jesus' victory in his "suit" with the world), and what "judgment" is (namely, the very situation in which the unbelieving world stands condemned (II, p. 31). That is, the eschatological occurrence which took place in Jesus' coming and going is to continue to take place in preaching. This continuing eschatological occurrence is the Spirit's activity in preaching.

As this occurrence takes place in the Spirit's "convincing," it likewise takes place in the brotherly love which also manifests itself in the fellowship of believers (13:35). For brotherly love, too, is an eschatological phenomenon (II, p. 82). The task, then, which the believers have received, and through which the Church's life in the world makes sense, is this: that it exist as a non-worldly eschatological entity within the world, having been "sent," as Jesus was (17:18), into the world from without. Delimited from the world as the Congregation of the "hallowed" (ἡγιασμένοι, 17:17, 19), a constant offense to the world and hence persecuted by it (15:18–16:4), nevertheless united with the Father and the Son, the Church constantly offers the world the possibility of believing (17:20–23). Since it is

Jesus himself who speaks in the Church's word, wherever it sounds forth it again and again becomes true that "... the hour is coming, and now is, when the dead will hear the voice of the Son of God and those who hear will live" (5:25). John indicates that the Church's word must sound forth ever the same yet in ever new form. How it may do so, the Gospel of John itself illustrates by the way in which it both adopts and sovereignly transforms the tradition.

8. All the foregoing (1–7) has more or less implied what needs to be said about the Johannine view of the *Church*. That it has not been treated as a topic by itself up to this point is due to the fact that John himself never takes the concept "Church" for a theme as Paul does. The Church is only indirectly dealt with, and the word ἐκκλησία does not occur at all (except in III Jn. 6 and 9f., where it does not mean "Church" but "a church"). No specifically ecclesiological interest can be detected. There is no interest in cult or organization.* But that does not entitle one to conclude that interest in the Church is completely absent. On the contrary, there is a lively interest in it, as I John in particular and also in their own way II and III John confirm. But John does not speak of the Church in the terminology that comes from the traditional account of the plan of salvation which is common to the Old Testament, Judaism, and the earliest Church. For this tradition, the Church (or Congregation in Jewish tradition)—an eschatological entity—is the People of God at the time of the End, in whom the history of salvation has reached its completion (§ 10). The terminology typical of this whole cycle of ideas is missing in John (§ 41, 2; II, p. 8). The Johannine terminology pertaining to the Church comes, instead, from the area of Gnostic thought. In it, the "pneumatics" (spiritual men), in whom dwell the pre-existent sparks of light (§ 15, 1 and II, pp. 13f.), constitute a potential unity which becomes reality through the fact that the Redeemer gathers together the scattered sparks of light and unites them with himself. This idea had already influenced the development of the Church-concept in Paul and elsewhere in Hellenistic Christianity (§ 15, 4e). It is at work in John, too. But it is significant that the term "body of Christ" (§ 34, 2), so important in Paul and the deutero-Pauline literature, never occurs in John's writings—and, in fact, that he has no designation in the singular

---

* In fact, from III Jn. one can deduce a Johannine opposition to the ecclesiastical organization which was then developing.

number for "Church" at all. Those who are bound together in the fellowship of the Church are termed Jesus' "disciples" (e.g. 13:35; 15:8), and his "friends" (15:13ff.), and are also termed, by a specifically Gnostic designation, his "own" (ἴδιοι 13:1, *cf.* 10:3f.). This peculiarity of calling it only by terms in the plural defines the Church as a Church of gathered individuals who become his disciples by their decision of faith (especially 6:60–71).

In a certain sense the Church is conceived in John as the "invisible Church," insofar as they who are "of the truth" belong to it, even though they have not yet heard his voice but are yet to hear it (18:37; *cf.* 10:3). They prove to be "his own" when the call goes out to them and they follow him (10:1–6). That is why a unity of his own in "one flock" is still a thing of the future (10:16; 17:20f.); to work toward it is a duty for those who already are believers (17:18). His own, scattered throughout the world, must be gathered together and led to unity with him (17:21f.). This process, however, has been set going by the coming of the Revealer (as in Gnosticism), and thus the invisible Church is gradually being realized in the visible Church of the disciples.

Negatively, this Church is already recognizable as a unity by the fact that it is delimited from the world, in fact exposed to its hatred (§ 50, 7 and especially 14:17, 19, 27; 15:18–16:11; 17:14, 16; I Jn. 3:1, 13; 4:4f.; 5:4). Positively, it is recognizable by the fact that it is the Church of those whose existence is eschatological, those whose freedom from the world and sin is founded upon their relation to Jesus as the Revealer (§ 50, 1–3 and 4). The unity in which they are bound together is primarily the unity of each individual with him, the "shepherd" (ch. 10), the "tree of life" (ch. 15). It is the unity of faith (§ 50, 6). But as their freedom from the world and from sin includes the imperative, "Keep yourself free!" (§ 50, 3), the fellowship of the believers with him is also their fellowship with each other which is governed by the commandment of love (§ 50, 4). It is not through a discipline of abstention from the world, an ascetic conduct of life, or a sacramental cult that this Church seeks to achieve its eschatological character, for it is the Church of the Word—the Word from which it lives, the Word which is also its commission to the world. Its life is impelled by the living Spirit within it: it is the power which brings forth both knowledge and the proclamation of the Word (§ 50, 7).

PART FOUR

THE DEVELOPMENT TOWARD
THE ANCIENT CHURCH

CHAPTER V

The Rise of Church Order and its Earliest Development

§ 51. Eschatological Congregation and Church Order

1. No human society can have permanence in history without regulations. Hence, it is self-explanatory that regulations gradually developed in the primitive Christian congregations—both for the constitution of the local congregations and for their relation to each other and to the totality of the Church. As the congregations grew and Christianity spread, these regulations were formed, unified, and solidified until the organization of the ancient catholic Church stood created, or, rather, had grown into being.

But is the Ecclesia in the New Testament sense a historical entity —a thing of history at all? Is it not, rather, the eschatological Congregation of those who are divorced from the world (§§ 6; 10, 4; 34)? Then would it not be a falling away from its own nature, if the Ecclesia should nevertheless come to constitute itself as an entity within the world, having, as such an entity, a history in which it works out its regulations? And what if these regulations become regulations of law enforced by compulsion; what if their execution becomes the concern of an office? Will they not then directly contradict the nature of the Ecclesia? For its regulations—if it be permissible to speak of such at all—are created from case to case by the free sway of the Spirit. In the Ecclesia can the leaders' authority have any other foundation than the gracious gift of the Spirit?

These synonymous questions are *the theme of the still unconcluded discussion once held between Rudolf Sohm and Adolf Harnack.* According to Sohm, any such thing as ecclesiastical law stands in contradiction to the nature of Ecclesia; with such a thing a notion (first visible in I Clem.) invades the Church that the authority of Spirit-endowed persons is the authority of office. But that is the sinful fall of the Church; by it she denies her own nature. Harnack endeavors to prove that, on the contrary, from the very beginning there were in primitive Christianity regulations which had the character of law and necessarily developed into full legal regulations, and that such regulations by no means need to contradict the nature of Ecclesia.

2. In order to judge the right and wrong of these mutually contradictory views we must make clear to ourselves *the difference between the Ecclesia as an historical phenomenon and the Ecclesia as the eschatological Congregation guided by the Spirit's sway*, which it understands itself to be. Harnack focuses upon the Ecclesia as historical phenomenon; Sohm understands it from the point of view of its own understanding of itself. As an historical phenomenon, the Ecclesia is subject to the laws to which all historical phenomena are subject, and its history is an object for historical, sociological, psychological consideration. Undoubtedly, as an historical religious society the Ecclesia is constituted by its members who join it by their own free decision (so long, at least, as there is still no such thing as à "folk-church," into which one is born). But the Ecclesia itself understands itself quite differently. That is, it understands itself as the eschatological Congregation of the "called," the "chosen," the "saints" (§ 10, 3), and the believer attributes his membership in it not to his own decision but to the call of God and to the sacrament of baptism, which (in Pauline formulation) incorporates him into the Body of Christ (§ 34, 2 and 3). Undoubtedly, insofar as the eschatological Congregation, which, *as such*, is invisible, is visibly embodied in an historical society, it cannot escape the force of historical laws. Nevertheless, one must certainly inquire whether and to what extent the Ecclesia's self-understanding is itself a factor that has determined its form and history. While Sohm professes to construe the form and earliest history of the Church purely on the basis of its understanding of itself, Harnack loses sight of that self-understanding and understands its form and history from historical and sociological motifs alone.

In point of fact *the Ecclesia's self-understanding was a decisively important factor.* That is most clearly recognizable by the fact that the union of the local congregations into the total Ecclesia, in which union the Christian religion is distinct from the Hellenistic mystery-congregations, was really caused not by the empirical facts and necessities of interchange, mutual help, or an urge toward power—

though such factors may, of course, have been incidentally at work— but rather by just that self-undestanding of the Ecclesia, according to which the total Church takes precedence over the local congregations (§ 10, 1, I, pp. 93ff.), no matter whether the Church-concept is oriented more toward the idea of the People of God or more toward that of the Body of Christ. For that reason the "autonomy" of the local congregations is no contradiction of the idea of the total Church; it cannot be, because in each local congregation the total Church presents itself.

But also *the incipient regulation of the local congregations* is determined by the congregation's understanding of itself as an eschatological community ruled by the Spirit. It is so determined, first, by the fact that out of this self-understanding *the exclusivity of the Christian congregations* results, giving them their special character over against the mystery-congregations (§ 10, 3), and by the fact that this exclusivity at the same time means that *delimitation from the "world"* (§ 10, 4) in which there originates a disciplining of life which will eventually lead to the development of the penance-discipline. It is so determined, secondly, by the fact that the characteristic way in which the church offices arose and took on form was founded upon the congregation's self-understanding. *The chief persons of authority are those endowed with gifts of the Spirit*, beside whom those who act for the external order and welfare of the congregation's life play at first a subordinate role. The character of those having Spirit-gifts is determined by the fact that the eschatological congregation knows itself called into existence by the proclaimed word (§ 8, 4; 34, 1 and 2), and therefore gathers about the word, listening and also speaking (I Cor. 14). The Spirit-endowed, then, are primarily *proclaimers of the word*, and that fact stamps the character of the incipient churchly office from the outset. Even when the sacrament, which stands by the side of the word, receives a greater weight in the self-understanding of the congregation and its leaders take on a priestly character, they nevertheless remain proclaimers of the word also, and the congregation continues to be the listening congregation gathered about the word.

3. In this sense Sohm's conception of the Church as a society constituted not by a code of law but by the sway of the Spirit must be considered valid. He is right, further, in maintaining that the congregation, so understanding itself, needs no law; in fact *that legal regulation contradicts the Church's nature—in case, that is, such law*

ceases to be regulative and becomes constitutive. Sohm's error, however, lies in his failure to recognize that a regulative legal provision not only does not stand in opposition to the Spirit's sway, but may actually be the creation of the Spirit. Quite rightly Karl Holl pointed out in refutation of Sohm that *the word of the Spirit-endowed, being an authoritative word, creates regulation and tradition.* What Paul writes to his congregations as one who claims to "have the Spirit of God" (I Cor. 7:40; *cf.* 14:37 and also 2:10ff.) creates tradition. And the author of the Apocalypse attributes canonical authority to his prophetic book (Rev. 22:18f.). The New Testament would never have been written, or passed on, or canonized as authoritative, if the charismatic word and regulative tradition were contrary to each other.

Sohm one-sidedly pictures the members of the Christian congregations as religious individualists and enthusiasts and one-sidedly conceives *the working of the Spirit* as taking place in inspirations of the moment. What Paul combats as a danger or what he at least restricts (I Cor. 12 and 14), Sohm regards, so to say, as the normal thing. No matter how much momentary inspiration may be characteristic of the word of the Spirit-endowed—*the word which they proclaim* does not derive its content from a revelation personally vouchsafed to them in inward illumination, but instead they proclaim "the word of faith" (Rom. 10:8), the "gospel" at whose center stands Christ and the occurrence of salvation in him: "the word of the cross," "the reconciliation." Richly varied as the form of that word may be—as the New Testament abundantly testifies—it is a definite word mediated by tradition; there never was a "gospel" without "tradition" (παράδοσις—see I Cor. 15:1f.).

The Spirit works, however, not only in the proclaimers of the word, but *also in the congregations.* And here again the Spirit's work manifests itself not only in momentary inspirations, remarkable psychic phenomena, and the capacity to do things that surpass the normal (§ 14, 1), but also in the order-creating activities of individual members, in their various services to the group, which Paul teaches his readers to regard as being spiritual gifts, too (I Cor. 12:5ff., 28; Rom. 12:7f.; see I, pp. 154, 336). The Spirit also works in the congregations in such a way that definite decisions are made and put into action. The Spirit founds in the beginning something like a *"congregational democracy,"* which is very well able to exist side by side with an "aristocracy" consisting of the Spirit-endowed. Of course, one cannot say that there was a democratic constitution as an institutional legal ordinance which guaranteed each individual his rights and assigned him his duties, so it would be better to call it a "pneumatocracy" or, less felicitously, a "Christocracy" (Eduard Schweizer). Nevertheless, such terms are not very clear, for neither pneumatocracy nor Christocracy is a genuine opposite to democracy (nor to aristocracy or monarchy, either). For the real question is just this: in what form will the rule of the Spirit, or of Christ, realize itself in history? At any rate, it is incontestable that the later order (in which congregational officials have superseded the Spirit-endowed, a monarchical episcopate has developed, and the distinction between priests and laymen has arisen) was preceded by an order that must be called democratic. For notwithstanding the authority of the Spirit-endowed—for this is not an authority of office—the congregation takes action as a totality. It not only has itself the charismatic right to "test" the charismatics (=the Spirit-endowed; see I Thess. 5:21; I Cor. 12:10, 14:29; Did. 11:7–12; Herm. mand. XI) but also sends out missionaries (Acts 13:2) or delegates (I Cor. 16:3; II Cor. 8:19, Acts 15:2, probably also Ign. Philad. 10:1; Sm. 11:2; Pol. 7:2). It holds sessions, sometimes court-sessions (I Cor. 4:3, 5:3f.) in which majority decisions may be reached (II Cor. 2:6). In Acts 6:2, 5, 15:22, 30 we evidently have a reflection of a practice by which recommendations or proposals offered by the leaders of the congregation are voted into force by the whole congregation. In I Clem. 54:2 the recalcitrant one is exhorted to do "that which is ordered by the congregation." Even when in the course of time installation of congregational officials arises, the congregation is evidently also active in the process, for in all probability it is from the congregation that the prophet-voices arise which point out the persons to be installed (I Tim. 1:18, 4:14; *cf.* Acts 20:28). At any rate, I Clem. 44:3 explicitly says that presbyters were appointed in the congregations by the successors of the apostles "with the approval of the whole congregation." And Did. 15:1 in harmony with this commands: "therefore appoint for yourselves bishops and deacons."

Hence, it is not justified to place the inception and development of church order and church office in such opposition to the sway of the Spirit as Sohm does. Intelligent conduct which arises from a recognition of what the situation demands does not exclude the possibility that the Spirit is working in such conduct. It is no less true that the services performed through the Spirit in and for the congregation do not contradict the nature of the Spirit simply because of being connected with an office. Such a conclusion would be necessary only if the Spirit's sway were regarded as restricted to the phenomena of an individualistic Spirit-possession. Early Christianity was spared from such a narrow view of the Spirit by the influence of Pauline and Johannine theology and, secondarily, by that of the synogogal tradition—or that of the Old Testament and Judaism.

The development about to be described, therefore, is viewed from the point of view of this critical question: were the incipient regulations appropriate to the nature of the Ecclesia as an eschatological congregation constituted by the word of proclamation?—or, to what extent were they appropriate, and how appropriate did they continue to be? This question includes the further question: did this budding ecclesiastical law have regulative character or constitutive, and did it retain its original character? But the rise of ecclesiastical law itself is regarded from the point of view of two questions: 1. From what time, and how, is the observance of regulations guaranteed by penalties? For as soon as that occurs, the regulations take on the character of legal regulations. 2. What are the sources of authority that establish regulations and watch over their observance? Are they the congregations—either each congregation, or the totality of all the congregations—or are they individuals either empowered by the congregation or authorized by some other kinds of power? If the authority behind the regulations is represented by individuals, then the ecclesiastical office arises.

§ 52. The Ecclesiastical Offices

1. Neither in the earliest Palestinian Congregation nor in earliest Hellenistic Christianity was there originally any thought of instituting church regulations or offices—which is just what one would expect in view of their eschatological consciousness of standing at the end of time. The consequence even of this single fact was that the earliest Church in Palestine at first remained within the regulations of the Jewish Congregation and had no intention to constitute itself a new religious community (§ 8, 1). Although baptism and the Lord's Supper already delimited the Palestinian Congregation from Judaism and later delimited the Hellenistic Church from heathen cults, still

neither in the Palestinian Church nor originally in the Hellenistic Church was there a priestly class. As late as I Pet. (*cf.* 2:5, 9) the Congregation is "a holy priesthood," "a royal priesthood"; i.e. all Christians have priestly quality. But to the extent that both branches of the Church had need of some sort of order and guidance, such was given by persons of authority who were still far from being officials. In the Palestinian Congregation these were Peter, John, and James, the Lord's brother (§ 8, 4); in the Hellenistic congregations they were, quite naturally, the "apostles" who had founded these congregations. Since the apostles are not resident in a particular congregation, we find in addition to them other proclaimers of the word: "prophets" and "teachers." Neither are these men officials. Rather, they are persons called individually by the Spirit, no matter whether they were settled in one congregation or whether like the apostles they wandered from place to place.

But presently there appears *in the early Congregation of Palestine the office of the "elders"* (§ 8, 4). There was little need to feel a conflict between this office and the persons of authority, because one of the latter, James, was in all likelihood also chairman of the board of elders. A council of "elders," as a matter of fact, is an institution in which respect for personal authority is united with the authority of office; such a council was an excellent means of enhancing the authority of leading persons. The formation of a board of elders, furthermore, could scarcely seem to the Christian Congregation to be anything out of the ordinary, because therein it was only following the pattern of the synagogue congregations.* The earliest Church at first took the form of a synagogue within Judaism, as is well known.

As for *the Christian congregations in the Hellenistic world,* which had developed out of synagogue-congregations or had attached themselves to such, much the same thing holds true. Here, too, "elders" led the congregations. This is clear from the fact that in the very sources where the adoption of synagogal tradition is evident (not in the Didache, however), *presbyteroi* (elders) appear as congregational leaders; it is so in Acts, James, I Clem., Hermas, and II Clem. (17:3–5). For the early period at least we may assume that the title denoted both office and age; it clearly does in I Pet. 5:1–5. In the

---

* See Schürer, *A History of the Jewish People in the Time of Jesus Christ,* II, part I, pp. 149ff.; Strack-B.IV 145; Joachim Jeremias, *Jerusalem zur Zeit Jesu,* II B (1937), 88ff.

partially or totally Gentile congregations the leaders bear the title *episkopos*, which is known to us in pagan Greek usage as the title of certain municipal officials and also of officers of associations and cultic societies.* Christian *episkopoi* appear for the first time at Phil. 1:1, and there *diakonoi* are named with them—a title which is likewise known to us as one used for municipal officials and for officers of associations.† It can be inferred from the Christian use of these terms that the activities which at first were voluntarily assumed by individuals on the basis of their personal authority gradually became the functions of formal officials. In place of the early informal designations "those who labor among you" (κοπιῶντες, I Thess. 5:12), "fellow workers" (συνεργοῦντες, I Cor. 16:16 and elsewhere), your "leaders" (or "chairmen" Heb. 13:7) there now appear the more formal ones, "elders" or "episkopoi" (and *diakonoi*, "assistants"); yet, in addition to these, more general designations continue to be used, such as ἡγούμενοι or προηγούμενοι ("leaders," I Clem. 1:3, 21:6; Herm. vis. III 9:7). The difference between presbyters and *episkopoi* is probably just a difference of terminology. Both titles alike evidently mean the leaders of the congregation—though it must be left open what powers and duties, and how many of them, were apportioned to the leaders in the one case and the other. It is probably a result of intercommunication between the congregations that here and there both titles were used side by side for the same persons, as in I Clem. and Hermas (*cf.* also Acts 20:17 with 20:28, where "guardians" translates *episkopoi* in RSV). This is particularly clear in the pastoral epistles. To their author the familiar title is evidently presbyter, elder. (I Tim. 4:14, 5:17, 19; especially Tit. 1:5). But when he specifies the qualifications for this office he takes over an already formulated tradition in which the qualifications for the office of *episkopos* were enumerated—and retains the latter title without changing it (I Tim. 3:2, Titus. 1:7). Probably a distinction in meaning between these two titles develops only when the monarchical episcopate arises. Then the *episkopos* is the chairman of the board of elders, a situation for which Ignatius is the earliest witness.‡

* See M. Dibelius on Phil. 1:1 in Lietzmann's *Handbuch*; H. W. Beyer in *ThWB* II, 908ff.

† See Dibelius in the preceding note, *op cit.*, same page.

‡ See M. Dibelius on Herm. sim. IX 27:3 in the supplement volume of Lietzmann's *Handbuch*; also W. Bauer on Ign. Mg. 2:2 in the same volume.

Within the framework of a theology of the New Testament it is not necessary to trace this development in detail, even so far as the paucity of sources grants us insight into it. In various regions it took place in varying ways and with varying speed. But the important thing is to clarify the character of this incipient office.

2. First, we must clarify *the distinction between the congregational officials and the "charismatics,"* who also play a leading role in the young congregations. This distinction has become common since the discovery of the Didache (1883) and Harnack's evaluation of it. It means that the congregational offices possess administrative and jurisdictional functions for each particular congregation, but that the elders and *episkopoi* are not proclaimers of the word—at least not by virtue of their office. Rather, it is the *apostles, prophets, teachers,* whom I Cor. 12:28 places at the head of the list of the "charismatics," who are *the proclaimers of the word.** These are in no sense officials of a specific congregation, but have their calling, or rather their "call," for the whole Church. Theirs is not an official activity, as we clearly see in the case of the apostles: they were called by the Lord and are not in charge of an office which must be filled again after their death. But the same is true of the prophets and teachers. They are called by the gift of the Spirit, and at first, at least, any member of the congregation may become the recipient of the gift (χάρισμα) of the Spirit. Neither is their commission restricted to that congregation to which they belong. As the Didache and Hermas show, they like the apostles may also travel as wandering preachers from congregation to congregation, especially after the apostles, along with the rest of the first generation, have died out.

In order to indicate this distinction there are those who term the "office" of the apostles, prophets, teachers, a "charismatic office" in contrast to the institutional office of the elders or episkopoi. But it would be better to avoid the term "office" for the proclaimers of the word. At any rate, one should not talk of a "double organization" (one for the specific congregation and one for the Church as a whole), for the work of the apostles, prophets, and teachers cannot be termed an organization. But it is correct to say that the activity of the elders and episkopoi is restricted to their specific congregation, while by

---

* Apostles and prophets, Acts 18:20, Did. 11; prophets and teachers, Acts 13:1, Did. 13:1f.; apostles and teachers, Herm. sim. IX 15:4, 16:5, 25:2; while in Herm. vis. III 5:1 apostles, bishops, teachers, and deacons are combined.

the person and the work of the apostles, prophets, and teachers the Ecclesia is represented as the *one* Church. But this oneness is at first not an organizational but a charismatic unity wrought by the Spirit.

In the fact that the activity of proclaiming the word, which we have seen really constitutes the Church (§ 8, 4; § 34, 1 and 2), is not at first tied to an office, we have solid evidence that *the Church at first knows no office or law by which it is constituted as the Church.* What there is of office and law—the institution of congregational officers (presbyters and episkopoi)—does not constitute the Church, but regulates the practical side of congregational life. Now, according to Paul's view the tasks and activities within the compass of congregational life (the "varieties of service," the "helps" and "administrations" I Cor. 12:5, 28 tr.) are also gifts of the Spirit. To that extent it may be justified to term the offices of "presbyter" and "episkopos" charismatic, but in so doing one must be aware that although this corresponds to Paul's specific understanding of the matter, it nevertheless does not agree with the oldest usage of Hellenistic Christianity (§ 14, 1, I, p. 154). This general Hellenistic usage agrees with the usual philologically established usage, according to which being empowered and commissioned by a *charisma* (supernatural gift) is in sharp contrast with natural endowment and legal commission. The charismatic (or "pneumatic") man, then, is the inspired man endowed with miraculous power.

Charisma (considered always as the miraculous gift bestowed by the Spirit) was capable of being regarded in three different ways: 1. as the power which manifests itself as the momentary, or violent, or extraordinary event (such as glossolalia or ecstasy) which occurs in specific miraculous phenomena; here a man's *charisma* is the particular miraculous deed accomplished through him. 2. As the power with which certain individuals (πνευματικοί) are endowed. 3. As the manifestation of that which is miraculous in respect of its significance (οἰκοδομή, edification). With the coalescing of the second and third viewpoints there arises the ecclesiastical conception of the *charisma* of office.

3. The *course of development* now is a double one. On the one hand, the charismatics, so far as they are proclaimers of the word, more and more become officials; that is, their *charisma*, which was originally given to the person, is now understood as an office–*charisma* conveyed by ordination (I Tim. 4:14, II Tim. 1:6). On the

other hand, the proclaiming of the word is transferred as a right or duty of office to the officials (elders or episkopoi) of the congregation (pastoral letters, Did., Herm.).

At the head of the charismatics stands the apostle. At first he was the proclaimer of the word called by the Lord or the Spirit (Rom. 10:14ff.; Mt. 28:18ff.; Lk. 24:46ff.; Acts 1:8, 13:2 and elsewhere), the missionary to the Jewish and to the Gentile world. He can be called "herald" (κῆρυξ), as his preaching can be called *kerygma* (herald-service, proclamation); see Rom. 10:8ff.; I Cor. 1:23, 9:27; I Tim. 2:7; II Tim. 1:11 and elsewhere). His designation as "sent man," "messenger" (שָׁלִיחַ, ἀπόστολος), was probably taken over from the Jewish institution of שְׁלִיחִים (messengers) of the Sanhedrin. But whereas the office of the Jewish שָׁלִיחַ expires with the performance of his errand, the Christian apostle remains what he became by his call. As the unmodified use of the word "apostle" indicates, his commission cannot expire. The apostle proclaims the risen Lord. Indeed, in the apostle, as the representative of Christ, the Lord himself encounters men. Not only Paul so formulates it (II Cor. 5:20), it is also expressed in the saying of Jesus at Mt. 10:40; Lk. 10:16; Jn. 13:20. Thus the concept of the apostle as the proclaimer sent out by the risen Lord is primarily determined by the *idea* of *authorization*; his word is the word legitimated by the Lord. In addition to this, *the idea of tradition* gradually achieves preponderance, an idea which, of course, was not absent at the beginning (I Cor. 15:3, 14f.). The "testimony" (μαρτύριον), which at first meant primarily an appeal as if by oath (I Thess. 2:12: "we *charged* you"), takes on more and more the meaning of "attestation," i.e. attestation of the facts experienced by the apostles as eye-witnesses, especially to the resurrection of Christ (Acts 1:22, 2:32, 3:15, etc.). The resultant narrowing down of the title "apostle," which originally was accorded to all missionaries, to include only the twelve (Paul is the only exception to this restriction) is clear evidence that the apostles were regarded as the guarantors of the Church's tradition. According to Eph. 2:20 the Church is built upon the foundation of the apostles and prophets; and the latter belong with the former as recipients of revelation (3:5). Christ established both, along with the evangelists, pastors, and teachers, as the authorized bearers of the tradition (4:11; *cf.* Herm. sim. IX 25:2). The apostles, of course, begin the list; their names, according to Rev. 21:14, are inscribed on the twelve foundation stones of the New Jerusalem's walls (see, further, § 55, 5). Especially significant is the legend of the election of a substitute for Judas Iscariot to the college of the twelve (Acts 1:21–26). Also indicative, probably, is the distinction made between apostle and evangelist (Eph. 4:11; *cf.* II Tim. 4:5; Acts 21:8); the latter title fell to missionaries as soon as the title "apostle" was reserved for the twelve. (It was not able to establish and maintain itself as a common title because the congregational officials gradually took over the function of proclaiming the word.) Since the apostles are regarded primarily as guarantors and mediators of the tradition, the Church's "deposit-in-trust" (παραθήκη I Tim. 6:20; II Tim. 1:12, 14 tr.), they come to be regarded in the same light as were the congregational officials, upon whom, next after the apostles, the responsibility for preserving the tradition rests. Hence, the notion can now arise that the apostles must have successors (pastoral epistles, Acts 14:23; I Clem. 44:2; see immediately below). The conception of apostleship as an office could find support in sayings which grant the apostle the right to support by the congregations (I Cor. 9:17–18; II Cor. 11:7–12; Lk. 10:7; for "teachers," Gal. 6:6) or also in the fact that the claim to be called an apostle was conditioned by the fulfilment of certain qualifications (I Cor. 9:1f.; II Cor. 3:2f.; 12:12).

Now comes a further development. The *apostolate* comes more and more to be seen from the standpoint of the organization of the whole Church and to be conceived as an office which, unlike that of the bishops and elders, pertains to the whole Church. This finds expression in the fact that the organizing of the individual congregations is attributed to the apostles. And this is not incorrect insofar as the apostles, as Paul's letters show, not only founded the congregations but thereupon claimed the right—though not a legal one—to guide them with advice and exhortation by letters and visits. In so doing they not only concerned themselves with right understanding of the faith and combatted heresy, but also worked for proper order (*cf.* I Cor. 4:15; 9:1f.; II Cor. 3:1–3; 10:13–16; Gal. 4:17–20; and compare the restraint that Paul exercises toward the congregation at Rome). But it is something new when *the appointment of elders and episkopoi is traced back to the apostles*. This is already done in Acts 14:23, and again in the pastoral epistles.

It is done indirectly in Tit. 1:5 by the order of the pretended apostle to the recipient that he appoint elders in every city. What "Titus," who is to act in the apostle's place, is considered to be, may probably be inferred from II Tim. 4:5: an evangelist. That is, he is practically an apostle himself except that after the reservation of the title "apostle" to the twelve and Paul (see II, p. 105), he can no longer receive that title. However that may be, the author of the pastorals does not venture to ascribe direct apostolic appointment to the elders and "bishops" who in his time are functioning as congregational officials, but injects Timothy and Titus, pupils of the apostle, as an intermediate link. It amounts to the same thing whether the author says the charisma of office was conferred upon "Timothy" by the laying on of the apostle's hands (II Tim. 1:6) or whether he says that it was mediated by the laying on of the hands of the presbytery (I Tim. 4:14), which was itself guided by "prophecy" (I Tim. 1:18, 4:14). Evidently the latter corresponded to the practice of the author's own time.

This view is fully developed in I Clem. Jesus Christ, commissioned by God, on his part commissioned the apostles (42:1f.). They then spread the proclamation through lands and cities and everywhere appointed bishops and deacons (42:4; 44:2) and authorized them to arrange for their own successors (44:2)—for which Scripture proof from the Old Testament is then provided (43). Here, then, the congregational office as obligatory for all congregations is traced back to the apostles; the latter, that is, appear as the organizers of the whole Church.

The decisive step has then been taken: henceforth the office is regarded as *constitutive of the Church*. The whole Church rests upon the office-bearers, whose office is held to go back in uninterrupted succession to the apostles (=the twelve). The tradition of the proclamation, and the succession which guarantees its continuity, are no longer left, as they originally were, to the sway of the Spirit (I, pp. 60f.) but are institutionally safe-guarded. The Spirit is henceforth bound to the office and is transmitted by a sacramental act, ordination by the laying on of hands (Acts 6:6; 13:3; I Tim. 4:14; II Tim. 1:6 perhaps also I Tim. 5:22). For a while the freely acting Spirit is still at work in this process. We see this in the fact that prophet-voices from the congregation precede the act of the laying on of hands (Acts 13:2; I Tim. 1:18; 4:14). We also see it in the further fact— which may amount to the same thing—that the predecessor does not simply name his successor, but that the congregation gives its approval (I Clem. 44:3).

In the case of ordination it is probable that synagogal tradition was influential. But more important is the insight that this development is understandable from the fact that *the proclamation of the word became the affair of the congregational officials.* For this, Did. 15:1f. is clear evidence. There it is explicitly said that the bishops and deacons perform the service of the prophets and teachers and are to be honored as these are. Such a situation had to come because the original apostolate gradually died out, also because the wandering prophets (and teachers) gradually became suspect (Did. 11, Herm. mand. XI), and, above all, because the danger of "heresy" became acute. This is already evident in "Paul's" speech to the elders of Ephesus, in which they are exhorted above all to protect the congregation from perverse teachers (Acts 20:28–30). The same is evident in the pastorals. The qualities demanded in them for elders or "bishops" pertain not only to their administrative tasks (such as "sensible," "hospitable," "no lover of money," etc., I Tim. 3:2ff.; Tit. 1:6ff.) but also to their activity as teachers ("an apt teacher," I Tim. 3:2; II Tim. 2:24; Tit. 1:9: "he must hold firm to the sure word as taught, so that he may be able to give instruction in sound doctrine and also to confute those who contradict it"; *cf.* II Tim. 2:24–26). Keeping watch over right doctrine and doing battle against false doctrine are particularly urged as duties upon Timothy and Titus (I Tim. 1:3; 4:6f., 11ff.; 6:3, 20; II Tim. 2:14ff.; 3:1ff.; 4:1ff.; Tit. 1:10ff.; 2:1ff., 15; 3:8ff.). Indeed, the charisma of office seems to manifest itself most particularly in their teaching activity, since after the exhortation "attend to the public reading of scripture, to preaching, to teaching" is added: "Do not neglect the gift you have" (I Tim. 4:13f.). In Hermas, though the duties connected with organization and charity are in the foreground, nevertheless the congregational officials are named in vis. III 5:1 in such close connection with the apostles and teachers that one must conclude that like the latter they, too, are proclaimers of the word, especially since for Hermas the apostles belong to a bygone time. Similarly, according to II Clem. 17:3–5 the elders are those who "put minds right" and "proclaim concerning salvation."

4. But in the formation of the congregational office still a further element comes in: namely, that the *bishops* become *the leaders of the*

sacramental cultus. This is all the more important the more the sacrament comes to be regarded, along with the word or even instead of the word, as the factor which is constitutive for the Church.

Of this, there is still nothing to be seen in the New Testament. We may assume that the direction of the congregational worship service and hence also the administering of the sacraments, except where everything was left to the sway of the Spirit in the charismatics, was in the hands of those who had a personal authority—"those who labor among you and are over you" (I Thess. 5:12, I Cor. 16:16, Rom. 12:8, etc.)—so far as there was any ordering direction in worship and the administration of the sacrament. For I Cor. 11:17ff., 12, and 14 show that at least at Corinth in Paul's time there was no such direction. Paul directs that "all things be done decently and in order" (I Cor. 14:40; *cf.* I Clem. 40:2). But if his admonition was to be carried out, it was soon necessary to designate persons to be responsible for it, just as in the mysteries of Andonia it was the business of the ῥαβδοῦχοι (staff-bearers) to see to it "that all things be done decently and in good order by those who are present" (Inscriptiones Graecae V 1, 1390 § 10). In the Christian congregations it was just this which became the concern of the *episkopoi.* The Didache evidently testifies to this when directly after the ordinance for the Lord's Day it says, "Therefore" (οὖν) choose for yourselves bishops and deacons. . . ." (15:1). Since it is said that these perform for the congregation the service of prophets and teachers, then evidently prophets and teachers—charismatics, that is—had at first been the leading persons in the celebrations of worship; so the prophets were explicitly permitted to say as many prayers of thanksgiving in addition to the liturgical prayers as they wished (10:6). Since I Clem. 44:7 terms the elders (or "bishops") "those who offer gifts," they are evidently the leaders of the celebration of the Eucharist. With some degree of probability it can be deduced that according to Hermas likewise the leadership of the sacramental cultus fell to the lot of the "bishops." At any rate, in Ignatius it is clear that the "bishop" (here already the monarchical bishop) is the administrator of the sacrament of the Lord's Supper (Eph. 5:1f., Mg. 7:1, Tr. 2:2, 7:2, Philad. 4f., 7:2). In Justin (Apol. I 65:3, 67), finally, the congregational leader (προεστώς) clearly stands forth as the leader of the congregational worship and of the cultic celebration.

This fact takes on special importance as soon as the cultus is no longer conceived as the self-presentation or the appearing of the eschatological Congregation, which in worship is filled with the powers of the Spirit as the firstfruit of coming salvation (Rom. 8:23; *cf.* Heb. 6:4f.), but, having as its focus not the word but the sacrament of the Lord's Supper, is conceived as an institution of salvation which mediates the "medicine of immortality" (Ign. Eph. 20:2; see § 13, 3, I, pp. 150ff.). Then eschatological consciousness is over-shadowed or supplanted by sacramentalism, and *the bishop* who leads worship and administers the sacrament *becomes the priest*, whose office gives him a quality which separates him from the rest of the congregation, making them laymen. This is all the more the case when the sacrament is conceived as a sacrifice. Such a conception is prefigured in the language in which the Didache and Ignatius describe worship, is further prepared for in I Clem., and then actually exists in Justin Martyr; for to him the Eucharist is a sacrifice (§ 13, 2, I, pp. 149f.).

Something decisive has occurred here. The order which regulates the cultus is now regarded as that which guarantees its efficacy. Thereby the persons who carry out the cultus achieve priestly character, and the distinction between priests and laymen, unknown to the New Testament and, indeed, contradictory to it, develops. The position that the leader of the cultus cannot be deposed (I Clem.) is not in itself a symptom for the rise of a divine ecclesiastical law, but its resting upon the priestly ordinances of the Old Testament is (I Clem. 43).

In view of the special character of the Christian Congregation, this has a far-reaching consequence. It brings it about that *the regulations of the Church all together become ordinances of divine law* and make the Church into an institution of salvation. For in all cults, even pagan ones (the mystery-cults, for example), cultic ordinances are, of course, conceived as those of holy law. But in the Christian Church that has other special consequences. The Church as an eschatological entity is lifted out of the profane regulations of the world, and hence, for the members of the Church, religion is not an isolated territory of their secular life which in other respects is geared into the regulations of the world. Rather, their life is completely determined by the fact that they belong to the Church. The Church's claim is a total claim, and it leaves no secular areas of life that could be subject to the claim of worldly law. While for Paul it was a misconception of the Church's eschatological character for a Christian to seek his rights from a worldly court, now what is true of the cultic ordinance is transferred to all the ordinances of life. They all participate in the sacral character of the cultic ordinance.

Of course, so long as primitive Christianity lives in the expectation of the imminent end of the world, it has no interest in regulating the orders of profane life, but takes these as they are (I Cor. 7:14–24), and leaves the control of them to the state (Rom. 13:1–7). But in the course of time the more development there is toward the formation of Christian regulations for living, the more the territory of divine law will expand outward from its center in the cultic ordinance. This tendency takes on concrete form by the fact that the Old Testament is taken over by the Church; hence, its legal regulations—since the ordinances of divine law cannot change—are regarded as authoritative. Naturally, these can only become pertinent for specific questions, such as that of matrimonial law. This development lies beyond the period of primitive Christianity and need not here be further pursued. It suffices to have pointed out the origin of the development.

We need further to consider only (1) that the execution of a regulation of life by legal ordinance requires the establishment of penalties (it will be shown in § 61 that the establishment of such penalties is already beginning in early Christianity) and (2) that ecclesiastical legal ordinances, because they require the power of compulsion, can really receive validity only by delegation of power from the state. But when the Church now conceives itself as the original source of legal authority, it necessarily comes into competition with the state and in the end has to develop the theory that it is the Church which delegates the state to exercise the power of compulsion.

§ 53. The Transformation of the Church's Understanding of Itself

This development, the outcome of which lies beyond the boundary of the New Testament, though it is presaged within it, is ultimately *a transformation in the Church's understanding of itself.* Originally the Church conceives itself as the eschatological people of God, the Congregation of the saints, those who are called out of the world and divorced from it. The Church senses this transcendent character of itself by the gifts of the Spirit which are at work in it. But the Spirit

is the earnest-money or the pledge of the coming glory, the eschatological fulfilment (I, p. 155). Hence, the Church lives in hope of the
fulfilment and documents its transcendent character in its exclusive-
ness and by the conduct of its members as "strangers" in the world
(§ 10, 3 and 4).

While the consciousness of being a non-worldly society belonging
to the other world and filled with its powers does not actually get
lost, it nevertheless suffers a peculiar transformation. In consequence
of the delay of the expected parousia *the transcendent character of the
Church* gradually comes to be seen not so much in its reference to
the future as *in its present possession of institutions* which are already
mediating transcendent powers in the present: a sacramental cultus
and finally a priestly office.

Of course, *that reference to the future* does not get lost, but it, too,
becomes peculiarly modified. The future salvation toward which
hope is directed comes to be seen less in the completion of the history
of salvation and the transformation of the world at the dawn of the
new age (as in Rom. 9–11 and 8:19–22) than in the future life of the
individual beyond death. Certainly the traditional picture of the end-
drama continues to be passed on, and at certain times and situations
may take on living power as in Rev. and I Pet. Still, the most important thing in the picture of the future is the expectation of the
resurrection of the dead and the last judgment (I, pp. 74–77); i.e.
interest is concentrated upon that which is decisive for the individual.
It is just this interest which at an early time finds solid formulation
in the statement about Christ as judge of the quick and the dead
(I, p. 78)—the only item in the second article of the Apostle's Creed
which deals with the eschatological future. And, correspondingly, the
third article of the Creed speaks of a hope only for the resurrection
of the flesh and life eternal.

Correspondingly, *the meaning of the sacraments* comes to be seen
in the fact that they mediate the powers of the future life to the
individual. The effect of baptism is the overcoming of death and the
acquisition of eternal life (I, pp. 140–142; see further Herm. vis. III
3:5: "Your life was and will be saved by water"). The Lord's Supper
becomes the "medicine of immortality" (I, pp. 147f.).

In Hellenistic Christianity this development is implicit from the
outset, as the practice of vicarious baptism indicates for the conception of baptism (I Cor. 15:29). The reason it is implicit is that in

addition to the conception of the Church as the People of God, the true Israel (I, p. 97), there came the interpretation of the Church as the sacramental unity of the "body of Christ" (I, pp. 178f.). Paul, it is true, knew how to unify the idea of the body of Christ with the idea of the Israel of God, since for him the body of Christ is precisely the eschatological Congregation (I, pp. 311f.) and the realm of Christ (I, p. 312). For him the eschatological future realizes itself in the way the baptized leads his life (I, pp. 312f.) and in the fellowship of life into which baptism unites believers (I Cor. 12:12–27; for the Lord's Supper, see I Cor. 10:17). Nor was his understanding of baptism surrendered in the school that followed him (Col. 3:1–17; Eph. 4:1–5, 21; Tit. 2:11–14). But the more the Christian's new way of life comes to be understood not as the demonstration of the new (eschatological) existence but as the condition for achieving future salvation (the latter especially in Hebrews; see 2:1–4; 10:19–31; 12:25–29 and see §§ 58, 59), the more this reference to the future loses the meaning it had had in Paul; the dialectic relation between indicative and imperative (I, p. 332) is surrendered. Then the effect of baptism is limited to forgiveness of the sins committed in one's pre-Christian period, and the problem of sins committed after baptism arises (§§ 58 and 59).

In John the idea of the eschatological People of God plays no role, and the term "Ecclesia" is missing (II, pp. 8, 91). And though for him the individual's salvation, his "life," is in the foreground, still he retained the idea of the unity of believers (§ 50, 8)—and did so even though he gave up founding it upon the sacrament (§ 47, 4). Along with the history-of-salvation perspective John also lacks the traditional Jewish-Christian eschatology (§ 45),* but not the believer's relation to the future. Like Paul, John understands the believer's existence as eschatological existence (§ 50, especially II, pp. 79 f.). However, the Gospel and Epistles of John did not at first influence the development of theology.

But when this Pauline-Johannine dialectic is missing and the knowledge is lost that the future so qualifies the present that believers already exist eschatologically now, understanding for the paradoxical quality of the Christian situation (I, pp. 95f.) gradually disappears,

---

* Ecclesiastical revision, however, endeavored to inject the traditional eschatology into the Gospel and the Epistles of John by means of certain glosses; see II, p. 39 and 85 footnote).

and the Church has changed from a fellowship of salvation to an institution of salvation, even when, and particularly when, it holds fast to the traditional eschatological conceptions. Its transcendence is understood no longer as pure reference to the future, but primarily as a sacramental quality. The Spirit is no longer the power that now and again breaks out in the "gifts"—the words and deeds and conduct of the believers—but is a power immanent in the institutions, particularly in the sacramental cult; it is the office-bearers' equipment for office. The officers have taken on the quality of priests, while it is only through their mediation that the Spirit is indirectly at work in the laymen.

2. But there is still another way in which this reference to the future is modified: the eschatological tension relaxes. The expectation of eschatological fulfilment is not simply given up, but the fulfilment of the hope is pushed forward into *a time that lies in the indeterminate distance*.

II Pet. 3:1–10 shows by its polemic against doubt of the coming of the promised parousia that there were even groups in which the glow of the expectation had gone out or was threatening to do so. The same doubt is combatted in I Clem. 23:3–5 and II Clem. 11 and 12. The exhortations to wait patiently likewise show that hope was in danger of exhausting itself: Jas. 5:7–11, Heb. 10:36, II Clem. 12:1, Herm. vis. III 8:9. The same thing is indicated by the exhortations to be awake and watching in such later synoptic passages as Mt. 13:33–37, Lk. 12:35–38, Mt. 24:43–51 and, outside the synoptics, Rev. 3:3, 16:15, Did. 16, and the exhortations of Hermas not to let the remaining interval before the impending end go by without repenting—for example, sim. X 4:4.

Admittedly, this was not a smooth and everywhere identical development. In times of peril and persecution the consciousness that the end is breaking in can vividly and passionately flare up, as in Rev. and I Pet. Again and again voices arise, crying: "The end of all things is at hand" (I Pet. 4:7), "Near is the day" (Barn. 21:3; *cf.* 4:3, 9), "the last times" (Ign. Eph. 11:1; *cf.* also Heb. 1:1; 9:26, Herm. sim. IX 12:3 and the eucharistic prayers of Did. 9f.). But at the same time the pastoral epistles and Acts show that to a large extent Christians are preparing for a rather long duration of this world and that the Christian faith, losing its eschatological tension, is becoming a Christian-bourgeois piety.

As a matter of course the preaching of the coming judgment belongs to the Christian proclamation for the author of Acts (17:30f.), to whom the "last days" of Joel 3 have become present reality in the pouring out of the Spirit (2:16f.). While Christ tarries in heaven Christians await "times of refreshing" (3:19), "times of restitution of all things" (3:21 KJ). Though it is first said that the predictions of the Old Testament apply to this "restitution," nevertheless the goal of the prediction is then regarded to be the historical coming of Jesus (v. 22). How different it is in I Pet. 1:1–12: Here the goal of prediction is "the sufferings of Christ and the subsequent glory" (the glorification of the risen Lord), and the intention of the reference to prophecy is not as in Acts 3:26 to make a moral appeal but to fortify the hope of the eschatological fulfilment. While Acts 3:20f. without any tone of impatient expectation says, "that times of refreshing may come. . . . and he (God) may send the Christ, Jesus, whom heaven must receive until the time of restitution," according to I Pet. 1:5 believers "are guarded through faith for a salvation ready to be revealed in the last time" and they rejoice in having "now for a little while to suffer various trials" (v. 6). Indeed, it is already characteristic that at the beginning of Acts impatient hope is corrected when the risen Jesus not only answers the question, "Will you at this time restore the kingdom of Israel?" by saying that the time for this is hidden from men, but also announces that the Christian mission must first be carried "to the end of the earth" (1:6–8).

By the pastorals, also, it is taken for granted that the life of believers is a life in hope (I Tim. 1:1, Tit. 1:2, 2:13, 3:7). They await "the appearing of the glory of our great God and Savior Jesus Christ" (Tit. 2:13, I Tim. 6:14, II Tim. 4:1), they hope for "life eternal" (I Tim. 1:16, 4:8, 6:12, 19), for "salvation" (I Tim. 2:15, 4:16, II Tim. 2:10), and fear the judgment (I Tim. 5:24, II Tim. 4:1; *cf.* I Tim. 6:9). But the historical coming of Jesus can also be called the "appearing" (ἐπιφάνεια) of Christ; already he has destroyed death through the Gospel and brought life and incorruption to light (II Tim. 1:10); already the promised "life" is present reality in the fact that the proclamation is present (Tit. 1:2f.); already God has "saved" us (II Tim. 1:9), having done so by means of baptism (Tit. 3:5). This, it is true, is thinking in the line of Paul's thought, to which the eschatological event takes place in the proclamation (§ 34, 1), but Paul's understanding of the eschatological character of the present has greatly paled (see below, § 58, 3m) and there is no longer a trace either of the tension between the present and the future or of longing for the fulfilment. Righteousness is no longer the eschatologically present essence of salvation but is now—side by side with εὐσέβεια ("religion, piety")—moral uprightness (I Tim. 6:11, II Tim. 2:22, 3:16). Similarly the "last days," in which false messiahs and false prophets according to apocalyptic prediction will appear (Mk. 13:21f. par.) are interpreted to be the present time with the false teachers that are appearing in it (I Tim. 4:1, II Tim. 3:1), much as in I Jn. 2:18. That the world is calculated to last for a considerable time yet is indicated by the prayer for the civil authorities—particularly its purpose-clause: "that we may lead a quiet and peaceable life in all piety and respectability" (I Tim. 2:2; the same conclusion is implicit in the traditional prayer for the civil government preserved in I Clem. 61). The grace of God, described as σωτήριος (full of salvation), is also called παιδεύουσα (educative)—educating the Christian: namely, to morally impeccable conduct (Tit. 2:12). The parenesis of the pastoral epistles agrees, offering as its norm a picture of Christian-bourgeois piety (§ 60).

3. So it is not surprising that the Christian Church conceives of itself *as a new religion* existing side by side with the Jewish and the heathen religion (the latter regarded as a unity). This found terminological expression peculiar to the book of Acts in the term "the Way." Saul goes as a persecutor to Damascus where he will perhaps find people "belonging to the Way," (9:2), and later he describes himself as one who "persecuted this Way to death" (22:4). The Jews in Ephesus "speak evil of the Way" (19:9), and a disturbance arises concerning "the Way" (19:23). The procurator Felix is informed about "the Way" (24:22). Everywhere this term ὁδός can be translated "direction, tendency," as in the eyes of the Jews this Christian "direction" is a "sect" (αἵρησις, 24:14). In point of fact, however, the Christian religion is meant, irrespective of whether Christian teaching or the Christian fellowship is uppermost in the author's thought. In the same sense Christians will later be spoken of as the "third kind" (I, pp. 107f.).

The author of Luke and Acts is guided in his presentation by *a conception of Christianity as an entity of world history*. In contrast to the other evangelists he endeavors as an historian to describe the life of Jesus in his Gospel. In the proemium he assures the reader that he has acted as a conscientious investigator in having taken pains with the sources (Lk. 1:1–4). And in the narrative itself he strives not only to give a better connected account than Mark, but also to bring the narrated events into chronological relation with world history. He is already doing this at 1:5 by dating Zacharias in the time of Herod, then especially by dating Jesus' birth (2:1–3) and again by dating the appearing of John the Baptist with a six-fold synchronism (3:1f.). It is also significant that in 21:20–24 he transforms the apocalyptic prediction of the "abomination of desolation" and its subsequent catastrophes (Mk. 13:14–20) into a prediction of the siege and destruction of Jerusalem by the Romans. In Acts correspondingly he offers a history of the earliest Church, the beginnings of Christian missions, and Paul's missionary journeys down to his imprisonment in Rome. The very fact that he writes an account of the origin and earliest history of the Christian Church—in which the eschatological Congregation, of course, would have no interest—shows how far removed he is from its own way of thinking. The fact that he wrote Acts as a sequel to his Gospel completes the confirmation that he has surrendered the original kerygmatic sense of the Jesus-tradition (§ 54, 3) and has historized it. Whereas for the eschatological faith not only of the earliest Church but also of Paul the history of the world had reached its end, because in Christ the history of salvation had found its fulfilment and hence its end, according to the viewpoint of Acts the history of salvation now continues. While for Paul, Christ, being the "end of the Law" (Rom. 10:4), is also the end of history, in the thought of Acts he becomes the beginning of a new history of salvation, the history of Christianity. Later on he will be regarded by universalistic thinking as the middle-point and turning-point of history.

The author of Acts further classifies Christianity as a religion within world history by letting Paul in the Areopagus-discourse appeal to heathen piety by the reference to an inscription on an Athenian altar and to the Stoic belief in God (17:23, 28). This amounts to acclaiming "heathen history and culture and the heathen religious world as Christianity's pre-history."* And the conception of the relation of Christianity to Judaism found in Acts corresponds to this: Paul's teaching on the Law is no longer understood, and Jewish history has simply become the pre-history of Christianity.

* See Vielhauer, "Zum Paulinismus der Apostelgeschichte," *Evangelische Theologie*, 1950–51, pp. 1–15.

It is further significant, finally, that at the climaxes of his narrative the author of Acts, following the pattern of ancient historians, puts into the mouth of Peter and especially of Paul speeches which express the situation-transcending significance of the event (10:34–43; 11:5–17; 15:7–11; 17:22–31; 20:18–35; 22:1–21).

CHAPTER VI

The Development of Doctrine

§ 54. Paradosis and Historical Tradition

1. According to Jude 3 Christian teaching is "the faith once for all delivered (παραδοθείση) to the saints"; according to II Pet. 2:21 it is "the holy commandment delivered (παραδοθείση) to them." And according to Pol. Phil. 7:2 "the word delivered (παραδοθείς) from the beginning."* The Christian Church, called by the word and ever and again reconstituted by the word, does indeed need *tradition* (I, pp. 59f.). Παραδιδόναι, "to pass on by tradition or as tradition," its noun παράδοσις "tradition" and παραλαμβάνειν, "to receive by or as tradition," are from the beginning technical terms for the tradition-process (I Thess. 2:13; 4:1; Gal. 1:9; I Cor. 11:2, 23; 15:1, 3; Phil. 4:9; and, after Paul, Col. 2:6; II Thess. 2:15; 3:6; Jude 3; II Pet. 2:21; I Clem. 7:2; Did. 4:13; Barn. 19:11), and παραθήκη is the term in the pastorals for the *deposit* of teaching offered by the tradition (I Tim. 6:20; II Tim. 1:12, 14; *cf.* 2:2), a juristic term perhaps intentionally chosen to avoid the term παράδοσις, which through Gnosticism had become suspect (v. Campenhausen). Usually the content of the "tradition" (or "deposit") is right teaching in contrast to false teaching; but it can also mean that which is ethically required (Did. 4:13; Barn. 19:11; I Clem. 7:2; and in II Pet. 2:21 probably both the ethical demand and the tradition of teaching are meant as one). The apostles' proclamation founded the tradition, and in the apostle concept the idea of tradition becomes the dominant factor (II, p. 105).

While every religion requires transmission, transmission or *tradition* in Christianity not only plays a special role but also takes on a peculiar character. In pagan religions transmission is confined

* Unfortunately, English lacks a verb on the same root as the noun tradition to show the intimate connection of the Greek verb παραδιδόναι with its noun παράδοσις (Tr.).

primarily to cultic acts and the liturgical formulas which accompany them; there may in addition be an etiological myth which tells of the origin of the cult. In a more developed stage cosmogonic myths may also enter in or replace the old formulas, as in the religion of Egypt or in so-called Orphism or in Gnosticism. Then one may properly speak of doctrine and theology, and these, too, may be transmitted as tradition. However, they are subject to great variability, as is indicated, for instance, in the manifold allegorizations of old myths in the Gnostic systems or in those of the Osiris myth (Plutarch: *De Iside et Osiride*).

The *Israelitic-Jewish religion* naturally also requires transmission of its cultic acts and liturgy. In addition, the transmission of laws regulating life plays a greater role in it than in most pagan religions, even where these have developed beyond the primitive stage (as was especially the case in the Greek world, where ethics became independent of the official religion). In Judaism the Old Testament tradition is supplemented by that of the scribes (sopherim) who were responsible for the interpretation of the old tradition in regard to its application in the present. Here, too, the terminology of "taking over" (παραλαμβάνειν, קִבֵּל) and "passing on" (παραδιδόναι, מָסַר) prevails. The decisive difference between the religion of the Old Testament and of Judaism and the pagan religions in respect to tradition is this: in the former the cultic-legal tradition is supplemented by an historical one. And this historical tradition has not merely the etiological function of explaining the origin and form of cult and rite but tells the history of the people, since here God is primarily the God of history who reveals Himself in the history of the people. In this respect, too, it is fundamentally different from the Greek world, in which the writing of history developed as secular history without connection with the official religion, although (as in Herodotus) the viewing of history was not necessarily devoid of religious reflection.

2. But what was the nature of tradition in earliest Christianity, and what meaning did it have? I Cor. 11:23–25 shows for the case of the Lord's Supper that *in Hellenistic Christianity* there was a *"tradition" of cultic formulas*: "for I received . . . what I also delivered to you, etc." (I, pp. 145f.). For the case of baptism, at the beginning there was only the naming of Christ over the one being baptized (I, pp. 137f.). There is no need here to deal with the further develop-

ment of the baptismal liturgy, which lies beyond the time of the New Testament (I, pp. 133f.); we need only to point out the origin of certain formulas which in part were later united and supplemented in the Apostles' Creed (i.e. the Symbolum Romanum).

A Christian *tradition* corresponding to the cult-myth is offered by Paul in I Cor. 15:3f. ("For I delivered to you . . . what I also received . . ."). It sums up in one short sentence the salvation-event which took place in Christ, his death and resurrection. The precipitate of *paradosis* is further found in statements about Christ as he "who is ready to judge the living and the dead" (I Pet. 4:5, etc.; see I, p. 78) and about his rising or his being raised from the dead (Rom. 10:9; II Tim. 2:8, etc.; see I, p. 80) and about his exaltation (I, p. 82). Sentences like Rom. 1:3f.; 4:24–26; I Cor. 8:6(?); I Tim. 3:16; 6:13; II Tim. 2:8; 4:1; I Pet. 1:20f.; 3:18f., 22; 4:5; Ign. Eph. 18:2; Tr. 9; Sm. 1:1f.; Pol. Phil. 2:1f., and others, are obviously citing or alluding to confessional formulas or hymns that had already become traditional. In addition to such christological formulas it is likely that others early took form which expressed monotheistic faith and later found solid shape in the first article of the Apostles' Creed (I, pp. 68–70).

Now when historical data like "descended from David" (Rom. 1:3) and "under Pontius Pilate" (I Tim. 6:13) occur in the christological formulas, that brings to light a characteristic difference between Christian confessional formulas and *paradosis* and those of the heathen: *the occurrence of salvation*, of which the Christian formulas speak, is peculiarly *bound up with history, world history*. It took place not in some mythical time, neither is it a timeless occurrence in some transcendent sphere, but it took place here on earth, and not long ago, either. The saving event of the crucifixion took place "under Pontius Pilate," the resurrection is testified by a series of people, "most of whom are still alive," and the list of their names is an appendix to the *paradosis* (I Cor. 15:5–8). That is, to the *paradosis* belongs history, an account about historical events. Hence, the conception of the author of Luke-Acts (II, pp. 116f.) in fitting the story of Jesus and the earliest period of the Church into the context of world history is understandable enough, even though in the process the eschatological character of this history gets lost.

The problem of the relationship between *history of salvation* and *world history*, or between *revelation* and *history*, is posed by the paradosis in which both are united—posed anew as compared with the Old Testament and Judaism. For historical tradition could no longer have the meaning which it had had in the Old Testament and Judaism. The revelation of God in Jesus was not an event in the history of the People, to which one could look back as to Moses' history, the exodus from Egypt, the seizure of Canaan, or the history of the judges and the kings. The "new covenant" (I, p. 98), unlike the old, is not the founding event of a people's history, but, however much it arises from a historical event, the death of Jesus, it is nonetheless an eschatological event, and the "People of God" with which this covenant is made is an entity not of world history but of eschatology (I, p. 98). Participation in the Lord's Supper makes the participant a member not of a national commonwealth but of the eschatological Congregation which sojourns in this world as in a foreign land (I, p. 100). For Christ is the end of history, and because he is thereby the fulfilment of the history of salvation it was possible for the Christian Church to take over the Old Testament with its historical account, but only by understanding Old Testament history as history of salvation in a new sense and by comprehending the Church's continuity with the history of Israel as the continuity of the divine plan of salvation which governs that history and has now reached its fulfilment (I, p. 97). So the story of Jesus and the call of the eschatological Congregation appeared as the fulfilment of the Old Testament's predictions, especially in Matthew's presentation. Such a view, however, was not inescapable. In contrast to Matthew, Mark did not write the story of Jesus with constant reference to prediction, and in John the history-of-salvation perspective is completely absent (II, p. 8).

Furthermore, it could happen that the history-of-salvation sense of Old Testament history got completely lost. It did when the figures of Israel's history were adduced, following synagogal tradition, as examples for pious or moral conduct or for patient suffering, as in I Clem. and also Jas. 5:10f., Heb. 11:17ff. Then, of course, the suffering Jesus could also be adduced as a model to follow, as in I Pet. 2:21, Heb. 12:2. The extent to which such a procedure forsakes the history-of-salvation point of view is shown by I Clem., which in addition to Biblical examples can also cite "examples of the heathen" (55:1f.).

At any rate, Old Testament history could not be continued as an historical account of the life of Jesus and the history of the Church unless their eschatological meaning were to be sacrificed, as was done in Luke-Acts (II, pp. 116f.).

3. But how much, and in what way, did faith have need of an account of historical events? Passages like II Cor. 5:18f.; 8:9; Phil. 2:6–11 indicate that it was possible *to formulate statements of the paradosis without mentioning historical facts.* So does Paul's attitude to the Palestinian Jesus-tradition, which he all but ignores (I, pp. 188f.), for it could lead to fixing one's attention upon the "Christ according to the flesh" whom Paul wants no longer to know (II Cor. 5:16; I, p. 294). In a way John indicates this, too, by his free treatment of the tradition and by the independent way in which he formed his Gospel (II, pp. 3f.). Altogether it is strange how little reference is made in apostolic and post-apostolic literature to Jesus' life—apart from the Gospels and Acts (see especially 2:22f.; 10:37–39) only at I Tim. 6:13 and Heb. 2:18; 4:15; 5:7; 12:2.

On the other hand, it is clear that passages like II Cor. 5:18f.; 8:9; Phil. 2:6–11 make sense only because they speak *at the same time of an historical person, Jesus.* And it is precisely the humanity of Jesus which is strongly emphasized in Phil. 2:7f.: ". . . becoming a man like other men and being recognized as truly human" (Weymouth; *cf.* Rom. 8:3; Gal. 4:4). The humanity of Christ—the fact, that is, that the saving event took place in the sphere of "flesh"—is essential: "He was manifested in the flesh" (I Tim. 3:16; *cf.* also Col. 1:22, Heb. 2:14; 5:7; 10:20; I Pet. 3:18; 4:1). For John, too, it is essential that Jesus was a man: "The Word became flesh" (1:14); he comes from Nazareth and his parents are known (II, pp. 41f.). To deny his humanity is a false teaching (II, pp. 40f.). Ignatius, also, like I John, combats the docetism of Gnostic heretics (Ign. Eph. 7, 18:2; Tr. 9–10; Sm. 1–3; 4:2; 5:2; 7:1).

But was it not enough merely to declare and insist upon the fact of Jesus' humanity? Was information about the manner of his historical life also necessary? Certainly Luke thought so and proceeded to give his Gospel a corresponding form (II, p. 116). In Paul, however, there is no trace of such an interest. When he refers to the obedience of Christ (Phil. 2:8; Rom. 5:19) or to his exemplary love (II Cor. 8:9; Rom. 15:3) he is thinking of the self-abasement and sacrifice of the pre-existent Christ and not of the concrete conduct of the historical Jesus. It is also something other than simple appeal to the historical Jesus when *"words of the Lord"* are appealed to, as is occasionally done by Paul (I, pp. 188f.). Outside of the Gospels, it is true, a saying of Jesus is directly cited only once in the New Testament (Acts 20:35), but there can be no doubt that sayings of Jesus were pretty generally passed on in the congregations, and certain quotations in the so-called Apostolic Fathers confirm that this was so. The logia-collection worked into Matthew and Luke was evidently soon superseded by the synoptic Gospels. It may still have remained in use here and there for a while, and we have no way of knowing whether, or to what extent, words of the Lord such as are quoted in Did. 1:3–6; I Clem. 13:2; II Clem. 2:4; Barn. 4:14; Pol. Phil. 2:3, and elsewhere, and others to which Ignatius occasionally alludes, come from oral tradition or from a written collection of sayings—it is at least doubtful whether they come from any one of our four Gospels. That such collections existed is also testified by papyrus finds.

But it is clear that the passing on of words of the Lord was motivated not by historical-biographical interest but by the practical concern to regulate the way of life of believers and to keep their hope alive. The one whom they heard speaking in the words was not the historical Jesus, but the Church's heavenly Lord. But then, we must ask, how is Matthew to be understood, who presents the words of the Lord in the framework of a history of Jesus? And above all how is Mark to be understood, who in his account also made use of words of the Lord but gave more room to the account of Jesus' deeds and his fate? It is in these two evangelists that it becomes clear to what an extent the historical tradition belongs to the kerygma or could be combined with it—and that it could be combined under various points of view.

That neither Matthew nor Mark wrote his Gospel out of historical interest, as Luke did, is clear; but they also differ from each other. Matthews presents Jesus as the one in whom the history of salvation has found its fulfilment. Running all through his Gospel is the demonstration that in the life and work of Jesus the predictions of the Old Testament are fulfilled: "This (or, all this) occurred in order that that which was spoken (by the Lord through the prophet) might be fulfilled" (1:22, etc.). But in addition he represents Jesus as the authoritative interpreter of the Law, or rather as the bringer of the new Torah, the messianic Torah, with his claim: "You have heard that it was said . . . but I say to you" (5:21–48). Insofar, then, as Matthew offers an account of the history of Jesus, he thereby makes visible the fact that eschatological salvation became history; the Jesus whom he depicts is to be understood not as a figure of world history but as its conclusion. Hence, in comparison with his source, Mark, he repeatedly enhances the divinity of the figure of Jesus (*cf.* especially 19:17 in contrast with Mk. 10:18). And then in depicting Jesus as the teacher of the Congregation he makes clear that this is the eschatological Congregation. Once more, his historical account expresses that fact (that eschatological salvation became history) by making the reader conscious that the present is eschatological in character; he does this by showing that the present stands under the dominion of the eschatological King, as his conclusion (28:18–20) clearly expresses: "All authority in heaven and on earth has been given to me," etc.

Mark in his own way also brings to view that fact that eschatological salvation became history. Fulfilment of prediction is of minor importance in his Gospel and occurs in pure form only at 4:12, though 7:6f.; 9:12; 11:9f.; 12:10f.* are related. Chief emphasis falls upon the miracles and miraculous events like the baptism and the transfiguration. In these the true nature of the Son of God, though in general hidden, appears—but only to the readers of the Gospel, for that nature was to remain hidden from his contemporaries (I, p. 32). While Matthew kept within the conceptual horizon of the Old Testament and Judaism, Mark expresses the kerygmatic character of the historical account in the manner of Hellenistic thinking: Jesus' life is not an episode of world history but the miraculous manifestation of divine dealing in the cloak of earthly occurrence. By including the debates of Jesus along with the miracles Jesus is presented less than in Matthew as teacher of the Church and more as the Son of God, who unmasks the anti-godliness of Jewish tradition. By giving baptism and the Lord's Supper their origin in Jesus' own baptism by John and in his last meal, Mark is likewise giving the history of Jesus the character of occurring revelation. By the account of the transfiguration, finally, he shows that only from the standpoint of faith in the risen Lord (9:9) can the "history" of Jesus be recognized as being in its inner nature epiphany of the Son of God.

4. Matthew and Mark, as we have just seen, made the historical account serviceable to the kerygmatic character of the "Gospel." But there was something intrinsically problematical in that procedure.

* Mk. 1:2f. is probably an ancient gloss.

The problem lay in the fact that both Mark and Matthew, following his lead, gave their writings the form of an historical presentation, a "life of Jesus," in which the single bits of the old tradition are united into a chronological-geographical continuity—and some of even the old bits of tradition themselves exhibit novelistic details which bear witness to a biographical interest on the part of the congregations which passed them on. This problem arises from the fact that the Christian Church, knowing itself to be the eschatological Congregation of men called out of the world and belonging to the coming aeon, was nevertheless not called by a revelation from the beyond—whether a revelation given in the pictures of ecstatic visionaries, or a revelation brought by some unconfirmable myth—but by an historical figure, Jesus, in whom it heard the word of God calling it. As it is the Church's duty to manifest its non-worldly character in its existence within the world, so it is also its duty not completely to sublimate into myth him who called it into existence—however much it may express his significance in the language of traditional mythology. The tradition about Jesus, therefore, has this special character: that it speaks simultaneously of the eschatological occurrence and of an historical occurrence. The question is whether this paradoxical character was maintained.

While in the presentation of Luke-Acts this paradox was resolved in favor of a theology of history which knows only a history of salvation unrolling as world history (II, pp. 186f.), it was also resolved in another direction by sacrificing from the kerygma its reference to the historical occurrence. This happened in Gnosticism. In it the occurrence of salvation is understood with a consistent one-sidedness as transcendental, and, in consequence of divorcing it from history, the occurrence of salvation becomes mythical. Unlike heathen Gnosticism, Christian Gnosticism naturally could not give up all connection with the historical person Jesus and thus transplant the occurrence of salvation into a mythical past. But it did surrender the historical reality of the Redeemer when it denied the identity of the Son of God with the historical Jesus by teaching either that the Son of God only temporarily—from the baptism of Jesus, say—united with the human Jesus and then left him before the passion, or that the Redeemer's human form was only seemingly a body (docetism).

This solution of the paradoxical problem inevitably seemed heretical to the majority of the congregations (I, p. 169; II, p. 40f.).

But the very writings that most emphatically assert against Gnosticism that "the Word became flesh" and see the incarnation of anti-Christ in those "who do not confess that Jesus Christ came in flesh"—John, I and II John, and Ignatius, too—demonstrate the relative appropriateness and the intent of Gnostic teaching; in opposition to a historizing of the eschatological occurrence, it expresses a legitimate interest of faith.

The meaning of that paradox was grasped most clearly of all by John and is most clearly set forth in his Gospel. In the very fact that he dealt so freely with the tradition of Jesus' life (II, pp. 3f.), he most sharply made clear the meaning it has for the kerygma by reducing the revelation of God in the man Jesus to the mere fact that He so revealed Himself (§ 48, 3, esp. II, pp. 67 and 69) and by uncovering in the most extreme fashion the paradox of "the Word became flesh" (§ 46, especially II, pp. 40f.)—the paradox that God's word went forth in a definite historical person and remains a present reality. He presents this person not as a reliably testified person of the past but as he is constantly present in the word which proclaims him in the power of the Spirit (II, p. 90). For John, therefore, the tradition is not historical transmission, which establishes the continuity of historical occurrence, but is the Church's preaching, in which Jesus is present in the Spirit (§ 50, 7). The succession which the kerygmatic tradition requires is here not yet conceived as an institutional one (as in Acts, the pastorals, and I Clem., § 52, 3) but as a free, Spirit-wrought succession. While Paul—inconsistently with his basic insight—still tries to guarantee the resurrection of Jesus by the enumeration of witnesses, as if it were an historically visible fact (I Cor. 15:5–8; see I, p. 295), John concludes his Easter-stories with the sentence: "Blessed are they who have not seen and yet believe" (20:29; see II, pp. 56f.).

§ 55. The Problem of Right Teaching and the Rise of the New Testament Canon

1. Christianity did not become a mystery-religion because in it salvation rests primarily not upon a sacramental cult which professes to mediate divine powers through material elements (I, p. 135), but upon the proclamation of the word, in which the grace of God by being proclaimed encounters the hearer and demands of him personal

faith. The proclamation, telling of God's deed in Christ, is at the same time personal address to the hearer; and at the same time as it brings knowledge of what God has done in Christ it also brings the hearer a new knowledge of himself. It is the "knowledge of the truth" which frees the hearer from "ignorance" and "error" (I, p. 67), and in which knowledge and acknowledgment are bound together into a unity. In the same way Paul understands the "knowledge" which he spreads abroad by his preaching (II Cor. 2:14; 4:6)—this knowledge means: "to gain Christ and be found in him" (Phil. 3:8f.).

This "knowledge" (whether ἐπίγνωσις or γνῶσις) scarcely differs in substance from "faith," except that it emphasizes *the element of knowing which is contained in the very structure of "faith."* This appears most clearly in John by the way in which he understands the relationship between "believing" and "knowing" (§ 49, 2). For the believer must, of course, understand what is proclaimed to him about God and Christ and also how his own situation is thereby qualified. The theological expositions in Galatians and Romans have no other purpose than to unfold the knowledge which is the concomitant gift of faith. Paul clearly saw that this knowledge is not merely capable of development, but also stands in need of development. Faith must prove itself to be living faith by reaching in each case a right judgment as to what is required of the man of faith, for whatever does not come from faith is sin (Rom. 14:23). Paul wishes for his readers that their power of judgment may grow and gain in certainty (Rom. 12:2; Phil. 1:9f.; Philm. 6; see I, pp. 326f.). Similarly Col. 1:9f. wishes: "that you may be filled with the knowledge of his will in all spiritual wisdom and understanding, to lead a life worthy of the Lord . . ." (*cf.* 3:10). Also similar are the prayer II Pet. 1:3 and the exhortations that correspond to it (1:5 and 3:18), and Barnabas wishes: "May God . . . give you wisdom, insight, knowledge, understanding of his just demands" (21:5); γνῶσις (knowledge) for him means not merely theoretical but also practical knowledge (5:4; 18:1; 19:1; *cf.* 16:9: "wisdom in regard to his just demands"). As Paul rejoices that such "knowledge" is alive and at work in the congregation (I Cor. 1:5; II Cor. 8:7; Rom. 15:14), so I Clem. praises the "complete and dependable knowledge" of that Corinthian congregation (1:2), and Did. 11:2 orders that wandering teachers are to be received if their activity is conducive to "increasing uprightness and knowledge of the Lord."

2. Such "knowledge" or "wisdom" is the knowledge of God's will; i.e. the power of judgment that lies within the Christian's ethical willing and which it is every believer's duty to cultivate and activate. To be distinguished from it is *a special "knowledge" or "wisdom"*; its content is the divine plan of salvation and the saving occurrence which is described in the kerygmatic formulations of the paradosis. Already to Paul the divine plan of salvation and its realization in Christ seemed a "mystery" (I Cor. 2:6f.; 15:51; Rom. 11:25); it seemed even more so to writers later than Paul (for Colossians and Ephesians, see no. 3, below; also II Thess. 2:7 [Rom. 16:25], I Tim. 3:9, 16; Rev. 10:7; Ign. Eph. 19:1; Mg. 9:1; Tr. 2:3). The formulations of the paradosis needed interpretation. Their concepts and statements were not only subject to various interpretations but they also led inevitably to further thinking, to questions: what theological and christological, cosmological and anthropological consequences necessarily result? Which ones are legitimate deductions? This is the origin of Christian theology. In the course of time Christians also had to come to terms with heathen thinking, its mythology and philosophy; there had to come a theology which finally in the apologetes became a sort of Christian philosophy.

This "knowledge," too, has its origin in faith, though it is not for all believers to develop such knowledge independently. That is a special gift not given to all (I Cor. 12:8). But whoever has it is to communicate it to others and these are to listen to him; indeed, he who has it may wish that all might achieve it (Eph. 1:17). This knowledge as well as that described under 1, above, also has a practical purpose, since in its light the situation of the Christian becomes clear, and in it he learns to understand himself. Thus the theological expositions of Galatians and Romans teach one to understand the emancipation of Christian existence from the Law and the cosmic powers; so do those of Colossians. Paul's discussion with his gnosticizing opponents in Corinth shows how one's understanding of "freedom" and "authorization" (ἐξουσία) leads to a particular way of living. The critical question for the development of theology is how far it sticks to being an unfolding of the knowledge contained in faith. That is equivalent to saying how far it is the explication of the kerygma and of Christian existence as it is determined by the kerygma. It has cut itself loose from its origin and become mere speculation or rational construction when it no longer rightly sees the connection between the knowledge of God and His dealing and the knowledge of the Christian's situation determined by it.

Motivation for the development of a Christian theology was furnished not only by the necessity of interpreting the kerygma but also by the Old Testament, which had been taken over by the Church and also required interpretation. II Pet. 1:20f. shows the embarrassment they were in; the readers are warned that the prophecy of Scripture is not to be interpreted in the light of one's private understanding but only in accordance with its pneumatic origin. We have already dealt in § 11 with the multiple possibilities and attempts at interpretation. Here we need only briefly consider what meaning the interpretation of the Old Testament had for the development of a Christian theology. The situation was not merely that the Church had to overcome the difficulties offered by the Old Testament, but also that the Old Testament could serve as a source of Christian "knowledge" when its mysteries were interpreted by means of allegory. For the author of Ephesians one such mystery is the saying in Gen. 2:24 which he interprets as applying to the union of Christ with the Ecclesia (5:31f.). The author of Hebrews (§ 11, 2c) is manifestly proud of what he is able to offer his readers in the way of knowledge. By his solemnly rhetorical introduction to his interpretation of the Old Testament cult and to his theory of the high-priesthood of Christ he is explicitly reminding the reader that his knowledge rises above the level of a Christianity that is primitive (5:11; 6:12). Though in Barnabas "knowledge" and "wisdom" play no role as technical terms, its author (§ 11, 2b) specifically calls his interpretation of the Old Testament "knowledge" (6:9; 9:8; 13:7; *cf.* "to know" 7:1; 14:7; 16:2; "to make known" 1:7; 5:3; "to make wise" 5:3). He praises the Lord "who placed in us wisdom and understanding of his secrets" (6:10), and he writes his book in order that the readers may go on beyond their "faith" to a "perfect knowledge" in order that faith and the Christian virtues may be enriched by the addition of "wisdom, prudence, understanding, and knowledge" (2:2f.). The allegorical method by means of which Hebrews and Barnabas and later Justin Martyr (§ 11, 2f.) get knowledge is also occasionally used by I Clem. (§ 11, 2d), though as a rule he uses the Old Testament as a book of ethical examples. He, too, calls his art of interpretation a γνῶσις (40:1: "we have looked into the depths of divine knowledge").

[130]

It soon became apparent that even authoritative Christian writings needed exposition. Understandably, such a need was first felt in regard to the Pauline letters, in which according to II Pet. 3:16 there is much that is hard to understand, giving rise to false interpretation by false teachers. Polycarp also confesses that neither he nor others are able completely to grasp the wisdom of the "blessed and renowned" Paul, but that his letters are able to bestow edification upon him who ponders over them. And can the treatment of the theme "faith and works" in Jas. 2:14–26 be understood in any other way than that it is a debate against misunderstood ideas of Paul? In the mind of the Church the interpretation of Paul is not an exegesis concerned with merely understanding his wording but is motivated by the practical interest of ascertaining the meaning of Paul's utterances for the present situation, or of preventing the misuse of them. Hence, interpretation of Paul can be undertaken by letting Paul speak anew—i.e. by writing a new letter in his name. Thus in a certain sense II Thessalonians is a commentary on I Thessalonians. For the expectation of the imminent end of all things expressed in the earlier letter—whether against a too enthusiastic eschatological mood or (more likely) against doubts that had arisen in view of the delay of the parousia—is restricted in the later letter: before the End comes all sorts of things must first take place (II Thess. 2:1–12).

We must mention, finally, the exposition of other texts of mysterious content or of apocalyptic pictures and terms. God's plan of salvation is a "mystery" (Col. 1:26f., Eph. 1:9, etc.); so are the apocalyptic seer's visions "mysteries," and he interprets them (Rev. 1:20, 17:5, 7) or he may only hint at their meaning (Rev. 13:18): "This calls for wisdom: let him who has understanding reckon the number of the beast." The name for the "understanding" of the mysterious "booklet" of which Hermas learns from the "old lady" who appears to him is $\gamma\nu\hat{\omega}\sigma\iota\varsigma$; and the cognate verb ($\gamma\iota\nu\dot{\omega}\sigma\kappa\epsilon\iota\nu$) constantly recurs in Hermas—the term means the process of understanding the visions and allegories (vis. III 1:2, 4:3; sim. V 3:1; IX 5:3, etc.).

3. This Christian $\gamma\nu\hat{\omega}\sigma\iota\varsigma$ (knowledge or understanding) which arises out of the elements discussed above leads before long to the problem of right teaching. *Paul* himself already knew two "wisdoms": the paradoxical wisdom of the cross and a wisdom available only to the "mature" ($\tau\dot{\epsilon}\lambda\epsilon\iota o\iota$) and penetrating into the depths of divinity

(I Cor. 2:6ff.; see I, pp. 181 and 327). The latter is certainly not the product of rational thought, for Paul attributes it to revelation by the Spirit (2:10), and in the end it also flows into a recognition of God's gift and of the situation of the believer (2:12; see I, p. 327). Still it is clear that in this wisdom fantasy and speculative thought are at work as well as motifs of the apocalyptic and mythological tradition. For a part of this wisdom is the mythological theorem of the deception of the "rulers" by the disguise of the pre-existent Christ (2:8; see I, pp. 175f.). Probably the notion of the fall and liberation of the creation, to which Paul allusively refers in Rom. 8:20ff., also goes back to such mythological tradition, and certainly secrets like the eschatological "mystery" of I Cor. 15:51ff. do; whereas the history-of-salvation mystery in Rom. 11:25ff. is derived from speculative fantasy.

Though Paul himself is already under the influence of *Gnostic thinking* (§ 15, 4), his correspondence with the congregation at Corinth permits us to see in young Christianity there were circles which had fallen under the power of such influence to such an extent that the Christian message was emptied of its true content or perverted. Such are the members of the congregation who boast of their "wisdom" and "knowledge" (I Cor. 1:18ff.; 8:1ff.); so are the apostles who have worked their way in from the outside—false apostles, to Paul (II Cor. 2:13)—for whom Paul claims to be a match in "knowledge" (II Cor. 11:6). The struggle between this gnosticizing wing and the ultimately victorious orthodoxy has not died out even after Paul's time. Its tenacity indicates that in circles of considerable extent there was a craving for a knowledge that would go beyond faith. That the "false teachers" opposed by I John were characterized by a claim to possess knowledge is indicated by the author's effort to make clear what "to know God" in reality means (2:3ff.; 3:6; 4:6ff.). Similarly, in his battle against Gnostic teachers Ignatius asks, "Why have we not all become wise, having received the knowledge of God— that is, Jesus Christ?" (Eph. 17:2). And he praises Christ who has "made wise" his readers—made them solid, that is, in the orthodox faith (Sm. 1:1). The false teachers in Thyatira, against whom Rev. 2:18–29 polemizes, evidently boasted of their knowledge of the "deep things of Satan" (or, in case this is a polemic distortion of their claim, what they really claimed was knowledge of the deep things of God). Col., the pastorals, Jude, and II Pet. also polemize against a gnosticizing Christianity.

One way of meeting this danger was *to reject such striving after knowledge altogether.* That is the attitude we meet in the pastorals. Here "false teaching" is not combatted with counter-arguments but all debate with it is declined: it is simply "falsely called knowledge." "Timothy" is advised to "charge certain persons not to teach any different doctrine nor to occupy themselves with myths and endless genealogies which promote speculation rather than the divine stewardship (*v. l.* training) that is in faith" (I Tim. 1:3f.; *cf.* 4:7; 6:20). Or he is exhorted: "Have nothing to do with stupid, senseless controversies; you know that they breed quarrels" (II Tim. 2:23; *cf.* 2:16; Tit. 3:9). He is to stick to "the words of the faith and of the good doctrine," the "sound words" of the Lord, the "sound doctrine" (I Tim. 4:6; 6:3; Tit. 1:9, etc.). Neither does Acts 20:29f. enter into discussion with the false teachers, but is content to call them "men speaking perverse things." Jude and its imitator, II Pet., deal still more summarily with the false teachers: here there not only is no suggestion of a refutation by argument, but they are directly accused of moral turpitude and immoral conduct. I Jn. also, unlike Paul, does not enter upon a theological discussion with the false teachers, but simply thrusts before these "antichrists" the statement of the true humanity of the Son of God. One may concede that he does offer a refutation to the extent that he makes clear the existential meaning of faith by uncovering the unity of indicative and imperative, the unity of faith and love (II, pp. 80–82), whereas Ignatius gets stuck in dogmatic polemics and stays there.

The method represented by the pastorals could be successful in limited circles at the most; for the urge for knowledge could not be rooted out—and, after all, was it not in itself legitimate? At any rate, such an urge is expressed in *Colossians* and *Ephesians* in their further development of Pauline motifs—in Col. in a struggle against false teachers, in Eph. in a non-polemic explication of Christian knowledge.

Colossians warns the reader against the "φιλοσοφία (literally "philosophy," but, of course, not Greek philosophy is meant but Gnostic speculation) and empty deception whose norm is human tradition and the elemental spirits of the universe, and not Christ," 2:8 tr.). Though the author does not carry out a true discussion in debate form and though it is almost entirely by indirection that he allows the opposing view to be recognized, he nevertheless sets up against it his own view of the theme under discussion—the relation of Christ to the angelic or cosmic powers—and is convinced that in Christ "are hid all the treasures of wisdom and knowledge" (2:3). Here "wisdom and spiritual understanding" (1:9 tr.) is by no means restricted to the judgment of the ethical will (see above, II, p. 129) but certainly includes a theoretical "wisdom" by which the "mystery" (the divine plan of salvation is often so termed: 1:26f., 2:2; 4:3) is unfolded by describing the cosmic status of Christ and by describing the reconciliation of the cosmos brought about by the work of salvation, a cosmos torn by recalcitrant powers and reconciled in the fact that the latter are overcome (1:15–20; 2:9–15). At the same time, the transcendent nature of the Ecclesia is characterized as that of the "body of Christ." The fact that the author in 1:15–20 made use of a pre-Christian hymn that had already received a Christian editing before him* proves to what an extent Christian craving for knowledge had already mingled with cosmological speculation.

The interest of the author of *Ephesians* is not polemic. But for him, too, God's plan of salvation is the "mystery" which was imparted by revelation to the Paul whose mask the author adopts (3:3; *cf.* 1:9; 6:19). By that which he writes the readers are to recognize what "insight into the mystery of Christ" he possesses (3:4) and how he is able "to preach . . . the unsearchable riches of Christ, and to make all men see what is the plan of the mystery" (3:8f.). He abundantly shares his knowledge with the reader, and while the author of Col. wishes his readers "wisdom and spiritual understanding to lead a life worthy of the Lord" (Col. 1:9f.), the author of Eph. wishes in the parallel passage "that God . . . may give you a spirit of wisdom and of revelation in the knowledge of him . . . that you may know what is the hope to which he has called you, etc." (1:17–19). Later he wishes that his readers may be able to comprehend "what is the breadth and the length and height and depth and to know the love of Christ which surpasses knowledge" (3:18f.). Like Col. (which he is probably using) he also describes the work and dignity of Christ in the cosmological terminology of Gnosticism (1:10, 20–22; 2:14–16). His theme, however, is not the reconciliation of the cosmos but the unity of the Church and Christ's relation to it (2:11–22; 4:1–16; *cf.* 5:29–32). For this he has at his disposal a special wisdom in scriptural interpretation by

* See E. Käsemann, *Eine christliche Taufliturgie*, in *Festschrift für Rudolf Bultmann*, 1949, pp. 133–148.

which he reads out of Ps. 68:19 Christ's descent to earth and his victorious ascent (4:8–10) and interprets the "great mystery" of Gen. 2:24 as applying to Christ and the Church (5:31f.).

4. The diversity of theological interests and ideas is at first great. A norm or an authoritative court of appeal for doctrine is still lacking, and the proponents of directions of thought which were later rejected as heretical consider themselves completely Christian—such as Christian Gnosticism (§ 15, 3). In the beginning, *faith* is the term which distinguishes the Christian Congregation from Jews and the heathen, not *orthodoxy* (right doctrine). The latter along with its correlate, *heresy*, arises out of the differences which develop within the Christian congregations. In the nature of the case this takes place very early; even Paul already curses the Judaizers who offer a "different gospel" in wanting to impose the yoke of the Law upon converted Gentiles (Gal. 1:6–9). He likewise polemizes against those in Corinth who deny the resurrection (I Cor. 15) and against the gnosticizing preachers who proclaim "another Jesus" (II Cor. 11:4). We have just shown (in 3, above) that battles with Gnosticism continued to be fought.

It is understandable that in such battles πίστις takes on the meaning of right belief (I, p. 90) and also that πίστις, retaining its primary meaning "the faith with which one believes," can come to mean the right kind of faith. It must be meant in one or the other of these senses when we hear of men who "have made shipwreck of their faith" or "have missed the mark as regards the faith" (I Tim. 1:19; 6:21), who "have failed the test in regard to faith" (II Tim. 3:8 tr.), or when in a (pretended) look into the future it is said of the false teachers: "some will depart from the faith" (I Tim. 4:1). At any rate, right doctrine is meant when the proper servant of Christ is described as "nourished on the words of the faith and of the good doctrine which you have followed" (I Tim. 4:6—here "faith" and "good doctrine" constitute a hendiadys). And the right kind of faith is meant when it is said of the false teachers: "They are upsetting the faith of some" (II Tim. 2:18). In Tit. 1:13 and 2:2 occurs the expression "to be sound (literally, "healthy") in faith," which evidently means to be orthodox, and from this expression the pastorals found a solid technical term for right doctrine: "sound (or "healthy") teaching" (I Tim. 1:10; II Tim. 4:3; Tit. 1:9; 2:1; *cf.* "sound λόγος," Tit. 2:9, which RSV renders "sound speech," but it may also mean doctrinally sound preaching; *cf.* also "sound words," I Tim. 6:3; II Tim. 1:13). The word *pistis* also contains the meaning "right doctrine" in Eph. 4:5, even though in the explanation "one Lord, one faith, one baptism . . ." faith evidently means primarily that confession of faith at baptism which Rom. 10:9 mentions. Nevertheless the word "one" in "one faith" indicates that in the author's mind hovers a contrast with other confessions (as does a contrast with other lords in the case of "one Lord"), and hence the idea of the *right* confession is also present. It means the same thing as is meant by the "faith of equal standing" (or "faith of the same sort," tr.) which the "Peter" of II Pet. 1:1 and his readers have received in common. Certainly right doctrine is meant by "the faith which was once for all delivered to the saints," Jude 3 (*cf.* Jude 20: "your most holy faith"; on the implications of "delivered" see § 54, 1).

In Rom. 10:9 *"to confess"* (ὁμολογεῖν) means: to make the baptismal confession, with no thought as yet of a *right* confession in contrast to a heretical one. Hebrews uses the word "confession" (3:1; 4:14; 10:23) in this same sense, though here the reader is urged to hold fast his confession in contrast to neglecting it or being anxious in regard to it. Mt. 10:32 ("confessing Jesus") already has this meaning and so do Jn. 9:22; 12:42 and Herm. sim. IX 28, 4 and 7 (where ὁμολόγησις also occurs). But "the good confession" of I Tim. 6:12 means the right confession in contrast to heresy, and the verb "confess" is often used with the same implication (I Jn. 2:23; 4:2: "that Jesus has come in the flesh"; 4:3; 4:15: "that Jesus is the Son of God"; II Jn. 7; Ign. Sm. 5:2: "that he was clothed in flesh"; Pol. Phil. 7:1).

Thus a *terminology* develops for indicating *orthodoxy*. Words with the prefix "ortho-" do not yet appear, for the ὀρθοποδεῖν of Gal. 2:14 ("walk straightly in regard to the truth of the gospel") is a purely figurative expression; likewise ὀρθοτομεῖν in II Tim. 2:15 ("rightly handling the word of truth"). In the apostolic and post-apostolic period the actual words "orthodox," "orthodoxy," and the verb "be orthodox" (ὀρθόδοξος, ὀρθοδοξία, ὀρθοδοξεῖν) do not yet occur; they belong to philosophic usage. And "dogma" (δόγμα) also occurs only in the general sense of "regulation," "ordinance," "directive" (Ign. Mg. 13:1; Did. 11:3; Barn. 1:6; 9:7; 10:1, 9f.).

To designate *false teaching, heresy*, formations with the prefix "hetero-" were immediately available: ἑτεροδιδασκαλεῖν ("to teach otherwise"—I Tim. 1:3; 6:3; Ign. Pol. 3:1; cf. Gal. 1:6; II Cor. 11:4), ἑτεροδοξεῖν ("to have other opinions"—Ign. Sm. 6:2), ἑτεροδοξία ("other doctrine"—Ign. Mg. 8:1). So were formations with the prefix "pseudo": pseudoprophet (I Jn. 4:1), ψευδοδιδάσκαλος, "false teacher," (II Pet. 2:1), ψευδοδιδασκαλία, "false teaching," (Pol. Phil. 7:2), ψευδολόγος "false word" (I Tim. 4:2). Αἵρεσις (hairesis, the Greek parent of our word "heresy") means in the beginning a school or party (Acts 5:19 "of the Sadducees"; 15:5 "of the Pharisees"; cf. 26:5) and in this sense can be applied by non-Christians to the Christian faith (Acts 24:5, 14; 28:22; RSV renders "sect"), then it also means a faction (Gal. 5:20; I Cor. 11:19). Even in II Pet. 2:1 the αἱρέσεις are not heresies but the factions evoked by the false teachers. The αἱρετικὸς ἄνθρωπος of Tit. 3:10, however, in the context can only be the heretic, and in Ignatius (Eph. 6:2; Tr. 6:1) αἵρεσις at least approaches the meaning "heresy"—the meaning which became the common one in the ancient Church—though perhaps all Ignatius means is "faction."

W. Bauer has shown that that doctrine which in the end won out in the ancient Church as the "right" or "orthodox" doctrine stands at the end of a development or, rather, is the result of a conflict among various shades of doctrine, and that heresy was not, as the ecclesiastical tradition holds, an apostasy, a degeneration, but was already present at the beginning—or, rather, that by the triumph of a certain teaching as the "right doctrine" divergent teachings were condemned as heresy. Bauer also showed it to be probable that in this conflict the Roman congregation played a decisive role. Later, but independently of Bauer, M. Werner* defended a similar thesis, regarding heresy as a symptom of the great crisis of the post-apostolic period, which, according to him, consisted of the fact that in consequence of the delay of the parousia a chaos of teachings arose. Since Christians wanted to hold fast to the tradition but now had to reinterpret it, a multitude of attempts at reorientation was called forth. "By the continuing delay of the parousia the inner eschatological logic, the dominating connectedness of meaning in the doctrine of Christ and salvation received from the apostles and Paul, is broken, and the several items and concepts of faith thereby lose their unambiguity" (pp. 131f.). All the attempts at reorientation were originally "heresies"—also the Christianity of the "great

* *Die Entstehung des christlichen Dogmas*, 1941, pp. 126–138. For Bauer, see *Rechtgläubigkeit und Ketzerei im ältesten Christentum*, 1934.

Church" which finally gained the day; the "great Church" is only the most successful heresy. In this thesis the influence of the non-occurrence of the parousia is obviously greatly over-estimated. Granted that this non-occurrence was one reason for the formation of heresies, nevertheless it was only one among others. Indeed, we probably ought to call this non-occurrence a *conditio sine qua non* rather than a positive cause. For the differentiation of the various shades of teaching did not first arise in the post-apostolic period but was already present in the time of Paul, who in Galatia, Corinth and elsewhere had to contend with "false teachers." The motifs of later heresies are already partially present in the Hellenistic Christianity of the apostolic period when the Christian message had penetrated the world of Hellenism from its mother-soil in Palestine and the influences of the mystery religions, particularly of Gnosticism, set to work. Christian Gnosticism is not the result of disappointed expectation of the parousia; rather vice versa, as the Corinthian letters already show, the rejection of realistic eschatology is a consequence of the Gnostic thinking which even then was penetrating into the Christian congregations.

5. In view of the differences in doctrine and of the conflict between them the question necessarily arose *concerning the authority which might determine "right" doctrine.* To whom could one appeal in a given case for the correctness of one's opinion? To the *Lord* himself? Appeal to a revelation directly accorded by the Lord or by the Spirit could only make the problem all the more delicate and the embarrassment all the greater. In this situation only such words of the Lord could claim authority as were regarded as vouched for as words of the historical or of the risen Jesus—but that means the factual authorities could only be the people who were bearers of reliable tradition, primarily *the apostles.* When Serapion (*ca.* 200 A.D.) says, "The apostles we accept as the Lord," he is only expressing what had long been taken for granted. The element of tradition had long ago become the decisive thing in the apostle-concept (§ 52, 3). According to Acts 2:42 what the Jerusalem Church held to was "the teaching of the apostles." Jude 17 refers the reader to the words of "the apostles of our Lord Jesus Christ" against the heretics; likewise II Pet. 3:2, where "the commandment of the Lord and Savior through your apostles" takes its place by the side of the canonical authority of the Old Testament prophets. How the authority of the Lord is

concentrated in the person of the apostles is shown by the ranging of the apostles with the Lord in I Clem. 42:1f.; Ign. Mg. 7:1; 13:1; Pol. Phil. 6:3.

It must be recognized, of course, that the apostles could become an indubitable authority only when with the disappearance of the first generation they themselves already belonged to the past, and the conflicts of the apostolic period in which Paul had been involved had died away. Another presupposition for such apostolic authority is the restriction of the title "apostle" to the twelve (§ 52, 3), for, of course, it was not possible to appeal with success to one of those missionaries who had earlier also borne the title apostle. When one appealed to individual apostles such as Peter or Paul (*cf.*, for example, Ign. Rm. 4:3), it was not as individualized and significant personalities that they were appealed to, but as undoubted authorities whose personal differences were of no concern. Apostolic authority is basically that of the college of the twelve, with which only that of Paul is considered equal. It is significant that the Church's first manual of ethics and congregational order was given the title "Teaching of the Twelve Apostles."

But how did this apostolic authority concretely present itself after the twelve and Paul were no longer alive? It was not adequate simply to appeal to the oral tradition by which the words of the apostles had come down to any particular present. At first, it is true, one could still name disciples of apostles and so-called "elders" who had still (actually or allegedly) associated with the apostles or at least with their pupils (Papias, Clement of Alexandria). But that this was an uncertain matter comes to light in the conflict with Gnosticism, for it, too, appeals to oral tradition, "the apostolic tradition which we, too, have received by succession" (Ptolemy to Flora, 10:5). It was Gnosticism particularly which made oral tradition suspect.

But there was a way out of this if one could point to certain persons as authorized bearers of the tradition, and one could. These persons were the congregational officials, *the bishops*, whose appointment, according to common conviction, went back to the apostles (II, pp. 106f.). They represent the legitimate "succession" (διαδοχή)*.

---

* This term first appears in Hegesippus (Eusebius, *Historia Ecclesiastica*, IV 22:3) and Irenaeus I 27, 1. Nevertheless, the cognate verb (διαδέχεσθαι) in this sense is already found in I Clem. 44, 2.

The address of "Paul" to the elders of Ephesus (Acts 20:18ff.) and also the pastorals and Ignatius show what significance the congregational office takes on as bearer and guarantor of the apostolic tradition in the struggle over right doctrine; it was not until the consolidation of the monarchical episcopate that this significance was fully established.

But apostolic authority also lives on in *the written tradition*, the weight of which could only become the greater when oral tradition came into discredit through the Gnostics. Around the middle of the second century words of the Lord in a written tradition already count as Scripture (II Clem. 2:4); the public reading of Gospels in worship is testified by Justin (Apol. I 67). In the book of Revelation it is presupposed that this book is to be read to the congregation (1:3). In the case of Paul's letters it had long been taken for granted that they were to be read in the worship service (I Thess. 5:27; Col. 4:16); at an early time they were exchanged by the congregations to which they had been addressed, and relatively early there must have been collections of Pauline letters. I Clem. 47 refers the readers to Paul and his first letter to the Corinthians. For Ignatius, as for Polycarp, Paul is an authority taken for granted. Jas. 2:14–26 and II Pet. 3:15f. testify that his letters were much read. It is due to the important role of apostolic literature that Paul, though not one of the twelve, nevertheless counts as an apostle—indeed in the end as *the* apostle. In his genuine letters the Church possessed truly apostolic writings, and how much it needed such is indicated by the deutero-Pauline literature which circulated under his name: II Thess., Col., and Eph. as well as the pastorals. So do other writings to which the names of other apostles were attached. Some of these were published under such pseudonyms: the letters of Peter and Jude, and James also, as written by a brother of the Lord, could be reckoned to the same class. Other writings of this sort were attributed to an apostle as an afterthought; such were the originally anonymous Epistles of John and the Epistle to the Hebrews and also the book of Revelation, whose author was some man named John. Then, of course, the Gospels that were in church use also had to be attributed to apostles (Matthew, John) or to disciples of apostles (Mark, Luke) and so did Acts as the sequel of one of them. The tendency at work here is testified, finally, by the fact that a work could be written with the title "Teaching of the Twelve Apostles."

The problem now, however, was the selection of those writings out of the swelling literary production which could count as apostolic. The historical process had to lead to *the formation of a new canon* which took its place beside the Old Testament canon. Within the framework of a theology of the New Testament the detailed stages of this process cannot be described.

Though they cannot be dealt with here, the chief questions are the following: How did it happen that four Gospels were taken into the canon and that the attempts to reduce their number from four to one, either by accepting only one (Luke by Marcion, Matthew by the Ebionites) or by the preparation of a Gospel harmony (Tatian), did not succeed? How did the delimitation of the "apostle" portion come about and why did contested writings like Heb. and Rev. achieve canonical standing while others like I Clem., Barn., and Herm. were excluded? In such decisions how important was the fact that congregations were simply accustomed to certain writings, and how important were criteria of content (such as was the case in the exclusion of the Gospel of Peter, concerning which Bishop Serapion convinced himself that it had to be rejected as Gnostic)?

The essential fact is that in determining what is to be regarded as authoritative apostolic tradition for the Church, the office of bishop and the weight of written tradition worked together. In the end the authority of the bishop-office decided the matter: for the Greek Church, the thirty-ninth paschal letter of Athanasius (367 A.D.) conclusively set the extent of the New Testament at twenty-seven writings, and in the West this decision achieved recognition through Pope Innocent I (405 A.D.).

Unity of doctrine was assured by the canon and not by some normative system of dogmatics. But that means this unity is *only a relative one.* For in point of fact, the canon reflects a multiplicity of conceptions of Christian faith or of its content. Hence, its inner unity becomes a question. At any rate, such inner unity as is there does not appear with the unanimity of dogmatically formulated propositions. Beside the synoptics, which even among themselves exhibit differences, stands John, and beside the Gospels as a whole stands Paul! On one side of Paul stands Hebrews, on the other James! These variations were not necessarily felt as opposites, and they were at first so felt only in border cases as in the question whether Heb.

and Rev. ought to belong to the canon. But in the course of history these differences inevitably worked out as opposites, and when it finally came about that the various Christian confessions and sects all appeal for authority to the canon, that is possible only because in each of them one of the various motifs contained in the canonical writings has become the dominant one. Hence, the judgment is valid: "The New Testament canon, as such, is not the foundation of the Church's unity. On the contrary the canon, as such—i.e. as a fact as it is available to the historian—is the foundation of the multiplicity of confessions" (Käsemann).*

§ 56. Motifs and Types

Before we set forth what themes engage the desire for knowledge it is advisable to cast a glance at the various motifs which determine theological thinking and at the various types in which they take form.

1. *A special influence emanates from the Pauline letters.* Upon the editing of the Gospels, however, the theology of Paul had no influence. The Paulinism which is occasionally supposed to be found in Mark is limited to ideas which are the common property of Hellenistic Christianity. But Luke also contains no specifically Pauline ideas. Matthew need not even be considered, and John is likewise independent of Paul—at the most it contains an echo of Pauline terminology in the antithesis Law—grace (§ 41, 2). Some echoes of the Pauline doctrine of rightwising are found in Acts (13:38f.; 15:8–10). Nevertheless, it did not occur to the author of Acts to utilize the Pauline letters for his presentation. Of the Apostolic Fathers, I Clement, Ignatius, and Polycarp show the influence of Paul.

It is due to the influence of Paul's letters, at least for the most part, that the letter form plays a dominant role in ancient Christian literature. Letters are written not only after the example of Paul (especially Ignatius) but also under his name, so that one may speak of a Pauline school, to which II Thess., Col., and Eph. and, more remotely, the pastorals belong (see II, p. 140). I Pet. too, though it was not placed under the name of Paul, also belongs here, whereas the remaining "catholic" letters are not influenced by Pauline theology but only demonstrate that the letter form had become

---

* In America one would add (or substitute): (and) of denominational types of theology (Tr.).

customary. It is especially characteristic that the tract which came
to be known as I Jn. cleverly imitates letter style in its introduction
and in what was presumably its original close (5:13).* The discourse
entitled Epistle to the Hebrews is provided with an ending which
belatedly gives the writing the appearance of being a letter (13:18–
25). Later falsifications further testify to the continuing influence of
Paul's letters; among such works are: III Corinthians (preserved in
Armenian and Latin), the letter to Laodicea (found in some Latin
Biblical MSS), the correspondence between Paul and Seneca, and the
Epistula Apostolorum (preserved in Coptic and Ethiopic; discussions
in letter form between Jesus and his disciples after the resurrection).

2. The *tradition of the Hellenistic synagogue*, already at work in
Paul himself, exerts greater influence in the pastorals. An important
document of the Christianity which arose out of the Hellenistic
synagogue is I Clem.; another is the Shepherd of Hermas, which comes
out of the Roman congregation. In the latter, Jewish tradition is
utilized to such an extent that it has been surmised—not without
probability—that its substructure is a Jewish document which has
received Christian editing. The same is true of James, in which that
which is specifically Christian is surprisingly thin. At any rate, a
Jewish catechism, the doctrine of the Two Ways, is worked into the
Did. (1–6, 16:3–8) and also into Barn. (18–20). In all these writings
it is especially the homiletic and parenetic tradition of the synagogue
which continues to operate; in addition to this, in Heb. and in Barn.
1–17 it is also the tradition of the Hellenistic-Jewish Scripture-
theology, *viz.*, its allegoristic exegesis (§ 11, 2b and c). In a somewhat
different way Matthew shows the after-effect of Jewish scribalism
in his proofs of prediction and in his conception of Jesus as the
bringer of the messianic Torah (II, p. 124).

In particular the *apocalyptic literature of Judaism* exercised great
influence. It is not only detectable in the whole epistolary literature
of the New Testament and not only led to the weaving in of apocalyptic tradition in Mk. 13 and Did. 16, but it also led to the writing
of a Christian apocalypse, that of John, in which, moreover, older
Jewish tradition was utilized. Hermas also professes to be an apocalypse, but in it the apocalyptic form is essentially only the framework
for hortatory remarks. This influence is further shown by the fact

* *Cf.* R. Bultmann, *Die kirchliche Redaktion des ersten Johannesbriefes. In
Memoriam Ernst Lohmeyer*, 1951, 189–201.

that Jewish apocalypses were taken over by Christianity and handed on down with editorial alterations of greater or less degree. The Apocalypse of Peter is a case by itself; here, in addition to the influence of Jewish tradition, another tradition is at work: that of an oriental eschatology which had penetrated into Gentile Hellenism bringing along its special notions of the world beyond and especially of the underworld.

3. In part by way of the synagogue, in part directly, comes the influence of *Hellenistic popular philosophy* in the diatribe with its natural theology and ethical parenesis, as we already saw it affecting Paul (I, pp. 71f.). This influence manifests itself especially in "Paul's" Areopagus discourse (Acts 17:22–29) and in the parenesis of the pastorals, but also in Jas., especially in 3:1–12 and on a large scale in I Clem. Later on, this influence comes to full development in the apologetes and in the so-called Epistle to Diognetus.

4. To conclude the list, the tradition of *Gnostic mythology and terminology* which had already affected even Paul and John continued to have effect. It did so not merely in the fact that the terminology of Gnostic dualism and of dualistic parenesis often occurs (I, pp. 173f.) nor merely in the fact that single motifs of Gnostic mythology occur as in Rev. and Herm. but primarily in the fact that central motifs of christology, ecclesiology, and eschatology were worked out in Gnostic terminology—as we find them in Col., Eph., and the letters of Ignatius. Also, in the production of apocryphal gospels and acts of apostles Gnostic influence was at work. At first the boundary between this literature and literature which was rejected as heretical by the school of thought that had come to dominate was fluid, and it took some time until apocryphal gospels and acts in which Gnostic fantasy was let loose were excluded.

§ 57. Theology and Cosmology

PRELIMINARY REMARK

It is characteristic that theological thinking in the post-apostolic period also was not guided by a striving after a dogmatic system but was determined by concrete occasions. Consequently, many themes which became important to a later time do not enter the field of reflection, and many ideas taken over from tradition as undiscussed presuppositions are not explicitly developed. Hence, it is not appropriate to offer here a summary of the theological thoughts of the New Testament organized according to traditional *loci* in the form of a dogmatic. The themes intertwine. Since practically all of them are to be heard in the central theme of christology, and since the christological ideas are developed not as free speculation but in the interest of soteriology, the right course seems to be to make this section primarily a presentation of christology and soteriology. But since in the background of all these ideas stands the idea of God, it is advisable to preface the section with a presentation of *theology* in its narrower sense. And since theology like christology was not speculatively developed but God was spoken of only in His relation to the world, the first theme will have to be that of theology and cosmology. In developing it, the intertwining of the themes will become apparent in the fact that theology and cosmology cannot be presented without considering certain christological ideas.

Although in this section and in the rest of the book the literature of the so-called Apostolic Fathers is cited more copiously than usual, our interest in so doing is not to depict the historical development, as such, but rather through a consideration of it to clarify the motifs governing the New Testament way of thinking and to uncover the problems that lie within that thinking. The more inclusive one's view of the total development, the more light falls upon the New Testament itself.

1. It is true that in opposition to Gentile polytheism it is again and again emphasized that only one is *God* (I, pp. 67f.); but the need to prove to sceptical douʰters or atheists that this God *exists* is not yet present. On the whole, it is the tradition of the Old Testament and Judaism that prevails when God is mentioned: God is the Creator and Lord of the world; He is the Judge before whose judgment-seat everyone will someday have to stand (I, pp. 73 and 75–77), but He is also the Father of Jesus Christ. As such a God He is praised in songs that come out of Christian worship or are patterned after such songs (Rev. 4:8, 11; 5:13; 15:3f.; Herm. vis. I 3:4; *cf.* I Clem. 33:2f.). Eschatological hymns which praise God's act of salvation in anticipation lie behind Lk. 1:46–55, 67–79 and perhaps also Rev. 11:15, 17f. Beyond this, thoughts taken from the natural theology of Stoicism are put to service, as they already had been in Paul, to describe the origin of the world out of God and His governance of the universe (I, pp. 70f.). Both motifs, the Hebrew and the Stoic, appear side by

side in I Clem. 33:3, for instance, as they do in the Areopagus discourse (Acts 17:24–29). As a matter of fact, natural theology is never treated by and for itself, as if in the interest of a theodicy, for instance; its ideas are only incidentally put to use. Thus the reference to the divine διοίκησις (governance) of the universe, I Clem. 20, is made in the service of an exhortation to peace and harmony, and in I Clem. 24 the reference to God's providence which makes itself known in the regular cycles of nature is forced to serve as proof for faith in the resurrection.

No necessity for a *theodicy* is felt; for to the problem of suffering a double answer is always possible. In keeping with the tradition of the Old Testament and Judaism it can be regarded as punishment for sin and hence as an instrument of God's discipline (Heb. 12:4–11; Herm. sim. VI 3–5, VII) or of His testing (Jas. 1:2f.; I Pet. 1:6f.; II Clem. 19:3f.). Or all evil can be attributed to Satan and the demons or to demonic powers of the cosmos, and here, too, the idea of testing—the eschatological πειρασμός (both "testing" and "temptation")—may be combined with it (e.g. Rev. 2:10, 3:10). Sufferings, especially those of persecution (Rev. and I Pet.) are the trials of the last days, in which faith must stand the test; they last only a little while, and so they can actually serve to strengthen hope (I Pet. 1:6f., 4:12–19, 5:10, Did. 16:5). In addition, one may find the specifically Christian thought that suffering brings one into fellowship with Christ (I Pet. 2:20f., 4:13). The depth of Paul's thinking on the subject (I, pp. 349ff.), one must admit, is never again reached; in the main, the idea gets no further than the notion of the suffering Christ as an example to be followed (I Pet. 2:21, 3:18, 4:1; Heb. 12:1f.; Ign. Eph. 10:2f.; Pol. Phil. 8:1f.).

No theoretical interest in God's general relation to the world, aside from the history-of-salvation relation, exists as yet, and the Stoic conception of the *logos*, which was later taken up by the apologetes, is not yet put to service to explain the relation of the transcendent God to the world—not by John, either, for the Logos (Word) of his prologue comes not from the philosophical but from the mythological tradition and is not used to serve the cosmological interest (II, p. 64). The same is true of the angels, who according to the tradition of the Old Testament and Judaism constitute, as it were, the courtiers of God (Heb. 1:4ff; 12:22; II Thess. 1:7; I Tim. 5:21; Rev. 5:11; 7:11; I Clem. 34:5; Herm. vis. II 2:7, sim. V 6:4, 7).

Through them God once upon a time caused the Law to be proclaimed (Acts 7:53; Heb. 2:2); they helpfully bring God's people protection and guidance (Acts 5:19; 8:26: 12:7; 27:23); in particular they mediate revelation (Rev. 1:1; 22:6, 16; Herm. mand. XI 9 and *passim*. Hermas is acquainted not only with an angel of repentance (vis. V 7, etc.) and one of righteousness (mand. VI 2:1ff.), but also with one in charge of the beasts (vis. IV 2:4) and of course Michael, too, as the angel who rules the People of God (sim. VIII 3:3). God also lets sentences of punishment be carried out by angels (Acts 12:23; Herm. sim. VI 3:2, VII 1f., 6) and in Revelation it is angels who set going each act of the eschatological drama (Rev. 5–20). They are only servants of God and must not be worshiped in any manner (Rev. 19:10; 22:8f.). There are, of course, other angels that do not serve God but are evil (Barn. 9:4; 18:1, Herm. mand. VI 2:1ff.). But we also hear of angels that have still another quite different meaning: the angelic beings of the cosmos whose origin lies not in the genuine Old Testament-Jewish tradition but in that of Gnosticism. These are the "angels, principalities, authorities, and powers" which are already found in Paul (I, p. 173); and they also include the "rulers of this age" (I Cor. 2:6, 8) and the "thrones" (Col. 1:16) and "dominions" (Col. 1:16; Eph. 1:21). Such beings, like other Gnostic motifs, had already been adopted by the Jewish apocalypses, the eschatology of which was shaped by cosmological speculation, as we have seen (I, pp. 172f.).

All such things, whether adopted from Jewish apocalyptic or from Gnostic tradition, even though they may not entirely have lost what cosmological meaning they once had, were nevertheless made *to serve the history-of-salvation understanding of the relation between God and the world*. If thought about them had been consistent, they would have called into question the idea of creation—as radical Gnosticism recognized. For the notion of the aeons and of Satan as well as that of the cosmic rulers originated in the mythology of a dualistic understanding of the universe. Nor can it be denied that the belief in creation was somewhat obscured by the acceptance of such dualistic notions; but—except in radical Gnosticism—it was not called into question.

Neither did the *figure of the devil*, which has its origin in the mythological dualism of Iranian religion, become, either in Judaism or in Christianity, the representative of a cosmic principle opposed to the divine world of light, but became, instead, an inferior opponent of God whose tempting and destructive power is, indeed, a constantly threatening danger. For Paul, Satan was essentially the tempter (I, p. 258). But just as even Paul could occasionally attribute to him the spoiling of his plans (I Thess. 2:18), so in the time after Paul the devil is held to be the instigator of all evil. He "prowls around like a roaring lion, seeking someone to devour" (I Pet. 5:8). He is the one "who has the power of death" (Heb. 2:14). He is Christ's antagonist who deceives the whole world (Rev. 12:9); he lurks behind the mysterious Antichrist (II Thess. 2:9) and behind "the beast" and the lying prophet of Rev. 13:2, 4. Above all, he is the instigator of sin. As once he seduced Judas (Lk. 22:3; Jn. 13:27; see II, p. 17), so now he is still the seducer (Acts 5:3; I Tim. 5:15; Ign. Eph. 10:3, 8:1; Herm. mand. IV 3:4, 6, V 1:3, etc.). The thing to be done is to resist him in faith (I Pet. 5:9; Eph. 4:14, 6:11; Jas. 4:7) and to beware of falling into his snare (I Tim. 3:6f.; *cf.* 6:9). A human tempter may be reviled as a "son of the devil" (Acts 13:10). Behind persecutions he is lurking, tempting people to apostasy (I Pet. 5:8f.; Rev. 2:10; Ign. Rom. 5:3). Naturally, it is also he who leads the teachers of error astray (II Tim. 2:26; Pol. Phil. 7:1). The heathen temple (of Zeus? of Augustus and Roma?) in Pergamun is his throne (Rev. 2:13), and even the Jewish synagogue may be called the "synagogue of Satan" (Rev. 2:9). It is characteristic that for Ignatius separation from one's bishop is service of the devil (Sm. 9:1), and that the cultic unity of the congregation breaks the devil's might (Eph. 13:1). Because whoever falls into his power thereby pulls down judgment upon himself, the devil's "snare" can also be called his "judgment" or "condemnation" (RSV I Tim. 3:6), and "Paul" can deliver the heretics up to Satan (I Tim. 1:20). Nevertheless, his end is certain (Rev. 20:2, 10).

Even in Rev., where the notions of apocalyptic mythology play their largest role, God still remains the "Almighty" ($\pi\alpha\nu\tau\omega\kappa\rho\acute{\alpha}\tau\omega\rho$—nine times in Rev., elsewhere in the New Testament only once [II Cor. 6:18]). Close to the beginning we read: " 'I am the Alpha and the Omega', says the Lord God, who is and who was and who is to come, the Almighty"—(1:8). Satan and his demonic helpers can therefore play only that role which God has appointed them in the eschatological drama. By a heavenly act like the opening of the book of fate (6:1ff.), the blowing of the seven trumpets (8:7ff.), the emptying of the seven bowls (16:1ff.), by the call, "Come!" (6:1), by the command of an angel (7:2; 10:1ff.; 14:15, 18; 19:17) the demonic powers are given the signal, so to speak, to begin their raging; and their lack of independent action is repeatedly marked by saying "and power was given them (or him)" (6:8, 9:3; 13:5, 7; *cf.* 9:11) or simply "it was given . . ." (6:4; 7:2; 9:5; 13:7, 14f.).

2. At the same time, there were circles in which *angelic beings of the cosmos* played a different role. The New Testament and the Apostolic Fathers, it is quite true, are free from that radical Gnosticism which even in Ptolemy's moderate form (I, pp. 112f.) refuses to ascribe the creation of the world to God and ascribes it to a subordinate or even inimical Demiurge instead (I, pp. 109f.). But when I Jn. 1:5 insists that God is pure light without any darkness, that is probably a polemic against a gnosticizing Christianity which has given up the idea of creation in favor of the idea of emanation. For according to the latter idea, if the lower world of darkness developed by a series of steps out of the world of light, then the darkness must ultimately have its origin in God. It is unlikely that the heretics against whom he is writing actually said that, themselves, but the author sees that that is the logical consequence of their thinking (I, p. 170).

The dualistic view of the world could also be combined with the belief in *creation* in such a way that a fall of the creation was assumed. This is directly said by the Jewish apocalypses (IV Ezr. 3:4ff.; 7:11f.; II Bar. 23:4; 48:24f.) and is allusively suggested by Paul also (Rom. 8:20ff.; I, p. 174). However, Adam's fall, especially its cosmic significance, at first plays no role in ancient Christian literature; only in I Tim. 2:14 is there a hint of it. But when Col. 1:20 nevertheless characterizes the work of Christ as "reconciling all things to himself" and Eph. 1:10 calls it "uniting all things in him," that presupposes that prior to Christ the world had fallen into disorder and contention. Here Biblical tradition has been forsaken and Gnostic mythology is at work. Col. shows that as in Paul and John Gnostic motifs on the one hand have been taken up and that on the other hand Gnostic teachings are being combatted.

Colossians is directed against a heresy which evidently combines speculations of a syncretistic, i.e. Gnostically influenced, Judaism with the Christian faith. In it the dignity and work of Christ are impaired by the veneration of cosmic powers, which are called "elemental spirits of the universe" (2:8, as in Gal. 4:3, 9), "angels" (2:18) and "principalities and powers" (2:10, 15). The author offers no extended description of this "elements"–doctrine. But when he describes the cosmic status of Christ (1:15–20)—quoting a traditional hymn (II, p. 134 footnote)—in whom all cosmic powers have their origin and continue to exist, and when he contrasts Christ with the elemental spirits, calling him the one in whom "dwells the whole fullness of deity bodily" (2:9), we can infer that the heretics must have ascribed to the cosmic powers some sort of participation in the divinity which —in the author's view—dwells in Christ alone, or must have transferred to them a portion of the lordship which is Christ's alone. They appear to have worshiped the angelic powers (2:18); at least they served them by subservience to their δόγματα—i.e. certain ritualistic or ascetic regulations (2:16, 20f.). For that reason, the author, equating such regulations (perhaps rightly) with demands of the Old Testament Law, reminds the reader that Christ has set aside the Law (" the bond which stood against us with its legal demands", 2:14), triumphed over the angelic powers, and stripped them of their power (2:9–15).

Now, it is not as if the author of Col. contested the existence of these cosmic powers. For him, they belong to the totality of the cosmos, whose structure he conceives to be "Christ's body," of which Christ himself is the "head." It is just this which that hymn in 1:15–20 says, and so does the statement of 2:9 that the fullness of divinity dwells in Christ as its body. When the author explains the "body of Christ" as "the Church" (1:18), he conceives the latter to be a cosmic entity that reaches out beyond the empirical Church. To this cosmic "Church," then, those angelic powers also belong. Christ, by being the head of this "Church," is also "the head of every principality and power" (2:10 tr.). It is clear that here a mythological cosmology has been taken over—already taken over in the Christian redaction of that hymn* and then taken over by the author himself—in order to describe the stature and the work of Christ in comprehensive fashion; and the effort to combine the cosmological terminology with traditional Christian terminology is apparent. Christ's work of cosmic reconciliation is at the same time the reconciliation, founded

---

* Detectable in its introduction, vss. 12–14, and in the insertion of "the church" in v. 18 and of the words "by the blood of his cross" in v. 20.

in the cross of Christ, by which the former enemies of God (the heathen world sunk in its sins) were reconciled with God (1:21f.). And when the heretic is described as one "not holding fast to the Head, from whom the whole body, nourished and knit together through its joints and ligaments, grows with a growth that is from God" (2:19), a mythical terminology in which the universe is conceived as an organism is being used to describe the believer's relation to Christ. But factually the exhortation to "hold fast to the Head," which is implicit in this description, means neither more nor less than what our author soon after says in Pauline terminology: "If then you have been raised with Christ, seek the things that are above, where Christ is, seated at the right hand of God. Set your minds on things that are above, not on things that are on earth" (3:1f.).

Matters are not basically different in *Ephesians*. Here, too, the cosmological terminology has been taken over with only this difference, that here the cosmology has been more consistently reinterpreted into a history-of-salvation meaning. In the process a strange mixture of cosmological and history-of-salvation terminology often results (e.g. 2:11–22). The author does not have to fight heretics, and only occasionally does he warn against false doctrines (4:14). With no sense of impropriety he takes over Gnostic concepts to describe the work of salvation. Having first described it as "redemption" through Christ's blood, which he explicitly defines as "the forgiveness of our trespasses," he then brings in the idea of the reconciliation of the cosmos (1:10). But when he applies this idea, he interprets it as the unification of Jews and Gentiles in one "body" (2:11–22). But this "body" does not consist of cosmic powers, but is identical with the "Church" (1:22f.). Yet he uses Gnostic terminology more copiously than Colossians does, especially the myth of the Redeemer's* descent to earth and his reascension (4:8–10), which the author derives by peculiar exegesis from Ps. 68:19, also the myth that the ascending Redeemer* tore down the wall of separation that divided the lower from the upper world (2:15)—for him, however, this has become only a metaphor. The author also utilizes the picture found in Col. 2:19

---

* The author wrote "Christ's" and "Christ," but inasmuch as the "myth" alluded to comes over from pre-Christian Gnosticism (see I, pp. 167, 175), the translator has taken the liberty of substituting "Redeemer"—whom the author of Ephesians, of course, equates with Christ (Tr.).

[151]

of the connectedness of the universe as that of a body growing as a unified organism, indicating as the goal of its growth: "upbuilding in love" (4:15f.). In doing so he confuses the figure by mixing the picture of the growing body with the picture of a structure being built (still more acutely in 2:21f.).

The cosmic powers figure in Eph. not as beings belonging to the total structure of the universe who by Christ have been drawn into the reconciliation of all things, but only as enemy powers. They have now been made subject to Christ who sits in glory at God's right hand (1:20-22); that is, Christ here (as in Col. 2:15) is conceived of as their conqueror. But they are still considered threatening powers, and the author classified them with the devil (6:11f.). Men of faith are indeed freed from their rule, to which they once were subject (2:2-6), but they still have a battle to fight against them (6:10-13). Basically, everything mythological or cosmological about the idea has been here given up; for in point of fact the rule of the powers consisted of the sins and lusts of the flesh (2:1, 3). Rescue from their rule was brought about by the mercy and grace of God and by faith (2:4, 8), a rescue which manifests itself in good works (2:10). The battle against these powers is fought by the faith which holds fast to God's word and by prayer, for that is what the armor described in 6:14-18 amounts to.

The Jewish apocalypses already betray a *feeling about the world* which Paul later shares—a feeling which is no longer determined purely by the tradition of the Old Testament faith in God and creation. It is the feeling of people who feel themselves prisoners in a world pervaded with sinister powers—or if not prisoners, at least strangers in an enemy's land. Upon the soil of such a feeling it is quite understandable that the dualism and mythology of Gnosticism could take root and become influential, and that redemption through Christ could be, and was, interpreted as emancipation from these cosmic powers. Though for the "heretics" Gnostic ideas became dominant, the deutero-Pauline literature shows how the intellectual power of Paul asserted itself there and prevented any such thing. For he himself had paralyzed the dualistic mythology by his ability to make it the expression of his understanding of human existence as an historical existence (§ 26, especially 3). It is an aftermath of this element in Paul which is at work in Col. and especially in Eph., though in neither is the depth of Paul's thoughts reached.

[152]

It was also an idea of Paul's that the work of Christ was a *victory over the cosmic powers* (I Cor. 2:6–8; 15:24–26), and even before Paul the idea had already been expressed in the Christ-hymn quoted by him at Phil. 2:10f. But the characteristic idea of Paul is the conception that although the cosmic drama—begun with the resurrection of Christ—is being played in the present, it is by no means already finished. Christ's battle against the powers fills the time between his resurrection and his parousia; not until the latter will the last enemy, death, be destroyed (I Cor. 15:20–27; *cf.* I, p. 347). This corresponds to the hope of Jewish and the earliest Christian eschatology, in which the close of the cosmic drama and the triumph of God and His Messiah still lie ahead. But in keeping with Gnostic thinking is the conception that Christ's resurrection, or—here more important—his ascent, is already the glorious victory over the cosmic powers. The formulation of Phil. 2:10f. leaves it unclear whether the homage of the powers is considered already present reality or as still a thing of the future. But Col. 2:15 clearly speaks of Christ's triumph as already achieved. This conception became traditional and left its expression in a series of liturgical formulas or hymns. The hymn which underlies I Pet. 3:18–22 presumably closed with the following sentence, which we reconstruct out of v. 19 and v. 22:

Πορευθεὶς (δὲ) εἰς οὐρανὸν ἐκάθισεν ἐν δεξιᾷ θεοῦ ὑποταγέντων αὐτῷ ἀγγέλων καὶ ἐξουσιῶν καὶ δυνάμεων.

("And going into heaven he sat down at God's right hand,
With angels, authorities and powers in subjection to him." tr.)

Pol. Phil. 2:1 quotes a liturgical text which speaks of believing in

"Him who raised our Lord Jesus Christ from the dead
And gave him glory and a throne at His right hand,
To whom are subject all things in heaven and earth."

Christ's glorious ascent to heaven is also described in the hymnic fragment quoted at I Tim. 3:16, for that is what "seen by angels" and "taken up in glory" allude to. "Seen by angels" has a parallel in Ignatius: "in the sight of those in heaven and on earth and under the earth" (Ign. Tr. 9:1), even though the object of that sight named here is his crucifixion and death, for they are meant as cosmic occurrences, as which they constitute a unity with his resurrection—or, rather, his exaltation. The point of view which lies behind all these formulations comes most extensively to view in Ign. Eph. 19:

"And hidden from the ruler of this world remained the virginity of Mary and her child-birth, likewise also the Lord's death—three loudly-crying mysteries that took place in the silence of God. How, then, did it become manifest to the Aeons? A star flashed forth in heaven outshining all the stars, and its light was indescribable, and its newness caused astonishment. (Not the star of Mt. 2:2 is meant, but the luminous ascent of Christ.) . . . Thenceforth all magic was destroyed and every fetter disappeared; malignity's ignorance was canceled, the old regime was annihilated, for God had revealed himself in human form (in Jesus' birth, which is the beginning of the cosmic drama) in order to bring about new, eternal life. That began which, for God, was already completed. Thenceforth all things (=the universe) were agitated, because this would lead to the destruction of death" (Blt., tr.). Here, as the closing sentence shows, the idea of victory already won is combined with that of the conquest of death yet to come, as elsewhere the idea of victory won is combined with the traditional proposition of Christ the Judge who is to come (I Pet. 4:5; Pol. Phil. 2:1; I, p. 78).

Jude 8–11 also shows how the cosmic beings occupy the thinking of believers. Here the heretics are accused of defiling the flesh, rejecting "lordship" (κυριότητα), and reviling the "glorious ones" (δόξας), whereas the archangel Michael did not presume to revile even the devil. This allusive description cannot be interpreted with certainty; nevertheless, it is clear that κυριότης and δόξαι denote angelic powers. Perhaps we have here a case opposite to that of the heretics of Col., who out of respect for the angelic powers regard all manner of ritualistic and ascetic regulations as binding, while the heretics of Jude in the consciousness of their freedom adopt the opposite attitude and are libertines. The author, who, of course, does not need to have belonged to the angel-worshipers combatted in Colossians, at least respects those powers.

CHAPTER VII

The Core of Development

§ 58. Christology and Soteriology

To the extent that christological ideas are inseparable from cosmological ones, it was necessary to discuss some of them in the preceding section. A further interwining of themes now becomes apparent in the fact that soteriology, which forms a unity with christology, cannot be set forth without an anticipatory treatment of the problem of ethics, because the understanding of salvation is intimately connected with one's conception of the foundation of Christian living.

1. In all congregations *Jesus Christ* was worshiped *as the bringer of salvation*. It is he who is confessed at baptism, he who is worshiped in the cult as the present Kyrios (I, pp. 124f.), he who is awaited as the coming Judge and Savior (I, pp. 78f.). How important the service of worship is, is shown by the exhortations to attend the gatherings for worship (Heb. 10:25; Did. 16:2; Barn. 4:10; II Clem. 17:3; Ign. Pol. 4:2), particularly to participate in the Lord's Supper (Ign. Eph. 13) and to pray together (Ign. Tr. 12:2). The cultus has power: "Be zealous, therefore, to gather more frequently together for God's Eucharist and to give praise. For when you frequently gather together, Satan's powers are annihilated and his destructive power is destroyed by your unity of faith" (Ign. Eph. 13:1). In worship songs are sung to the praise of God and Christ. Paul already presupposes that "psalms" are sung in worship (I Cor. 14:26) and Col. 3:16 urges the singing of Spirit-given psalms, hymns, and songs; *cf.* Eph. 5:19, which is similar. Ignatius not only figuratively says that concord and the Congregation's harmony of love are a song of praise to Christ (Ign. Eph. 4:1), but also presupposes that in worship songs of praise and supplication were sung (Rom. 2:2; 4:2). In addition to (or combined with) hymns in praise of God, there were Christ-hymns. One example is the hymn which Paul quotes in Phil. 2:6–11, others are

[155]

the many hymnic fragments or sentences of liturgy which here and there are woven into the epistles and other writings.

The motifs seen in Phil. 2:6–11 are found, singly or together, in many places: the incarnation of the pre-existent one, the cross, and the exaltation. Incarnation and exaltation are sung in I Tim. 3:16. The exalted Christ and Christ the Judge to come are sung in Pol. Phil. 2:1 (see II, p. 153). If I Pet. 1:20, 3:18, 22 may be combined as fragments of a confession of faith, then it contains all three of those motifs plus a statement of the purpose of Christ's passion: it was "for sins . . . that he might bring us to God" (3:18; see also II, p. 153). I Pet. 2:21–24 perhaps also comes from a hymn; here the theme is the vicarious suffering of Christ. Christ's cosmic significance and his work of redemption is the theme of Col. 1:13–20 (from a baptismal hymn?), while Ign. Tr. 9:1f. deals with Christ's incarnation and with his resurrection which will be followed by the resurrection of the faithful. Rev. 5:9, 12 is a song of praise to "the Lamb that was slain" and by his blood obtained salvation. The salvation brought by Christ is described in I Clem. 36:1f.—evidently sentences out of a liturgy:

"Through him we fix our gaze on the heights of heaven,
   Through him we see the reflection of His (God's) faultless and
      lofty countenance,
   Through him the eyes of our hearts were opened,
   Through him our foolish and darkened understanding blossoms
      toward the light,
   Through him the Master willed that we should taste the
      immortal knowledge."

The *titles* which are given to Christ are manifold. He is the Son of God (I, pp. 128f.), the Lord (I, pp. 124f.), the Savior (I, p. 79; II, p. 158), the Judge (I, p. 78); but the old title Son of Man is no more to be found (I, pp. 79f.). In place of it other designations occasionally appear such as Pioneer (of life or of salvation; see Acts 3:15; 5:31; Heb. 2:10; 12:2; II Clem. 20:5) and High Priest (Heb. 2:17; 3:1, etc.; I Clem. 36:1; Ign. Philad. 9:1; Pol. Phil. 12:2), but also Teacher (I Clem. 13:1; Ign. Eph. 15:1; Mg. 9:1f.).

As for *Christ's person*, the reflections about his relation to God which later occupied the ancient Church are still far off. God is his Father whom he obeys (Ign. Sm. 8:1; *cf.* Mg. 7:1); the designation of

Christ as God occurs almost solely in Ignatius (see I, p. 129). Just as remote in this period are reflections about the relation between the divine and the human nature in Christ. The belief that the pre-existent one became man and was re-exalted to glory at God's right hand was sufficient. Only the miracle of his birth from a virgin here and there occupies the imagination of a writer (Mt. 1:18–25; Lk. 1:34f.; Ign. Eph. 18:2; 19:1; Sm. 1:1). Measured by later ways of putting the question the generally dominant christology would have to be called a Spirit-christology rather than adoptionistic. Only in Hermas do the motifs of an adoptionistic and of a Spirit-christology combine (sim. V), and there the combination is decidedly unclear.

The *work of salvation* as a whole consists of Christ's incarnation, his passion and death, his resurrection and exaltation, but sometimes one item, sometimes another, may be mentioned or emphasized. By and large, however, the chief emphasis lies upon his passion and death. Christ's death is the sacrifice made for us (I, p. 85). It is in this sense that his blood poured out for us is mentioned (I, p. 85), or the cross (Col. 1:20; 2:14; Eph. 2:16; Barn. 9:8; 12:1; Ign. Eph. 9:1; Tr. 11:2, etc.), or his suffering (πάσχειν: Mk. 8:31; Lk. 24:46; Acts 3:18; 17:3; Heb. 2:18; 9:26; I Pet. 2:19, 21; Barn. *passim*, II Clem. 1:2; Ig. Sm. 2:7; 7:1, etc.) or his sufferings (παθήματα: Col. 1:24; I Pet. 1:11; 4:13; 5:1; Heb. 2:9f.; I Clem. 2:1) or his passion (πάθος, very often in Ignatius). He is "the Lamb that was slain" (Rev. 5:6ff., etc.; *cf.* Acts 8:32; I Pet. 1:19; 2:22ff.; I Clem. 16:7; Barn. 5:2; 8:2). The salvation wrought by Christ's sacrifice is generally termed forgiveness of sin, release (ἀπολύτρωσις, "redemption"), rightwising ("justification"), sanctification, or purification, when it is being described in its effect upon believers (I, p. 85). In addition, it is termed victory over the cosmic powers, especially over death (see II, pp. 153 f.). The benefit of the work of salvation is appropriated by baptism, the effect of which is termed as a rule forgiveness of sin (I, p. 136). Baptism is probably always in mind when forgiveness of sin is mentioned, even though it may not be explicitly named (e.g. Lk. 24:47; Acts 2:38; Herm. vis. III, 3:5).

2. But the *concept of salvation* is unambiguous only insofar as it in any case means life and rescue from death.

II Tim. 1:10 formulates it thus: Christ is he "who abolished death and brought life and immortality to light. . . ." It is in this sense that Christ is the Savior ("rescuer"—II Tim. 1:10; Tit. 1:4, 2:13, 3:6; Acts 5:31, 13:23; II Pet. 1:1, 11, 2:20, 3:2–18; Ign. Eph. 1:1; Mg. intr., Philad. 9:2; Sm. 7:1; Pol. Phil. intr.; II Clem. 20:5; see I, p. 79) or the pioneer of salvation (Heb. 2:10) or of life (Acts 3:15; *cf.* 5:31), the "source of eternal salvation" (Heb. 5:9). In him salvation is given (II Tim. 2:10, 3:15; *cf.* Acts 4:12). He rescues from death because he himself conquered death (Heb. 2:14f.; Rev. 1:18; Barn. 5:6f.; *cf.* I Pet. 1:3, 21). The Christian message, accordingly, is called the "gospel of salvation" (Eph. 1:13), the "word of salvation" (Acts 13:26; *cf.* Heb. 2:3); its content is the "way of salvation" (Acts 16:17). "Salvation" and "life" are identical, and both may be combined in a hendiadys (Ign. Eph. 18:1; II Clem. 19:1).

But here *the views of salvation differentiate themselves* according to what is regarded to constitute the power of death and hence what kind of salvation or life corresponds to it; and further—related to this—according to whether the rescue is considered to be solely future or already present; and, finally, according to how the mediation and appropriation of salvation is conceived.

Whatever else it means, death is probably always also thought of as the literal end of natural life. Paul, however, had understood this "natural" life not as a mere phenomenon of nature, but as the human person's activity within his own history (I, pp. 209f.). Neither had he understood death as a mere event of nature, but simultaneously understood it as the already present nothingness of a life estranged from God (I, pp. 246ff.). Consequently, he had also understood the life conferred by Christ as a present reality given to a Christian in the gift of righteousness (I, p. 279), not, of course, as simply a state of being but as that freedom from sin which contains within itself the ethical imperative, and which maintains itself in hope, in the conquest of suffering and fate, and in emancipation from the world and its powers (§ 40). For Paul, that is, "life" is paradoxically a present reality. In substance the same is true of John (§ 42 and § 50, 3). To what extent has this Pauline and Johannine understanding of "life" (and "death") been retained?

Statements predominate in which *salvation is conceived as a thing of the future*. It is for "salvation" that Christ will someday appear for the benefit of those who await him (Heb. 9:28), who, by the power of God through faith are preserved "for a salvation ready to be

revealed in the last time" (I Pet. 1:5; *cf.* 1:9; 2:2). Whoever calls upon
the name of the Lord will (quoting Joel) be saved (Acts 2:21; *cf.* 15:11,
16:30f.).

It will be by repentance and the fear of God that one will be
saved (Herm. mand. IV 3:7; VII 1, IX 6; *cf.* sim. I 11, IX 12:3; II
Clem. 8:2, 13:1). Women will be saved by the bearing of children
(I Tim. 2:15). The future tense of "save" or "be saved" is also
used elsewhere: I Tim. 4:16; II Tim. 4:18; Did. 16:5; Barn. 1:3;
Ign. Pol. 1:2; very frequently in II Clem. e.g. 4:2, 14:1.

Life is likewise often spoken of *as a life that is yet to come*—for
instance when the "crown of life" is promised (Rev. 2:10; Jas. 1:12),
or in the expression "hope of life (eternal)" (Tit. 1:2; Barn. 1:4, 6;
Herm. sim. IX 26:2; *cf.* 14:3) or "the life which lies ahead" (Ign. Eph.
17:1), or when "salvation" and life" are combined (Ign. Eph. 18:1).

In general "life eternal" is understood (otherwise than in
John) as the life to come (I Tim. 1:16, 6:12; Tit. 1:2, 3:7; Acts
13:46, 48; Jude 21; Herm. vis. II 3:2). The verbal expression
"live forever" has the same meaning (Barn. 8:5, 9:2, 11:10f.).
But "life" alone (Herm. vis. I 1:9) or "to live," by itself, (Heb.
12:9; Barn. 6:17; Herm. vis. III 8:5; mand. IV 2:3f., XII 6:3)
also means the same thing. The future meaning of the following
expressions is clear: "to obtain life" (Herm. mand. III 5; sim. VI
5:7; *cf.* "to obtain glory, honor," etc., I Clem. 54:3; Herm. mand.
IV 4:2; sim. V 3:3) and "to inherit eternal life" (Herm. vis. III
8:4; *cf.* "heirs of eternal life," Tit. 3:7). To "inherit salvation"
(Heb. 1:14, tr.) or "inherit the blessing" (I Pet. 1:4, tr.) also
refers to future life. Just as this "inheritance" can be called
"imperishable" (ἄφθαρτος, I Pet. 1:4), so in place of being called
"life (eternal)" it may be called "incorruption" (ἀφθαρσία; Eph.
6:24; Ign. Philad. 9:2; II Clem. 20:5), or "incorruption" and
"life eternal" may be combined with each other (Ign. Pol. 2:3;
II Clem. 14:5; *cf.* "life in immortality," I Clem. 35:2).

But in other passages "*salvation*" or "*life*" is meant as *present life*.
Just as believers may be called "those who are being saved" (σωζόμενοι,
Acts 2:47; I Clem. 58:2) or even "those who have been saved"
(σεσωσμένοι, Eph. 2:5; Pol. Phil. 1:3), they may also be called "the
living" (II Clem. 3:1). God's deed rescued them. It is God who
"delivered us from the dominion of darkness and transferred us to
the reign of his beloved Son" (Col. 1:13, tr.). How that deliverance is

to be understood is shown by the remainder of the sentence: "in whom we have redemption, the forgiveness of sins" (1:14). In so writing, the author probably has baptism in mind—in keeping with the likelihood that the hymn which he adapts in vss. 15–20 comes out of a baptismal liturgy. From the fact that he prefaces the hymn with the statement: "giving thanks to the father, who has qualified you (*v. l.* us) to share in the inheritance of the saints in light" (v. 12), we see that he so relates present and future salvation as to regard the state of present salvation as an anticipation of that future salvation which is guaranteed by baptism. So, in spite of 1:14, true "life" is, itself, still future; as 3:3 puts it, it is "hid with Christ in God" and, further, "When Christ who is our life appears, then you will also appear with him in glory" (3:4). Consequently, the author can say that the Gospel proclaims "the hope laid up for you in heaven" (1:5; *cf.* 1:23, 27).

What we have here observed in Col. is typical. In similarly paradoxical manner Eph. speaks of the present reality of salvation: "but God . . . even when we were dead through our trespasses, made us alive together with Christ . . . and raised us up with him and made us sit in the heavenly places in Jesus Christ" (2:5f.). This author, too, is thinking of *baptism* (*cf.* 5:26), and present salvation is anticipatory of the future; for the content of the "illumination" brought by the Gospel is knowing "what is the hope to which he has called you . . ." (1:18; *cf.* 4:4). That the deliverance was accomplished by baptism is said in many places (Tit. 3:5; I Pet. 3:21; Barn. 11:11; Herm. vis. III 3:5; mand. IV 3:1; sim. IX 16:2ff.). It is just because baptism has taken place that it can be said of the deliverance ("salvation") that it has already occurred (*cf.* in addition to the last list of passages: II Clem. 1:4; 2:7; 3:3; 9:2, 5; Herm. sim. VIII 6:1; IX 26:8).

Just as the acquisition of salvation can be attributed to baptism, so it can also be attributed to being "*called*," without any substantial difference in meaning, for by his "calling" the Christian is called into the Church, and he is received into the Church by baptism. (In Hermas κλῆσις—"calling"—is actually a direct designation of baptism; mand. IV 3:6; *cf.* 3:4; sim. VIII 11:1; sim. IX 14:5). The "saved" or the "living" therefore may also be called "the called" (Heb. 9:15; Herm. sim. IX 14:5) or "the called, sanctified ones" (κλητοὶ ἡγιασμένοι, I Clem., intr.). God, or Christ, called them "into his marvelous light" (I Pet.

2:9), "from darkness into light" (I Clem. 59:2; *cf.* II Clem. 1:2, 8). They were called "to the peace of Christ . . . in one body" (Col. 3:5; *cf.* Eph. 1:11 in the text of ADG it, 4:4), to "eternal life" (I Tim. 6:12), to "the obtaining of glory" (II Thess. 2:14; *cf.* I Pet. 3:9, 5:16). Κληθῆναι ("to be called") often occurs without any complement (Eph. 4:1; II Tim. 1:9; I Pet. 1:15; II Pet. 1:3; II Clem. 2:4, 7, 5:1, etc.); so does κλῆσις ("calling": Eph. 1:18, 4:1, 4; II Thess. 1:11; II Tim. 1:9; Heb. 3:1; II Pet. 1:10; I Clem. 46:6; Herm. mand. IV 3:6; sim. VIII 11:1). The relation of the believer to the future is perhaps more strongly expressed by his "calling" than it is by the term "deliverance"; at least it is in II Thess. 1:11, or in expressions like "the hope of your calling" (Eph. 1:18) and "the calling of his promise" (Barn. 16:9); *cf.* also the "heavenly call" of Heb. 3:1.

3. The decisive question now is how *the relation between salvation's present reality and its futurity is conceived.* Has the dialectic understanding of this relation, such as we found it in Paul and John been retained? Is it still understood that it is the situation of the Christian to be in that peculiar "betweenness"—between "no longer" and "not yet" (see I, p. 322)? In very general terms it may be said that through the call into the Church, through the present forgiveness of sin mediated by baptism, the possibility of future salvation is bestowed; and likewise that the present stands under the ethical imperative, the fulfilment of which is the condition for achieving future salvation. But the real question is: is future life regarded as already a present reality in the very fulfilling of the imperative? To ask it differently: which is true—that the forgiveness mediated by baptism is conceived as absolution from the debts contracted up to the time of baptism and from the punishment they deserve? or that it is conceived as emancipation from the power of sin?

a. The problems involved in the situation may perhaps be made clearest by examining an extreme case. Such is the *Shepherd of Hermas.* Here we read (vis. III 3:5): "your life was saved and shall be saved through water"—the baptism which has saved you will bring about your future salvation. But this is dependent upon a pure conduct of life. The "heavenly letter" which Hermas receives, assures him: "But what saves you is the fact that you have not fallen away from the living God, and your sincerity, and your great continence. These things have saved you on condition that you persevere in them, and they save all who do likewise and walk in innocence and sincerity" (vis. II 3:2 tr.). Baptism brings about salvation only insofar as it frees one from his previously committed sins (mand. IV 3:1–3; 4:4) and thereby makes possible a new beginning for his life; but henceforth he must lead his life on his own responsibility in obedience to the commandments of God which Hermas constantly urges upon his readers. In the end, then, not baptism but his own good conduct saves the believer. For good conduct, "life" is promised (e.g. mand. III 5, IV 2:4, XII 6:3). No wonder that the problem of sins committed after baptism then arises. The revelation which Hermas professes to have received is just this: that after the benefit of the first repentance (at baptism) has been trifled away, now one last time before the impending end the possibility of repentance has been given by God (vis. II 2:4–8, mand. IV, 3, sim. IX 26:6). The Christian stands, indeed, between the past and the future, but this "between" is only a chronological one; it is a between-time, an interval which must be utilized for repentance. The whole book is a call to repentance, and the author is at pains to show that "repentance" is an "insight," the effect of which is to cause the sinner to recognize and repent his sins and to walk henceforth according to the commandments of God (mand. IV 2:2–4, etc.). It is characteristic of Hermas that for him "Faith" is one of the virtues (mand. VIII 8f., XII 3:1, sim. X 4:2), in fact, the chief virtue to which Continence, Simplicity, Knowledge, Innocence, Reverence, and Love are "daughters." But this *pistis* is nevertheless nothing other than faith in the one God (mand. I).

b. The exhortations of *James* also are pervaded with reference to the coming retribution and the judgment. He takes it for granted that the Christian is subject to the Law, the authority of which he emphasizes with the adjectives "perfect" and "royal" (1:25; 2:8), and that the Law, as a whole, must be observed (2:13f.). Why he also calls it "Law of freedom" (1:25; 2:12) is a riddle.* At any rate, the Pauline idea of freedom is just as remote from the author's mind as is Paul's concept of faith. Works of good conduct are required, and of the "doer of the Law" it is said: "he shall be blessed in his doing" (1:25).

This attitude finds its strongest expression in the polemic against a point of view which claims that salvation is awarded

* "Law of freedom" is probably a Jewish term; it seems that it occurs three times in the "Dead Sea Manual of Discipline" (M. Burrows, *Dead Sea Scrolls* II 2, 1951). *Cf.* E. Stauffer in *Th. L. Z.* 77 (1952), 577ff.

to a faith that is without works (2:14–26). The fact that the author polemizes against the proposition that Abraham was justified by faith alone makes it likely that that point of view is supposed to be Paul's or that of some group claiming Paul as its authority. If so, Paul's concept of faith is thereby utterly misunderstood. For Paul would certainly have agreed with the proposition that a faith without works is dead (2:17, 26) but never in the world with the thesis that faith works along with works (2:22). James can so speak only because he understands by faith merely the theoretical conviction of the existence of the one God, a belief which even the demons have (2:19).

Every shred of understanding for the Christian's situation as that of "between-ness" is lacking here. The moralism of the synagogue-tradition has made its entry, and it is possible that James not merely stands in the general context of this tradition but that its author took over a Jewish document and only lightly retouched it (see II, p. 143).

c. To this type belongs also *the Didache,* in the first part of which a Jewish catechism for proselytes is woven in (see II, p. 143), and which contained ethical commandments and prohibitions according to the scheme of the "Two Ways," and which the author enriched by interpolating words of the Lord. Naive belief in retribution dominates the exhortations, and the conclusion of the book, which refers to the coming judgment and exhorts the reader to "be watchful" (16:1) and promises salvation to those who "endure in their faith" (16:5), probably also comes out of the Jewish catechism.

d. *Barnabas,* too, took over that Jewish catechism (18–21). Its author also stands within the tradition of the Hellenistic synagogue with his allegoristic method of interpreting the Old Testament (§ 11, 2b). Nevertheless, his understanding of Christian existence, no matter how inconsistently he carries it out, goes beyond that of Herm., Jas., and the Did., and approaches that of the deutero-Pauline writings; this is all the more noteworthy in that the author is not under the influence of Pauline theology. It is true, he knows the forensic concept of "righteousness" (13:7, following Gen. 15:6; otherwise, he uses "righteousness" in the ethical sense: 1:4, 6; 5:4; 20:2—likewise "righteous": 10:11; 19:6), but Christians are not, for him, already rightwised (4:10; *cf.* 15:7). Salvation is a future thing (6:17–19; 15:5–9); believers are already at the last time (4:3, 9; 21:3) and have to prepare themselves by conscientious fulfilment of "the new law of our Lord Jesus Christ" (2:6), or of the "ordinances" (2:1; 10:11, etc.) or "commandments" (4:11; 16:9, etc.) "of the Lord" —for the judgment according to one's works lies ahead (4:12; *cf.* 15:5; 21:1, 3), the judgment which Christ as the coming Judge will hold (5:7; 7:2). The call to repentance, however, is missing; "repentance" occurs only once (16:9), but there it evidently means baptismal repentance.

Nevertheless, the present existence of Christians is already a new one. They are the "new People" (5:7; 7:5), the "People of the inheritance" (14:4), the "holy People" (14:6) to whom God's covenant pertains (13, 14)—in contrast to the Jewish people, which never had a true covenant with God (§ 11, 2b). The Christians' situation has become a new one by the fact that Christ, the Son of God, came and revealed himself in the flesh (5:6, 10f.; 6:7, 9, 14; 12:10), suffered for us on the cross and died (5:1f., 12f.; 7:2f. 12:1ff.), and thus by his blood (5:1) achieved for us the forgiveness of sins (5:1f; 7:3, 5) and by his resurrection destroyed death and gave us life (5:6; 7:3; 12:5). By these means he "renewed" us so that we now have the souls of children; he "created us anew" (6:11, 14; 16:8). His work is appropriated by us in baptism (11:8, 11; *cf.* 8:3; 16:9), which establishes a new life by the gift of the Spirit (1:2f.). Hence, the Christian can be called "a spiritual temple being built for the Lord" (16:10), and yet can be exhorted: "Let us be spiritual, let us be a perfect temple for God" (4:11, tr.). Otherwise, however, the Spirit plays no essential role, and the contrast between flesh and spirit occurs only at 7:3, where Christ's flesh is called "the vessel of the Spirit" (*cf.* 11:9). *Pneuma* denotes mainly the prophetic spirit of the Old Testament, except where the author is speaking non-technically of the "spirit" or "spirits" of his readers (*cf.* 11:11 where "in the spirit" parallels "in the heart"—a parallelism missed by Lake's translation). The new existence of Christians as "God's temple" is described in 16:9: "His word of faith, his call of promise, the wisdom of the ordinances, the commandments of the teaching, he himself prophesying in us, he himself dwelling in us, he leads us who were enslaved to death— opening the door of the temple (that is, the mouth) and giving us repentance—into the incorruptible temple."

Corresponding to the fact that in this description the "word of faith" stands first, "faith" is again central where it is said of the Christians "we are made alive" (N.B.: not "rightwised") by faith in the promise and by the word" (6:17). The "word" which is to be believed (9:3; 11:11) contains, of course, the message of Christ's work, which is the object of "believing" (7:2). But Christian existence can also be described as "believing God" (16:7) and occasionally also by just the noun "faith" (4:9) or just the verb "believe" (3:6 and 13:7 quoting Gen. 17:4f. and 15:6). Nevertheless, the concept of "faith" is not emphasized, nor is it sharply outlined; it is not placed in contrast to "works." The term "grace" correspondingly scarcely plays a role; it is used of Old Testament prophecy (5:6) and of baptismal grace (1:2); the content of the cross (9:8) and of preaching (14:9 quoting Is. 61:1f.) is "grace" (also used in a formula of greeting at the close, 21:9). In the obviously traditional triad "faith, love, hope" (1:4, 6; *cf.* 11:8), which are descriptive of Christian existence, the terms are not sharply distinguished from each other; according to 1:4 "faith" and "love" dwell in the Church "in the hope of his life," and according to 1:6 "the hope of life" is the beginning and end of faith. The new covenant is to be sealed in the heart "in the hope which belongs to faith in him" (4:8). Faith, for Barnabas, evidently is essentially hoping trust (*cf.* 12:7), a meaning that is also apparent in the fact that to believe in Jesus and to hope in him are interchangeable expressions (*cf.* 6:3 with 6:9; 11:11; 12:2f.; 16:8); in reference to God the verbs can also interchange: 19:7 uses "hope in God" in place of "believe in God." If faith's helpers are "fear" and "patience" (2:2), that points to a meaning of "faith" that lies in the same direction

But more important and more characteristic is the connection between "faith" and "knowledge." The author writes to his readers "in order that along with your faith you may have your knowledge complete (or perfect)" (1:5). The content of this "knowledge" is "the way of righteousness" (5:4), which primarily means the knowledge, given by the Old Testament, of that which is past, present, and future (1:7; 5:3), along with which, of course, knowledge of the "ordinances" is also given (21:5; *cf.* 6:9; 19:1). This knowledge is the new knowledge given by God, who is called He "who placed in us wisdom and understanding of his secrets" (6:10; *cf.* 5:3; 7:1). It is conferred upon him who has faith and virtue (2:3). Because "knowledge" and "teaching" constitute a unity, God can also be called He "who placed the implanted gift of his teaching in us" (9:9).

All in all, the understanding of Christian faith is less legalistic in

Barn. than in Herm., Jas., and the Did. The paradox of Christian existence between "no longer" and "not yet," and hence the determination of the present by the future, is not clearly set forth, it is true, yet occasionally it is involuntarily expressed. The exhortation "let us become spiritual" (4:11) is directed to such as have already received the Spirit and are "the temple of God." And it is as men "made alive by the word" (6:17) that they will receive the life to come.

e. Related to Barnabas is *Hebrews*. For its author, too, the life of the believer stands essentially under the demand of God. Responsibility has become greater for Christians than it was for Israel (2:2f.; 10:26–31; 12:25). God is an unbribable judge (4:12f.), and it is a fearful thing to fall into His hands (10:31). But the relation of the present to the future goes beyond the relation between human conduct and divine retribution, because the present is in a certain sense already a time of salvation. The believers' present situation is characterized by the fact that they are "those who have once been enlightened and have become partakers of the Holy Spirit, and have tasted the goodness of the word of God and the powers of the age to come" (6:4f.). And yet—does all this solemn description really mean anything more than that they have been baptized? Otherwise the essential description given of the present is that it is the time of the New Covenant (8:6–13; 10:15–18) which came into being by the sacrifice of himself which Christ as High Priest made, so that the entrance to the sanctuary stands open (10:19f.) and believers, freed from the fear of death (2:14f.), now have access to God and "confidence" and "hope" (3:6; 4:16; 6:11, 18; 7:19, 25). They can confidently approach the "throne of grace" (4:16—in prayer is probably meant, after all; *cf.* 7:25; 10:22). Nevertheless, the Christian is conscious of his accountability to the heavenly Judge, and the resultant paradox is misunderstood if one regards the new thing in the present reality of salvation to be that it contains the possibility, after the release (by baptism) from one's past sins, of achieving salvation by the Christian's new kind of conduct.

The problem of sins committed after baptism did not, in itself, oppress the author. To be sure, "deliberate" sins are unforgivable (10:26–31), and for grave sins, especially that of apostasy, there is no possibility of repentance (6:4–6; 12:16f.). The intercession of Christ for the believers (7:25; *cf.* 2:17) apparently means no more than that they can receive forgiveness for occasional sins. Unlike Hermas, the author does not call his readers to repentance; evidently the baptized have repented once for all (6:1, 6). He does call them to "endurance" (ὑπομονή, 10:36; 12:1), to hold fast to their "confidence" and "hope" (3:6, 14; 6:11; 10:23, 35); the really sinful sin is precisely that of apostasy. In harmony with this conception is Hebrew's concept of faith (I, p. 91). "Faith" first means, of course, acceptance of the missionary message (6:1; 11:6), then also trust (10:22), but above all it means faithfulness, fidelity (6:12; 10:22, 11 *passim*, 13:7; it is synonymous with ὑπομονή, "endurance," *cf.* 10:35–39) and hope (11 *passim*).

The "faith" by which the "righteous one" will live (10:38) is his "endurance"; the faith by which Abel was approved as "righteous" (11:4) can hardly be defined in any other way than simply belief in God. The contrast between "faith" and "works" plays no role in Heb.; neither does "rightwising by faith" or Paul's "righteousness from God." (*Dikaiosyne* in Heb. means "uprightness" in 1:9, 11:33, 12:11; or "the right," 5:13; or the "justice" of a ruler, 7:2; only once does it mean the substance of salvation: the "righteousness" which Noah achieved by virtue of his obedience, 11:7). The believer's trust, it is true, is toward the grace of God, and in 12:15 "grace" evidently means saving grace—probably also in 13:9 and 10:29. But the contrast between "grace" and "works" is missing; and in 4:16, where "grace" and "mercy" are co-ordinated, that is the grace of God which the one praying hopes to find "in time of need"—i.e. help in each particular time of need. What is important to the author is, rather, that Christians are "purified" and "sanctified"—i.e. by baptism. Christ's blood "purifies our conscience from dead works in order that we may serve the living God" (9:14 Blt.; *cf.* 1:3, 10:22; for "sanctify," which according to 9:13f. is synonymous with "purify," see 2:11, 10:10, 14, 29, 13:12). No reconciliation between these indicatives and the imperative "strive . . . for sanctification" (12:14 tr.; *cf.* 12:10) is attempted, nor between the two uses of τελειοῦν. This word means in 9:9 (*cf.* 9:14) and 10:1, 14 just what καθαρίζειν and ἁγιάζειν mean: "dedicate" or "sanctify"; but in 11:40 and 12:23 (*cf.* 12:2) it means "bring to completion or perfection" (the verb has this meaning even where applied to Christ: 2:10, 5:9, 7:28). The explanation for this double usage is that the dedication proleptically places the dedicated into heavenly existence, i.e. separates him from the world's

THE CORE OF DEVELOPMENT

sphere, desecularizes him. But the inner connection between the desecularization which takes place in the dedication and the desecularization which is to be brought about by one's own effort (13:13f.) is not made evident by the author. The imperative is here not truly founded upon the indicative. The purification of the conscience in 9:14 (*cf.* 10:2, 22) is simply the forgiveness of former sins conferred in baptism, and the "good conscience" of the baptized consists in their desiring to "act honorably in all things" (13:18). Of dying and rising with Christ there is no mention. The cross of Christ is referred to as an example for the Christian to follow (12:2f., 13:13). The author does know of "distributions of the Holy Spirit" (i.e. gifts distributed by the Holy Spirit), 2:4, and knows that in baptism the Spirit is given (6:4), and says (10:29) that he who has fallen away from the faith has insulted the "Spirit of grace." But the Spirit which is the power of Christian living (Paul's view) is not what he is talking about. Instead he is trying to teach the believer to understand the woes that come upon him as the discipline of God (12:4–11).

Because the dialectic relationship between imperative and indicative has been lost from sight, salvation is really only future, and the present simply stands under God's demand; insofar as the present is a "between," it is only a between-time, an interval that will last for a little while longer, in which by his "endurance" the believer must hold out (10:36, etc.). It is significant that the problem of legalism does not concern the author; all that interests him about the Torah is the sacrificial-ceremonial law which he interprets allegorically (§ 11, 2c).

f. The opening section of *II Peter* creates a first impression that its author has an understanding of Christian faith that goes beyond the field of legalistic moralism; for it is also true that the influence of the synagogue tradition is scarcely detectable in II Pet. In 1:3–11 the ethical imperative is given its foundation in the indicative—out of the "faith" by which the divine gift was accepted a whole chain of attitudes or modes of acting is derived: "virtue—knowledge—self-control—steadfastness—godliness—brotherly affection—love." But the unfolding of these modes of acting is made the responsibility of the believer's own σπουδή (effort, diligence)—the Spirit is mentioned only in 1:21, where it means that which inspires prophecy—and this "effort" has for its goal the confirmation of one's "call" and "election" (1:10). In point of fact, for this author God's gift is limited to His calling the believer to future salvation (1:3f.), or one might also say limited to baptism, which cleanses one from his former sins (1:9). When the author is defining the purpose of the promises given in God's call ("in order that you may share a divine nature, escaping the worldly corruption that lies in desire," 1:4, tr.), it is not clear whether his intention is to describe the present state of the Christian or to describe future salvation. Even if the former is his intention the present reality of salvation is still not conceived as a paradoxical one but as a quality of one's nature (a quality acquired through baptism). At any rate, in spite of all the author's high words about the already received gift of God (1:3f.), for him salvation lies basically in the future. For his purpose in writing is clearly to combat doubt about the coming of Christ (1:16; 3:4, 12) and to impress upon his readers the seriousness of the coming judgment and their consequent responsibility to lead a pure life (3:14, 17f.).

The situation is much the same in *Jude*, except that his exhortation looks forward not like II Pet. to "the day of judgment and destruction of ungodly men" (II Pet. 3:7) but to "the mercy of our Lord Jesus Christ" which will bestow upon us "eternal life" (Jude 20f.). That such expectation is founded upon pure living is the indirect implication not only of his description of the heretic's blasphemous way of life which the judgment will condemn, but also of the closing doxology with its confidence that God will keep the readers faultless and unblemished (24).

g. There is a clear-cut peculiar kind of Christian legalism in *II Clement*. The document bearing this title is an exhortatory and penitential sermon which looks forward to the coming judgment and the salvation promised to the pious. Judgment will be according to one's works (6:9; 11:6; 16:3; 17:4) and the whole life of a Christian must be an athlete's "contest" and for victory in it a crown beckons (7:1ff.). But the author's exhortation is motivated by reference to the Christian's present as it is conditioned by the work of Christ. Though "salvation" is mostly conceived as future (e.g. 19:3, "that we may be saved at the end"), believers are nevertheless already saved (3:3; 9:2). Christ who came as the "savior" and the "pioneer of incorruption" (20:5) saved them (1:4, 7; 2:7; 9:5); he called them (1:2, 8, etc.); he suffered for their sake (1:2). Believers are his "body" (14:2), that is, "the Church," which, as spiritual Church, was pre-existent and with the appearing in the flesh of the spirit-Christ has now likewise appeared in the flesh (14:1ff.). Those received by baptism into the "Church" must now keep pure their baptism or "seal" (6:9; 7:6; 8:6). They must give thanks for the gift of salvation and requite it (ἀντιμισθία, 1:3, 5; 9:7; 15:2) with a confession which consists in deeds (3:1ff.; 4:1ff.) and repentance (9:8). To keep baptism or "the seal" pure also means "to keep the flesh pure" (8:4, 6; 9:3; 14:3); i.e. to renounce the world and its desires (5:4; 6:4; 16:2, etc.) and to lead one's life in good works, in "uprightness," as one who is "upright," "holy," "reverent" (6:9; 11:7; 12:1; 15:3; 19:2f., etc.). Though love (ἀγάπη, 4:3; 9:6; 12:1; 13:4; 15:2; 16:4) is also regarded as a "virtue" (10:1), yet for II Clem. the characteristic virtue is ἐγκράτεια (self-control, abstinence, continence—4:3; 15:1), which even goes to the extent of sexual asceticism (12:5).

It is possible to find in II Clem. a founding of the imperative upon the indicative, but the Pauline paradox of it is lacking, and consequently so is the paradoxical realization of the future in the present. Here, too, then, the "betweenness" of Christian existence is that which determines only its chronology and not its character.

How far removed the author is from Paul may also be seen from the fact that though he occasionally speaks of temptation, to which he himself, being "altogether sinful" (πανθαμαρτωλός, 18:2), is also subject, he does not speak of the power of sin nor of its cancellation. "The flesh" for him is not an evil power, but is the sphere of the earthly (5:5, 8:2, 9:1ff., 14:3ff.), and as he urges men to "keep the *flesh* pure," he also teaches the resurrection of the "flesh" (9:1ff.). Similarly, *pneuma* is not the eschatological gift and power but indicates anything that is of heavenly nature (9:5, 14:1ff.). "Righteousness" is not the very substance of eschatological salvation (the cognate verb, δικαιοῦσθαι, "rightwise," never occurs), but is the uprightness that must be practised ("do righteousness", 11:7, 19:3) and the δίκαιοι (in Paul: "the righteous") here are really the good (11:1, 17:7, 20:3). The combination of δίκαιος with ὅσιος ("pious") is significant of their related meanings (5:6, 6:9, 15:3), and the occurrence of the terms εὐσεβής, εὐσέβεια, θεοσέβεια ("pious," "piety," "piety toward God"—the latter almost = "religion"; *cf.* RSV I Tim. 2:10—II Clem. 19:1, 4, 20:4) is also characteristic. Significant by comparison with Paul is the author's moral consolation in regard to suffering: if piety were already to receive its reward now, we would be practising trade and not religion (20:4); and he accompanies his exhortation to renounce the world with the consoling assurance: "the sojourn of this flesh in this world is slight and short of duration" (5:5; *cf.* 6:6, 7:1). Religious enthusiasm and charismatic phenomena are also completely lacking.

The Christianity of II Clem., then, is no less a legalistic one than is that of Herm., Jas., Did., Barn., and Hebrews, differing from theirs only in the fact that its legalism (as in II Pet. and Jude) is less shaped by the synagogue tradition and is more strongly influenced by certain Hellenistic tendencies of asceticism and flight from the world.

h. The *Letter of Polycarp*, consisting essentially of ethical exhortations ("concerning uprightness", 3:1), is the document of a Christianity estranged from the world and conditioned by hope in the future (8:1). Christians still live in the present age and look for the age to come (5:2). They hope for the resurrection of the dead (2:2; 5:2) and look ahead to the coming judgment which Christ will hold (2:1; 6:2; 11:2). Doubt of the resurrection and the judgment is combatted as heresy (7:1). In this present time the Christian's relatedness to the future must be carried out in the form of renunciation of the world: ἀπέχεσθαι ("to refrain from . . ." 2:2; 5:3; 6:1, 3; 11:1f.) and ἀπολείπειν ("to put aside", 2:1; 7:2) are the key words that pervade the exhortations; worldly desires are to be rooted out (5:3; *cf.* 7:1 and "continence" in 4:2). Thus the future conditions the present only negatively; of the idea that the future also positively conditions the present because the future is paradoxically present, there is no trace. The statements about Christ—that he came in the flesh (7:1) and suffered and died for us and our sins (1:2; 8:1; 9:2), that he arose and is exalted to be the ruler and judge (1:2; 2:1f.; 9:2)—amount only to this: that by them Christian hope in the coming resurrection is well founded (2:2; 8:1). There is no mention of the Spirit as the eschatological gift and the power of the new life, nor of the charismatic gifts. Christ, characteristically, is termed our "pledge" (of righteousness) who died for our sins (8:1). Similarly there is also no mention of *Sarx* as the power of sin. An echo of Gal. 5:17 is heard in the formulation, "every lust wars against the Spirit (spirit?)," in which it is doubtful whether the Holy Spirit is meant or merely man's better self (as in the quotation from Mk. 14:38 at 7:2). At any rate, Holy Spirit (πνεῦμα ἅγιον) does not occur. Nor is the present reality of future life through the sacraments touched upon; the sacraments are not mentioned.

Although the author knows some Pauline letters, Paul's doctrine of justification is echoed in 1:3 only: "knowing that by grace you are saved, not by works but by the will of God through Jesus Christ" (dependent upon Eph. 2:5, 8f. ?). The author does not speak of "being rightwised" (nor of "salvation" or of "being saved") and uses δικαιοσύνη (with the possible exception of 8:1) only in the sense of ethical "uprightness" (2:3, 3:1, 3, 4:1, 9:1f.); except in 1:3 "grace" occurs only in the closing wish (which is known to us only in Latin translation). *Pistis* in the Pauline sense plays no role; the word (usually absolute) is most frequently used: to denote Christianity 1:2 (the verb "believe" in the same way, 5:2), often in combinations: with "hope" and "love" 3:2f.; with "love" and "purity" 4:2; with "uprightness" 9:2; with "patience" 13:2; its object is often given by an εἰς ("in"): "in the Lord" 1:2 (?) ,13:2; "in him who raised the Lord" 2:1, 12:2; by an objective genitive: 4:3. Christian teaching may be called "the word concerning truth" 3:2, "the word handed down to us from the beginning" 7:2, "the word of righteousness" 9:1.

The statements about Christ's suffering and dying for our sins of course imply the thought of forgiveness brought by Christ; but the problem of post-baptismal sins does not engage the author. He knows that we all "owe the debt of sin" and hence must hope for future forgiveness at the judgment (6:1f.). That the sinner must repent is said in connection with a particular case (11:4); otherwise, "repentance" and "repent" are not mentioned. But forgiveness will be granted in the judgment only to those who serve Christ "with fear and reverence" (6:3). Exhortations to serve God or Christ in fear (2:1, 4:2, 6:3), to fulfill the "commandment of uprightness" (3:3), to obey the "word of uprightness' (9:1), to do the will of Christ or God and to walk in his "commandments" (or "worthily of his commandment" 2:2, 4:1, 5:1) run all through the letter. This manner of "walking" is concretely described in virtue-catalogues and especially in vice-catalogues (4:3, 5:2f., 6:1f.). Wives and widows are exhorted on the Haustafel pattern (4:2f.), as are the deacons, the youths and the maidens (5:2f.), and then the elders (6:1). Once he uses a word of the Lord for his parenesis (2:3—see Mt. 7:1f., Lk. 6:37f., or perhaps I Clem. 13:2). That the "commandment of uprightness" culminates (or is summed up) in "love" is. said in 3:3: "for he who has love is far from all sin" (a quotation?). Furthermore, "love" in combination with "faith" and "hope" characterizes Christian existence (see foregoing paragraph).

Throughout this book, then, the life of the Christian is understood as a preparation for coming salvation made by fulfilling the "commandments," by a way of life which renounces the world. The present is not understood as already full of the future's power and Paul's founding of the imperative (upon the indicative) has been forgotten. An echo of it can be found, if one likes, in 2:1, where the reminder, "by grace ye were saved" (1:3) is followed by the exhortation: "therefore . . . serve God." Anyway, a clear echo does occur in 8:1f., where after reference has been made to Christ's suffering for our sins we read: "Let us then be imitators of his endurance" (*cf.* 10:1). But that the believer is set free to the freedom of obedience, is a lesson the author did not let Paul teach him; in fact the term "freedom" (ἐλευθερία) is completely missing.

i. The threatening judgment which *the Revelation of John* proclaims in chapters 6–18 (–20) is the judgment over the world at enmity with God. It threatens the Church, too, one must admit: that is why it is admonished, especially in the letters to the seven churches in chapters 2, 3 (especially 3:2f.; later also 16:15), to be watchful and true to the faith. But it is primarily to comfort and strengthen it that the Church is made to contemplate the coming judgment. This very fact indicates that in a certain sense the author knows of a future power at work in the present—that sense, however, goes no further than this: that the hope in which the Church lives is certain of fulfilment. This certainty finds expression in the hymns and triumph-songs sung in heaven in praise of God's eternal reign and of His and "the Lamb's" eschatological victory (*cf.* especially 11:15, 17f.; 12:10f.; 19:1f., 6–8) and, at the end of the book, in the fact that future salvation is beheld in the picture of the New Jerusalem which is already present in heaven and is only awaiting the hour, so to speak, to let itself down upon the earth (21:1–22:5). Such a hope, one readily sees, harmonizes with thoughts of Paul (Rom. 8:24f., 31–39), for whom "faith" is simultaneously "hope" (§ 35, 3); and in the hope which faith is, the Church already has in its possession, as it were, a present treasure, which, for all its poverty, makes it rich (2:9), while the seemingly wealthy one is in reality poor (3:17). But for Paul future life is nonetheless present reality in a different way, inasmuch as Paul understands suffering as the weakness in which the power of the Lord comes to perfection (I, pp. 349–51). It may be that such an understanding can be surmised behind the words of

Rev., but it is never put into words—for this reason, if for no other, that as suffering the author has one-sidedly in view the sufferings of persecution (2:3, 9f.; 6:9; 7:14; 12:12, 17; 13:7). For him the consolation consists in the fact that the "crown of life"—heavenly reward—is certain for him who is faithful (*passim*—e.g. 2:10; 7:13–17; 14:3; 22:14) and, beyond that, that the Church will be preserved in the midst of the terrors of the end (3:10; 7:1–8; 14:1–5). In addition, the idea occurs that suffering is a salutary discipline (3:19).

The certainty of this hope is founded upon the death of Christ, "the Lamb that was slain" (5:6, 9; 13:8), whose blood redeems and cleanses (5:9; 7:14). What sort of relationship exists between Christ and his own is a question that cannot be clearly answered, because the author does not reflect about it; at any rate, the verb "believe" is not used to denote that relationship. *Pistis* occurs a few times (2:13; 13:10; 14:12; combined with "love" 2:19), but with the meaning "faithfulness," just as $\pi\iota\sigma\tau\acute{o}\varsigma$ means the faithful, dependable one (2:10, 13; 17:14). Christ himself is the "faithful (or "reliable") witness" (1:5; 3:14) and the words of the book are "reliable and true" (21:5; 22:6 tr.). *Pistis* is usually combined with "endurance" (2:19; 13:10; 14:12), and the praise of "endurance," or exhortation to show endurance, pervades the whole book. Worthy of the highest praise is he who has carried "endurance" to the point of martyrdom (2:13; 6:9–11; 7:9–17). Christ's word is the "word of endurance" which is to be held fast (3:10; *cf.* 3:3, 8), and it means the same thing when the author urges the "keeping" of the words of his book (1:3; 22:7, 9); likewise the exhortation to "hold fast what you have" (2:25; 3:11). "Holding fast the name" (2:13) has its negative parallel in "not denying the name" (3:8) or "the faith" (2:13). One must also "keep my works" (2:36) or "keep the commandments of God" (12:17; 14:12), or, in figurative language, "keep one's garments" (16:5). Besides "endurance," "works" are demanded (2:2, 19). According to his works each man will be recompensed (2:23; 20:12f.; 22:12); and the works of those who die "in the Lord" will follow them (14:13). By the words of the heavenly Lord, "I know your works," the churches receive comfort or warning as the case may be (2:2; 2:13, variant reading, 2:19; 3:1, 8, 15); they are urged to do "works" (2:5, 26, etc.) or are praised for their works (2:2, 13, 19) or rebuked for them (2:19, 22; 3:1f., 15); and condemnation, correspondingly, will fall upon unbelievers for their works (9:20f.; 16:11; 18:6). By the "works" that are required of Christians pure conduct is meant—not only according to ethical commandments (3:4?; 21:8, 27; 22:15) but also according to ritualistic commandments (2:14, 20); but one of the "works" demanded is undoubtedly faithfulness to the faith. But as there is a call for faithfulness there is also a call for repentance (2:15, 16; 3:3, 19; cf. 2:21f.; 9:20 f.; 16:9, 11).

The Christianity of Revelation has to be termed a weakly Christianized Judaism. The significance of Christ is practically limited to this: that he gives the passionate eschatological hope a certainty which the Jewish apocalyptists lack. To him as Lord over life and death (1:17f.; 2:8), as the heavenly comforter and ruler, is transferred what Judaism says of God. What gives the impression that the present is already illumined by the light of the future is the certainty of eschatological hope and the conviction that the end is near at hand (22:10 "the time is near"; 22:12: "behold, I am coming soon"). But the peculiar "between-ness" of Christian existence has not been grasped. In fact, not even in the chronological sense does the present possess the character of an interval, because the author does not reflect about the past which in Christ has been brought to its end and out of which believers have been transplanted into a new beginning. Hence the present is understood in a way not basically different from the understanding of it in the Jewish apocalypses: namely, as a time of temporariness, of waiting. The clear symptom of this understanding is the fact that *pistis* is essentially conceived as "endurance," as in Judaism.

k. Wherever the Pauline tradition continues effective, particularly in *Colossians* and *Ephesians*, there prevails a situation decidedly different from that in Revelation and in all the other writings considered up to this point. In these two writings the basic (i.e. non-chronological meaning of the "between"-situation is grasped, for the determination of the present by the future is grasped. The chronological sense of the Christian's "between-ness" plays a slighter role here simply because the nearness of the parousia is not discussed. Of course, that does not mean that the reference to the future which belongs to Christian existence has disappeared. "Hope" is not seldom mentioned; it is directed toward the prospective "revealing" of Christ (Col. 3:4), before whom believers will someday stand as saints (Col. 1:22f.). Hope also looks forward to the life which with Christ will then be revealed (Col. 3:3f.), to the salvation prepared in heaven

(Col. 1:5; Eph. 1:18), to the rewarding of all good deeds (Eph. 6:8). "This aeon" will be followed by the age "which is to come" (Eph. 1:21; *cf.* 2:2). Nevertheless, more emphasis falls upon salvation as a present state than upon an anticipation of future salvation (II, p. 160). Present conduct, it is true, may also be regarded as the condition for receiving future salvation—perfectly legitimately when such conduct is synonymous with "abiding in the faith" (Col. 1:23 tr.), less legitimately, from the standpoint of faith in God's grace, when the ethical exhortation is supported by a reference to reward (Col. 3:24).

But the thing characteristic of both Col. and Eph. is that the present is conceived as a time of salvation brought about by God's deed in Christ—a time of salvation, that is, in view of the fact that the cosmic powers have been disarmed (Col. 1:20; 2:15; see II, p. 153). By appropriating this occurrence through baptism (Col. 2:12; *cf.* 2:20; 3:3; Eph. 4:5), believers are emancipated from domination by the powers, from the "dominion of darkness," and transferred to the Reign of Christ (Col. 1:13). This "redemption" of theirs is the "forgiveness of sins" (Col. 1:14; *cf.* 2:14; Eph. 1:7; 5:26)—but not as if their life were now placed under an imperative, the fulfilment of which would be the condition for obtaining salvation, but rather thus: that with forgiveness the might of sin is broken and in their obedient conduct Life has become a present reality. Believers have died with Christ, been buried and raised with him, made alive (Col. 2:12f., 20; 3:3). Upon this indicative the imperative is founded (Col. 3:5ff., 12ff.; Eph. 4:1ff., 17ff., 25; 5:8ff.; *cf.* Col. 1:21f.; Eph. 2:5f.). The idea is peculiarly formulated in Eph. 2:10: we, saved by God's grace, are "his workmanship, created in Christ Jesus for good works, which God prepared beforehand, that we should walk in them." The formulation of Col. 3:2f. is especially clear: "Set your minds on things that are above, not on things that are on earth. For you have died, and your life is hid with Christ in God." The paradox: present, and yet future—or, future, and yet present—is here recognized. That paradox is preserved also in the fact that in spite of—or, rather, just because of—the Christian's having died with Christ the author still exhorts: "Put to death therefore what is earthly in you" (Col. 3:5; *cf.* Eph. 4:22), and that in spite of their emancipation from the evil powers believers are charged with the duty of fighting against them (Eph. 6:10ff.). The quality of being constantly menaced, which Christian living has, is clearly seen. There is, it is true, no mention of the "flesh" which strives against the "Spirit" (Gal. 5:17) nor of temptations (neither πειράζειν, "to tempt," nor πειρασμός, "temptation," occurs). The "flesh" with its "desires" (or "lusts") is regarded as done away with in baptism (Col. 2:13; Eph. 2:3), yet, in spite of that, exhortation to do battle against the desires and the vices does not drop out, but, having received a foundation in the indicative, remains. The conception that evil is one coherent power, and that the life of the believer consequently is a constant battle, finds expression in mythological language in the exhortations of Eph. 6:10–20: the devil and the demonic powers must be resisted and fought as with soldier's weapons. (The whole sphere of beings and things at enmity with God is occasionally also called "world," κόσμος, in the Pauline and Johannine sense: Col. 2:8, 20; Eph. 2:2; 2:12?). The Spirit given in baptism is the guarantee (ἀρραβών) of future salvation (Eph. 1:13f.); but it is also the power that is bestowed in the present in the process by which one constantly becomes new (Eph. 3:16; 4:23), and this Spirit must not be "grieved" (Eph. 4:30) by bad living.

"In Christ"—Paul's own phrase to denote Christian existence —occurs here in various ways. In a set formula (Col. 1:2; Eph. 1:1), it means "Christian." As in Paul, it may mean the fellowship with Christ established by baptism (Col. 2:12; Eph. 2:6, 10, 13, 3:6). The same is probably also meant in Col. 1:28, 2:9f., Eph. 1:10, 2:15, 21f.; in all these cases the Gnostic conception of the cosmic Anthropos which underlies the phrase (*cf.* especially Eph. 4:13) comes into view. Several times "in Christ" has a representational meaning: "in—i.e. *with*—Christ" salvation is given, Col. 2:3, Eph. 1:3, 6; 2:7; 4:32; but it may also be that the ἐν is meant to be instrumental, as it probably is in Eph. 1:20, 2:15 (i.e. "*by* Christ"). "Chosen *in Christ*" seems to have a special meaning: through the fact that Christ was chosen before all time by God, believers in him are also chosen—Eph. 1:4, 9; 3:11. Nevertheless, the phrase in liturgical language had evidently already crystallized into a set formula (*cf.* Eph. 3:21) so that frequently its exact sense can scarcely be determined.

Salvation has become available through preaching, the "word of truth," the "Gospel" (Col. 1:5; Eph. 1:13), which has revealed the hidden secret (or mystery) of God (Col. 1:25ff.; 4:3; Eph. 3:1ff.; 6:19); consequently, this "word" of preaching must be kept alive in the Church (Col. 3:16). In that word, or in the knowledge which results from it, salvation is present reality. To denote this knowledge a whole series of terms is used: γνῶσις (knowledge) and ἐπίγνωσις (full knowledge), σοφία (wisdom), σύνεσις (understanding), φρόνησις (comprehension, insight).

In distinction from Paul, "believe" and "faith" play a relatively unimportant role. "Believe" never occurs in Col., and in Eph. only at 1:13, 19, where the πιστεύσαντες or πιστεύοντες are simply "the Christians" (I, p. 90). The use of *pistis* varies. Sometimes it means the Christian religion, "Christianity" (Col. 1:23; Eph. 1:15, 3:12) or the degree to which one exhibits Christianity, especially in combination with "love" (Col. 1:4; Eph. 1:15). *Pistis* may then be followed by a phrase of specification, though only rarely: just once by εἰς (which in Paul occurs after "believe" but never after "faith")—"in Christ" (Col. 2:5)— by ἐν (=εἰς) Col. 1:4: "in Christ Jesus"; Eph. 1:15: "in the Lord Christ Jesus" (in Paul perhaps at Gal. 3:26; in the pastorals at I Tim. 3:13; II Tim. 3:15); once by an objective genitive, Col. 2:12: "faith in (lit. "of") the working of God"; but never by the objective genitive so frequently found in Paul, "faith *of* Jesus (Christ)," meaning "faith *in*."

Often *pistis* probably places more emphasis upon "faith" as a subjective attitude (Col. 2:7; Eph. 3:17, 6:16–23); in other places it has the objective meaning, so that *pistis* means belief, the "confession" or "creed" of the Christian, as in the characteristic juxtaposition "one Lord, one belief, one baptism" (Eph. 4:5, tr.—from liturgical tradition?) and perhaps in Eph. 4:13. Only once does *pistis* occur in combination with "grace" in the Pauline antithesis to "works" (Eph. 2:8f.; *cf.* 2:5); however God's "grace" bestowed in Christ or the Gospel is mentioned a few times (Col. 1:6; Eph. 1:6f., 2:7; *cf.* 4:7). But it is characteristic that in such phrases they do not use Paul's typical verb "rightwised" (by "grace" or "faith") but "saved" (σεσωσμένοι)— indeed the verb δικαιόω (to rightwise) is missing in both writings. In Col. "righteousness" (δικαιοσύνη) is also missing; it does occur in Eph. (4:24, 5:9) but not in the forensic sense denoting the essence of (eschatological) salvation, but as an ethical term, i.e. "uprightness" (similarly τὸ δίκαιον Col. 4:1; Eph. 6:1, "justly," "right"), appearing at Eph. 4:24 in combination with ὁσιότης ("piety"), a word, not found in Paul, which corresponds more or less with the εὐσέβεια (godliness, piety, religion) of the pastorals.

The thought that what distinguishes Christian existence is specifically knowledge, and that knowledge consequently must be constantly growing, is especially characteristic of Col. and Eph. God's deed of grace, which takes effect in preaching, is a causing to know ("make known" Col. 1:27; Eph. 1:9; 6:19), just as by revelation the apostles were "caused to know" the "secret" or "mystery" of the plan of salvation (Eph. 3:3f., 5) which constitutes the subject and content of preaching (Col. 1:25–27; 4:3; Eph. 1:9; 3:9; 6:19). The content of the "secret" is nothing other than God's plan of salvation (Col. 1:26; Eph. 1:9f.; 3:9f.) or, as it may also be phrased, simply: "Christ, in whom are hid all the treasures of wisdom and knowledge" (Col. 2:3; *cf.* 1:27). The content of the knowledge mediated by preaching is then at the same time Christ's love which surpasses all knowledge (Eph. 3:19); but God's will which demands worthy living (Col. 1:9f., 28; 4:5; Eph. 5:17) is also what that knowledge knows.

The authors may also say—summing up, as it were—that salvation is present in the Ecclesia as the "body of Christ," into which believers have been taken up by baptism (Col. 1:18, 24; 2:19; 3:15; Eph. 1:21f.; 2:6; 5:23, 30). Not that that is a guarantee, for the Church must prove that it really is the body of Christ by holding fast to Christ the Head of the body (Col. 2:19) in the unity of love (Col. 3:14f.; Eph. 4:2f.)—also in suffering for the Church (Col. 1:24), in mutual instruction and admonition (Col. 3:16), and in the thanksgiving and the songs of the assembled congregation (Col. 1:12; 2:7; 4:2; especially 3:16; Eph. 3:21; 5:19f.). Interest in the Church is more prominent in Eph. than in Col. not only because the union of Jews and Gentiles (as Christians) into one temple of God is a special theme of Eph. (2:11–22), but also because it is an important thought for its author that the Church is founded upon "the holy apostles and prophets" (2:20; 3:5) and is directed by them along with the evangelists, pastors, and teachers (4:11). The ancient catholic Church's idea of authority is beginning to come alive; nevertheless, the Church's leaders still have no priestly character; their office is that of preaching the word. Neither is there any mention yet of a special Church discipline. The members are to train one another (Col. 3: 13–16; Eph. 4:2f., 32; 5:19–21). Though the life of believers is released from worldliness ("desecularized") because it is the life of men who have died with Christ, who have renounced and are to renounce their former way of life (Col. 1:21; 3:5ff.; Eph. 2:1ff.), who are no longer oriented toward the "things that are on earth" but toward those "that are above" (Col. 3:2; see above), and because it is a life lived within the Church, nevertheless it is not a life that flees the world. The ascetic and ritualistic regulations of the heretics are opposed (Col. 2:16, 21; see II, p. 150). It is a pious life, borne up by brotherly love, in the forms of bourgeois existence; the pattern for it is provided (as in the pastorals) by the Haustafeln (Col. 3:18–4:1; Eph. 5:22–6:9).

It cannot be denied that in Col. and Eph. there is a certain doctrinarianism and moralization in their understanding of salvation. The nature and origin of sin are not grasped with such depth as in Paul and John. Sin is regarded as a sinister power, it is true; but its essence is seen only in a life of vice—pagan living is described in catalogues of vice (Col. 3:5, 8; Eph. 2:1ff.; 4:18f.). Consequently, *pistis* also is not understood with such radicality as in Paul and John. Their language also is to a large extent conventional; it is nourished by the Pauline tradition and—especially in Eph.—by liturgical tradition. Nevertheless, fundamental motifs of Paul's theology remain alive in them, particularly in their understanding of the believer's paradoxical situation "between the ages," in their understanding of the present's reference to the future, and in their basing the imperative upon the indicative.

1. Related to Col. and Eph. is *I Peter*; in it, however, the Christian's relation to the future is more prominent. Hope for coming salvation is predominant (1:3ff., 13; 3:9; 4:13; 5:4), yet not so as to exclude thinking of the judgment (4:6, 17ff.). In fact, even the expectation that the End is near is still (or once more) alive (4:7). Consequently, divorce from the world is also more prominent. (But the Pauline and Johannine use of the term κόσμος is lacking; and the term αἰὼν οὗτος—"this world" and also "this age"—is not found.) Christians are often described as "holy"; this is not a mere technical designation but an expression of the fact that they no longer belong to the present world. The Christian Church is a "spiritual house," a "holy priesthood," a "holy nation" (2:5, 9f.), designations that include responsibility for holy conduct (1:15). Toward the world Christians must know themselves to be "aliens" and "exiles" (2:11; *cf.* 1:1, 17). The present has the character of the temporary (1:17), though this idea is used mainly as consolation in the sufferings of the present (1:6; 5:10). But the "between-ness" in which believers now stand is not mere chronology. For inasmuch as they are already

"holy," one may say that salvation has a present reality. They are made holy (sanctified) by the Spirit conferred in baptism, which bestows upon them the efficacy of Christ's blood (1:2; *cf.* 1:18–21). Baptism, which receives its power from the resurrection of Christ (3:21; 1:3), rescues them and gives them a new relation to God (3:21).* So they are born again (or begotten anew 1:23). But 1:3 significantly adds that it was to a "living hope" that God caused them to be reborn (or begot them). Hence the present reality of salvation manifests itself in the fact that they are hopers: their "faith," as such, is "hope."

But the present reality of salvation is also clearly shown in that new conduct in which one's renunciation of the world is to be carried out (1:13ff.; 2:1ff.; 4:1ff., 7ff.). The sacrament of baptism did not simply bestow upon the believer a new nature, the possession of which guarantees future salvation; rather, all the way through we find the indicative furnishing the basis for the imperative in genuinely Pauline fashion (1:13ff., especially v. 15; 1:23; 2:11, 24; 3:9); once the Pauline motif of "freedom" also occurs (2:16). On the other hand, an exhortation is occasionally supported by a reference to the approaching End (4:7; 5:6). The idea of the Spirit given at baptism is not, as it is in Paul, made to bear fruit in parenesis; and "flesh" as the power of sin is mentioned allusively at the most (2:11: "abstain from the passions of the flesh"); and sin is recognized only in a life of vice (2:1; 4:2f., 15), in the passions (1:14; 2:11; 4:2f.), which, significantly are called "human passions" (4:2). So it is not surprising that *pistis* except where it means confident hope (1:9, 21), has the general meaning: "the Christian faith"—with here and there the nuance of "loyal faith" (1:5, 7; 5:9; the verb πιστεύω with the same nuance: 1:8; 1:21 in text of א C 33)—and the "believing" (πιστεύοντες) or the "faithful" (πιστοί) are simply the "Christians" (1:21; 2:7; *cf.* 5:12). The antithesis of "faith" to "works" is lacking; it is said, rather, that God judges each man according to his "work" (1:17), and believers are to distinguish themselves by their "good works" (2:12). Mention of God's "grace" does occur. It is spoken of as the grace given by God through Christ (1:10; 3:7; 5:12) or the grace to be expected in the future revealing of Jesus Christ (1:13) or as the varied grace of God which manifests itself in charismatic gifts (4:10;

* The words συνειδήσεως ἀγαθῆς ἐπερώτημα εἰς θεόν probably mean: the prayer which issues from a consciousness of the purity acquired through baptism.

cf. 5:10) or in strength to endure undeserved suffering (2:19). But "grace" no longer has the specifically Pauline meaning. Neither is "rightwising" mentioned; δικαιοσύνη is here not "righteousness" but "uprightness" (2:24; 3:14) and δίκαιος means the "upright," "innocent" one (3:12; 4:18).

The Pauline idea of suffering and dying with Christ is modified in a strange manner. To interpret suffering in persecution as a sharing in the sufferings of Christ (4:13) is not in itself un-Pauline. But the genuinely Pauline thought is echoed only at 4:2: *viz.*, that fellowship with Christ's suffering takes place in the decision of faith and hence is a goal ever to be won or, better, is a process constantly taking place in the life of the believer (I, pp. 349f.). Elsewhere the author understands that thought thus: that a connection with Christ is brought about by the suffering of Christians because following Christ brings with it the suffering of persecution. Hence the crucified Christ is not the "power and wisdom of God" (I Cor. 1:24) but the pattern for the believer's suffering (2:21ff.: 3:18)—though, of course, he leaves intact the (traditional) statement that Christ's death was a death for our sins (1:18f.; 2:21, 24; 3:18). The thought that taking up the cross is radical divorce from the world and the giving up of all boasting (Gal. 6:14; Phil. 3:3ff.; I Cor. 1:18ff., etc.) has been lost. In fact, suffering is regarded at all only as innocent suffering resulting from human malice or from the enmity of the heathen to the Christians (3:13ff.; 4:12ff.)—similarly πειρασμός is never used as "temptation" but always means "trial," the trial of sufferings.

Eschatological consciousness with its aloofness from the world is more prominent in I Pet. than in Col. and Eph. (and the pastorals), a fact that is certainly conditioned by the situation of threatened and in part actual persecution of the Christians by the heathen. This gives the parenesis its peculiar character. Both the admonitions to obey the public authorities (2:14–17) and the Haustafeln (2:18–3:7) exhort the reader not only to a decent and clean bourgeois life but to a specifically Christian attitude: by his good conduct the believer is to bring honor to the faith and be prepared to endure. The admonition to patient endurance runs through the whole writing (1:6f.; 2:20f.; 3:16f.) and with it the exhortation to love (both ἀγάπη and φιλαδελφία, 1:22, 2:17; 3:8; 4:8). In addition, the admonition to "humility" is characteristic (3:8; 5:5f.). Not only in these admonitions to brotherly love but also in special admonitions the thought is expressed that the Church's nature as a "holy priesthood" realizes itself in a Church life ruled by brotherly love: each is to serve the whole with his special gift (4:10f.). The "elders" receive a special exhortation in this direction (5:1–4), and so do the "younger men" (5:5).

m. In a different way, more or less in the same direction as in Col. and Eph., the Pauline tradition works on in the *pastoral epistles.* Here the expectation of the future parousia has lost still more of its tension, and the Christian faith is becoming a piety which, though it by no means surrenders its aloofness from the world, nevertheless is making a place for itself within the framework of bourgeois living. It is characteristic that though there are echoes of some Pauline ideas, other important concepts of Paul's theology have either disappeared or have lost their old meaning. Thus "to save" (and "be saved") has taken the place of "rightwise" (and "be rightwised"); and "salvation" has replaced "righteousness" (II, p. 115).

Only in Tit. 3:7, echoing Paul, does "rightwised by his grace" occur. Otherwise δικαιοῦν does not occur except in the quotation I Tim. 3:16, where its passive is used of Christ and means not "rightwised" but "vindicated." Δικαιοσύνη means "uprightness" —to it one is trained by Scripture (II Tim. 3:16), for it one must strive (I Tim. 6:11; II Tim. 2:22), as reward for it a wreath (crown) stands in prospect at the end (II Tim. 4:8). The δίκαιος, correspondingly, is the "upright" man (I Tim. 1:9; Tit. 1:8).

"To believe" very rarely occurs, and, when it does, not in Paul's sense, as the combination of πιστεύειν with ἐπί and the dative suffices to indicate (I Tim. 1:16, a construction found in Paul only within the repeated quotation at Rom. 9:33; 10:11). Paul's πιστεύειν εἰς ("believe in" followed by accusative) and πιστεύειν ὅτι ("believe that . . .") do not occur. Πιστεύειν in the pastorals means "trust, depend upon" (I Tim. 1:16; II Tim. 1:12; probably also Tit. 3:8 with θεῷ as object). Πίστις occurs frequently and sometimes has the complement "in Christ Jesus" (I Tim. 3:13; II Tim. 1:13; 3:15), but in general it has the worn-down meaning of "Christianity," "Christian religion"; as the context may demand, it can mean the subjective faith with which one believes or faith as the object which one believes, "belief" (*cf.* I Tim. 1:5; 2:15; 3:9; 5:8; 6:12; II Tim. 1:5; 4:7; Tit. 1:1), in fact it can actually mean "right doctrine," orthodoxy.

Characteristic expressions are the set formula ἐν πίστει= "Christian" (I Tim. 1:2, 4; Tit. 3:15; *cf.* "in a common faith" Tit. 1:4). Another formula is "faith and love" (I Tim. 1:14; II Tim. 1:13) as a designation for the state of being a Christian. *Pistis* is, above all, proper faith in contrast to a wrong kind, both in the subjective sense of the right quality or degree of faith and in the objective sense of right doctrine (see II, p. 135). As the right quality or degree of faith, *pistis* loses its character of that which is the basis of Christian existence and becomes a virtue. The very fact that it can be given the adjective "unfeigned" (ἀνυπόκριτος, I Tim. 1:5; II Tim. 1:5), which Paul gives only to "love" (Rom. 12:9; II Cor. 6:6; *cf.* I Pet. 1:22), is indicative. This "unfeigned faith" may indeed appear as the root of "love" (I Tim. 1:5) but coupled with a "pure heart" and a "good conscience." Especially characteristic are combinations with other virtues: with "love" I Tim. 1:14; II Tim. 1:13, also Tit. 2:2 which also adds "steadfastness" (ὑπομονή), and I Tim. 4:12, where "faith" and "love" are combined with "conduct" and "purity." In I Tim. 6:11 "faith" even appears as one member in a whole catalogue of virtues: "uprightness, godliness, faith, love, steadfastness, gentleness." II Tim. 2:22 and 3:10 are similar.

The characteristic designation of the Christian attitude is εὐσέβεια, "the attitude pleasing to God," "piety."

The substantive occurs ten times, the verb (εὐσεβεῖν) at I Tim. 5:4, and the adverb (εὐσεβῶς) at II Tim. 3:12 and Tit. 2:12. The adjective is missing but is replaced by ὅσιος "holy" or "pious" (I Tim. 2:8; Tit. 1:8). Like *pistis*, "piety" can mean simply "Christianity"—I Tim. 3:16, 6:3; II Tim. 3:5.

Piety makes itself known in respectable conduct (I Tim. 2:2; 5:4; 6:11; II Tim. 3:12; Tit. 2:12) such as is described in the Haustafeln (I Tim. 2:8–15; 6:1f.; Tit. 2:2–10). So it is the opposite of a former heathen life of vice (Tit. 3:3). It is the renunciation of "irreligion" and "worldly passions" (Tit. 2:12; I Tim. 6:9; II Tim. 2:22; 3:6; 4:3), yet it bears no traits of a flight from the world but is characterized by a "sensibleness" (σωφροσύνη) which avoids licentiousness and excess (I Tim. 3:3, 8; Tit. 1:7; 2:3) and is frugal (I Tim. 6:6–10) but still does not practice asceticism (I Tim. 4:4f., 8; 5:23; on the subject of marriage, see § 60, 5).

Such "piety" holds promise both for the present life and for the life to come (I Tim. 4:8). For believers are waiting for the "appearing" of Christ (I Tim. 6:14f.; II Tim. 4:1; 4:8?; Tit. 2:13), they have the hope of eternal life (Tit. 3:7; 1:2; II Tim. 1:1), the recompense which "on that Day" the Lord as Judge will provide for faithfulness to the faith (II Tim. 4:8; *cf.* 4:1). Nevertheless, the present no longer stands in the eschatological tension that Paul knew; instead the Church has settled down to the prospect that the world will last a while yet (II, p. 116). When it is time to do so, God will bring to pass the appearing of Christ ("at the proper time," I Tim. 6:15). It is never said that this event lies near ahead, but neither can one detect any such thing as disappointment at the delay of the parousia. It is significant that the eschatological term ἐπιφάνεια ("appearing") can also be used in this literature to denote the historical appearing of Christ (i.e. Jesus) upon earth (II Tim. 1:10; *cf.* Tit. 2:11; 3:4). Reference to the future recedes behind the consciousness of present salvation. The pastorals know, in fact, that the present is under grace, which once was hidden but now with the "appearing" of Christ has been revealed (II Tim. 1:9f.; Tit. 1:2f.; 2:11). They also know the importance of the Gospel as the proclaimed word by which salvation was and continues to be revealed (II Tim. 1:10; Tit. 1:3; *cf.* I Tim. 3:16) and know what importance preaching has for the Church (I Tim. 5:17; II Tim. 2:15; 4:2; Tit. 1:9; *cf.* also I Tim. 2:7; II Tim. 1:11; 2:9; 4:17). They also know that not our works but grace saved us (II Tim. 1:9; Tit. 3:7). It becomes ours through baptism, and baptism gives us a new possibility of life as it does in Hermas and Hebrews, but not as a new chance by the forgiveness of our former sins ("forgiveness of sins" is lacking in the pastorals as in Paul!) but as the "working of regeneration and renewal in the Holy Spirit" (Tit. 3:5).

The paradox of Christian existence— a new existence within this old world (Tit. 2:12)—is here grasped: in other words the qualitative (and not merely chronological) sense of the Christian's "betweenness" is grasped. The present has not come under a new bondage to the Law, although as in Herm., Barn. and Heb. it is subject to new conditions, but is under the sway of the Gospel in which grace has come to be a present reality (II Tim. 1:9f.; Tit. 1:3). God gave the Spirit which is characterized by power, love, and self-control (II Tim. 1:7); it also aids the Christian in fulfilling his duty (II Tim. 1:14). The period of religious ecstasy, however, is past; particular charismatic gifts are not mentioned except that of office (the preaching-teaching office—I Tim. 4:14; II Tim. 1:6, probably also II Tim. 2:1, translating χάρις not as "grace" but as "gift"). The life of the believers, accordingly, is beginning to be subjected to an ecclesiastical discipline not only in the fact that the congregational officers rebuke and correct teachers of error (II Tim. 2:25; Tit. 1:9, 13) and, if need be, excommunicate them (I Tim. 1:20; Tit. 3:10f.), but also in the fact that they supervise the ethical life of the members and keep them in control (I Tim. 5:3–16, 19f.; II Tim. 4:2; Tit. 2:15). Thus, somewhat as in Col. and Eph. the present reality of salvation is incorporated, so to speak, in the Church, which is "the pillar and bulwark of the truth" (I Tim. 3:15). Nevertheless, the concept Ecclesia is not emphasized as it is in Eph. (the word Church occurs in the pastorals only in I Tim. 3—vss. 5, 15, and 16), and there is no mention of the "body of Christ."

The Christianity of the pastorals is a somewhat faded Paulinism—nevertheless, the Pauline tradition works on in it. The way in which grace is spoken of does not sound very Pauline, it is true; nevertheless, it is understood in Paul's sense as a power that transforms our present living when Tit. 2:11f. describes it as that which "trains" us to "godly living." For here the imperative is understood to be founded upon the indicative, even though the Pauline paradox is not expressed. Grant all the following: (1) that the believer's divorce from the world is not grasped with such radicality as it was by Paul, because the depth of Paul's understanding of sin (and hence also of faith) is no longer grasped; (2) that κόσμος (I Tim. 1:15; 3:16; 6:7) no longer means "world" in Paul's sense except in the adjective "worldly" (Tit. 2:12); (3) that the struggle between "flesh" and "Spirit" is not mentioned ("flesh" never occurs at all except in the quotation I Tim. 3:16); (4) that dying with Christ to live with him is not found, and that Paul's resulting description of Christian life as a living "in Christ" occurs at the most in II Tim. 3:12, if it does there.* Nevertheless, for all its plodding one-sidedness, it is a legitimate extension of Paul's thinking to understand grace as a power that molds everyday bourgeois living; and when this everyday living is placed under the light of grace something also remains of Paul's "as if . . . not" (I Cor. 7:29ff.; I, p. 351f.).

---

* "In Christ" otherwise is an adjectival complement to "faith" (see above, II, p. 183) or to both "faith" and "love" (I Tim. 1:14; II Tim. 1:13), or, as in Col. and Eph. (see II, p. 177), it has representational meaning (II Tim. 1:1, 9, 2:1, 10).

11. Closely related to the pastorals is the *First Letter of Clement*. It, too, is under the influence of the Pauline tradition, though much more under that of the Hellenistic synagogue, so that of genuine Paulinism there is little or almost nothing left. It is quite a problem to say what it really is that makes I Clem. a Christian document. Is it anything more than the consciousness of being certain of God's grace, thanks to the occurrence of salvation in Christ? That is to say, is it anything more than a "Church"–consciousness (see I, p. 37f.), such as the Jewish congregation also had, but a consciousness now made alive, strong, and certain?

As in the pastorals, though looking to the eschatological future has not been given up, the eschatological tension has disappeared. Hope, it is true, is not infrequently mentioned; in fact "hope" can denote the Christian attitude as a whole (51:1: "the common ground of our hope," tr., 57:2). But the hope in God (59:3) which Christians have in common with the pious men of the Old Testament (11:1; *cf.* the quotation from Ps. 31:10 in 22:8 and from Prov. 1:33 in 57:7) is for the most part simply trust in God; in this sense πιστεύειν ("to trust") and "to hope" may be combined, as the nouns *pistis* ("trust") and "hope" also may (12:7; 58:2). The statement made of God, "he is near" (21:3; 27:3), does not refer to the proximity of the End but means God's omnipresence, and the congregational prayer (59–61) comes to a close without any eschatological look toward the future. But, of course, the author can also speak of the coming Reign of God (42:3; 50:3); the Lord (God? Christ?) will suddenly come (23:5, after Is. 14:1; Mal. 3:1); the judgment is to come (28:1f.) and it will requite men according to their works (34:3 quoting Is. 40:10, etc.). There is no delineation of the events of the End at all and the glory of the salvation to come is only mentioned in allusions (34:7f.; 35:3f.). Only in the truth of the belief in resurrection is any living interest shown. The doubts about it are refuted (23–26), and it is significant that the chief role in this argumentation is played not by the raising of Jesus but by proofs taken from nature (alternation of day and night, of seed-time and harvest, the Phoenix), seconded by words of Scripture and a reminder of God's truthfulness—while the raising of Jesus is only cited as the "first-fruits" of the "coming resurrection" (24:1) without being meant in the sense of I Cor. 15:20.

For the Christian Church salvation is in a certain manner present reality: it is, in just the fact that it is conscious of being the Christian

Church. The technical term "Church of God" occurs, it is true, only in the conventional salutation; otherwise *ecclesia* means only a particular congregation (44:3, 47:6). But the author calls Christians by the old titles of the eschatological Congregation. They are "called" and "sanctified" (salutation), they are "the holy portion" (30:1); God made them the "portion of his choice" for Himself (29:1) and sanctified them through Christ (59:3); hence they are the "chosen (of God)" (1:1; 2:4; 6:1; 46:4; 49:5; 58:2; 59:2) or the "chosen by God through Jesus Christ" (50:7), "the called by his will in Jesus Christ" (32:4; *cf.* 59:2; 65:2; also 46:6: "one calling in Christ"). They are the "flock" of Christ (16:1; 44:3; 54:2; 57:2).

As these expressions show, it was through Christ, our "means of salvation" (36:1), that salvation was brought about. He is the foundation of the Christian's relationship to God, because through him God chose (50:7) and called (59:2; 65:2) us and bestowed upon us right knowledge of Himself (36:1f.). He is the gate of righteousness into life (48:2–4). One's gaze is to be fixed upon his sufferings (2:1), his blood (7:4). (The cross is not explicitly named, but his blood is: 7:4; 12:7; 21:6; 49:6. His sufferings, furthermore, are described not according to the synoptic tradition but according to Is. 53, ch. 16). All such expressions are already highly formalized into set phrases; the author can only say in general that Christ's blood was given "for us" (21:6; 49:6; *cf.* 16:7 modeled on Is. 53:6)—as he also says of heathen heroes for their peoples (55:1)—that it brought us "redemption" (12:7) and gave the whole world the "grace of repentance" (7:4; *cf.* 8:1).

Though the possibility of repentance has always existed (7:5ff.; 8:1ff.), it has once more become actual to the present by the death of Christ. There is no explicit reference to baptism whatever; the only presupposition mentioned for forgiveness is repentance. And repentance, one must recognize here, is connected with the fulfilment of the commandments. In fact, it can be said that the "commandments" of Christ (37:1) as the "yoke of his grace" (16:7) represent the soteriological meaning of the present. Thus the ethical demands, or the virtues that correspond to them, are called the "paths of blessing" (31:1), and among the "blessed and wonderful gifts of God" appears "continence in holiness" along with terms which denote the possession of salvation: "life in incorruption, splendor in righteousness, truth in boldness, faith in confidence" (35:1). To that extent it might be said that for the author indicative and imperative constitute a unity. Such a unity is also expressed in the sentence: "Being, therefore, a holy portion, let us do all that belongs to sanctification" (30:1 tr.). But this unity is not the paradoxical unity of the future and the present. Rather, it is the same unity as in Judaism, for with the consciousness of being God's chosen, holy People it also combines knowledge of its responsibility and its obligation to holy conduct. Hence the significance of Christ consists, on the one hand, in his having given the Church by his death the consciousness of being the Congregation of the elect, the People of God (59:4, 64) and, on the other hand, of his therefore being the teacher and law-giver of the Church.

Christ is the teacher who taught "gentleness and long-suffering" (13:1). There is constant mention of his "commandment" (ἐντολή), his "injunctions" (παραγγέλματα), "orders" (προστάγματα), and "just demands" (δικαιώματα) (2:8; 13:3; 27:2; 37:1; 49:1). But his "injunctions" are identical with the old commandments of God, "the glorious and venerable rule (κανών) of our tradition" (7:2). As one may speak of Christ's "orders," one may therefore also speak of God's "orders" (3:4; 40:5; 50:5; 58:2), "just demands" (58:2), and "statutes" (νόμιμα, 1:3; 3:4; 40:4). The only difference is in the name appended: Christ's or God's. In substance it remains the same whether one fixes his regard on Christ (2:1; 7:4; 36:2) or on God (19:2; cf. 34:5). Pistis (or πιστεύειν, which usually is used absolutely) may have Christ for its object (22:1: "in—ἐν—Christ"; never εἰς, never χριστοῦ as objective genitive) but more frequently God is the object (3:4; 27:3; 34:4, and, of course, everywhere where the faith of pious men of the Old Testament is mentioned). The meaning proper to Christian "faith" cannot assert itself under such circumstances.

The problem of legalism, therefore, does not exist for the author, although he took over from Paul the thought that we are rightwised ("justified") not by our works but by faith (32:4). He can both quote Gen. 15:6 like Paul (10:6) and also say that "Abraham performed (ποιήσας) uprightness and truth through trust" (31:2, tr.). Δικαιοσύνη and δίκαιος (the latter co-ordinated with ὅσιος—almost="proper"—, with "innocent," or with "pious," 14:1; 46:4; 48:4; 62:1) are ethical terms for the author (cf. δικαιοπραγία, "just dealing", 32:3), even though he defines the "gate of uprightness standing open into life"

as the "gate in Christ" (48:2–4—see especially the expansion in 48:4).
It is self-evident, therefore, that in this document *pistis* cannot have
the Pauline (or Johannine) meaning. Except where it means trust in
God (see especially 26:1; 35:5—πιστῶς) and is related to "hope" (see
above, II, p. 187), *pistis* is only one of the many virtues (1:2; 35:2;
62:1) and is specifically paired with "hospitality" (10:7; 12:1). It
can also mean simply the Christian attitude as a whole (5:6; 6:2; 27:3)
and so be equivalent to εὐσέβεια, "piety" (*cf.* 1:2 with 22:1; 11:1
with 10:7; 12:1—εὐσέβεια also at 15:1; 61:2; 62:1) or to "holiness of
soul" (29:1; *cf.* 48:4; 60:4; he is fond of ὅσιος, "holy": 2:3; 6:1; etc.).
So, in a faded sense, *pistis* can mean "Christianity" (22:1; *cf.* similar
use of the verb "believe": 12:7; 42:4).

Neither "sin" nor "flesh" is mentioned as a power to which man
has fallen victim. Of the Holy Spirit, or the "Spirit of grace" it is
said that it has been given to the Church. The apostles also worked
by its power (42:3; 47:3), and the author writes his own letter "through
the Holy Spirit" (63:2). But nowhere do we hear of the struggle
between flesh and Spirit, nor is the Spirit appraised as the "firstfruit" or "guarantee" of the final consummation of salvation. For
the most part, *pneuma* is the Spirit which inspires the words of the
Old Testament (8:1; 13:1, etc.). Ecstatic possession by the Spirit has
disappeared; the Spirit that was given to the Church is conceived
as working in the virtues (2:2). God's "grace" is the saving grace
which brought the new possibility of repentance (7:4; 8:1) or grace in
an altogether general sense (30:3) in which the pious men of the Old
Testament also shared it (50:3; 55:3). In the plural it means God's
favors in general (23:1). The Pauline antithesis between "grace" and
"works" is not present, nor is that between "faith" and "works."
Only in the conventional closing greeting does "the grace of our
Lord Jesus Christ" appear. Once χάρισμα (gift) occurs (38:1) meaning,
as in I Pet. 4:10, the gift given to an individual which is to be used
to the advantage of the fellowship. "Knowledge," which is often
mentioned, is not a special gift and has no specific content (unless
perhaps in 48:5, but the meaning here is obscure) but is Christian
knowledge in general (1:2; 36:2; 41:4; 48:5; *cf.* also the verb "know":
7:4; 59:3; ἐπίγνωσις 59:2; ἐπιγινώσκειν 32:1) or, specifically, the understanding of the Old Testament (40:1)—by which, however, he does
not mean the art of allegory as Barnabas does.

Inasmuch as the Church was called by Christ and looks forward to the coming Reign of God, the Church stands in an intermediate time; and since there is present enjoyment of the "blessed and wonderful gifts of God" (35:1), it might be said that this "between-ness" determines not merely the chronology but also the character of Christian existence. But it disintegrates into a mere temporariness, more or less as in the book of Revelation, because, despite what the author says of Christ, he does not bring to expression how it is that in Christ anything really decisive took place, founding a new relation to God. Ultimately, the only relation to God that the author knows is the old one, for the characteristics of Christian existence are also attributed to the pious men of the Old Testament: "piety," "faith," "hope," and "repentance." As God's "injunctions" are the same for Christians as for the Old Israel, so the virtues of Christians are none other than those of the pious men of the Old Testament, who, indeed, are to be regarded as patterns for Christians to follow. Ultimately, all that Christ has done is to strengthen and make certain the Church's consciousness of being the Church, so that from the author's point of view Christ has his appropriate title when he is called "protector and helper of our weakness" (36:1).

o. *Ignatius* represents a completely different type from all the writings so far considered. Like the last few types described he also is under the influence of Paul's theology. But this takes on a special form with him because his antecedents lie not in the tradition of the synagogue but in the thought-world from which John also came (§ 41, 3), a fact which accounts for many points of contact between him and John.* Salvation is called by Ignatius, as by John, usually "life," and also "truth."

"Life" without a modifier Mg. 9:1; "true life" (τὸ ἀληθινὸν ζῆν) Eph. 11:1, Tr. 9:2 (in apposition to "Christ" Sm. 4:1); "true life" (ζωὴ ἀληθινή) Eph. 7:2; "our inseparable life (ζῆν, likewise in apposition to "Christ") Eph. 3:2; "our life through all (time?)," epithet of Christ, Mg. 1:2; "life eternal," Eph. 18:1; Pol. 2:3; equivalent to these expressions are the terms (lacking in John) "immortality" (Eph. 20:2) and "incorruption," Eph. 17:1; Mg. 6:2; Philad. 9:2; Pol. 2:3. The opposite term is "death" (*passim*) which, in turn, for its opposite may have "truth" (Sm. 5:1; Pol.

* It has often been asserted (most recently by Christian Maurer, *Ignatius von Antiochien und das Johannesevangelium*, 1949) that Ignatius is dependent upon John. But such is not likely the case.

7:3). In parallel meaning we find "light of truth," Philad. 2:1, and
"pure light," Rom. 6:2; the Church can be termed "enlightened"
(φωτισμένη) Rom. intr.

"Life" is a thing of the future ("the life which lies before you,"
Eph. 17:1) and Christ can be called our "hope" (Eph. 21:2; Mg. 11,
etc.) as well as our "life." And the Gospel is called "the Gospel of the
common hope" (Philad. 5:2), as the Christian faith can be called
simply: "hope" (Mg. 9:1). That which is hoped for is the "rightwising"
that is to come (Philad. 8:2), or especially the resurrection (Tr. 9:2;
Eph. 11:2; Tr. intr., Rom. 4:3; Sm. 5:3; Pol. 7:1), or the gaining of
"pure light." A special technical term for the object of hope is
"attaining to God" (θεοῦ τυγχάνειν or ἐπιτυγχάνειν); this usually
refers to what Ignatius expects as the fruit of his martyrdom (Eph.
12:2; Mg. 14, etc.), but it is also the hope of all Christians (Eph. 10:1;
Mg. 1:2; Sm. 9:2; Pol. 2:3).

But the traditional picture of early Christian eschatology has to
all intents and purposes disappeared. We read once, it is true: "These
are the last times" (Eph. 11:1). Nevertheless, calling salvation
"immortality," "incorruption," and "attaining to God" indicates
that the hope here implied is a hope for the salvation of the individual.
The two aeons are not mentioned. Even though Satan is called "prince
of this αἰών" (Eph. 17:1; 19:1; Mg. 1:2, etc.) this is no exception, for
the time-aspect of the concept is subordinate here, while the contrast
between this world and the other world is emphasized, as the
parallelism of "this aeon" to "the world" in Rom. 6:1 indicates. Of
the old apocalyptic pictures, at least that of the judgment and the
"wrath to come" is retained (Eph. 11:1; Sm. 6:1); the idea of coming
reward and punishment is used (Eph. 16:2; Mg. 5:1; Sm. 9:2). But of
the future coming of Christ there is at the most a single allusion (Pol.
3:2). The "coming of the Savior" (Philad. 9:2) is not the eschatological
coming but the entrance into history of Jesus, who "in the end was
made manifest" (Mg. 6:1); through him "grace" came (Sm. 6:2) and
became a present reality (Eph. 11:1; Mg. 8:1). The cosmic catastrophe,
which apocalyptic eschatology expected to occur in the future, has
already taken place in the birth, death, and resurrection of Jesus
(Eph. 19; cf. Mg. 11, Tr. 9; Philad. 8:2; Sm. 1; see II, pp. 153f.). So
salvation is present now. Since Christ is our life (Eph. 3:2; Sm. 4:1),
then to be in Christ already means to be in life. Believers are

"members" of Christ (Eph. 4:2; Tr. 11:2) or "branches of the cross" (Tr. 11:2); as those who are united in the Ecclesia they are the body of Christ, of which he himself is the head (Sm. 1:2; Tr. 11:2). Whereas they are in life, the heretics are already in death; they are "clothed with death" (νεκροφόροι, Sm. 5:2; *cf.* Philad. 6:1). "To live after the manner of men" (Rom. 8:1; 6:2) would in reality be to die, while to die the death of a martyr means to live (Rom. 4:3, 6; *cf.* Mg. 5:2). Indeed, not until one belongs to Christ does one even *exist* (Mg. 10:1). The existence of the heretics is only a "semblance" (δοκεῖν, Sm. 2, Tr. 10) of existing.

But with this individualistic piety there is combined an ecclesiastical piety: salvation is available to the individual in the Church. That is why the unity of the Church and the unity of each congregation under the guidance of its one bishop is one of the chief concerns of Ignatius (Eph. 4:2; Mg. 6:2; Sm. 8:2, etc.). In the united congregation the power of prayer is mighty (Eph. 5:2) and Satan's power is overcome (Eph. 13:1). Baptism plays a curiously unimportant role in Ignatius (Eph. 18:2; Sm. 8:2; Pol. 6:2); the Eucharist plays a far greater one as the "medicine of immortality" (Eph. 20:2). To partake of it the congregation ought to gather more frequently (Eph. 13:1. Philad. 4). In the Eucharist the eschatological occurrence takes place as present event (Eph. 13:1f.), and it brings about "union" (ἕνωσις) with the flesh and blood of Christ (Philad. 4; Sm. 7:1).

Still, it would be wrong to conceive the Christianity of Ignatius as being mere sacramentalism in the sense that receiving the sacrament guarantees salvation. The peculiar thing is that Ignatius considers the believer's whole life to be stamped by sacramental union with Christ, receiving thereby a sacramental character, so to speak. For this thought Ignatius uses Paul's formula "in Christ" not only to designate the coming fulfilment as one that takes place in Christ (Eph. 11:1; Rom. 4:3, etc.), but also to describe the conditioning of present living by fellowship with him (Eph. 1:1; 8:2; 10:3, etc., see below). But union with Christ is determined by his paradoxical nature— Christ who was the pre-existent Son of God (Mg. 6:1; 7:2; 8:2), became man, suffered, died, and rose again. He was "God humanly manifested" (Eph. 19:3), a paradox that is emphasized again and again (especially Eph. 7:2) and is passionately defended against the denials of the heretics. Everything depends upon the reality, the actuality of the humanity and the suffering of Christ and upon the

[193]

reality of his resurrection (Tr. 9f., Sm. 2f., 7:2). The resurrection itself is physical, of the flesh: the risen Christ ate and drank with his disciples "as a person in the flesh, though spiritually he was united with the Father" (Sm. 3:3, tr.; *cf.* 12:2). Just for the sake of this paradox Christ is also called "God" (Eph. intr., 1:1; 15:3, etc.), though, of course, God is his Father, and he is the Son (Eph. 2:1; 4:2, etc.) subordinate to his Father (Sm. 8:1; Mg. 13:2), but joined with Him in unity (Mg. 7:1; Sm. 3:3, etc.). He is the will (γνώμη, Eph. 3:2) of God, his "word proceeding from silence" (Mg. 8:2; *cf.* Rom. 8:2; Philad. 9:1 for similar metaphors).

Christ, both God and man at once—everything hangs upon this paradox, because through it man, too, can attain to a paradoxical existence: the correlate to "God became man" is "man becomes God." Ignatius avoids, it is true, the actual word θεωθῆναι ("be deified"). But other expressions do service for it: (ἐπι)τυγχάνειν θεοῦ ("attain to God" but also: to get, or obtain, God; see above, II, p. 192), θεοῦ μετέχειν ("to have, partake of, or enjoy God"), θεοῦ γέμειν ("be full of, or filled with, God," Mg. 14), "to be (or become) God's" (Mg. 10:1; Rom. 6:2; 7:1). The formula "in Christ" (see above) is interchangeable with "in God" (Eph. 1:1; Mg. 3:1; Pol. 6:1); and the phrase "Christ in us" (Mg. 12; Rom. 6:3) has its parallel in "God in us" (Eph. 15:3). Christians are both θεοφόροι ("wearers of God") and χριστόφοροι ("wearers of Christ"); they are θεοδρόμοι (literally "God-runners," prob. = "soarers to God," Philad. 2:2; Pol. 7:2).

The Christian's new mode of being can be indicated, as in Paul, with the term *pneuma*. Christians are contrasted to non-Christians as the "spiritual" to the "carnal" (σαρκικοί Eph. 8:2; the opposite to "spiritual" can also be "human", Eph. 5:1; *cf.* "in human fashion," Tr. 2:1; Rom. 8:1). The chains which Ignatius wears as a "captive in Christ" (Tr. 1:1, etc.) are "spiritual pearls" (Eph. 11:2). But Ignatius differs from Paul in the fact that for Ignatius "the flesh" is merely the sphere of the earthly, the visible (Mg. 3:2), the evident (φαινόμενον, Rom. 3:3; Pol. 2:2), the sphere of transitoriness and death, and not also the power of sin; for in place of "flesh" he can say "matter" (ὕλη, Rom. 6:2; *cf.* 7:2). Of course, the sphere of the earthly can become a sinister power to a man if he lets himself be led astray to think or act "according to the flesh" (Mg. 6:2; Rom. 8:3; Philad. 7:1). But the term "flesh" serves Ignatius primarily to describe the paradoxical nature of human existence as being both "spiritual" and "of the flesh" at once. By the fact that Christ is "both flesh and Spirit" (Eph. 7:2), or that his resurrection is "both of flesh and of Spirit" (Sm. 7:2), "flesh" has been rendered capable of union with "Spirit." Ignatius wishes for the congregations a "union with the flesh and spirit of Jesus Christ" (Mg. 1:2; cf. Mg. 13:2); he wishes for the Ephesians that they may "abide in Jesus Christ both physically (σαρκικῶς) and spiritually" (Eph. 10:3); he wishes for the Magnesians that in all they do they may have success "in the flesh and in the spirit" (Mg. 13:1; cf. further: Tr. intr., 12:1; Sm. 1:1; 13:2; Pol. 1:2; 2:2; 5:1). This paradox is expressed with particular clarity when Ignatius says: "They who are carnal cannot do spiritual things, neither can they who are spiritual do carnal things" and shortly thereafter assures them, "But even what things you do according to the flesh are spiritual, for it is in Jesus Christ that you do them all" (Eph. 8:2).

Since "flesh" is the sphere of death, the union of "flesh" and "spirit" made possible by Christ can also be understood as the uniting of death and life. For Christ, Ignatius says, is "true life in death" (Eph. 7:2); that is why in his passion he calls us to himself as his members (Tr. 11:2).

"The distinction of the Gospel" over the Old Testament dispensation is "the coming, the passion, and the resurrection" of Christ (Philad. 9:2; cf. Eph. 20:1; Sm. 7:2). By his "passion" he gave the baptismal water its power (Eph. 18:2); his "cross" is the elevator (μηχανή) which lifts believers to God (Eph. 9:1). Christ's passion, death, and resurrection are understood as events which continually condition Christian existence, not as an occurrence of the past the benefit of which is appropriated in baptism as the cancellation of one's former sins. The phrases which express this traditional view occur very rarely in Ignatius. The phrase "for us" (referring to the suffering and dying of Christ) appears only in Rom. 6:1 and Sm. 1:2; "for our sins" only at Sm. 7:1. (Otherwise, neither "sin" nor "sinner" occurs; the verb "sin" appears only in the characteristic sentence: "No man who professes faith sins," Eph. 14:2.) By this omission Ignatius is also spared from limiting the effect of the salvation-occurrence to the cancellation of sins committed in one's pre-Christian period.

The Christian's fellowship with the suffering and dying of Christ is described with a variety of expressions, such as "to suffer with him" (Sm. 4:2), "to die through him in his passion" (Mg. 5:2, etc.). Christians are "branches of the cross"

(Tr. 11:2); they are "nailed to the cross" (Sm. 1:1). Ignatius says of himself: "My selfish love (ἔρως) is crucified" (Rom. 7:2). In addition compare, for example, Eph. intr., 1:1; Tr. 4:2; Rom. 4:3, and for its paradox, the closing salutation: "in the name of Jesus Christ and in his flesh and blood (which is) both a passion and a resurrection having the nature of both flesh and spirit" (Sm. 12:2 tr.).

Beyond doubt Ignatius thinks that the Christian's sharing of death and life with Christ is brought about by the sacraments (see above II, p. 193). But this sharing with Christ gives the whole of life a sacramental character, though in a different way than in Paul. For the latter, "being crucified with Christ" (Rom. 6:6; Gal. 5:24; 6:14) constantly takes place in the battle against sin and in renunciation of the world. Not so Ignatius. For him it takes place in literal suffering and in the willingness to die as the imitation of Christ (Sm. 5:1; Mg. 5:2). From this view comes Ignatius' craving for martyrdom (especially in Rom.); for not until he is martyred will that be truly actualized which was potentially or approximately given in the sacrament and in the conduct of his life. Not until his martyrdom will Ignatius be truly an "imitator of the passion of my God" (Rom. 6:3), even though all Christians may be called, or ought to be able to be called, "imitators of God" (Eph. 1:1; 10:3; Tr. 1:2; Philad. 7:2). While every Christian is a "disciple of Jesus Christ" (Mg. 9:1; 10:1; Rom 3:1; Pol. 2:1), nevertheless it is the martyr who is the true disciple (Eph. 1:2; 3:1; Tr. 5:2; Rom. 4:2; 5:1, 3; Pol. 7:1).

Furthermore, the ethical life of believers is conditioned by this sacramental fellowship, although Ignatius does not call it dying and rising with Christ. One must not merely be called a "Christian," but must also "live according to Christianity" (κατὰ Χριστιανισμόν, Mg. 4; 10:1; cf. Rom. 3:2f.; Pol. 7:3).

Christian living is rarely described concretely. Usually Ignatius simply refers to the "commandment(s) of Christ" (Eph. 9:2; Rom. intr.; Philad. 1:2), for Christ is for him also the "teacher" (Eph. 15:1; Mg. 9:1); or he refers to the "ordinances" (δόγματα) of the Lord and the apostles" (Mg. 13:1). He evidently presupposes something like a catechism of Christian living. Specifically, he admonishes his readers to love for the brethren and unity (Mg. 6:2; Tr. 8:2; Philad. 8 and elsewhere), to prayer for non-Christians and to patient endurance of scorn and injustice

(Eph. 10), to worthy conduct which will not offend the heathen (Tr. 8:2). It is characteristic of him that his warnings against heresy outweigh his ethical parenesis. "To be firm in the faith" (Eph. 10:2) is the thing that counts.

Again and again "faith" and "love" are named as marks of Christianity (Eph. 1:1; 9:1; 14:1f.; 20:1; Mg. 1:2, etc.); "faith" is the "flesh," "love" the "blood" of Christ (Tr. 8:1). In this combination "faith" generally means, probably, the acceptance of right doctrine or the holding fast to it. But in Ignatius faith as orthodoxy is not to be separated from faith as an attitude of life, the will to share in suffering with Christ; thus Ignatius can speak of "believing in his death" (Tr. 2:1) or believing "in the blood of Christ" (Sm. 6:1).

The source of "faith" or "believing" lies, as we have seen, in the mystery of Christ's death and resurrection (Mg. 9:1). The opposite of "faith" is an un-faith (ἀπιστία, Eph. 8:2; Mg. 5:2) for which the cross is a "scandal" (Eph. 18:1). The "disbelievers" (ἄπιστοι) are heretics who deny the reality of Christ's passion (Tr. 10:1; Sm.2) and by their "false teaching" corrupt "the faith for the sake of which Jesus Christ was crucified" (Eph. 16:2). This is the "teaching of the prince of this world" (Eph. 17:1), while the true teaching is the "doctrine of incorruption" (Mg. 6:2).

Beyond doubt right faith for Ignatius is not merely assent to dogmatic propositions but is an existential attitude.* But nowhere in his letters does "faith" have that meaning which Paul expresses by contrasting "faith" and "works." Only the (Pauline) motif of rejecting "boasting" and "being puffed up" occasionally occurs (Eph. 18:1; Mg. 12; Tr. 4:1; 7:1; Sm. 6:1; Pol. 4:3; 5:2), but the opposite is not "faith" but "non-boasting" (ἀκαυχησία, Pol. 5:2) and "humility" (Tr. 4:2) or "being modest" (Mg. 12) and "restraining one's self" (Tr. 4:1). Ignatius also catches up Paul's expression "I am not thereby rightwised" from I Cor. 4:4 (tr.), applying it to his own progress toward martyrdom (Rom. 5:1). He hopes to be "rightwised" by the death and resurrection of Christ and by faith (Philad. 8:2). But these are rare echoes of Pauline language. "Righteousness" as designation for the essence of salvation never occurs at all; its adjective (δίκαιος) in Ignatius refers to moral uprightness (Mg. 12 quoting Prov. 18:17; used also in a play on words Eph. 1:1—see

* I.e. an attitude which involves the whole being and the whole doing of the believer (Tr.).

Bauer *ad loc.* in Lietzmann's *Handbuch*). As "flesh" does not mean the power of sin (see above II, p. 194), neither does Spirit mean the power behind ethical conduct, but means the other-worldly sphere (see above, II, p. 194), or is used in conventional phrases. However, Ignatius does speak of God's "grace" as a power at work in the Church (Sm. 9:2, Rom. intr., Mg. 8:2)—a power, furthermore, which is specially incorporated in the congregational officers (Mg. 2; Pol. 1:2). χάρισμα ("gift") he uses in the same sense (Sm. intr.; Pol. 2:2). Otherwise "grace" is God's, or Christ's, gracious will (e.g. Rom. 1:2; Philad. 8:1; 11:1; Sm. 11:1) or, in an objective sense, is the salvation wrought by God (Eph. 11:1; Mg. 8:1; Sm. 6:2). But "grace," like "faith," never stands in antithesis to "works."

Ignatius has here been treated at considerable length. That was necessary partly because from him a light is cast backward upon the theology of Paul, partly because Ignatius, in contradistinction to all other writers of early Christianity after Paul and John, is a figure having originality. But it was primarily necessary because through him the problems clearly emerge which confronted a genuine appropriation of the Christian kerygma which had received its first theological explication at the hands of Paul. Almost everywhere else Christian faith sank back into legalism, even though Col., Eph., and I Pet. as well as the pastorals hold fast to some motifs of Paul's theology and make them effective. But Ignatius learned from Paul to understand Christian faith as a truly existential matter. He did not reach emancipation from Hellenistic dualism, it is true—on the contrary, it is within such dualism that he understands the antithesis of "flesh" and "Spirit." Since he knows "flesh" not as the power of sin but only as the sphere of transitoriness and death, he did not grasp the meaning of Paul's doctrine of justification ("rightwising" by faith) nor of his concept of "faith." Neither does he understand Paul's concept of Christian "freedom," for to his mind "freedom" is to be achieved only after death (martyrdom)—Rom. 4:3. Nor did he understand Paul's concept of the Christian's relation to the suffering and dying of Christ, but understood it to be an imitating of Christ. But Ignatius did comprehend the paradoxical character of Christian existence: an existing between "already" and "not yet." In fact, because he did not take over the apocalyptic doctrine of the two aeons, for him that "between-ness" shrinks to the time between the believer's baptism and death (or, rather, resurrection) and consequently well-nigh loses its chronological sense and to a considerable extent becomes that which determines the character of Christian existence. Legalism is no problem for Ignatius. The reason for that is not (as it generally is with other writers) that he thinks legalistically and hence does not find it problematical that fulfilling the "(new) law" is the condition for achieving future salvation. Rather, the reason for it is that it would never occur to him that salvation might be won by one's own merit. That which is new in the Christian situation lies, for him, not in the granting of a new chance but in the transformation of one's existence. For him the effect of the salvation-occurrence is not limited to the cancellation of past sins but is a power experienced in the present. Though the traditional eschatology plays no role in Ignatius' thought, he nevertheless understood Christ as the eschatological event. Hence he knows the dialectic of Christian existence: the paradox that it unites indicative and imperative. Christians who are "disciples" or "imitators" of God or Christ (Mg. 10:1; Eph. 1:1; Tr. 1:2) must nevertheless still become such (Mg. 9:1; Eph. 10:3; Philad. 7:2). By the indicative they may be described as "belonging to God" (ὄντες θεοῦ, Eph. 8:1), or as "in all ways adorned by the commandments of Jesus Christ" (Eph. 9:2), but they can likewise be admonished by the imperative as people who have yet to become "sanctified in all things" (Eph. 2:2). The paradox of Gal. 5:25 reappears in this form: "Since you are perfect, then also strive after perfect (deeds)" (τέλειοι ὄντες τέλεια καὶ φρονεῖτε, Sm. 11:3 tr., to which he immediately adds, "For if you desire to do well, God is ready to help you." *Cf.* Eph. 15:3; Mg. 12).

4. In the preceding survey we have examined a certain body of literature. We did so under a guiding question: how is the present conceived to be related to future salvation, and in what way is the Christian situation understood to be that peculiar situation of "between-ness"? The answers yield a series of differences, an abundance of nuances. In some writings there is no understanding of that "between-ness" at all. In them the present is not conceived as a period basically new as compared with the past, but is a temporary and preparatory period quite as in Judaism. Of this sort are Jas., Did., Rev., and I Clem. In most other cases, however, the present is distinguished from the past as something made new by the coming of Jesus, or by his death and resurrection. Nevertheless, here the "between-ness" of the present is conceived as that which determines

only the chronology of the Christian situation and not its character; it is the period of a new chance for man's effort in behalf of his future salvation—ultimately, therefore, here, too, only a temporary and preparatory period. Only where the Pauline tradition continues to work controllingly does the basic (non-chronological) sense of that "between-ness" come forth—radically in Ignatius, with some power also in Col., Eph., and I Pet. and more weakly in the pastorals and even in Barn., though he is not under the influence of Paul. The basic sense has completely paled down in Herm. and Heb., in both of which, as in I Clem., Jas. and Did., the synagogue-tradition has become dominant. But even where the synagogue-tradition is weak or missing, as in II Pet., Jude, and Pol., the same is true.

The more prominent the chronological meaning of the believer's "between-ness" becomes—even to the point of becoming its sole meaning—the more salvation's present reality comes to be seen solely in the fact that one's former sins are canceled by the work of salvation (Jesus' death and resurrection) appropriated in baptism, and that thereby the possibility of a new beginning is conferred upon the present. This possibility, however, is understood to mean that now by obedience to God's demands a man can successfully exert himself to fulfil the condition for attaining future salvation: do the good works on the basis of which he will be acquitted in the judgment by God (or Christ), who will judge according to works. This legalism is not relinquished but is at the most only modified when the Spirit's assistance in this human effort is mentioned, or when the consciousness is alive that Christians are the new People of God (especially Barn. and Heb.), called, and in an anticipatory sense "saved" (II, p. 159), and hence also have hope. Neither is it any relinquishing of legalism when a possibility exists of obtaining God's forgiveness by repentance for sins committed after baptism. That the question concerning such a possibility can arise (Herm. but also Heb.) is a clear symptom of legalistic thinking. It is significant how rarely faith in the radical sense, as we find it in Paul and John, is understood as a new relation to God. As a rule *pistis* is understood as trust in God, as confident hope, or as patient faithfulness. Even in Col. and Eph. and in the pastorals Paul's antithesis of "faith" to "works" is only faintly echoed; otherwise it is entirely lacking (for which in Ignatius there is a special reason; see II, p. 199) or is simply reproduced in conventional phrases (I and II Clem.). Man is thrown back upon his own strength and nothing remains of the insight, "if anyone is in Christ, he is a new creation" (II Cor. 5:17). The consequence of this is probably clearest in I Clem. For him the difference between Christians and the pious men of the Old Testament disappears.

5. What does this mean for *christology*? The Christ who is worshiped in the cultus as the present Kyrios (II, p. 155) is truly thought of as Lord of the present only when the present is understood as made absolutely new by him—i.e. when Christ's appearing is understood in Paul's sense (Gal. 4:4, etc.) and John's (Jn. 5:25, etc.) as the eschatological event which terminated the old world and when, correspondingly, Christian existence is understood as divorced-from-the-world, eschatological existence. The decisive question is whether this end which has been imposed upon the world is understood only chronologically as the end of the course of time or whether it is also and essentially understood as the end of the worldliness of man, who, having become, as a believer, a new creature, has stepped over from death into life. This qualitative meaning of the eschatological occurrence had been completely cut loose from the chronological meaning by John (§ 45, 3), while in Paul the two are still combined. The radicality of John is well-nigh achieved by Ignatius, while Paul's understanding is to some degree preserved in Col. and Eph. and even in the pastorals. Hence in them, too, the salvation-character of the present is seen in the fact that in the present the word of the proclamation is sounding forth (II, pp. 177, 185)—i.e. that here, as in Paul (I, p. 302), Christ is present in the proclaimed word. Everywhere else Christ's eschatological significance (except where it entirely disappears, as in Jas. and Herm.) is seen only in the fact that he will (soon) put the world's temporal course to end when he returns to hold judgment and bring salvation. As the coming Judge he is, consistently, for the present time the teacher and law-giver, not the founder of a new relation to God. Paul's expression "in Christ," which denotes the believer's present existence, is still found in this sense in Col. and Eph. but is also already becoming a conventional phrase meaning "Christian" (II, p. 177). As such a formula it is used in the pastorals (II, pp. 186f.) and in I Pet. (3:16; 5:10, 14), rather often in I Clem., and once in Pol. (1:1). Once in Rev. the phrase "in the Lord" (14:13) occurs. "In Christ" does not occur in Heb., Barn., Jas., Did., II Pet., II Clem., or Herm. Only in Ignatius does it have once more its old strength (II, p. 193).

[201]

Participation in the suffering and death of Christ meant, in Paul, the shaping of Christian living by that divorce from the world which is to be constantly accomplished in the battle against sin (Rom. 6:6; Gal. 5:24; 6:14). It still has this meaning in Col. 2:12, 20; 3:3, perhaps in II Tim. 2:11f., and certainly in I Peter 4:1f. But already in I Pet. there is combined with it the idea of the *imitatio Christi* (II, pp. 182f.), which later is so important in Ignatius (II, p. 195). In this idea of imitation Christ is not regarded as the eschatological emancipator but as an example (so also in I Clem. 16:17; Pol. 8:2). While for Paul sharing the suffering and death of Christ is at the same time a present sharing of his life (II Cor. 4:8ff., etc.), in the notion of imitation the life is the future life which is to be conferred at the resurrection.

The presence of Christ here and now—where it is anything more than his presence as teacher, law-giver, and example—according to Col., Eph., and the pastorals is experienced in the proclaimed word; but otherwise it is experienced in the cult, particularly by receiving the sacraments of baptism and the eucharist. Since the sacraments have their foundation in the death and resurrection of Christ, in a certain sense they give present reality to the salvation-occurrence by mediating its benefit: the forgiveness of sins and the gift of eternal life (Ignatius).

Except in Ignatius *the incarnation* of the pre-existent Son has no significance of its own but is only the necessary presupposition for his passion and death or also for his activity as teacher and founder of the Church by his commissioning of the apostles. In Ignatius, as a consequence of his conception of "flesh" and "spirit," the incarnation has a special meaning; by it that which is of the earth and the flesh is enabled to participate in that which is otherworldly and spiritual (II, pp. 193f.). The incarnation regarded as an act of obedience and love, which is the dominant view in Paul and John (Phil. 2:8; Rom. 15:3; II Cor. 8:1; Gal. 2:20; Jn. 3:16, 4:34, 12:49f.; I Jn. 4:9), has disappeared except for a remnant (Sm. 8:1; Mg. 7:1).

The more Christian faith degenerates into legalism, the more Christ's significance is reduced to that of being at work in the Church's sacrament. The less Christ is felt to be present in the proclaimed word, the more the Church becomes a sacramental institution of salvation (II, p. 114). Christology, as soon as it ceases to be naive and becomes a matter of reflection, will have to find its task in furnishing a foundation for the sacramental significance of Christ.

CHAPTER VIII

The Problem of Christian Living

§ 59. The Understanding of the Imperative

1. The problem of Christian living, among other problems, was present to the Church from the beginning (§ 10, 4; § 11, 3c)—not only and not primarily as a problem of the practical side of living, but mainly as a problem of the Christian's understanding of himself. The problem was set by the paradoxical situation of the Church: as the eschatological entity which it is it belongs not to the old but to the future world and yet must lead its life within the old world between "no longer" and "not yet." As a new life no longer belonging to the old aeon it can be described in the indicative; but as long as it must be led in the old world, it stands under the imperative. As new life it stands under God's grace; as life within the old world it stands under His law, under ethical demand (§ 11, 3c). The problem therefore resolves itself into this question: how is the relation between the present and the future, between the indicative and the imperative, understood? Paul had solved the problem by his understanding of Christian freedom (§ 38) and had conceived the relation between the present and the future as a dialectic one (§ 40)—and John likewise (§ 50). The question was whether or not this understanding would be retained—whether Christian freedom would be understood as the freedom to obey, obedience itself then being understood as the gift of grace or of the Spirit, or whether obedience would be conceived as an accomplishment and hence as the condition to be fulfilled in order to obtain salvation (I, pp. 119f.), and then whether the imperative would receive again the character of a law in the sense that had been demolished in Paul's doctrine of justification: the character of a way to salvation.

In most essentials the answer to these questions has already been given in the discussions of soteriology (§ 58) because on account of

[203]

the peculiar nature of the Christian understanding of salvation the themes of soteriology and ethics cannot be separated. They cannot be separated because the question of the relation between present and future salvation is most intimately bound up with the question of the relation between indicative and imperative. In our discussion it developed that the Pauline tradition is still alive only in Col., Eph., I Pet., and, more weakly, in the pastorals, and that everywhere else a sinking back into legalism takes place except in Ignatius, who, while he has learned decisive things from Paul, nevertheless reinterprets him under the influence of sacramental thinking. The fact is that on the average the insight of Paul and John that the occurrence of salvation means eschatological occurrence was not grasped; instead it was reduced to an event—the death and resurrection of Jesus—the effect of which, when appropriated in baptism, is to cancel the sins of the past. The man who is purified from his former guilt has henceforth the chance of a new beginning but is now left to rely on his own strength to become worthy of the coming salvation by his obedience. The knowledge that the gift of grace (Paul) or of God's love (John) makes a man radically new is lost. Gone is the knowledge that a man without God's grace is a victim to the power of sin and death, that he has lost his freedom and is living in disobedience to God even if his conduct be correct, because God's law is to him a means of asserting himself before God. Vanished is the knowledge that his release from the powers that controlled him is a release to genuine obedience, but that he is never cast loose from the giving and forgiving grace of God nor left to rely upon his own strength.

2. Hence *the failure to see any longer man's radical fallen-ness to* the power of sin, falsehood, darkness is an understandable development. The conversion of the heathen was regarded—both from the Gentile-Christian and the Jewish-Christian view-point—as the acquiring of a new and correct knowledge of God, as the transfer from the "darkness" of "ignorance" and "error" into the light of the knowledge of the one God (§ 9, 2; *cf.* especially II Clem. 1:6f.), and at the same time as a turning away from a life sunk in vices (§ 9, 3), which, as such, is a life under the power of death. Rescue from this death occurs by the forgiveness of sins which is made available by Christ's death and is appropriated in baptism (I, pp. 84f., 136f.). The last statement also applies, of course, to the Jews who turn to the Christian faith.

The "*slavery*" into which man prior to faith has fallen is no longer understood as slavery to sin (and the Law) as it is in Paul and John (Gal. 4:24; 5:1; Rom. 6:16–20, 8:15; Jn. 8:32–36), but to "death" and "corruption" (Heb. 2:15; II Pet. 2:19)— a view that is likewise found in Paul, it is true (Rom. 8:21). The only exception is Tit. 3:3 ("slaves to various passions and pleasures"). "*Freedom*" in I Pet. 2:16 perhaps means freedom from the Law and from sin; in Ign. Rom. 4:3; Pol. 4:3 it means freedom from death. Otherwise, the term "freedom" as a mark of Christian existence no longer occurs at all unless one is inclined to find it in the heretics' slogan at II Pet. 2:19. On the "law of freedom (or "liberty")" Jas. 1:25, 2:12, see II, p. 162 footnote.

In no case is conversion understood as the radical transformation of the old man. There are indeed echoes of Paul's thought of the destruction of the "old man" (Rom. 6:6; 7:6; I Cor. 5:7f.) and also of the "newness" ($\kappa\alpha\iota\nu\delta\tau\eta\varsigma$) of Christian life (Rom. 6:4). But the paradox of the statements: "If anyone is in Christ, he is a new creation" (II Cor. 5:17; *cf.* Gal. 6:15) and: "our inner (man) is being renewed every day" (II Cor. 4:16; *cf.* Rom. 12:2) is scarcely understood any longer. Only rarely is there a train of thought in which there is any grasp of man's renewal in the sense of Paul's understanding of indicative and imperative. The clearest case of this sort is Col. 3:1ff.: "If then you have been raised with Christ, seek the things that are above . . . for you have died . . . put to death therefore your members that are on the earth . . . having put off the old man . . . and having put on the new man which is being renewed; . . . put on then . . ." (*cf.* 2:12f.). In Tit. 3:3–7 the paradox is also still preserved in that the imperative is founded upon the "renewal" brought about by the "Holy Spirit." In Eph. 2:1–10 the quoted sentences from Colossians are echoed, but their paradox is now only weakly expressed: "you who were dead through your trespasses and sins . . . he made alive together with Christ . . . created in Christ Jesus for good works." Likewise in the admonition of Eph. 4:22–24: "Put off your old man . . . and be renewed in the spirit of your minds and put on the new man created after the likeness of God. . . ." The catch-word "renewal" is echoed in Heb. 6:6; but here the meaning of renewal as including the imperative is given up when it is said that after baptism it is impossible to "restore again ($\pi\acute{\alpha}\lambda\iota\nu$ $\dot{\alpha}\nu\alpha\kappa\alpha\iota\nu\acute{\iota}\zeta\epsilon\iota\nu$) to repentance" the (grave) sinners. And the threat of divine retribution, which he says is so much more terrible for Christians than for Jews (2:2f.; 10:28f.; 12:25), indicates that the author did not understand the Christian's radically different standing before God. If either of them understood it, it was rather the author of Barnabas: "Because we received the remission of sins and hoped in the Name, we have become new, created again from the beginning" (Barn. 16:8). Or again (6:11): "Since, then, he made us new by the remission of sins, he made us another type, that we should have the soul of children, as though he were creating us afresh." But because the author knows nothing of present righteousness (4:10), neither did he understand the renewal radically. This judgment is not altered by his term "the new law of our Lord Jesus Christ" (2:6), for this consists of "ordinances" and "commandments," as we have seen (II, p. 164). Even when Christians are called the "new People" (5:7; 7:5), this "new" denotes only the chronological not the qualitative newness of the eschatological Congregation. Hermas, too, speaks of the renewal which (by baptism) the Christian has experienced (vis. III 8:9: "the renewal of your spirits") or which he now receives by the Lord's revelation and call to repentance (vis. III 12:3; sim. VIII 6:2; IX 14:3; *cf.* VI 2:4). But precisely by speaking of the renewal now made possible for one last time he shows that he does not understand renewal in Paul's sense. If for him Christ is the "new door" (sim. IX 12:1–3), he is so only in the chronological sense.

A particularly revealing passage is Herm. mand. XII 3:4–5:4: Hermas has learned from the "Shepherd" what the commandments of God are and confesses in fright: "But I do not know whether these commandments can be kept because they are exceedingly difficult." But he has to be told in answer that he is mistaken—rather, the commandments are easy, and merely to regard them as difficult is already a sin. If a man only desires to do so from his heart, he can keep them; since man received from the Creator lordship over the world, why shouldn't he also have the strength to keep the commandments? If he only does not fear the devil, the devil will flee before him!

An understanding for "the old has passed away, behold, the new has come" (II Cor. 5:17)—i.e. for the total otherness of the Christian situation—is really found only in Ignatius. He really understood the salvation-occurrence as eschatological and consequently grasped the paradox of Christian existence. He understood the release of man from his old nature not as release from the power of flesh and sin, it is true, but as release from transitoriness and death (II, p. 195). That is understandable from a recognition of Ignatius' different presuppositions: the Hellenistic-Gnostic dualism, out of which he comes, and his sacramentalism. Elsewhere than in Ignatius understanding for what Paul and John called sin gets lost in moralistic-legalistic thinking—essentially under the influence of the synagogal tradition.

The manner in which *sin* is generally spoken of indicates that the radical fallen-ness of man outside of Christ is no longer seen. Almost nowhere is sin any longer regarded as a unified power, or, seen from man's side, as a unified attitude toward living; only in Colossians and Ephesians is sin still seen as a power that threatens even the Christian (II, pp. 176f.). Of course, we often hear of "sins" (ἁμαρτίαι and ἁμαρτήματα) and "transgressions"; and such confessions as the following occur: "my sins are many and manifold" (Herm. mand IV 2:3), or "I myself am altogether sinful (πανθαμαρτωλός) and have not yet escaped temptation" (II Clem. 18:2), or "we all owe the debt of sin" (Pol. Phil. 6:1). But practically never is sin mentioned as a power that dominates man; at the most sin is regarded as a unity in Heb. 9:26; 12:1, 4 and Pol. Phil. 6:1. When the men prior to Christ are regarded as sinners whom he came to save, the authors are thinking of the heathen life of vice (I Tim. 1:9; *cf.* Col. 1:21; 3:7f.; Eph. 2:3; Tit. 3:3; I Pet. 1:14, 18; 4:3); they were "dead in trespasses" (Col. 2:13; Eph. 2:1, 5; *cf.* Herm. sim. IX 16:3ff.), their "works" were "dead" (Heb. 6:1; 9:14; said of sinful Christians, Herm. sim. IX 21:2; *cf.* Rev. 3:1).

If we leave Ignatius out of account (II, p. 195), *the flesh* also is scarcely spoken of in the Pauline sense any longer, either. In Col. 2:11, 13 "flesh," if not the power of sin, is at least the sphere of sin: in baptism took place "the putting off of the body of flesh," and God made alive those who were dead "in trespasses and in (?) the uncircumcision of the flesh" (*cf.* Jude 23). A number of times the "desires of the flesh" are mentioned (Eph. 2:3; I Pet. 2:11; II Pet. 2:18; Did. 1:4; Barn. 10:9). But otherwise *sarx* now means as in Ignatius only the sphere of the earthly, that which is of the body.

Thus *sarx* is used neutrally, e.g. in II Clem. 8:2; Herm. vis. III 9:3, mand. III 1 and elsewhere. It is several times said that Christ revealed himself and suffered in the flesh (Barn. 5:6, 10ff., 6: 7, 9, etc.; II Clem. 9:5; Herm. sim. V 6:5ff.) or that man must not defile his flesh but keep it pure (II Clem., see II, p. 170; Herm. mand. IV 1:9; sim. V 7:1f.; *cf.* "pure in the flesh" I Clem. 38:2). Paul's "according to the flesh" no longer occurs at all as the characteristic of sinful conduct; to denote a natural relationship (I, pp. 236f.) the phrase still occurs but only in Col. 3:22, Eph. 6:5 (the earthly—κατὰ σάρκα—masters, i.e. masters of slaves) and I Clem. 32:2 (Jesus, Abraham's descendant "according to the flesh"). II Clem. like Ignatius, teaches the resurrection of the flesh (9:1ff.).

Hence, *the contrast between "flesh" and "Spirit"* in Paul's sense no longer plays any role but only denotes the contrast between the earthly and the divine (the other-worldly). This is true not only in Ignatius but also elsewhere—e.g. I Tim. 3:16; Barn. 7:3; II Clem. 9:5; 14:3ff.; Herm. sim. V 6:5ff., etc.; Col. 2:5 is somewhat different. More frequently found is the contrast "world—God," which may be expressed in full (Jas. 4:4; Ign. Mg. 5:2; Rom. 2:2) or only implied by speaking of "this world" (Eph. 2:2; Did. 10:6; Barn. 10:11; II Clem. 5:1–5 "this world of the flesh"; 8:2; 19:3; Ign. Mg. 5:2; Herm. vis. IV 3:2–4, sim. V 5:2), or by simply using "the world" in a derogatory sense (Jas. 1:27; 4:4; II Pet. 1:4; 2:20; Ign. Rom. 3:2f.; 7:1; Pol. Phil. 5:3). In such cases "world" for the most part does not mean a power inimical to God (which it clearly does mean in Jas. 4:4) but the sphere of the earthly, and the usage is less indicative of man's being fallen or threatened than of the negativity of ethical demand—as when "worldly passions" are mentioned (Tit. 2:12; II Clem. 17:3; *cf.* Pol. Phil. 5:3: "the lusts that are in the world") or simply "worldly things" (κοσμικά, II Clem. 5:6).

The contrast between *the present and the future aeon* lives on in some writings. It may be explicitly formulated (Eph. 1:21; II Clem. 6:3; Herm. sim. III–IV) or only one or the other may be named: "this" or "the present" aeon (I Tim. 6:17; II Tim. 4:10; Ign. Rom. 6:1; Pol. Phil. 5:2; 9:2, frequently in Hermas—"ruler of this world" several times in Ignatius), or only "the coming aeon" (Heb. 6:5: "the age to come," ὁ μέλλων; Herm. vis. IV 3:5: "the coming, ἐρχόμενος, aeon"; Barn. 10:11: "the holy, ἅγιος, aeon"; II Clem. 19:4: "the age without sorrow," ἀλύπητος). This usage, too, is characteristic for negative ethics, as one may see especially clearly in Hermas who

* The antecedents of the pronouns in I Clem. 32:1, 2 are far from clear. Perhaps 32:2 refers to Jacob, not Abraham (Tr.).

warns against the "lusts" (and "deceptions") of this aeon (mand. XI 8, XII 6:5; sim. VI 2:3; 3:3, etc.) or against its "vanities" (mand. IX 4, sim. V 3:6), its "wickednesses" (sim. VI 1:4) and its "occupations" (mand. X 1:4). One's belonging to the coming aeon appears essentially as the obligation to free one's self from the old world by obedience to the "new law of the Lord" (Barn. 2:6), to its "commandments" and "ordinances" and by renunciation of "fleshly" or "worldly" desires. The indicative upon which this imperative is founded is limited to the fact that former sins are forgiven: henceforth the baptized man is on his own responsibility and must fulfil the condition for achieving future salvation by his own good works. The consciousness of being freed from the power of sin and of being borne up by the strength of the Spirit is in the process of getting lost.

Freedom from sin is understood in the moral sense: as sinlessness. Therefore, where the contrast between the past and the present is taken seriously, the problem of post-baptismal sins—at least the grave ones—necessarily arises along with the question whether there is a possibility of renewed repentance (Heb., Herm.). Though it is true that in parenesis the contrast between "once" and "now" plays a great role (I, pp. 105f.). But where the contrast is only that between one's present baptismal purity and one's former sins, and is not a description of a once hidden salvation now revealed, a motivation for the imperative is furnished by means of an indicative, but their paradoxical relation to each other is not expressed. Sinlessness has thereby become a task to be accomplished; and to the extent that sinlessness shows itself to be unfulfillable or unfulfilled, refuge is sought in repentance and divine forgiveness. For by and large this is assumed without reflection to be an existing possibility—an assumption which is also an aftermath of the synagogal tradition. While Herm. calls men to repentance because that possibility is now once again opened to them but for the last time, II Clem. is a penitential sermon with the presupposition that repentance is possible at any time. The cry, "Repent!" pervades the letters to the seven churches in Revelation, and the repentance of Christians is dealt with in II Tim. 2:25; I Clem. 57:1; 62:2; Did. 10:6; II Pet. 3:9; Ign. Philad. 3:2; 8:1; Sm. 4:1; 5:3;, 9:1. In I Clem. 7–8 we hear of "repentance" as a possibility existing for Christians as it once did for the pious men of the Old Testament. Even though it is occasionally said that an opportunity for repentance is given us only so long as we tarry on earth (II Clem. 8:1–3; 16:1; Ign. Sm. 9:1), it is clear that repentance is now still constantly possible, a situation for which II Pet. 3:9 explicitly gives the long-suffering of God as the reason. Like repentance, forgiveness, too, always stands open (Jas. 5:15; Pol. Phil. 6:2).

Repentance is, of course, the condition for forgiveness (expressly stated in Ign. Philad. 8:1). Occasionally forgiveness is conditional to the requirement that man fulfil the commandments of God in love (I Clem. 50:5), for "love covers a multitude of sins" (I Pet. 4:8; Jas. 5:20; I Clem. 49:5; 50:5; II Clem. 16:4). The same thing is also accomplished by "doing good" (Pol. Phil. 10:2; Barn. 19:10; Did. 4:6); indeed, according to II Clem. 16:4 almsgiving is as good as repentance and better than prayer and fasting. Herm. sim. V 1 goes even further: here ritual fasting is rejected, and the teaching is presented that the genuine way to "fast" is to fulfil the commandments. In sim. V 3:7, contrariwise, fasting is approved but is put to charitable service: the food saved by fasting is to be turned to the benefit of widows, orphans, and the destitute. Such passages indicate that there were Christian circles in which fasting was deemed meritorious; in Pol. Phil. 7:2 it appears in combination with prayer, and in Did. 8:1 the Christian fast on Wednesday and Friday is contrasted with the Jewish fast on Monday and Thursday. A somewhat different case is the fast which is a preparation for the receiving of revelation (Herm. vis. II 2:1, III 1:2, 10:6f.) or for baptism (Did. 7:4). Suffering, too, if it leads to repentance, has a sin-canceling effect, so Hermas says (vis. III 7:6, sim. VI 3–5, VII); I Pet. 4:1 is hardly interpretable in this sense, but perhaps Jas. 5:14–16 is.

In the congregational prayer at I Clem. 60:1 forgiveness is implored under appeal to divine mercy. As in I Jn. 1:9, the confessing of sin is often mentioned (Jas. 5:16; I Clem. 51:3; 52:1; Barn. 19:12; Did. 4:14; 14:1; II Clem. 8:3; Herm. vis. I 1:3; III 1:5f.; sim. IX 23:4). Probably such confession is generally presupposed.

3. Corresponding to the fact that sin is no longer taken with radical seriousness, neither is *the grace of God* any longer radically understood. The "grace" of God is, indeed, often mentioned, but the antithesis of "works" to "grace" is only rarely echoed (Eph. 2:5, 8f.; II Tim. 1:9; Tit. 3:5, 7).

Quite often divine "grace" in a very general sense is mentioned (II Thess. 1:12, 2:16; I Tim. 1:14; Acts 11:23; 14:26;

15:40; I Clem. 30:2f.; 50:3; II Clem. 13:4; Ign. Sm. 12:1; Pol. 2:1; Herm. mand. X 3:1). In such cases "grace" · is scarcely distinguishable from "mercy" (ἔλεος, I, pp. 282f.). "Grace" and "peace" are often combined, both in greetings (I Tim. 1:2; II Tim. 1:2; Tit. 1:4 *v.l.*; II Jn. 3; Ign. Sm. 12:2) and elsewhere (Heb. 4:16); the place of "grace" can be taken by "mercy" (Eph. 2:4; Tit. 3:5). "Grace" may also be seen in God's granting of repentance (I Clem. 7:4, where, unlike Acts 5:31; 11:18, the author evidently is not thinking of baptismal repentance alone).

In general "grace" denotes the saving grace manifested in Christ (e.g. Tit. 2:11). The Christian message can be called the "Gospel" or "the word" of "grace" (Acts 20:24, 32). To become a Christian can be termed a hearing and understanding of God's grace (Col. 1:6). To be a Christian is to have come under the "yoke of grace" (I Clem. 16:17) or be under "present grace" (Ign. Eph. 11:1; *cf.* I Pet. 5:12). Heretics "have divergent notions (ἑτεροδοξοῦντες) concerning the grace of Jesus Christ" (Ign. Sm. 6:2); the sin of apostasy is called insulting "the Spirit of grace" (Heb. 10:29). "Grace" appears to be conceived as a power which aids one to a proper Christian attitude, in such expressions as say that the Church has received the "Spirit of grace" or "the grace of the spiritual gift" (I Clem. 46:6; Barn. 1:2) or that it is full of the "grace of God" (Ign. Rom. intr.). *Cf.* also I Clem. 23:1; 46:6; Barn. 1:3; on grace as a power see also I Clem. 55:3.

It is evident now that *pistis* (and its verb *pisteuein*) also cannot here mean, as in Paul, the obedience which faith is, but—except where it means hopeful trust or fidelity—is becoming a historical term, so to speak, a term for becoming or being a Christian or also for Christianity in the sense of the content of its belief (II, pp. 135f.). When the antithesis between "works" and "faith" gets lost, it is not surprising that the demand for good works (and warning against evil ones) is everywhere heard—in the pastoral epistles as in I and II Clem. and Barn. For the judgment and its retribution will turn out according to one's works (I Pet. 1:17; Rev. 2:23; I Clem. 34:3; Barn. 4:12; II Clem. 6:9, etc.). Jas. 2:24 explicitly assures the reader that man will be "justified" by works and not by faith alone (*cf.* I Clem. 31:2). Therefore, Hermas begs the "Shepherd" to instruct him "that I may know what works I must do in order to have life" (mand. IV 2:3, tr.; *cf.* VIII 8) and he constantly receives instruction about "wicked works" and "upright" ones, about the "works of God" and those "of the devil," etc. Certainly, exhortation to good work and reference to the judgment also occur in Paul (I Cor. 15:58; II Cor. 5:10; see I, pp. 320f., 332f., 337f.). But now that takes on another meaning because the imperative no longer has its foundation in the indicative as it did in Paul; because "grace" is no longer conceived in Paul's radical sense (I, pp. 289f.); and because the Spirit is no longer understood as uniting in itself both power and norm (I, pp. 336f.). Symptomatic of this change in meaning is the fact that "repentance" and "forgiveness of sins" which Paul almost never mentions (I, pp. 287, 317) now become prevalent.

As the term "faith" loses its Pauline (and Johannine) meaning, so does the term "*righteousness.*" "Righteousness of God" in Paul's sense is no longer found at all (on Jas. 1:20; II Pet. 1:1, see I, p. 285). Also the unmodified noun "righteousness" and the unmodified verb "be rightwised" are only rarely used in the forensic-eschatological sense, and even then it is not always clear whether the reference is to the rightwising of the believer which has already occurred (certainly so in Tit. 3:7; perhaps in I Clem. 35:2) or to the rightwising which is to come (Barn. 4:10, where it is said in so many words that we are not yet "made righteous"; 15:7; Pol. Phil. 8:1; Ign. Philad. 8:2; II Clem. 11:1; probably also I Clem. 30:3; 32:4). In the majority of cases *dikaiosyne* and *dikaios* denote moral uprightness (§ 58, 3 *passim*). When Polycarp writes "concerning *dikaiosyne*" (Pol. Phil. 3:1) that means that he is giving an ethical parenesis.

Dikaiosyne as uprightness or moral conduct—see, for instance: Eph. 4:24; 5:9; I Tim. 1:9; 6:11; II Tim. 2:22; 3:16; Acts 13:10; Jas. 5:6, 16; I Pet. 3:12; II Pet. 2:7f.; Rev. 22:11; Barn. 1:6; 19:6; Pol. Phil. 9:2; mostly so in I Clement, consistently so in Didache and II Clement, almost always so in Hermas. The following expressions are typical: "do, ποιεῖν, uprightness," already found in I Jn. 2:29; 3:7, 10, then in Rev. 22:11; I Clem. 31:2; II Clem. 4:2; 11:7; "practice, ἐργάζεσθαι, uprightness" Acts 10:35; Heb. 11:33; I Clem. 33:8 ("work a work of uprightness"), often in Hermas (e.g., mand. VIII 2: "practice great uprightness"): "do, πράσσειν, uprightness" II Clem. 19:3. (*cf.* δικαιοπραγία, "exercise-of-uprightness," I Clem. 32:3); "to will upright things" Herm. vis. I 1:8; "way of uprightness" II Pet. 2:21; Barn. 1:4, 5:4; II Clem. 5:7; "reward of uprightness," Did. 5:2; Barn. 20:2; II Clem. 20:4. *Dikaiosyne* as the summation of all "virtues" (ἀρεταί), Herm. mand. 1:2, sim. VI 1:4; combined with "virtue" (ἀρετή), Herm. mand. XII 3:1, sim. VIII 10:3. The "angel of uprightness" and the "angel of wickedness" stand opposed to each other in Herm. mand. VI 2:1ff. *Dikaiosyne* as a virtue is often mentioned with one or more other virtues; e.g. with "love," II Clem. 12:1, with *pistis* (probably "fidelity") Pol. Phil. 9:2, with "hope" and *"pistis"* Barn. 1:6, with "purity" Herm. sim. IX 16:7, with "truth" I Clem. 31:2; Herm. sim. IX 25:2, or in a catalogue of virtues I Clem. 62:2; Herm. mand. VI 2:3, VIII 10, XII 3:1; with "humble" Did. 3:9; Barn. 19:6, with "worthy," σεμνός, Herm. sim. VIII 3:8. Particularly characteristic is the combining of "uprightness," "upright" or "uprightly" with ὅσιος ("devout," "pious") or its derivatives: I Clem. 14:1; 48:4, II Clem. 5:6; 6:9; 15:3, or with the equivalent adverb εὐσεβῶς, "piously," Tit. 2:12; I Clem. 62:1.

This terminology reveals that an ideal of moralistic piety is beginning to replace and to a considerable extent already has replaced the eschatological consciousness and endowment with spiritual gifts. As in Judaism it is the ideal that the servants of God shall live in piety and the fear of God as the condition for participating in future salvation. As *dikaiosyne* in the sense of right conduct takes on the meaning of "piety," so the number of expressions which denote "piety" increases.

The terms εὐσέβεια ("piety, religion" and the corresponding adjective and verb) and θεοσέβεια (once) do not occur in the New Testament until the pastorals and II Pet., then they become frequent in I and II Clem. Ὅσιος, "devout," and ὁσιότης, "devoutness" occur in the New Testament only in Eph. 4:24 and the pastorals, but are common in I and II Clement. Σεμνότης, "reverence" already emerges in the New Testament at I Tim. 2:2, occurs rather often in I Clem., and then is a great favorite with Hermas, for whom Reverence, personified, is one of the seven virgins (=virtues) who are building the tower of the Church (vis. III 8).

The use of *"fear (of God)"* and "to fear (God)" is especially revealing. Paul, too, sometimes speaks of the "fear of God" (Rom. 3:18 quoting LXX Ps. 35:2) or "of the Lord" (II Cor. 5:11), but the expression does not become a technical term for the Christian attitude until it appears in Acts 9:31, in the interpolation II Cor. 7:1, and, as "fear of Christ," in Eph. 5:21. The unqualified word "fear"

is used with the same meaning in I Pet. 1:17; 3:2, 16 (combined with
πραΰτης, "gentleness"), Jude 23. Later "fear of God" (or "of the
Lord") and "fear," unqualified, frequently occur in I Clem., Barn.,
Pol., and especially in Herm., who treats at length the two kinds of
fear—of the Lord and of the devil (mand. VII). In the New Testament
the verbal form, "to fear God (or "the Lord"), aside from the technical designation of proselytes or semi-proselytes as "God-fearers,"
is still only seldom used as a characterization of the Christian
attitude (Col. 3:22; I Pet. 2:17; Rev. 11:18; "to fear thy name"
Rev. 19:5; *cf.* 14:7; 15:4), then it becomes more frequent in I
and II Clem. and Herm. The related designation of the pious as
"slaves of God" or "of Christ" likewise becomes more and more
frequent.

Within the New Testament the term "slave of God" (or "of
Christ" or "of the Lord") occurs in the word-play of I Cor. 7:22
but not yet in the technical sense. In the technical sense (approximately equivalent to "Christian") it occurs in Col. 4:12; Eph.
6:6; II Tim. 2:24; I Pet. 2:16; Rev. 1:1; 7:3; 19:2, 5; 22:3. To be
distinguished from this is the use of the term as a title for
distinguished persons like Moses (Rev. 15:2), the prophets (Rev.
10:7; 11:18), and the apostles (current in Paul and then present
in Tit. 1:1; Acts 4:29; Jude 1; II Pet. 1:1). "To serve (or to be a
slave of) δουλεύειν, God" occurs only at Mt. 6:24=Lk. 16:13.
"To serve Christ" or "the Lord" is a term not unknown to Paul,
but one which he uses comparatively seldom and then only when
it is specially motivated by the context (Rom. 7:6 [25]; *cf.* 6:6;
Gal. 4:8f.; I Thess. 1:9). As characterization of the Christian
attitude: Col. 3:24; Acts 20:19. In Hermas "slave" (or "servant")
"of God" is a current term for "Christian"; it also occurs in the
congregational prayer I Clem. 60:2; also in II Clem. 20:1. Likewise,
"serving God" or "the Lord" is common in Hermas; it is also
found in I Clem. 26:1; 45:7; II Clem. 11:1; 17:7; 18:1; Pol. Phil.
2:1; 6:3. In Hermas the term is so worn down that he can also
say "serve faith" (mand. IX 12), "serve good things" (neuter,
mand. VIII 8), "serve the virtues" (vis. III 8:8), "serve the good
desire" mand. XII 2:5, 3:1). But nowhere except in I Pet. 2:6 is
the paradox grasped as in Paul (I Cor. 4:19; Gal. 5:13) that this
slave-existence is at the same time an existence as a free man.
That is, nowhere else is it radically understood what it means
to be a "slave of God" or of "Christ"; nowhere else is the
moralistic sense of "servitude" overcome.

4. Both in terminology and in substance it is *the influence of the synagogue* that is here at work pushing aside the theology of Paul (and of John). Not only in Heb. and Barn., in Rev., Jas., and the Did., in I Clem. and Herm. is the tradition of the synagogue dominant —partly in the form of written sources—but it is also detectable in the deutero-Pauline literature: Col., Eph., the pastorals, and I Pet. The Church is on the way to straying into a religious moralism. Besides the writings of Paul and John the forces which work against this are two. On the one hand there is the tradition of Jesus' preaching contained in the synoptics; its radical demand for obedience and its message of grace could hamper the development of moralism, but it could also come to be of service to such a development. On the other hand there is the Kyrios-cult and sacramentalism. *The effect of Jesus' preaching* remained at first remarkably weak. Is it detectable at all in any other way than that the love-commandment generally appears as the highest of the ethical demands? At any rate, it is striking that sayings of Jesus are extraordinarily seldom quoted.

Paul rarely quotes words of Jesus (I, pp. 188f.); elsewhere in the New Testament a saying of Jesus is quoted only at Acts 20:35 and perhaps at I Tim. 5:18 in case the "scripture" here quoted is intended to be Lk. 10:7. In Jas. there are perhaps some allusions to words of Jesus (e.g. 5:12), but no quotations. After the New Testament the only quotation of considerable extent is Did. 1:3–6; quotations of smaller extent: Did. 8:2 (the Lord's prayer), 9:5; 15:3f.? (in addition perhaps a few allusions: 11:7; 13:1; 16:1f.?); I Clem. 13:2; 46:8; Pol. Phil. 2:3; 7:2; in II Clem. rather numerous (2:4 as "scripture"; 3:2; 4:2, 5; 5:2–4; 6:1f.; 8:5; 9:11; 12:2 quite apocryphal, 13:4; 14:1?). In Ignatius there are at the most a few allusions (Eph. 14:2; Pol. 2:2; Sm. 1:1?). Barnabas places Old Testament sayings or sayings that he himself has formed upon the lips of Jesus (7:5, 11), but quotes none of the words of Jesus known to us in the tradition; allusions to such: 5:9; 7:9?; 21:2?. Hermas once expressly adduces a saying of Jesus (sim. IX 31:2) and several times is perhaps alluding to a saying of Jesus (mand. IV 1:6; sim. IX 20:3?; 29:1–3). Nevertheless, words of Jesus, as papyrus finds prove, must have circulated abundantly in the congregations. Those which are quoted by the so-called Apostolic Fathers are all incorporated in ethical parenesis.

At any rate, only *the Kyrios-cult with its sacramentalism* directly constitutes a real counterbalance to moralism. That is clearest in Ignatius, for whom the effect of baptism does not lie exclusively in the cancellation of former sins: in union with the Eucharist it gives the entire Christian life a sacramental character (II, pp. 193 f.). Nevertheless, Ignatius is the only one after Paul and John who grasped the fact that Christian existence is transcendent in character and is determined by the Spirit, even though he understands divorce from the world not primarily as freedom from the power of sin but as freedom from transitoriness. It is also significant that he is almost the only one for whom the Eucharist plays a role, whereas even in Colossians and Ephesians, in which sacramentalism and the pneumatic character of the Ecclesia do also come into play, only baptism is mentioned. In the context of regulations for the congregation the Did. naturally gives directions not only for baptism but also for the Eucharist (9–10, 14:1) and in the eucharistic prayer of thanksgiving we read: "but to us thou hast given the gift of spiritual food and drink and of life eternal through thy Servant (or Child)" (10:3). Otherwise, the Eucharist is only seldom mentioned (Acts 2:42; 20:7; Jude 12). Of course, the celebration of it is everywhere presupposed, and it is likely included among the "sacrifices" and "services" of I Clem. 40:2. As Justin Martyr and the well-known letter of Pliny show, it is an identification mark of the Christian congregations. But there is nothing to indicate that it was significant for the self-understanding of Christian existence. In spite of that, however, it must have been one factor among others that gave the Church the consciousness of being a fellowship borne up by forces that are not of this world.

For the Church is also conscious of having been called by divine grace and of having been given the Spirit (see above, II, p. 200.) Though it is difficult to say how "grace" and the "Spirit" determine Christian existence when they are not understood in Paul's sense, the conviction is still there that they manifest themselves in Christian conduct (II Tim.:7; I Clem. 2:2; Barn. 1:2ff.; Ign. Sm. intr.). And though no unity is achieved between such statements and the imperatives in which the winning of salvation is made dependent upon one's own effort, such statements nevertheless testify to a consciousness of being borne up. This consciousness finds manifold expression; for instance: Col. 1:12–14, 24; 2:10–15; Eph. 1:6–14; 2:1–9; Tit. 2:11–14; I Pet. 1:3–12; 2:7–10; II Pet. 1:3f., in the triumph-

songs of Revelation (II, p. 173), I Clem. 36:1f. (II, p. 188), Barn. 16:9
(II, p. 164), II Pet. 1:6f. It is alive in the consciousness of belonging
to the Ecclesia (Col., Eph., the pastorals, I and II Clem.) or to the
new People of God (I Pet., Heb., Barn.).

Neither is the knowledge lost that the activity of grace and the
Spirit manifests itself in the capacity (and the obligation which it
involves) given to the individual to exert himself on behalf of the
congregation, as the following passages show: Eph. 4:7; I Pet. 4:10f.;
I Clem. 38:1f.; 48:5f.; Did. 1:5. Do miraculous phenomena such as
healings (I, p. 154) still occur? If they do, they play no role in the
literature, at any rate (Heb. 2:4 is speaking of the past). In quite
general terms Ignatius mentions spiritual gifts (χαρίσματα) that were
given to the congregation or its bishop (Sm. intr., Pol. 2:2); in so
speaking, he is thinking, immediately at least, of the manifestation
of Christian and dutiful conduct. It may be that he also includes
experiences of pneumatic inspiration in the service of worship such
as the one he reports of himself (Philad. 7:1f.; *cf.* Rom. 7:2) and
certainly also includes the singing of "psalms, hymns, and spiritual
songs" of which Col. 3:16 and Eph. 5:19 speak (Ign. Eph. 4:2; Rom.
2:2). The old activity of Christian prophets (I, pp. 41 and 154) lives on
(Eph. 2:20; 3:5; 4:11; I Tim. 1:18; 4:14; Rev. 2:20; 22:6, 9; Did. 11–13;
15:1f., Herm. mand. XI) but it begins to be suspect, as the Did. and
Herm. and also Rev. 2:20 indicate, and one must take care to distinguish the genuine from the false prophets. Books of revelation also
continue to be written, as Rev. and Herm. show, but reflection on
the part of the author (especially in Herm.) outweighs the prophetic
inspiration.

According to Did. 15:1 the place of the prophets (and teachers)
is being taken by the congregational officials, and the direction of
development is that the "gift" is becoming the official equipment of
these officers (§ 52, 3). But the consciousness of belonging to a fellowship filled with pneumatic forces lives on even when these forces are
administered by an ecclesiastical institution—in fact, in just such a
situation it may become especially strong and certain. And this
consciousness creates a compensation for the consciousness of being
under the demand of the imperative and left to one's own efforts for
salvation. An organic unity of both motifs—though not in Paul's
sense—will be achieved only when the sacrament of penance develops,
a sacrament by which the effect of baptism can be again and again

renewed. And it sounds almost like a reference to that which is to come when I Clem. 7:4 calls the "grace" given the world by Christ's death the "grace" (or "gift") "of repentance"; for under this term the author understands not baptismal repentance alone. But until the time when "repentance" will be regulated by the sacrament of penance, the Church will be afflicted by the inner contradiction which exists between having its conduct placed under the "new law" with its "ordinances" and "commandments, on the one hand, and the claim or the assurance, on the other hand, that in baptism it has received the Spirit which makes life new.

§ 60. The Content of the Ethical Demand

1. What is the content of the "new law"? What do the "commandments," the "ordinances," and the "commands" (προστάγματα) demand? What must one do to obey?

The consciousness of belonging to the Ecclesia, which by its very nature does not belong to the world, the consciousness of the Church's separateness and its delimitation from the world remained alive generally (§ 10, 3 and § 53, 1). Consistent with this is *the basic character of the ethical demand*. Its immediate character is *negative*: they who (by baptism) are purified and sanctified are called to purify and sanctify themselves (§ 10, 4) to renounce "worldly" or "fleshly" desires and refrain from all evil (see especially I, pp. 104f. and what is said at II, p. 208 concerning "world," κόσμος).

In *catalogues of vices* lists are made, as they already were by Paul, of the desires and sins that one must avoid (I, p. 72). Frequently, as already in Gal. 5:19–23, they are paralleled with a contrasting *catalogue of virtues* (Col. 3:5–14; Eph. 4:31f.; I Tim. 6:4–11; Jas. 3:15–18; *cf.* also I Clem. 35:5; II Clem. 4:3; Herm. sim. IX 15: opposed to the twelve virtue-virgins stand twelve women clad in black, the vices); but the catalogues of virtues may also stand by themselves (Eph. 4:2f.; II Pet. 1:5–7, Herm. vis. III 8). Side by side with these catalogues or mingled with them there are also *lists resembling catechisms* of commandments and prohibitions according to the scheme of the "two ways," the ways of life and death or of light and darkness. This scheme, like the catalogues, was taken over from the Hellenistic synagogue. In Did. 1–6 and Barn. 18–20 a catechism for proselytes arranged according to this scheme has been worked in.

Into it words of Jesus have been inserted in Did. 1:3–6. Similarly
sayings of Jesus also appear elsewhere in parenesis (II, p. 215). As a
matter of course Old Testament sayings of an exhortatory or threatening character are also adopted (I Pet. 3:10–12; Jas. 4:6; Heb. 3:7–11;
10:37f.; 12:12; I Clem. 8:4; 14–15; Barn. 2:10; 3:3–5; 4:11, etc.). The
vices listed include typical sins such as sensual greed and sexual
passion, envy and covetousness, wrath, hatred, evil words and lying,
etc. The listing is not determined by any systematic order nor are
the several vices or virtues derived from a principle, an ethical ideal.
The listing is loose, guided by associations of content or form.

In addition to pareneses offered in the form of catalogue or
catechism there is also *the developed parenesis*. The warning against
vices and the admonition to exercise the virtues in I Clem. is developed
with homiletical breadth according to such catch-words as "jealousy"
(3–6), "humility" (13–16), "harmony" (20–22). In the process,
examples from the Old Testament are abundantly given, but also
some from the present and even from heathen saga and history (e.g.
3–6, 11–16, 20–22, 55). Developed parenesis also occurs in James, the
author of which dwells rather long upon single themes (2:1–13:
partiality; 3:1–12: sins of the tongue; 3:13–18: conceit over wisdom;
4:1–5: contention and desire for the world; 4:13–17: admonitions to
business men; 5:1–6; warnings to the rich). Especially in the *Mandata*
Hermas describes virtues and vices with their blessing or terrifying
consequences, often in dialogue-form. He contrasts against each other,
for example: "simplicity" and "evil-speaking" (mand. II), "truth"
and "falsehood" (mand. III), "purity" and "adultery" (mand. IV),
"long-suffering" and "quickness to wrath" (mand. V), "grief" and
"joyfulness" (mand. X); or he describes the two kinds of "fear"—of
God and of the devil (mand. VI) and likewise the two kinds of
"temperance" (mand. VIII), and of "desire" (mand. XII), and of
"luxury" (sim. VI).

2. Seen as a whole all the separate commandments stand under *the
demand for sanctification*: the renunciation of "the world," of one's
former (heathen) way of life, and of the fleshly desires. Now the
decisive question is whether this demand for sanctification is understood and unfolded solely, or at least in essence, in the negative sense,
resulting in asceticism and hence in the ideal of the individualistic
holiness of the *homo religiosus*—or whether, as in Paul (§ 38, 3), it
simultaneously has a positive sense as the demand which points the

individual into fellowship with others, in which he is to do the good in selflessness. As long as "the world" is understood as the sphere of sin which by men's own fault has become a power over them (§ 26, 2 and § 44), the demand for renunciation of the world will be a genuine ethical demand, and the unity of the negative and the positive sense of sanctification will be preserved. It is probably necessary to acknowledge that from the beginning both tendencies—the purely negative and the also positive—are present and competing with each other, for even in Paul a dualistic-ascetic motif is already at work, as we have seen (I, p. 202). Historically regarded, it is a question of how the influences of the synagogal tradition and of popular-philosophical (Stoic) ethics, on the one hand, and of Hellenistic-Gnostic dualism, on the other hand, work with each other or against each other. In the course of time two different types of Christian piety develop, depending upon whether the one or the other of these two tendencies preponderates; for the most part, however, the boundary between them cannot be sharply drawn.

That unity stands forth, preserved, where the catalogue of vices is paralleled by a corresponding catalogue of virtues (see above, II, p. 218), but also wherever the admonition to abstain from the "passions of the flesh" has the demand for "good works" combined with it, as I Pet. 2:11f. formulates it (*cf.* Tit. 3:8). It is generally so in the pareneses of Col. and Eph., of the pastorals, Heb., Jas., I Clem., and Pol. to the Philippians. The preponderance of the positive sense of sanctification also expresses itself in the fact that the positive sense is developed by means of a host of single terms and instructions, while only a few terms are on supply to denote the negative sense. Those used for the negative sense, in addition to the general ones like "faithfulness" ($\pi\acute{\iota}\sigma\tau\iota\varsigma$), "uprightness," "piety" ($\epsilon\dot{\upsilon}\sigma\acute{\epsilon}\beta\epsilon\iota\alpha$), "reverence" ($\sigma\epsilon\mu\nu\acute{o}\tau\eta\varsigma$), are: $\dot{\epsilon}\gamma\kappa\rho\acute{a}\tau\epsilon\iota\alpha$ "self-control" in general, often specifically "continence"), $\dot{\upsilon}\pi o\mu o\nu\acute{\eta}$ ("patience," "endurance"), $\dot{a}\kappa\alpha\kappa\acute{\iota}\alpha$ ("innocence"), $\dot{a}\pi\lambda\acute{o}\tau\eta\varsigma$ ("simplicity," "generosity"), $\dot{a}\gamma\nu\epsilon\acute{\iota}\alpha$ ("purity") —though in individual cases where they are used one can be in doubt whether they mean more the Christian's negative relation to the world or whether they have a reference to living in fellowship with others.

Particularly indicative of the double-sidedness of the ethical demand is the virtue of "self-control" ($\dot{\epsilon}\gamma\kappa\rho\acute{a}\tau\epsilon\iota\alpha$) only rarely used in the New Testament but later more frequently named, which primarily denotes the negative side of sanctification. But it scarcely stands out as the one dominant demand; rather it is cited, as it already is in Gal. 5:23, as one virtue among others in catalogues of virtues (Tit. 1:8; II Pet. 1:6; I Clem. 30:3; 35:2; 38:2; 62:2; 64; II Clem. 4:3; Barn. 2:2; Pol. Phil. 4:2; 5:2). Nevertheless, a pre-eminent importance is ascribed to it when according to Acts 24:25 the moving theme of Paul's address before Felix and Drusilla is "righteousness and self-control." Likewise, when II Clem. 15:1 designates the author's intention in writing by saying that he has given the readers weighty advice "concerning self-control," which also is in harmony with his admonition to "keep the flesh pure" (II, p. 170). Or again when Hermas (mand. I 2, VI 1:1) regards the first commandment after that of "faith" and "fear (of God)" to be "self-control" or when in the dance of the Virtues "Self-control" is the daughter of "Faith" and the foremother of all the ensuing Virtues (vis. III 8:4ff.; *cf.* sim. IX 15:2). Even by Hermas, however, "self-control" is conceived not as asceticism but rather as abstinence "from all evil," and its opposite is "doing good" (mand. VIII); though it must be granted that ascetic features are not lacking in Hermas (vis. II 2:3, sim. IX 11; see below).

The positive sense of abstinence from the world comes out in one way in the fact that practically everywhere "good works" are demanded, but above all it comes out in the fact that among all the commandments the love-commandment occupies the highest place. The demands for living in fellowship all stand ultimately under the commandment of love. It appears in almost all pareneses and only in the writings which are most dependent upon Jewish tradition (such as Rev., Heb., Jas., and Herm.) is it more rarely found, while it occurs frequently within the circle of Pauline influence. "Love" (noun or verb) often appears in catalogues of virtues, frequently receiving in them a special accent by being placed at the beginning of the list (as in Gal. 5:22 and II Clem. 4:3) or at the end. Thus the list in Col. 3:12–14 closes with the sentence: "And above all these (put on) love, which is the uniting-band of perfection" (tr.). "Love" is at the end of the series at II Pet. 1:5–7, and in Herm. vis. III 8:5, 7 it is the last-named of the Virtues (*cf.* sim. IX 15:2; 18:4). I Clem. 49 is a panegyric on love (under the influence of I Cor. 13), the bond which unites us with God, and 50:1 draws this conclusion: "See . . . how great and marvelous love is! Nor is there any describing of its perfection" (tr.). "Love" is often used with "faith" as if to denote the essence of Christianity (I Tim. 1:14; 2:15; 4:12; II Tim. 1:13; 2:22; Barn. 1:4; 11:8; II Clem. 15:2; Herm. sim. IX 17:4). This is especially frequent in Ignatius who asserts in Sm. 6:1: "For the whole of the matter is faith and love, than which nothing is more highly esteemed" (tr.) (*cf.* Eph. 14:1f.; Philad. 9:2). Occasionally "hope" is associated with them, resulting in the triad of I Cor. 13:13; it is so in Pol. Phil. 3:2f., at the end of which we read: "for he who has love is far from all sin" (*cf.* Barn. 1:4–6; Heb. 10:22–24). Other combinations also occur (with "sanctification" I Tim. 2:5; with "purity" I Tim. 4:12; Pol. Phil. 4:2; with "fear" I Clem. 51:1; with "righteousness" II Clem. 12:1). That love brings about forgiveness of sins is often said (II, p. 210). Barnabas addresses his readers as "children of love" (9:7; 21:9), and in Ignatius "love" is the bond which binds the congregation together into the unity of a choir (Eph. 4:1f.; Rom. 2:2) and also the bond which unites the writer with his readers (Eph. 1:1; Tr. 12:3). Demonstration of love is what all the single virtues ultimately are: "mildness," "long-suffering," "meekness," "humility," "harmony," "compassion," "brotherly love," "hospitality"; also: "helping each other" ($\dot{a}\nu\tau\acute{\epsilon}\chi\epsilon\sigma\theta\alpha\iota$ $\dot{a}\lambda\lambda\acute{\eta}\lambda\omega\nu$) and "forgiving one another" and conducting one's self as one who is $\dot{a}\nu\upsilon\pi\acute{o}\kappa\rho\iota\tau\sigma$ ("un-hypocritical," "genuine"), "peaceful," "reasonable," "docile," "merciful," etc. All such virtues are singled out *not as traits of character but as modes of conduct in fellowship with others.* They are not derived from an ideal picture of humanity or personality, even when here and there Greek virtues are taken over such as $\sigma\omega\phi\rho\sigma\sigma\acute{\upsilon}\nu\eta$ ("prudence" and "moderation"), $\alpha\dot{\iota}\delta\acute{\omega}$ ("modesty"), $\dot{\epsilon}\pi\iota\epsilon\acute{\iota}\kappa\epsilon\iota\alpha$ ("reasonableness") or the term $\kappa\acute{o}\sigma\mu\iota\sigma$ ("that which is comely or becoming") and $\kappa\sigma\sigma\mu\epsilon\hat{\iota}\sigma\theta\alpha\iota$ ("to be adorned"; see below). There is no thought of character-education, just as there is none of education in general.

Now one must, of course, concede that such virtues for the most part have a *negative character* in that they ultimately demand one thing: selflessness, the waiver of one's own advantage and one's own right—and that they have *purely formal character* in that they do not set up concrete goals of action, do not sketch a program for molding society. But in both respects they are the appropriate explication of the love-commandment because by its own nature it will not tolerate formulated positive determinations (§ 2, 4) if it is not to relapse into law. It is completely described both in the "Golden

Rule" (Mt. 7:12) as well as in Paul's sentence "Love does no wrong
to a neighbor" (Rom. 13:10). For in both cases action arising from
love is guided not by looking toward some "work" (ἔργον) that is to
be accomplished but by asking what needs and troubles of my
neighbor or of society encounter me in any particular here and now.
Christian freedom must also prove itself in just this situation: the
Christian must be able to judge without a legal statute what God's
will demands of him at any given moment. Whether the liberty and
the duty to do this "distinguishing" (δοκιμάζειν, Rom. 12:2; Phil.
Phil. 1:10; § 39, 1) for one's self will continue to be held fast, is just
the question. The explicit admonition to distinguish "what is pleasing
to the Lord" is found after Paul only in Eph. 5:10; it may be permissible to discover it in Barn. 21:6 also: "And be taught of God,
seeking out what the Lord requires of you." But it may probably be
regarded as implicitly contained in the purely negative and formal
exhortations—at least to a large extent.

3. However remote any notion of an ideal picture of human
personality may have been as a point of reference for orienting
conduct, other ideal pictures did force their way in: *the ideal of
perfectionism and the ideal of holiness as a personal quality.*

The more the ethical demands made of the Christian come to be
regarded as the "commandments," the "commands" and "ordinances," which must be fulfilled as the condition for obtaining life
or salvation—and the more conduct is governed by the notion of
merit and by consideration of the judgment according to one's works
—the more there develops a striving after perfection. Then the
waiver of self demanded by the commandment of love is no longer
motivated by interest in one's neighbor and interest in fellowship
with others but by interest in one's own salvation. This can come to
the surface anywhere, but it appears in particularly crass form in
Hermas (e.g. mand. II, 4–6, sim. I, V 3:7f.). The influence of Hellenistic dualism, especially of the Gnostic kind (I, pp. 107, 173–175)
operated in the same direction as the notion of merit. The demand
for holiness changes its meaning just as the demand for love does,
and there arises the notion of holiness as a quality to be won by
renunciation of the world.

One consequence of perfectionism and the striving after holiness
is that the demand for *asceticism* becomes a temptation. That this
demand had been raised at an early time is indicated by the very

passages which polemize against it or at least admonish the ascetic
to modesty about his asceticism. I Tim. 4:3 is directed against the
heretics "who forbid marriage" and demand "abstinence from
foods" (*cf.* 2:15; 5:23; Tit. 1:14f.; perhaps also Col. 3:16–23, where it
is not clear whether it is truly ascetic tendencies that are being
combatted or merely ritualistic ones). But such a writing as II Clem.
with its demand "to keep the flesh pure" (8:4; 14:3) and its ideal of
celibacy or virginity (12:5) indicates where this path is leading.
Perhaps by the "virgin (men)" who "have not defiled themselves
with women" Rev. 14:4 means ascetics. In any case Herm. sim.
IX 11 proves that the practice of "subintroduction" (I, p. 103 n.)
which comes to view at Corinth as early as Paul's time (I Cor. 7:25,
36f.) continues to exist. Indications that Hermas himself is not far
from such tendencies are not only his designation of himself as
"Hermas the abstinent" (or "continent"), vis. I 2:4; *cf.* II 3:2, and his
admonition: "Keep this flesh of yours pure and undefiled" (sim. V 7),
but also the role which "abstinence" and "purity" and also "desire"
in specific reference to sexual life play in his book, and likewise his
interest in the question of marriage (the "wife" of Hermas shall
become his "sister," vis. II 2:3; and in mand. IV 1 and 4 marriage is
advised against).

The demand for asceticism as a demand applying to all Christians
did not establish itself, but as a commandment which individuals
take upon themselves, it was not contested. And the admonitions
that the ascetic is not to be haughty (I Clem. 38:2; 48:6; Ign. Pol.
5:2) indicate by themselves that the way is being prepared for the
differentiation of two levels of morality. But it is not merely this
striving after ascetic holiness which leads to the differentiation of a
perfect holiness from a lower level of morality: perfectionism operates
in the same direction. For it necessarily quickly became evident that
the demand for "abstinence" in the sense of consistent refraining
from all worldly needs, pleasures, and occupations was not universally
practicable—as the pastorals and Hermas illustrate. Therefore, it
cannot surprise us that the concept of "perfection" ($\tau\epsilon\lambda\epsilon\iota\acute{o}\tau\eta s$,
$\tau\acute{e}\lambda\epsilon\iota o\nu$) takes on a new meaning. In Mt. 5:48 $\tau\acute{e}\lambda\epsilon\iota o s$ (Lk. 6:36 has
a different word) seems still to be used in the sense of Hebrew שָׁלֵם or
תָּמִים (whole and complete, whole-hearted, without breach or inner
dividedness). In Mt. 19:21 (not found in Mk. 10:21) it means, on the
contrary, "perfect" in the sense of perfectionism; likewise in Did.

1:4; 6:2, in the latter of which two levels of morality are clearly
distinguished. Though Paul had used τέλειος not with the Semitic
but with a Greek meaning, he meant by it not "perfection" but
"adulthood" (I Cor. 14:20; Phil. 3:15); the same meaning appears in
Heb. 6:1. But Ignatius urges for perfection (Eph. 1:1; 15:2; Sm. 11:2f.);
in him the negative admonition to divorce from the world quite
overweighs the positive admonition to love, and for him the ideal
of the *homo religiosus* is embodied in the figure of the martyr. Hermas,
too, takes the pre-eminent rank of the martyr for granted (vis. III
1:9–2:1; 5:2; sim. IX 28:1ff.); and in other ways, too, he differentiates
two levels of morality, for he not only distinguishes the upright from
those who need repentance (vis. III 5:3f.) but also recognizes a
meritorious conduct which goes beyond the measure of the required
(sim. V 2:4ff.; 3:3ff.).

4. Side by side with these tendencies, which find their fulfilment
in the notion of holiness and in the differentiation of a double morality
in the ancient Church, there runs another hortatory tendency of
which the Haustafeln and the pastoral epistles as a whole are
typical. In it the conception comes to light that the Christian conduct
of life derives its Christian character not from the fulfilling of special
moral demands and from an idea of perfection or holiness upon which
they depend, but from *following such simple ethical demands as can
be familiar to anyone*. Here Paul's admonition is followed: "whatever
is true, whatever is respectable, whatever is right, whatever is
innocent, whatever is well-regarded, whatever is reputable—anything
that is a virtue, anything that deserves praise—think about it"
(Phil. 4:8 tr.). The specifically Christian element in this can only lie
in the fact that just as all the commandments of the Torah are fulfilled in the demand for love (according to Rom. 13:8–10; Gal. 5:14)
so every "virtue" is understood as a requirement of love and is to
be fulfilled by the power of love. Though a distinction from Greek
ethics is present in the fact that "virtue" is not considered from the
viewpoint of shaping character but rather under that of brotherly
fellowship (in Pauline language: of "edification," οἰκοδομή), it is also
clear that these demands in themselves require nothing which a
heathen's judgment would not also acknowledge to be good. If the
Christian Church is to bring honor to God or to the Christian faith
by its ethical conduct (a view already present in I Thess. 4:12; I Cor.
10:32 and then in Col. 4:5; I Tim. 3:7; 6:1; Tit. 2:5; 8:10; I Pet. 2:12,

15; 3:1, 16; I Clem. 1:1; 47:7; Ign. Tr. 8:2), then agreement between the moral standards of Christians and those of the heathen is presupposed.

Futhermore, Christian exhortation ingenuously takes over from *the ethics of popular philosophy* and from the store of ideas of *bourgeois morality* certain concepts and patterns of arrangement.

The schemata of moral teaching, particularly Haustafeln (schedules of household duties), such as Hellenistic Judaism had already taken over from the hortatory practice of Hellenism, are now impressed into Christian service. Such lists of duties are found in I Tim. 3:2ff.; Tit. 1:5ff.; Pol. Phil. 5:2, where the qualifications for "bishops" and "deacons" are enumerated. Especially favored are the "Haustafeln": Col. 3:18–4:1; Eph. 5:22–6:9; I Tim. 2:8–15, 6:1f.; Tit. 2:2–10; I Pet. 2:13–3:7; Did. 4:9–11; I Clem. 21:6–9; Pol. Phil. 4:2–6:2; Barn. 19:5–7 (woven into the parenesis); the praise of the Corinthian congregation, I Clem. 1:3, also follows this pattern.

The terms *"virtue," "what is proper"* (τὸ καθῆκον), and *"conscience"* (I, p. 71), all of which had already appeared in Paul, continue to occur. Especially significant is the increasingly frequent mention of "good conscience" (συνείδησις ἀγαθή, καθαρά, and the like): I Tim. 1:5, 19; 3:9; II Tim. 1:3; I Pet. 3:16, 21; Heb. 13:18; Acts 23:1; 24:16; I Clem. 1:3; 41:1; 45:7; II Clem. 16:4; Ign. Tr. 7:2; Pol. Phil. 5:3; corresponding mention of "bad (πονηρά and the like) conscience": I Tim. 4:2; Tit. 1:15; Heb. 10:2, 22; Barn. 19:12; Did. 4:14; Herm. mand. III 4.

A general characterization of Christian conduct is furnished by the terms δικαιοσύνη and εὐσέβεια—terms which on Hellenistic honorific inscriptions customarily described reverent, virtuous conduct and now also count as Christian virtues (II, p. 213). Also σεμνότης and σεμνός are taken over as designations of dignity and respectability (II, p. 213). Likewise σωφροσύνη ("prudence") is taken up among the Christian virtues: I Tim. 2:9, 15; Acts 26:25; I Clem. 62:2, 64, Ign. Eph. 10:3 (σώφρων, "prudent, sensible" I Tim. 3:2; Tit. 1:8; 2:2, 5; I Clem. 1:2; 63:3; "prudently, soberly," Tit. 2:12; σωφρονεῖν, "to be prudent, sober, sensible" in Paul at Rom. 12:3, then in Tit. 2:6; I Pet. 4:7; I Clem. 1:3; Pol. Phil. 4:3; *cf.* II Tim. 1:7; Tit. 2:4). Ἀιδώς ("modesty") is still rare (I Tim. 2:9; Heb. 12:28, *v.l.*) and so is χρηστότης ("mildness, kindness") as a Christian virtue (Col. 3:12; Eph. 4:32; I Clem. 14:3); less rare is ἐπιείκεια ("reasonableness, considerateness"; also ἐπιεικής, "reasonable")—already used by Paul, Phil. 4:5, it also occurs in I Tim. 3:3; Tit: 3:2; I Pet. 2:18; Jas. 3:17; I Clem. 1:2; 21:7; 30:8; 56:1; 58:2; 69:2; Ign. Eph. 10:3; Philad. 1:1f. A word which occurs in honorific inscriptions as a virtue, especially as a womanly virtue, κόσμιος ("decent, proper, moral") was also taken over into Christian usage: in I Tim. 2:9 as a virtue of women: in 3:2 named after σώφρων ("prudent") as a qualification for the "bishop" (*cf.* also κοσμεῖσθαι—which in these places ought perhaps to be translated not "be adorned," but "be kept in order"—I Clem. 2:8; 33:7; Ign. Eph. 9:2).

5. *The extent of the departments of living* toward which moral reflection and parenesis are directed is still a decidedly limited one. This is only natural because the Christian faith is in the main still restricted to people in humble circumstances or at least to the lower middle class. Their interests, it is true, already include, in addition to those of their own immediate circle of living, those of property and business. There are even slave-holders among them. But to undertake great enterprises, in particular to take a responsible part in politics, is still far from their mind, nor have they any such ambition. They also lack any regard for the problems and tasks of social life.

In *the high esteem for marriage* and in the views about *the disciplining of married life* the tradition of the Old Testament and Judaism, or the influence of the Hellenistic synagogue, is undoubtedly at work; also at work in addition to this is the influence of Stoic morality, for which purity of marriage and the rejection of fornication and adultery belong to the demands that are taken for granted (see especially Musonius and Epictetus).

Among the chief vices combatted in the catalogues of vices and elsewhere are "fornication," "adultery," "uncleanness" and the like. The rejection of adultery plays an especially prominent role in Hermas (mand. IV). In the Haustafeln husbands are admonished to love their wives, wives to obey their husbands, children to obey their parents, parents to be kind to their children (Col. 3:18–21; Eph. 5:22–25; 6:1–4; I Tim. 4:11; Tit. 2:4f.; I Pet. 3:1–7; *cf.* I Clem. 1:3; Ign. Pol. 5:1). Women are admonished to be modest and chaste and are warned against personal vanity (I Tim. 2:9; Tit. 2:4f.; I Pet. 3:3f.; I Clem. 1:3; 21:7; Pol. Phil. 4:2). Their duty to bear children is emphasized in I Tim. 2:15; 5:14, probably in opposition to Gnostic-ascetic tendencies (I Tim. 2:15; 5:14), the influence of which is detectable in the exaggerated demand for chastity in II Clem. and Herm., but on the whole these tendencies were rejected. They remain only in the advice against remarrying (as in I Cor. 7:11, 39f.; perhaps I Tim. 5:9, and Herm. mand. IV 4)—either after divorce or after the death of the first mate—and also in the fact that remarriage is evidently forbidden to the "bishop" or the "deacon" (I Tim. 3:2, 12; Tit. 1:6). The duty of training children to piety is often emphasized (I Tim. 3:4, 12; Tit. 1:6; especially I Clem. 21:8; Pol. Phil. 4:2; Did. 4:9; Barn. 19:5) and on occasion reference is made to the good tradition of a family (II Tim. 1:3–5, 16; 3:14f.). Even though the responsibility for the family, of which Hermas so often emphatically speaks (vis. II 2 and 3, sim. VII and elsewhere), is only a symbol for responsibility for the Christian Church, such symbolism nevertheless presupposes that duty to one's actual family is vitally felt.

Even living together in the more comprehensive community has, as it were, the character of living in a family. As parents and children are admonished to fulfil their duties toward each other, so old and young within the congregation are admonished (I Pet. 5:1–5, where the "elders" are both the "older ones" and the "presbyters," the leaders of the congregation; further: I Clem. 21:6; *cf.* 1:3; Pol. Phil. 5:3; 6:1; II Clem. 19:1). The leaders of the congregation are correspondingly directed to behave rightly toward old and young and to admonish them to perform their duties (I Tim. 5:1f.; Tit. 2:3–8). Special mention is made of duties toward widows, but also of the right conduct that is expected of them (I Tim. 5:3f.; Ign. Pol. 4:1; Pol. Phil. 4:3; Herm. mand. VIII 10, sim. IX 27:2). Providing for widows and orphans is often mentioned as a duty (Jas. 1:27; Barn. 20:2; Ign. Sm. 6:2; Pol. Phil. 6:1; Herm. vis. II 4:3, mand. VIII 10, sim. I 8, V 3:7; IX, 27:2). At an early time there was already an officially recognized status of "widow" which was marked off by special rights and duties (I Tim. 5:9ff.), and it appears to have been possible for virgins, too, to be taken into this class (Ign. Sm. 13:1). In gnosticizing circles women played a role as prophetesses or teachers as in the early period (Acts 18:26: Priscilla; Acts 21:9: Philip's four daughters as "prophesying virgins"). In the trend within the Church which had become dominant this role was denied them (I Tim. 2:1f., the interpolation I Cor. 14:34f.; Rev. 2:20). Applying to all members of the congregation and particularly to its officials we find exhortations to love, kindliness, and humility and also to agreeableness and truthfulness, and warnings against anger and envy, gossiping and lying, uncleanness and drunkenness. That the virtues demanded are "bourgeois" ones is not surprising; nevertheless, it is striking that while there is admonition to "good works," there is only rarely an exhortation to diligent toil (in Paul I Thess. 4:11f.; then also II Thess. 3:6–12; Did. 12:3f.), and that such exhortation represents this toil as having charity or penance for sins as its purpose (Eph. 4:28, Barn. 19:10). Negative exhortation preponderates: one must not walk ἀτάκτως ("lazily"; "in idleness," II Thess. 3:6, 11), not "be a busybody" (περιεργάζεσθαι, II Thess. 3:11; I Tim. 5:13), not be a "meddler in others' affairs" (I Pet. 4:15, tr.: ἀλλοτριοεπίσκοπος);* in short, it is the admonition to ἡσυχία ("quietness") or ἡσυχιάζειν ("to live quietly")—see I Thess. 4:11; II Thess. 3:12; I Tim. 2:2, 11f.; I Pet. 3:4; Did. 3:8; Barn. 19:4; Herm. mand. V 2:3–6, VI 2:3, VIII 10, XI 8. The ambition of the Congregation is none other than that which is given as the purpose of praying for the officials of the state: "that we may lead a still and quiet life in all piety and respectability" (I Tim. 2:2 tr.).

Christian conduct toward non-Christians is sketched in the advice given at Tit. 3:1f.: "Admonish them to submit to authorities and officials, to obey, to be prepared to do any good work, to defame no one, to keep from quarreling, to be reasonable, and in every respect to behave agreeably toward all men" (Blt., tr.). On the attitude toward the state, see below. The admonition to be kind to non-Christians and the warning not to repay evil with evil is urged in I Pet. 3:15f. (probably already in 3:9 also) and Ign. Eph. 10:2f. A special admonition to such conduct is laid upon Christian wives toward their heathen husbands (I Pet. 3:1f.); a corresponding admonition is addressed to Christian slaves (I Pet. 2:18f.). Christians in general are to bring honor to God and to their faith by the way they live (II, p. 225). The Church's prayers include intercession for all men (I Tim. 2:1; I Clem. 60:4; Ign. Eph. 10:1; Pol. Phil. 12:3).

How far the Christian Church was from thinking of remolding the world, of adopting an economic or political program, is indicated by its attitude toward property, slavery and the state. As for the matter of *property*, the picture of the original Church's "love-communism" sketched in Acts 2:45; 4:32–35 stands isolated in the

---

* The meaning of the compound can only be conjectured (Tr.).

tradition and is representative only insofar as it is a pattern for the love which is prepared to bring about that "equality" of which Paul speaks in II Cor. 8:13f.: the surplus of one man is to supply the need of another. The custom of setting aside money for the needy on Sunday (I Cor. 16:2) became the fixed practice of taking up a collection in the Sunday worship-service, which is placed at the disposal of the congregation's leader for charity (Justin Martyr, apol. I 67:6). "Love-communism" of this sort always remained a voluntary matter; just as Paul neither knew a "command" to this effect (II Cor. 8:8) nor wished that giving should be done "reluctantly or under compulsion" (II Cor. 9:7), neither did the succeeding period. Therefore, it is no surprise to discover that in that succeeding period economic equality does not exist in the congregations but rich and poor are found side by side. But we can well understand that a distrust of wealth arises (Jas. 2:1–7) and that admonitions to the rich and warnings against acquisitiveness and greed increase in number (I Tim. 6:6–10, 17–19; Jas. 5:1–6; Heb. 13:5; Herm. vis. III 6:5–7, sim. I, VIII 9:1, etc.). Especially Hermas exhorts his readers to charity, which benefits the rich man himself, because the poor man's prayer of thanksgiving ascends in his favor (vis. III 9:2–6, mand. II 4–6, VIII 10, especially sim. II). Hand in hand with the warning against wealth goes that against business and worldly "pursuits" and "occupations" (II Tim. 2:4; Jas. 4:13–16; Herm. vis. I 3:1, III 6:5, mand. III 5, X 1:4f., sim. IV 5, VI 3:5, VIII 8:1f., IX 20:1f.).

In the matter of *slavery* Paul's standpoint is maintained (I Cor. 7:21f.; *cf.* Philemon); i.e. so far as it is a matter of this world's social order, the slavery question does not exist for the Christian Church. The fact that slavery exists is accepted as a part of the given world order which it is not the task of Christians to alter. Hence it also causes no offense that there are Christian masters who own slaves. But the Christian faith's independence from and superiority to the world's order demonstrate themselves in the fact that within the Church the difference between master and slave has no validity because both, as Christians, are brothers. Nevertheless, the slaves must not deduce from that fact a right to be disrespectful to their Christian masters (I Tim. 6:1f.; Ign. Pol. 4:3) nor raise a claim to be bought free at the expense of the congregation (Ign. Pol. 4:3). For the masters, whether Christian or heathen, are their masters only κατὰ σάρκα, "according to the flesh"—on the world's plane—(Col. 3:22;

Eph. 6:5); their true master is Christ, and in fear of him they are to serve their earthly masters faithfully as if it were a service rendered to their true Lord (Col. 3:22–25; Eph. 6:5–8 *cf.* I Tim. 6:1f.; Tit. 2:9f.; Did. 4:11; Barn. 19:7). They are patiently to endure whatever unjust treatment they may experience and remember the innocent suffering of Christ (I Pet. 2:18–25). But the masters are also correspondingly admonished to grant their slaves whatever is right and fair (Col. 4:1), not to deal threateningly with them (Eph. 6:9; Did. 4:10; Barn. 19:7), and not to be haughty toward them (Ign. Pol. 4:3).

As for *the Christian relation to the state*, here, too, it holds true that the Christian is to submit to it as a given order, for it was instituted by God (as in Rom. 13:1–7, so also in I Clem. 61:1). The Christian owes it obedience (Tit. 3:1; I Clem. 60:4) even when, and precisely when, he is under its suspicion as a Christian (I Pet. 2:13–17; 4:16). At an early time the Christian Church took over from the synagogue the custom of praying for the civil authorities (I Tim. 2:1f.; I Clem. 61:1f.; Pol. Phil. 12:3). The author of Acts takes pains to emphasize the loyalty of Christians to the state and to prove the assertion that they were enemies of the state to be a Jewish slander (18:12ff.; 21:27ff.; 23:29; 25:18f.; 26:31). The hatred toward Rome which breaks out in Rev. rests not upon a rejection of the existing civil order on principle but upon indignation over its demand of emperor-worship, at which Christian obedience naturally draws the line. For that reason one must not regard the attitude of Revelation as contradictory to the general Christian acknowledgment of the civil order. This order is simply not questioned, but it belongs, of course, to the transitory orders of this world. Consequently, no obligation is felt to take over responsibility for it or for the just administration of it—a situation for which one of the causes, of course, is the fact that the Christians still belonged primarily to those social classes for which such responsibility was out of the question.

§ 61. Church Discipline

1. Concern for *the purity of the Church* has its foundation not merely in the individual's interest in salvation but is also a concern of the Church as a whole, for it as a whole is supposed to be and professes to be the Congregation of the saints. It lies in its own interest, therefore, to develop a discipline which by admonition or

punishment trains the individual members and in the extreme case eliminates unworthy members. But the purity of the Church is endangered not only by unethical conduct of its members but also by false teaching. This, too, ranks as sin (see especially Ignatius), and it accords with Jewish tradition that a causal connection like that between heathenism and a life of vice (I, p. 72) is seen between false teaching and the vices, as the polemic found in the pastorals and Jude and II Pet. indicates.

Responsibility for the purity of the Church resides at first—and in a certain sense we may say continually—*in all members of the congregation*. As Paul had admonished the Thessalonians: "Exhort one another and build one another up" (I Thess. 5:11, tr.) and specifically: "set right the idle" (5:14, tr.) and as he had assumed in the Roman Christians the ability to "set yourselves right" (νουθετεῖν ἑαυτούς, Rom. 15:14, tr.), so similar admonitions continue to be given: "to set yourselves (or ἀλλήλους, "each other") right" (Col. 3:16; I Clem. 56:2; II Clem. 17:2); "to exhort" (παρακαλεῖν, Heb. 3:13; 10:25; Barn. 19:10; Herm. mand. VIII 10, XII 3:2); "to reprove" (ἐλέγχειν, Did. 15:3; *cf.* 2:7; 4:3; Barn. 19:4; also Eph. 5:11, but this probably refers not to erring Christians but to pagans; to whom Jude 22 refers is not clear). Fathers and mothers, specifically, have the duty of disciplining their children or their family (παιδεύειν, see Eph. 6:4; I Clem. 21:8; Pol. Phil. 4:2; Herm. vis. II 3:1f.; νουθετεῖν, "correct, set right" Herm. vis. I 3:1f.); older persons have the same duty toward younger persons (I Clem. 21:6).

But this task pertains particularly to certain responsible persons, especially to *the leaders of the congregations* whose duty it is to "admonish," as the pastorals again and again urge (I Tim. 4:13; 5:1; 6:3; II Tim. 4:2; Tit. 1:9; 2:6, 15; also Ign. Pol. 1:2), and this is given as their purpose in writing by the author of Hebrews (13:19, 22) and repeatedly by Ignatius (Eph. 3:2; Mg. 14:1; Tr. 6:1, etc.). Upon the leader of the congregation falls the duty of παιδεύειν ("correcting, disciplining," II Tim. 2:25; Herm. vis. III 9:10; *cf.* sim XI 31:5f.), or of νουθετεῖν ("setting right,"—the same term as in I Thess. 5:12— presupposed to be the leader's duty in Col. 1:28; Acts 20:31; II Clem. 17:3; 19:2 and exercised as his duty in I Clem. 7:1) or of ἐλέγχειν ("reproving, rebuking," I Tim. 5:20; II Tim. 4:2; Tit. 1:9, 13; 2:15).

2. In particularly bad cases *the sinner* (or the teacher of error, as the case may be) *must be excluded from the congregation*—whether it

be because his sin is so great as to make association with the sinner utterly impossible or because the attempts at admonishing and correcting him have been in vain. From Rev. 2:14f., 20f. it is to be gathered that heretics must be excluded; from Rev. 22:15, that all gross sinners must. Paul himself had already demanded that the evil-doer who was "living with his father's wife" be "delivered to Satan" (I Cor. 5:1–5)—which must mean be excommunicated. The author of the pastorals similarly says that he has delivered two heretics to Satan (I Tim. 1:20), while the "Paul" of II Thess. 3:6, 14f., though he does forbid the readers to associate with the sinner, nevertheless evidently means this only in a limited and temporary way, for he says: "Do not regard him as an enemy, but set him right as a brother" (tr.). The advice given in Pol. Phil. 11:4 is similar. II Tim. 2:25f., too, admonishes the leader of the congregation to correct the heretics in kindness in order that they may come to repentance and knowledge and escape the devil's snares. But in case kindly correction fails, exclusion must follow, according to Tit. 3:10. That is probably also the meaning of Jude 22f., but they are verses having a very uncertain text-transmission. In Did. 14:2 temporary suspension of association with people who are quarreling is demanded until they are reconciled with each other; in 15:3 association with a member who has wronged another is likewise forbidden until he has repented. Jas. 5:19f. also admonishes Christians to lead back the brother who has wandered away from the truth (*cf.* II Clem. 15:1). The same attitude toward a sinner is recommended by Herm. mand. IV 1:9, but Ignatius advises that one should not even speak with heretics either in private or in public (Sm. 7:2; *cf.* Eph. 7:1).

Definite rules soon had to be created both for the *restitution* of a temporarily excluded member and for the *conclusive exclusion of* a notorious and incorrigible sinner (or heretic), but in the sources at our disposal there is little to be learned about such rules. We probably can assume that at first it was the assembled congregation that made the decision on conclusive exclusion, as Paul had demanded of the Corinthians (I Cor. 5:4f.). The presupposition for the restitution of a repentant sinner was certainly from the outset a confession of repentance made before the congregation. So we read in Did. 4:14: "In the congregation you shall confess your transgressions and not proceed to your prayer with a bad conscience," even though here those who are to be received back after temporary exclusion are not

[233]

thought of as especially grave sinners. (The same direction is found in Barn. 19:12, but in this case "in the congregation" is lacking.) The confession of sin demanded of the rebels at Corinth in I Clem. 51f. is surely meant to be one to be made before the whole congregation. The same thing is to be deduced from Ign. Philad. 3:2, where we hear of those who "having repented come to the unity of the Church," and from 8:1, where repentance is described as a "repenting to the unity of God and (to) the bishop's council." Since the restitution was undoubtedly confirmed by admitting the penitent to the congregation's service of worship and specifically to the Lord's Supper, it is to be assumed that that is just where the confession of repentance was made. This may also be gathered, probably, from the fact that according to Did. 14:1 the whole congregation is to confess its "transgressions" before participating in the Eucharist (in some such way as in the prayer of I Clem. 60:1f.); this must apply, then, all the more to the graver sinners. They may be meant by the call which precedes the celebration of the Eucharist: "If anyone be holy, let him come (to the Eucharist); if he be not, let him repent" (Did. 10:6). In Herm. vis. III 1:5ff. Ecclesia raises Hermas, who has confessed his sins, from his knees. Is this scene composed on the pattern of a liturgical usage in which the sinner after confessing his sins before the congregation was raised up and comforted by the leader of the congregation? And is the angel of repentance in Hermas patterned after the congregational officer effecting the acceptance of the penitent? When Hermas is ordered to communicate the instructions he has received from the lady Ecclesia (vis. II 4:3) to Clement and to the "elders who preside over the congregation," the purpose surely is that they may act according to them. Aside from this we learn nothing further of any officially granted absolution (see vis. II 2:4f.) from this early period.

3. But it was inevitable that the question of *distinguishing between light and grave sins* should soon arise. In I Jn. 5:14–21, a supplement made by some ecclesiastical revision, verse 16 distinguishes between sins that are "not mortal" ($\mu\dot\eta\ \pi\rho\grave{o}s\ \theta\acute{a}\nu\alpha\tau\text{o}\nu$) and those that are "mortal" ($\pi\rho\grave{o}s\ \theta\acute{a}\nu\alpha\tau\text{o}\nu$), and for the latter even intercession is declined. What sort of sins that means, is not said. The ideal of a sinless Church naturally could not be maintained: it was necessary to be content with an average uprightness on the part of the members of the Church. In distinction from "deliberate" sins

(Heb. 10:26) one could put up with "unintentional" sins (I Clem. 2:3) as inevitable, and one could trust that the congregation's general confession of sin and prayer for forgiveness would bring about forgiveness. Only notorious heresy and gross moral trespasses inevitably remained an offense, particularly apostasy and denial of the faith in times of oppression. The excommunication of "heretics" certainly did not always take place by an explicit ban such as I Tim. 1:20 presupposes and Rev. 2:14f., 20 demands. The "heretics" probably often removed themselves from the "orthodox" congregations on their own volition (*cf.* I Jn. 2:19), claiming orthodoxy for themselves and accusing the others of heresy. III John and Ignatius give us some idea of how such splits inevitably arose.

There were grave sins which caused temporary exclusion but which could be forgiven after confession and repentance. Evidently of this sort at first were adultery and fornication, as their position in the catalogues of vices and also the admonitions referring to them indicate. That they were regarded in many circles as unforgivable may be taken to be indicated by Heb. 12:16f.; 13:4, and by the later practice of the Church down to the edict of Callixtus (217/18 A.D.). Murder, which like the two vices just mentioned was later reckoned among the mortal sins, is at first scarcely mentioned; it is named only in traditional lists of commandments and vices (Did. 2:2; 3:2; 5:1f.; Barn. 19:5; 20:1f.). The sin of apostasy does play a role, however. To a large extent it evidently was regarded as unforgivable (Heb. 6:4–8; 10:26–29) and later was considered a mortal sin for which until the Decian persecution no forgiveness was granted. Hermas still regards apostasy and denial of the faith as forgivable, even though it is the gravest of sins (*cf.* sim. VIII 6:4, IX 18:3; 19:1), but he considers it unforgivable only in the case of impenitence (vis. III 7:2; *cf.* vis. III 5–7 as a whole, sim. VIII 6:4–6). Hermas does know of sinners so hardened that repentance is denied them (sim. IX 6:2; 19:1). Nevertheless, in general and in keeping with the purpose of his book of repentance, he proclaims the possibility of repentance for all sinners (*cf.* especially sim. VIII 11:1–3) and while he does distinguish various classes of sinners (*cf.* especially vis. III, sim. VIII and IX) he still does not know any basic distinction between light sins and mortal sins. This distinction, suggested in I Jn. 5:16 and Heb. 10:26, is likewise unknown in the other writings of the apostolic and post-apostolic period. I Clem.'s call to repentance knows no limitation (chapters 7 and 8), neither does that of II Clem. Even Ignatius assumes the possibility of repentance for the heretics (Philad. 3:2; 8:1; Sm. 5:1; 9:1), though he considers it difficult (Sm. 5:3).

The direction that further development would have to take is clear. To distinguish between light and grave sins imperils from the outset the radical understanding of sin, as it had been conceived by Jesus, Paul, and John. But that understanding is completely surrendered when this distinction is combined with a distinction between two kinds of repentance. Though the latter distinction is not made in so many words, factually it is nevertheless made in the fact that for the grave sins an official ecclesiastical repentance (penance) comes to be required. For this is quite another thing from the repentance to which all Christians are again and again called (II, p. 209), quite another thing from the penitent disposition in which the congregation prays for forgiveness of its sins (I Clem. 60:1; Did. 14:1). Inasmuch as with the penetration of legalism into the Church the genuine understanding of grace like that of sin was lost (§ 59, 3), the sinner who was excluded from the fellowship of the Church now had to be regarded as one no longer standing under the forgiving grace of God. What he had been given in baptism, he had lost. If the Church then in view of his penance granted him forgiveness and took him back into its fellowship, this act, so far as its meaning is concerned. necessarily became a repetition of his baptism. Since baptism was a sacrament, the churchly institution of penance also necessarily became a sacrament. When this development should have taken place, the Church's character as institution of salvation (II, pp. 110. 202) would be complete.

Epilogue*

1. The Task and the Problems of New Testament Theology (the Relation between Theology and Proclamation)

The science called New Testament theology has the task of setting forth the theology of the New Testament; i.e. of setting forth *the theological thoughts of the New Testament writings*, both those that are explicitly developed (such as Paul's teaching on the Law, for example) and those that are implicitly at work in narrative or exhortation, in polemic or consolation. The question may be raised whether it is more appropriate to treat the theological thoughts of the New Testament writings as a systematically ordered *unity*—a New Testament system of dogmatics, so to say—or to treat them in their *variety*, each writing or group of writings by itself, in which case the individual writings can then be understood as members of an historical continuity.

The second procedure is the one chosen in the treatment here offered. By this choice the opinion is expressed that there can be no normative Christian dogmatics, in other words, that it is not possible to accomplish the theological task once for all—the task which consists of unfolding that understanding of God, and hence of the world and man, which arises from faith, for this task permits only ever-repeated solutions, or attempts at solution, each in its particular historical situation. Theology's continuity through the centuries consists not in holding fast to once formulated propositions but in the constant vitality with which faith, fed by its origin, understandingly masters its constantly new historical situation. It is of decisive importance that *the theological thoughts be conceived and explicated as thoughts of faith*, that is: *as thoughts in which faith's understanding of God, the world, and man is unfolding itself*—not as products of free speculation or of a scientific mastering of the problems involved in "God," "the world," and "man" carried out by the objectifying kind of thinking.

Theological propositions—even those of the New Testament—can

* The Epilogue reproduces with slight alterations and additions my contribution to the volume honoring Maurice Goguel, *Aux sources de la tradition Chrétienne*, published by Delachaux et Niestlé in 1950 (Neuchâtel and Paris).

[237]

never be the *object* of faith; they can only be the *explication* of the understanding which is inherent in faith itself. Being such explication, they are determined by the believer's situation and hence are necessarily incomplete. This *incompleteness*, however, is not a lack to be remedied by future generations, each generation supplying what is still lacking, so that by an ever-continued summation a complete dogmatics would finally result. Rather, the incompleteness has its cause in the inexhaustibility of believing comprehension, which must ever actualize itself anew; this incompleteness consequently signifies a task and a promise. Furthermore, my understanding of myself in my world of work and destiny by the light of a love conferred upon me or of a responsibility entrusted to me is necessarily always incomplete. It is self-evident, for example, that the New Testament's thought about the state and society are incomplete because the possibilities and the problems of forms of the state and society which history has introduced in the meantime could not be present to the minds of the New Testament authors. It is likewise clear that the world of modern science and technology imposes upon believing comprehension new tasks which could not yet occur to minds of the New Testament period. Therefore the theological thoughts of the New Testament can be normative only insofar as they lead the believer to develop out of his faith an understanding of God, the world, and man in his own concrete situation.

But from the fact that theological statements are by nature the explication of believing comprehension it also follows that *these statements may be only relatively appropriate, some more so, others less so.* The possibility exists that in some of them the believing comprehension may not be clearly developed, that it may be hindered—bound perhaps by a pre-faith understanding of God, the world, and man and by a corresponding terminology—and consequently may speak of God's dealing and of the relation between God and man in juristic terms, for instance. Or it may speak of God's relation to the world in mythological or cosmological terms which are inappropriate to faith's understanding of God's transcendence. Or the consequence may be that it expresses God's transcendence in the terminology of mysticism or of idealistic thinking. From this possibility arises the task—even in the case of the New Testament writings—of *content-criticism* (Sachkritik) such as Luther, for example, exercised toward the Epistle of James and the Revelation of John.

But the most important thing is that basic insight that the theological thoughts of the New Testament are the unfolding of faith itself growing out of that new understanding of God, the world, and man which is conferred in and by faith—or, as it can also be phrased: *out of one's new self-understanding.* For by the believer's new understanding of himself we, of course, do not mean "understanding" as in a scientific anthropology which objectifies man into a phenomenon of the world, but we do mean an existential understanding of myself which is at one with and inseparable from my understanding of God and the world. For I am I, of course, not as an isolable and objectifiable world-phenomenon but I am I in my particular existence inseparably bound up with God and the world.

If the scientific presentation of the theological thoughts of the New Testament has the task of pointing them out as the unfolding of believing self-understanding, it then presents *not the object of faith but faith itself* in its own self-interpretation. But here arises the real problem of the presentation! For can one concentrate upon faith without seeing at the same time that toward which it is directed, its object and content?

For in the New Testament, faith is not understood as a self-understanding arising spontaneously out of human existence but as an understanding made possible by God, opened up by His dealing with men. Faith is not choosing to understand one's self in one of several possible ways that are universally available to man but is man's response to God's word which encounters him in the proclamation of Jesus Christ. It is *faith in the kerygma,* which tells of God's dealing in the man Jesus of Nazareth.

When, therefore, the science of New Testament theology seeks to present faith as the origin of the theological statements, it obviously must present the kerygma and the self-understanding opened up by it in which faith unfolds itself. And that is just where the problem lurks! For both the kerygma and faith's self-understanding always appear in the texts, so far as they are expressed in words and sentences, already interpreted in some particular way—i.e. in theological thoughts. Although there are single statements in the New Testament which can be designated as specifically kerygmatic, even they are always formulated in a particular theological terminology—take, for instance, that simplest sentence, "Jesus, Lord" (II Cor. 4:5), for it presupposes a particular understanding of the term "Lord."

Therefore, it is *not possible simply and sharply to distinguish kerygmatic statements in the New Testament from theological ones,* nor to derive from the New Testament a self-understanding not formulated in theological statements. Nevertheless, he who sets forth a New Testament theology must have this distinction constantly in mind and must interpret the theological thoughts as the unfolding of the self-understanding awakened by the kerygma if he is to avoid conceiving them as an objectifying kind of thought cut loose from the act of living, no matter whether such thought be attributed to the intellect or to "revelation." For when revelation is conceived as an arrangement for the impartation of teachings, these teachings have the character of the objectifying thought of science, a kind of thought which dims their existential reference to living into a mere object of thought—but then they are pseudo-scientific teachings. Such a procedure leads to the misunderstanding that theology, conceived as the "right teaching," is the object and content of faith, when actually it is only the kerygma that may be regarded as the "right teaching" which is the object and content of faith. Though the propositions of philosophy, so far as they contain truth, are in themselves "right teaching," the propositions of theology are not themselves "right teaching" but, so far as they contain truth, teach what the "right teaching" is—a teaching which is not found by investigation but is given in the kerygma. But the kerygma is just what theology can never seize in definitive form; it can always take hold of it only as something conceptually stated, and that means as something already theologically interpreted.

This state of affairs reveals itself in its problematical character all the more when the theologian holds fast to the insight that faith can be nothing else but the response to the kerygma, and that the kerygma is nothing else than God's word addressing man as a questioning and promising word, a condemning and forgiving word. As such a word it does not offer itself to critical thought but speaks into one's concrete existence. That the kerygma never appears without already having been given some theological interpretation rests upon the fact that it can never be spoken except in a human language and formed by human thought. This very fact confirms its kerygmatic character; for it makes clear that the statements of the kerygma are not universal truths but are personal address in a concrete situation. Hence they can appear only in a form molded by an individual's understanding of his own existence or by his interpretation of that understanding. And correspondingly they are understandable only to him who is able to recognize the kerygma as a word addressed to him in his situation—to recognize it immediately only as a question asked him, a demand made of him.

Differently expressed: the kerygma is understandable as kerygma only when the self-understanding awakened by it is recognized to be a possibility of human self-understanding and thereby becomes the call to decision. For the theological investigator obviously cannot presuppose his own faith as an epistemological instrument and make use of it as a presupposition for methodical work. What he can and should do is keep himself ready, open, free. Or, better, keep himself questioning—or knowing the questionability of—all human self-understanding, in the knowledge that existential* understanding of one's self (in distinction from existentialistic† interpretation of Man's being) is real only in the act of existing and not in the isolated reflection of thought.

2. The History of New Testament Theology as a Science

A survey of the history of New Testament theology as a science may clarify the problem.‡ Its origin lies in the "Collegia biblica" ("Biblical collections") of the *old-Lutheran orthodoxy*, those collections of scriptural quotations which as "dicta probantia" were intended to furnish the scriptural proof for the statements of dogmatics. In them, passages of the Old and the New Testament are indiscriminately arranged according to the *loci* of dogmatics as, for instance, in **Sebastian Schmidt's** *Collegium biblicum, in quo dicta Veteris et Novi Testamenti juxta seriem locorum communium theologicorum explicantur* (1671; 2nd ed., 1689). They take for granted the assumption that both the statements of dogmatics and the teaching of Scripture are, as "right teaching," the object and content of faith. That is, kerygma

---

* German text: *existentiell*. See the following note (Tr.).

† German text: *existential*. The terminology of existentialism thus far devised in English is highly unsatisfactory. This might be a useful way of distinguishing between these perplexing twin words (Tr.).

‡ Amos N. Wilder also develops the problems of New Testament theology by means of a survey of its history in the volume edited by Harold R. Willoughby, *The Study of the Bible Today and Tomorrow* (University of Chicago Press, 1947), pp. 419–436.

EPILOGUE

and theology are naively identified with each other. In *pietism* it is just the same, except that here, where the title "Biblical Theology" is first encountered,* scriptural doctrine was treated independently of dogmatics.† The theologians of the *Enlightenment* continue in the same direction, and for them scriptural doctrine set free from dogmatics is the critical norm by which dogmatic theology is to be measured. Even the titles of some of these works are eloquent: in the years 1771–75 **G. T. Zachariae** published his *Biblische Theologie oder Untersuchung des biblischen Grundes der vornehmsten theologischen Lehren* (*Biblical Theology, or Investigation of the Biblical Foundation of the Most Eminent Theological Doctrines*). In 1787 appeared **Johann Philipp Gabler's** *Oratio de iusto discrimine theologiae biblicae et dogmaticae regundisque utriusque finibus* (*A Discourse on the Proper Distinction between Biblical and Dogmatic Theology and the Boundaries to be Drawn for Each*). When **Lorenz Bauer** gave separate treatment to *Theologie des Alten Testaments* (*Theology of the Old Testament*) 1796–1803 and *Theologie des Neuen Testaments* (*Theology of the New Testament*) 1800–02, this very separation indicates a parting from dogmatics and an intention to present the theology of Scripture as an historical phenomenon. Likewise, **Martin Leberecht de Wette's** *Biblische Dogmatik des Alten Testaments und Neuen Testaments, oder kritische Darstellung der Religionslehre des Hebraismus, des Judentums und des Urchristentums* (*Biblical Dogmatics of the Old and New Testament, or Critical Presentation of Hebrew, Jewish, and Early Christian Teaching on Religion"*) 1813. More and more it is taken for granted that Christianity is the rational religion—proved to be so by the right interpretation of Scripture. For it is maintained that interpretation has to demonstrate that everything in Scripture which contradicts the principles of reason and experience is accommodation to "erroneous folk-concepts."

It is fully clear that here as in old-Lutheran orthodoxy New Testament theology is regarded as the right doctrine, except that here this doctrine is not founded upon the authority of Scripture but is worked out by rational thought and is only rediscovered in Scripture

* As the title of C. Haymann's book, *Biblische Theologie*, 1708.

† Example: A. F. Büsching, *Epitome theologiae e solis sacris literis concinnata* (*Epitome of theology compiled from the Sacred Writings alone*), 1756; *Gedanken von der Beschaffenheit und dem Vorzug der biblisch-dogmatischen Theologie vor der scholastischen* (*Thoughts upon the nature of biblical-dogmatic theology and its superiority to the scholastic*), 1758.

[242]

—regardless of how much Christian tradition may be at work in that which it was thought possible to establish as the content of rational thought. Like orthodoxy, the Enlightenment is also unaware of theology's reference to the kerygma, only now one can no longer say that kerygma and doctrine are identified with each other, because Biblical doctrine is regarded as an historical ("symbolical") embodiment of rational truths and hence cannot be the authority for faith. In reality the Enlightenment walked to its consistent end the path which orthodoxy had begun. The two agree in not seeing the difference between theology and kerygma and in confusing approval of theological statements with faith in the kerygma. For both viewpoints these theological statements have the character of general, timeless truths. The difference is only that for orthodoxy the theological statements are utterances of Scripture conceived as authority, while for the Enlightenment they are truths founded upon reason and discovered by rational thought. That is, whereas for the Enlightenment the kerygmatic character of "right teaching" has altogether disappeared, it is retained by orthodoxy to the extent that for it the theological statements of Scripture are authority and are regarded as the object and content of faith—though it thereby misunderstands both kerygma and faith.

With the Enlightenment there took place not only a parting from the authority of Scripture but also another change. If right interpretation of Scripture is to demonstrate the Christianity to which it bears witness to be the rational religion, then this interpretation must peel off everything local and temporal, everything individual and particular, in order to win that which is timelessly general. But quite understandably attention is more and more directed at just those things; for general truth is known beforehand, and a historical presentation can only be made, of course, from individual phenomena determined by their time in history. Thus, those presentations of New Testament theology arise which are (1) interested in the individual differences of the New Testament authors, differences which they characterize as so many "concepts of doctrine," and which (2) place the various formations of New Testament thought into a context of historical relations. Finally—and in this respect the tradition of the Enlightenment works on in the nineteenth and twentieth centuries—New Testament theology comes to be understood as a phenomenon of the history of religions, and it is then no longer proper, so it seems, for the science which presents it, being an historical science, to be interested in the question of truth.

This development might have been prevented if the work of **Ferdinand Christian Baur** had been destined to exercise a decisive influence.* Unlike the Enlightenment, Baur did not distinguish between eternal rational truths of timeless character and their imperfect, time-bound formulation which an enlightened reason overcomes, but sees (following Hegel) that truth always and everywhere can be grasped only in a particular historical form and that it unfolds itself as *the* truth only in the totality of the historical course of development. The subject in which and to which this development takes place is the human mind, and history is "the eternally clear mirror in which the mind regards itself, contemplates its own image, in order to be what it is in itself and also for itself, for its own consciousness, and to recognize itself as the moving power of that which has historically come to be."†

Since, therefore, historical reflection is the way to grasp the truth, then historical investigation of the history of Christianity—primarily of its origin and hence of the New Testament—is the way to grasp the truth of Christian faith, a truth which for Baur is unquestionably no other than the truth of the human mind in general. Hence New Testament theology must understand the interpreting of the New Testament to be the unfolding of Christian consciousness, which is itself understood as a decisive stage in the process by which the human mind comes to itself.

With this view Baur hit upon the real meaning of New Testament theology in the respect that it is the explication (in thought) of believing self-understanding. Though orthodoxy had solidly retained the insight that by the New Testament a word that man is to believe is said to him, orthodoxy nevertheless replaced the kerygma with theological doctrine and made the latter the object of faith; Baur overcomes this danger. But by reducing faith's self-understanding to a consciousness which arises in historical development out of man himself so that in him the mind comes to consciousness of itself, he eliminates the kerygma. Yet he does this not as rationalism does—its thinking knows no authority—but in such a way that history itself

---

* After Baur's death (1860) his lectures on New Testament theology were published by his son (1864).

† F. C. Baur, *Lehrbuch der christlichen Dogmengeschichte*, 1847, p. 59.

becomes authority and takes the place of the kerygma through the fact that he regards backward-directed reflection upon history as the way by which the mind of man comes to itself.

The fruitful way in which Baur put the question was already lost by his followers. They retained the conception of history as a process of development and likewise the concrete view of history which Baur had drawn up according to Hegel's scheme of thesis, antithesis, and synthesis: out of the struggle of the Torah-free Gospel of Paul (thesis) with the Torah-bound Jewish Christianity (antithesis) there finally emerged in a series of compromises the ancient Catholic Church (synthesis). But after Baur the question of the meaning of history and of historical reflection got lost. The work of investigation proceeded in the direction that had been taken by the Enlightenment— except that belief in the eternal verities of reason, or the consciousness of having definitively recognized them, got lost, and the Christian faith was no longer regarded as the "rational" religion. That meant, then, that investigation fell victim to a historism which conceived early Christianity and with it the New Testament as a phenomenon within the closed continuum of world history linked together by cause and effect.

The logical consequence would have been a complete relativism. This consequence was avoided by idealistically interpreting history's course of development as one having meaning: even without binding one's self to Hegel's philosophy of history one could perceive the power of the mind at work in history and could believe in a progress in which the eternal verities and norms are more and more clearly grasped. Under the influence of romanticism one could also conceive personality as a history-forming power. Thus this period found in the teachings of the New Testament the expression of the Christian *Weltanschauung*—which it described as "religious-ethical"—and saw the significance of Jesus in the fact that he was the proclaimer of religious-ethical truths and that he effectively and uniquely embodied them in his own person. Representative examples of this conception are **H. J. Holtzmann's** *Lehrbuch der Neutestamentlichen Theologie* (1896–7, 2nd ed., 1911), a model of critical conscientiousness, and **Paul Wernle's** sprightly and impressive book *Die Anfänge unserer Religion* (1901, 2nd ed., 1904).

A decisive turn, the importance of which could not at first be foreseen, took place in the *history-of-religions school*. **William Wrede's** essay *Über Aufgabe und Methode der sogenannten neutestamentlichen*

Theologie (*Concerning the Task and Method of So-called New Testament Theology,* 1897), may be regarded as the statement of its program. Wrede combatted the method of "concepts of doctrine" because he contended that an intellectualistic understanding of Christianity underlies it; after all, Christian faith is religion and not a system of thoughts! The scientific task, he therefore maintained, is to present as New Testament theology the living religion of earliest Christianity. Obviously, a right insight was here at work in that theological teachings were understood as an expression of faith and not as the object of faith—now understood, however, not as the unfolding of believing self-comprehension but as subsequent reflective thinking about the objects of faith. The connection between the act of living and the act of thinking was here torn apart, as Adolf Schlatter used to say.

The cause of this shortcoming lies in the fact that a clear concept of faith and religion was missing. There was only an awareness that religion is not a theoretical attitude, but that it is a feeling, that it is piety; and there was an awareness that it can take form in various types. It can appear as a trust in God. And since it is taken for granted that God is the holy will which determines and demands the good, trust in God includes the consciousness of ethical obligation, and from such trust flows a positive relation to the world as the place in which the ethical will must prove itself in the execution of concrete tasks. But religion can also be "redemption-religion." In it the thought of the demanding will in the concept of God recedes behind the thought of transcendence. A negative relation to the world is the result, and this piety which flees from the world can intensify itself to the point of mysticism. However, the idea of redemption can also be taken up into that religion of trust in God and of a feeling of duty as the idea of redemption from sin. Accordingly, **Heinrich Weinel** in his *Biblische Theologie des Neuen Testaments* (1911; 4th ed., 1928) against a background of orientation in the general history of religions presents Jesus' "religion" as an "ethical religion of redemption" in contrast to that "mythical religion of redemption" ("esthetic religion" in the first edition), motifs of which, he concedes, then united themselves in various ways with that of Jesus in the "religion" of earliest Christianity. **Julius Kaftan** also conceives the religion of the New Testament as an ethical religion of redemption (forgiveness of sins) in his concise and spirited treatment: *Neutestamentliche Theologie im Abriss dargestellt* (1927). In **Wilhelm Bousset's** brilliant *Kyrios*

Christos (1913; 2nd ed., 1921) the religion of earliest Christianity appears, on the contrary, as essentially a cult-piety which sent forth as its flower: mysticism. One-sidedly but powerfully the basic idea is here carried through; and because many things are here seen in a new way, the problems which are active in New Testament theology emerge into a new light.

In the history-of-religions school, religion had been recognized as an independent force, the essence of which does not lie in acknowledging general timeless truths, whether they be mediated by a supra-natural "revelation" or discovered by rational thought. Religion is rather—for the intention of the history-of-religions school can evidently be so interpreted—an existential attitude. And though the legitimate meaning of the theological statements was not grasped by its adherents, they were nevertheless evidently on the right path.

An indication that they were on the right path is the fact that in the exegetical labor of this school those terms which are characteristic of religion as an independent attitude directed toward the transcendent God and distinct from every worldly attitude were grasped anew. Decisive for the discovery of the importance of eschatology to the New Testament was **Johannes Weiss'** *Jesu Predigt vom Reiche Gottes* (1892; 2nd ed., 1902). Another important insight was that *pneuma* in the New Testament does not mean "mind, spirit" as understood by the Greeks and by idealism but does mean the miraculous working of the transcendent God, as was first shown by **Heinrich Gunkel** in his book, *Die Wirkungen des Heiligen Geistes nach der populären Anschauung der apostolischen Zeit und nach der Lehre des Apostels Paulus* (1898; 3rd ed., 1909). Various works of **Wilhelm Heitmüller** pointed out the meaning and importance of the sacraments to earliest Christianity,* and in connection with them a new insight into the meaning of Ecclesia was won and also into the peculiar nature and significance of the idea "church" in earliest Christianity.†

It was only natural that in addition to the research of the historical school and of the history-of-religions school the work of conservative

---

* *Im Namen Jesu.* An investigation of the New Testament from the linguistic and history-of-religion standpoint, in particular concerning Christian baptism, 1903. See also his articles "Abendmahl" and "Taufe" in *RGG* I and V (1909 and 1913).

† *Cf.* Olof Linton, *Das Problem der Urkirche in der neueren Forschung*, 1932. Since then various essays by Maurice Goguel in the *Revue d'Histoire et de Philosophie religieuses*, 1933, 1938, and Nils Alstrup Dahl, *Das Volk Gottes: Eine Untersuchung zum Kirchenbewusstsein des Urchristentums*, 1941.

scholars under the influence of the orthodox tradition continued, and likewise that in their discussions with those of other trends they were also considerably influenced by the questions and the results of those others. In the tradition of the "concept-of-doctrine" method stand the very carefully written *Lehrbuch der Biblischen Theologie des Neuen Testaments* by **Bernard Weiss** (1868), 7th ed., 1903—English translation: *Theology of the New Testament*, 1892, from the third German edition) and the concise *Grundriss der neutestamentlichen Theologie* by **Theodor Zahn** (1928). More deeply influenced by modern statements of the questions involved, yet conservative in its results, is the *Theologie des Neuen Testaments* by **Paul Feine** (1910; 8th ed., 1950). It is significant that both B. Weiss and P. Feine later added to their presentations of New Testament theology a book on the "religion" of the New Testament.* It can scarcely be claimed that in these works new insights into the problem of the relation of theology to the kerygma were opened up. Nor can that claim be made for the *Theologie des Neuen Testaments* by **Friedrich Büchsel** (1935; 2nd ed., 1937), even though it bears the sub-title, "Geschichte des Wortes Gottes im Neuen Testament" ("History of the Word of God in the New Testament"), for the theological teachings are not differentiated from the kerygma which the word is, but are, themselves, taken to be God's word. Neither is **Ethelbert Stauffer's** very original *Theologie des Neuen Testaments* (1941; 4th ed., 1948) determined by that problem. Stauffer does indeed break away from the "concept-of-doctrine" method and from the notion of schematic development. After a short survey of the "course of development of primitive-Christian theology" he sets forth the thought-world of the New Testament as a unity under the title, "The New Testament's Christocentric Theology of History" and thus transforms theology into a religious philosophy of history.

A place by itself in this whole development is occupied by **Adolf Schlatter**. His book *Der Glaube im Neuen Testament* (1885; 4th ed., 1927) can in itself be termed a New Testament theology *in nuce*. It was followed by his *Theologie des Neuen Testaments* (1909–10).† He

*B. Weiss, *Die Religion des Neuen Testaments*, 1903, 2nd ed., 1908 (English translation: *The Religion of the New Testament*, 1905). P. Feine, *Die Religion des Neuen Testaments*, 1921.

† In 1921 the two volumes of this work appeared under new titles: *Die Geschichte des Christus* and *Die Theologie der Apostel*.

set forth his conception of the task in a small volume, *Die Theologie des Neuen Testaments und die Dogmatik* (1909). He marks off the boundaries of his own position against three frontiers: against the "statistical" inventories of New Testament thoughts found in ortho-doxy, against the rationalistic "concept-of-doctrine" method, and against the history-of-religions school. He accuses them all, rightly, of separating the act of thinking and the act of living. But he does not see the unity of these two acts as Baur did in the fact that theo-logical thoughts are the explication of man's understanding of him-self as mind (reason). For Schlatter understands man from the standpoint of his will and sees the origin of his thoughts to lie in his willing and his acting. "They (i.e. the "men of the New Testament") frustrate the attempt to separate the act of thinking from the act of living, and that is why they do not even create the appearance of laying before us timeless items of knowledge independent of historical conditions. Rather, their labor of thought stands in conscious and independent combination with their willing and acting; this labor has its foundation and its material in their experiences and serves them as a means for carrying out their profession. Their thoughts are components of their deeds and hence of their history. Therefore, the task of New Testament theology is not yet exhausted by setting up a catalogue of the thoughts of Jesus and his disciples. By doing this an historical caricature easily arises: a sum of abstract, timeless 'doctrines,' which are conceived as the content of a consciousness cut off from willing and acting. But Jesus and his disciples did not carry their thoughts within them in this form. In order to observe rightly we must make clear to ourselves the context which engenders their thoughts and into which their thoughts immediately return as the basis for what they proceed to do."* From this it also follows that the presentation must distinguish the individual "metaphors of teaching" (Lehrtropen), in order to make clear that primitive-Christian history "has its basis in those events which constitute the personal life-situation of the individual."†

Such sentences might be understood in the sense of historical relativism, but, of course they are not so meant. What Schlatter terms the "experiences" of the "men of the New Testament" which are the foundation and the material for the formation of their

* *Neutestamentliche Theologie*, I, pp. 10f.
† *Das Neue Testament und die Dogmatik*, p. 40.

thoughts, or what he terms "personal life-situation" has its origin in the encounter with the person of the historical Jesus. Primitive-Christian history begins with the "inward life of Jesus himself,"* that is, with the fact that Jesus knows himself to be the "Christ" and works as such. Now, inasmuch as encountering Jesus and acknowledging him as "Christ" is faith, the theological thoughts consequently are the unfolding of faith, each thought called forth by a concrete historical task. And we may probably add, keeping within Schlatter's intent, they are the unfolding of the new self-understanding which is conferred with and by faith; for we may probably assume that Schlatter took it for granted that faith includes an understanding in which a man understands God, the world, and himself anew.

In spite of all this, it seems to me that Schlatter did not clearly see the problem of the relation between theology and the kerygma. What he does not see is that it is in the kerygma that the historical Jesus first appears as the "Christ." Consequently, in his thought the place of the kerygma is taken by the historical Jesus—under the assumption that Jesus can be made visible as the "Christ" by historical investigation, whereas in reality at the most a messianic consciousness might be made visible in this way. That is probably the reason why in all questions of historical criticism, particularly in regard to the literary-critical investigation of the Gospels, Schlatter is subject to peculiar inhibitions, and why he wants to interpret the formation of theological thought in the New Testament one-sidedly out of the Old Testament-Jewish tradition in which Jesus himself stands, failing to recognize the importance of Hellenistic syncretism. The kerygma of the Church then factually becomes a passing on of historical tradition; that is, the passing on of the picture of the historical Jesus (that picture as Schlatter happens to see it), in which Jesus is thought to be already perceptible as the "Christ." The peculiar problem how Jesus the proclaimer comes to be "Christ" the proclaimed is thereby covered over and by just this covering the peculiar essence of the kerygma is also obscured.

The presentation of New Testament theology offered in this book stands, on the one hand, within the tradition of the historical-critical and the history-of-religion schools and seeks, on the other hand, to avoid their mistake which consists of the tearing apart of the act of

* *Ibid.*, p. 60.

thinking from the act of living and hence of a failure to recognize the intent of theological utterances.

Since the New Testament is a document of history, specifically of the history of religion, the interpretation of it requires the labor of historical investigation. The method of this kind of inquiry has been worked out from the time of the Enlightenment onward and has been made fruitful for the investigation of primitive Christianity and the interpretation of the New Testament. Now such labor may be guided by either one of two interests, that of reconstruction or that of interpretation—that is, reconstruction of past history or interpretation of the New Testament writings. Neither exists, of course, without the other, and they stand constantly in a reciprocal relation to each other. But the question is: which of the two stands in the service of the other? Either the writings of the New Testament can be interrogated as the "sources" which the historian interprets in order to reconstruct a picture of primitive Christianity as a pheno-menon of the historical past, or the reconstruction stands in the service of the interpretation of the New Testament writings under the presupposition that they have something to say to the present. The latter interest is the one for which historical labor is put to service in the presentation here offered.

But that is just the reason why it was so urgent to interpret the theological thoughts of the New Testament in their connection with the "act of living"—i.e. as explication of believing self-understanding. For they can claim to have meaning for the present not as theoretical teachings, timeless general truths, but only as the expression of an understanding of human existence which for the man of to-day also is a possibility for his understanding of himself—a possibility which is opened to him by the New Testament itself, in that it not only shows him that such self-understanding is the reply to the kerygma as the word of God addressing him, but also imparts to him the kerygma itself.

To make clear this believing self-understanding in its reference to the kerygma is the task of a presentation of New Testament theology. This clarification takes place directly in the analysis of the theology of Paul and John. It takes place indirectly in the critical presentation of the development toward the ancient Church, because in this development both the problems of believing self-understanding and the problems of the kerygmatic formulations conditioned by such self-understanding become visible.

Bibliographies

For §§ 41–50 as a whole. In addition to the commentaries* on John and the relevant sections in the theologies of the New Testament, see the following for the history of investigation. *English:* B. W. Bacon: *The Fourth Gospel in Research and Debate,* 2nd ed., 1918; W. F. Howard: *The Fourth Gospel in Recent Criticism and Interpretation,* 1931.

Non-English: P. H. Menoud: *L'évangile de Jean d'après les recherches récentes,* 2nd ed., 1947; J. Behm: "Der gegenwärtige Stand der Erforschung des Johannesevangeliums" in *Theologische Literaturzeitung* 73, 1948, pp. 21–30.

For the characterization of the Fourth Gospel as a whole. *English:* J. E. Carpenter: *The Johannine Writings,* 1927; R. H. Strachan: *The Fourth Gospel: Its Significance and Environment* (the third edition is undated; the second edition was of 1943); W. F. Howard: *Christianity According to St. John,* 1943; William Temple: *Readings in St. John's Gospel,* 1945.

Non-English: Alfredo Omodeo: *La mistica Giovannea,* 1930; William Wrede: *Charakter und Tendenz des Johannesevangeliums,* 2nd ed., 1933.

§ 41, for section 1. *English:* F. W. Worsley, *The Fourth Gospel and the Synoptists,* 1909; P. Gardner-Smith: *St. John and the Synoptic Gospels,* 1938; Erwin R. Goodenough: "John a Primitive Gospel," *JBL* LXIV, 1945, pp. 145–182.

Non-English: Hans Windisch: *Johannes und die Synoptiker,* 1926; also, "Die Absolutheit des Johannesevangeliums," *Zsyst Th.* 5, 1928, pp. 3–54; T. Sigge: *Das Johannesevangelium und die Synoptiker,* 1935.

§ 41, for section 3. *English:* C. F. Burney: *The Aramaic Origin of the Fourth Gospel,* 1922; J. de Zwaan: "John Wrote in Aramaic," *JBL* LVII, 1938, pp. 155–171; Hugo Odeberg; *The Fourth Gospel,* 1929; E. C. Colwell: *The Greek of the Fourth Gospel,* 1931.

Non-English: A. Schlatter: *Sprache und Heimat des vierten Evangelisten,* 1902; R. Bultmann: "Die Bedeutung der neuerschlossenen mandäischen und manichäischen Quellen für das Verständnis des Johannesevangeliums," *ZNW* 24, 1925, pp. 100–146; F. Büchsel: *Johannes und der hellenistische Synkretismus,* 1928; Lothar Schmidt: *Johannesevangelium und Religionsgeschichte,* 1933; Ernst Percy: *Untersuchungen über den Ursprung der Johanneischen Theologie,* 1939 (concerning which see R. Bultmann: review in *Orientalistische Literaturzeitung,* 1940, pp. 150–175); Eduard Schweizer: *EGO EIMI,* 1939; K. Kundsin: *Charakter und Ursprung der johanneischen Reden,* 1939.

* Though this book will be read mainly by readers who do not easily read German, it may not be superfluous to call special attention to Bultmann's own commentary on John, *Das Evangelium des Johannes,* 1941–47 (2nd ed., 1950) in which many assertions in this section of the book are treated in detail (Tr.).

BIBLIOGRAPHIES

§§ 42–44. Besides the literature cited above for the characterization of John as a whole, see: *English:* B. F. Westcott: *The Revelation of the Father*, 1884; G. B. Stevens: *The Johannine Theology*, 1894.

Non-English: Erich von Schrenk: *Die johanneische Anschauung vom Leben*, 1898; F. Büchsel: *Der Begriff der Wahrheit in dem Evangelium und in den Briefen des Johannes*, 1911; J. B. Frey: *Le Concepte de "Vie" dans l'Évangile de Saint Jean* (Biblica I), 1920, pp. 37ff.; Hans Pribnow: *Die johanneische Anschauung vom "Leben,"* 1934. See also the articles in *ThWB* on ἀλήθεια, ζάω, θάνατος, φῶς, ψεῦδος; F. Mussner: *Die Anschauung vom Leben im 4. Evg., 1950.*

§§ 45–48. *English:* R. H. Charles: *A Critical History of the Doctrine of a Future Life* (Jowett Lectures, 1898–99), 1899, pp. 362–376; E. von Dobschütz: *The Eschatology of the Gospels*, 1910, pp. 187–202; H. A. Guy: *The New Testament Doctrine of the Last Things*, 1948, pp. 159–172.

Non-English: R. Bultmann: '*Die Eschatologie des Johannes-Evangeliums*' (*Glauben und Verstehen I*), 1933, pp. 134–152; Doris Faulhaber: *Das Johannesevangelium und die Kirche*, 1935; B. Aebert: *Die Eschatologie des Johannes*, 1937; Alf Corell: *Consummatum est. Eskatologi och Kyrka i Johannesevangeliet*, 1950; Jacques Dupont: *Essais sur la Christologie de S. Jean*, 1951.

§ 45. *English:* G. B. Stevens: *The Johannine Theology*, 1894, pp. 74–126; H. R. Mackintosh: *The Doctrine of the Person of Jesus Christ*, 1912, pp. 94–121; A. E. J. Rawlinson: *The New Testament Doctrine of the Christ* (Bampton Lectures), 1926, pp. 199–228; R. H. Strachan: *The Historic Jesus in the New Testament*, 1931, pp. 128–222.

Non-English: W. Lütgert: *Die Johanneische Christologie*, 2nd ed., 1916; W. Bousset: *Kyrios Christos*, 2nd ed., 1921, pp. 154–183; Ernst Gaugler: *Das Christus-zeugnis des Johannesevangeliums* (*Jesus Christus im Zeugnis der Heiligen Schrift und der Kirche*, second supplement to *Evangelische Theologie*), 1936, pp. 34–67.

§ 46. To the literature for § 45, add for section 2: G. P. Wetter: *Der Sohn Gottes*, 1916; for section 4: Oscar Cullmann: *Theologische Zeitung* 4, 1948, pp. 360–72.

§ 47 as a whole. Hugo H. Huber: *Der Begriff der Offenbarung im Johannesevangelium*, 1934. For section 4: J. M. Creed: "Sacraments in the Fourth Gospel," in *The Modern Churchman* 16, 1926, pp. 363–372; C. T. Craig: "Sacramental Interest in the Fourth Gospel," *JBL* LVIII, 1939, pp. 31–41; Oscar Cullmann: *Urchristentum und Gottesdienst*, 2nd ed., 1950; H. Clavier: "Le Problème du rite et du mythe dans le 4. Evg.," *R.H.Ph.Rel.*, 1951, 275–292.

§§ 49–50. *English:* W. H. P. Hatch: *The Idea of Faith in Christian Literature from the Death of Paul to the Close of the Second Century*, 1926; J. O. Buswell: "The Ethics of 'Believe' in the Fourth Gospel," in *Bibliotheca Sacra* 80, 1923, pp. 28–37.

Non-English: Adolf Schlatter: *Der Glaube im Neuen Testament*, 4th ed., 1927; Rafael Gyllenberg: *Pistis* (in Swedish), 1922; J. Huby: "De la connaissance de foi chez S. Jean," in *Recherches de Science religieuse* 21, 1931, pp. 385–421; the article πίστις in *ThWB*.

§ 50 as a whole. D. Faulhaber (see under § 45). For section 4: J. Moffatt: *Love in the New Testament*, 1929; C. R. Bowen: "Love in the Fourth Gospel," in *Journal of Religion* 13, 1933, pp. 31–41; W. Lütgert: *Die Liebe im Neuen Testament*, 1905; Herbert Preisker: *Das Ethos des Urchristentums*, 2nd ed., 1949. For section 7: see the literature for § 14 and also M. Goguel: *La notion johannique de l'Esprit*, 1902; J. G. Simpson: "The Holy Spirit in the Fourth Gospel," in *Expositor* 9, Ser. IV, 1925, pp. 292–299; H. Windisch: "Jesus und der Geist im Johannesevangelium," in *Amicitiae Corolla for R. Harris*, 1933, pp. 303–318; Anton Fridrichsen: "Die Kirche im 4. Evangelium," in *Schwedische Theologische Quartalschrift* 16, 1940, pp. 227–242.

§§ 51–53 as a whole. See the literature for §§ 8 and 10. Concerning the literature down to 1932, see: Olof Linton: *Das Problem der Urkirche in der neueren Forschung*, 1932. Out of the earlier literature, see especially Harnack: *Die Mission und Ausbreitung des Christentums in den ersten drei Jahrhunderten*, 4th ed., 1924 (for the title of an English translation of an earlier edition of the same work, see the literature for § 9); Alfred Loisy: *L'Évangile de l'Église*, 5th ed., 1929; B. H. Streeter: *The Primitive Church studied with special Reference to the Origin of the Christian Ministry*, 1929; F. J. Foakes-Jackson: *The History of the Christian Church from the Earliest Times to A.D. 461*, 1933, Chapter X; Ernst Troeltsch: *The Social Teaching of the Christian Churches* (German, 1912; translated by Olive Wyon, 1931, reprint 1949); Rudolf Knopf: *Das nachapostolische Zeitalter*, 1905, pp. 147–222. Out of the abundant literature since 1932, see Karl Müller and H. von Campenhausen: *Kirchengeschichte* I, 1, 3rd ed., 1941, pp. 116–126; Otto Michel: *Das Zeugnis des Neuen Testaments von der Gemeinde*, 1941; Eduard Schweizer: *Das Leben des Herrn in der Gemeinde und ihren Diensten*, 1946; especially Maurice Goguel: *L'Église primitive*, 1947. See also the special literature for the following paragraphs:

§ 51. *English:* Walter Lowrie: *The Church and Its Organization: An Interpretation of Rudolph Sohm's Kirchenrecht*, 1904; A von Harnack: *The Constitution and Law of the Church in the First Two Centuries* (translated by F. L. Pogson, edited by H. D. A. Major), 1910; Thomas M. Lindsay: *The Church and Ministry in the Early Centuries* (Cunningham Lectures), 1902, 2nd ed., 1903, pp. 1–36.

Non-English: Rudolph Sohm: *Kirchenrecht* I, 1892; the same: *Wesen und Ursprung des Katholizismus* (*Abhandlungen der sächsischen Gesellschaft der Wissenschaften, Philosophisch-historische Klasse* 27, 10), 1909, 2nd ed., 1912; A. von Harnack: *Entstehung und Entwicklung der Kirchenverfassung und des Kirchenrechts in den ersten drei Jahrhunderten* (for English translation, see preceding paragraph), 1910; Erich Foerster: *Rudolf Sohms Kritik des Kirchenrechtes*, 1942; Karl Holl: "Der Kirchenbegriff des Paulus im Verhältnis zu dem der Urgemeinde," in *Sitzungsbericht der preussischen Akademie der Wissenschaften*, Berlin, 1921 (reprinted in Holl's *Gesammelte*

BIBLIOGRAPHIES

Schriften II, 1928); Wilhelm Mundle: "Das Kirchenbewusstsein der ältesten Christenheit," *ZNW* 22, 1923, pp. 20–42; H. von Campenhausen: "Recht und Gehorsam in der ältesten Kirche," *Theol. Bl.* 20, 1941, pp. 279–295; the same: *Kirchliches Amt nnd geistliche Vollmacht in den ersten drei Jahrhunderten*, 1953.

§ 52. See the general literature for §§ 51–53; also the following: *English:* B. H. Streeter: "The Rise of Christianity," in *The Cambridge Ancient History*, Vol. XI, especially pp. 286–293; T. M. Lindsay: (see § 51), pp. 69–217; A. C. Headlam and F. Gerke: "The Origin of the Christian Ministry," in *The Ministry and the Sacraments*, 1937, pp. 326–367.

Non-English: K. L. Schmidt: "Le Ministère et les Ministères dans l'Église du Nouveau Testament," in *Revue d' Histoire et de Philosophie Religieuses*, 1937, pp. 313–336; Ph.-H. Menoud: *L'Église et les Ministères selon le Nouveau Testament*, 1949. For section 2: F. V. Filson: "The Christian Teacher in the First Century," *JBL* LX, 1941, pp. 317–328. For section 3: A. Fridrichsen: *The Apostle and His Message*, 1947; Johannes Munck: "Paul, the Apostles and the Twelve," in *Studia Theologica* III, 1950, pp. 96–110. *Non-English:* H. von Campenhausen: "Der Christliche Apostelbegriff," in *Studia Theologica* I, 1948, pp. 96–130; the same: "Lehrerreihen und Bischofsreihen," in *In Memoriam Ernst Lohmeyer*, 1951, pp. 240–249; J. Brosch: *Charismen und Ämter in der Urkirche*, 1951; H. Greeven: "Propheten, Lehrer, Vorsteher bei Paulus," *ZNW* 44, 1952, 1–43.

§ 53. *English:* T. M. Lindsay (see § 51), pp. 169–210; E. F. Scott: *The Nature of the Early Church*, 1941; G. Johnston: *The Doctrine of the Church in the New Testament*, 1943; F. C. Grant: *An Introduction to New Testament Thought*, 1950, pp. 268–299; Oscar Cullmann: *Christ and Time* (translated by F. V. Filson), 1950.

Non-English: M. Goguel: "Eschatologie et apocalyptique dans le Christianisme primitif," in *Revue d'Histoire et de Philosophie Religieuses*, 1932, pp. 381–434, 490–524; A. Fridrichsen: "Église et Sacrement dans le Nouveau Testament," in *Revue d'Histoire et de Philosophie Religieuses*, 1937, pp. 337–356; H. D. Wendland: *Geschichtsanschauung und Geschichtsbewusstsein in Neuen Testament*, 1938; O. Bauernfeind: "Die Geschichtsauffassung des Urchristentums," *Zsyst Th.* 15, 1938, pp. 347–378; Martin Werner: *Die Entstehung des christlichen Dogmas*, 1941; Ph. Vielhauer, "Zum Paulinismus der Apostelgeschichte," *Ev. Theol.*, 1950–51, pp. 1–15; M. Dibelius: *Aufsätze zur Apostelgeschichte*, 1951 (especially pp. 108ff.); G. Bornkamm: "Die Verzögerung der Parusie," in *In Memoriam Ernst Lohmeyer*, 1951, pp. 116–126; R. Bultmann: "Der Mensch zwischen den Zeiten," in *Man in God's Design*, 1952, pp. 39–59.

§§ 54–58 as a whole. *English:* B. H. Streeter: *The Rise of Christianity* (see above, bibliography for § 52), 1936; C. H. Dodd: *The Apostolic Preaching and Its Development*, 1936, 6th ed., 1950; C. T. Craig: *The Beginning of Christianity*, 1943; F. V. Filson: *One Lord, One Faith*, 1943; A. M. Hunter: *The Unity of the New Testament*, 1943; E. F. Scott: *The Varieties of New Testament Religion*, 1943.

BIBLIOGRAPHIES

Non-English: A. Loisy: *La naissance du Christianisme*, 1933; J. Lebreton and J. Zeiller: *L'Église primitive*, 1938; R. Asting: *Die Verkündigung des Wortes im Urchristentum*, 1939; J. Gewiess: *Die urapostolische Heilsverkündigung nach der Apostelgeschichte*, 1939; M. Goguel: *L'Église primitive*, 1947; the same: *Les premiers temps de l'Église*, 1949; Hannelore Schulte: *Der Begriff der Offenbarung im Neuen Testament*, 1949.

§ 54, for section 1. *English:* G. F. Moore: *Judaism* I, 1927, pp. 251–262. *Non-English:* G. van der Leeuw: *Phänomenologie der Religion*, 1933, § 64, 4; W. G. Kümmel: "Jesus und der jüdische Traditionsgedanke," *ZNW* 21, 1922, pp. 1–34; 22, 1923, pp. 257–279; 24, 1925, pp. 193–202; O. Cullmann: *Die ersten christlichen Glaubensbekenntnisse*, 1943; J. de Ghellinck: "Les origines du symbole des apôtres," in *Nouvelle revue de theologie*, 1945, pp. 178ff. For section 3: M. Dibelius: *From Tradition to Gospel*, 1934; R. Bultmann: *Die Geschichte der synoptischen Tradition*, 2nd ed., 1931; Joachim Jeremias: *Unbekannte Jesusworte*, 1951.

§ 55. A. von Harnack: *History of Dogma* (translated from the third German edition by Neil Buchanan), 1895, Vol. I, Chapter III. *Non-English:* Walter Bauer: *Rechtgläubigkeit und Ketzerei im ältesten Christentum*, 1934; M. Werner: (see lit. for § 53); G. van der Leeuw: (see lit. for § 54). For section 5: *English:* P. R. Williams: *Authority in the Apostolic Age*, 1950, especially pp. 42–74. *Non-English:* A. von Harnack: *Die Briefsammlung des Apostels Paulus und die anderen vorkanonischen Briefsammlungen*, 1926; H. Strathmann: "Die Krisis des Kanons in der Kirche," in *Theol. Bl.* 20, 1941, pp. 295–310; O. Cullmann: "Die Pluralität der Evangelien als theologisches Problem im Altertum," in *Theologische Zeitung* I, 1945, pp. 23–42; H. von Campenhausen: (see lit. for § 52); W. G. Kümmel: "Notwendigkeit und Grenze des neutestamentlichen Kanons," *ZThK* 47, 1950, pp. 277–312; E. Käsemann: "Begründet der neutestamentliche Kanon die Einheit der Kirche?", *Ev. Theol.* 11, 1951–52, pp. 13–21. In addition, see the histories of the canon, especially those within the various introductions to the New Testament.

§ 56. For section 2. *English:* Sir Robert Falconer: *The Pastoral Epistles*, 1937; B. S. Easton: *The Pastoral Epistles*, 1947.

Non-English: O. Michel: "Grundfragen der Pastoralbriefe," in the *Wurm-Festschrift*, 1949; F. Spitta: *Studien zum Hirten des Hermas* (*Zur Geschichte und Literatur des Urchristentums* II), 1896; Arnold Meyer: *Das Rätsel des Jakobusbriefes*, 1930; H. Weinel: "Die spätere christliche Apokalyptic," in *Eucharisterion* II, *Festschrift für H. Gunkel*, 1923, pp. 141–173; A. Dietrich: *Nekyia*, 1893; M. Dibelius: "Paulus auf dem Areopag" in *Aufsätze zur Apostelgeschichte*, 1951, pp. 29–70; see also Dibelius' commentaries on James (Meyer's *Kommentar*) and on the pastoral epistles (Lietzmann's *Handbuch*).

For section 4. *English:* William Manson: *The Epistle to the Hebrews*, 1951; E. F. Scott: *The Epistles of Paul to the Colossians, to Philemon, and to the Ephesians*, 1930 and later reprints; C. R. Richardson: *The Christianity of Ignatius of Antioch*, 1935.

BIBLIOGRAPHIES

Non-English: H. Schlier: *Religionsgeschichtliche Untersuchungen zu den Ignatiusbriefen*, 1929; the same: *Christus und die Kirche im Epheserbrief*, 1930; E. Käsemann: *Leib und Leib Christi*, 1933; the same: *Das Wandernde Gottesvolk: Eine Untersuchung zum Hebräerbrief*, 1939; K. L. Schmidt: *Kanonische und apokryphe Evanglien und Apostelgeschichten*, 1944.

§ 57. *English:* F. C. Grant: *An Introduction to New Testament Thought*, 1950, pp. 99–143.

Non-English: H. Schlier and E. Käsemann (see lit. for § 56); G. Bornkamm: "Die Häresie des Kolosser-Briefes," in *Theologische Literaturzeitung* 73, 1948, pp. 11–20; R. Bultmann: "Bekenntnis- und Liedfragmente im ersten Petrusbrief," in *Coniectanea Neotestamentica* XI, 1947, pp. 1–14; H. Bietenhard: *Die himmlische Welt im Urchristentum und Spätjudentum*, 1951; G. Lindeskog: *Studien zum neutestamentlichen Schöpfungsgedanken I*, 1952.

§ 58. See the literature for § 57; also: V. Taylor: *Forgiveness and Reconciliation*, 1908; F. C. Grant: *An Introduction to New Testament Thought*, 1950, pp. 187–276; W. Bousset: *Kyrios Christos*, 2nd ed., 1921; H. Windisch: *Taufe und Sünde im ältesten Christentum*, 1908; O. Cullmann: *Christ and Time*, 1946.

For section 3: E. F. Scott (see § 56, section 4).

Non-English: Ernst Percy: *Die Probleme der Kolosser- und Epheserbriefe*, 1946; H. Schlier and V. Warnack: *Die Kirche im Epheserbrief*, 1949; J. Klevinghaus: *Die theologische Stellung der Apostolischen Väter zur alttestamentlichen Offenbarung*, 1948; W. Wrede: *Untersuchungen zum ersten Klemensbriefe*, 1891; A. von Harnack: *Der erste Klemensbrief*, S. A. Berlin, 1909, pp. 38–63. Literature on Barnabas in H. Windisch, Supplement Volume III to Lietzmann's *Handbuch*, 1920; also P. Meinhold: "Geschichte und Exegese im Barnabasbrief," *Zeitschrift für Kirchengeschichte*, 1940, pp. 255–303. On the abundant literature for Ignatius see W. Bauer in Supplement Volume II to Lietzmann's *Handbuch*, 1920; also Th. Preiss: "La Mystique de l'Imitation et de l'Unité chez Ignace d'Antioche," *Revue d'Histoire et de Philosophie Religieuses* 18, 1938, pp. 197–241; K. H. Schelkle: *Die Passion Jesu in der Vekündigung des N.T.*, 1949.

§§ 59–61 as a whole. *English:* E. von Dobschütz: *Christian Life in the Primitive Church* (translated by George Bremner, edited by W. D. Morrison), 1904. A. von Harnack (see lit. for § 9); F. C. Grant: *An Introduction to New Testament Thought*, 1950, pp. 300–324; C. H. Dodd: *Gospel and Law*, 1951; Vincent Taylor: *Forgiveness and Reconciliation*, 1946.

Non-English: R. Knopf: *Das nachapostolische Zeitalter*, 1905, pp. 417–444; R. Asting: *Die Heiligkeit im Urchristentum*, 1930; M. Goguel: *L'Église primitive*, 1947, pp. 508–540; H. Preisker: *Das Ethos des Urchristentums*, 1949.

§ 59. See the literature for § 58.

§ 60. Ernst Troeltsch (see under §§ 51–53); Igino Giordani: *The Social*

Message of the Early Church Fathers (translated by A. I. Zizzamia with *imprimatur*), 1944; M. S. Enslin: *The Ethics of Paul*, 1930.

Non-English: See the general literature for §§ 59–61, to which add pp. 105–137 in Knopf and pp. 541–600 in Goguel. In addition: K. Müller and H. von Campenhausen: *Kirchengeschichte* I 1, 3rd ed., 1941, § 6, 9 and § 23; H. von Campenhausen: *Die Idee des Martyriums in der alten Kirche*, 1936; the same: *Die Askese im Urchristentum*, 1949; H. Windisch: *Imperium und Evangelium*, 1931: H. Schlier: "Die Beurteilung des Staates im Neuen Testament," *Zwischen den Zeiten* 10, 1932, pp. 312–330; K. Pieper: *Urkirche und Staat*, 1935; E. Stauffer: *Gott und Kaiser im Neuen Testament*, 1935; the same: *Christus und die Cäsaren*, 1948; G. Kittel: "Das Urteil des Neuen Testaments über den Staat," *Zsyst Th.* 14, 1937, pp. 651–680; K. L. Schmidt: "Das Gegenüber von Kirche und Staat in der Gemeinde des Neuen Testaments," *Theol. Bl.* 16, 1937, pp. 1–16; F. J. Leenhardt: *Le Chrétien, doit-il servir l'état?* 1939; O. Eck: *Urgemeinde und Imperium*, 1940; W. Bieder: *Ekklesia und Polis im Neuen Testament und in der alten Kirche*, 1941; M. Dibelius: *Rom und die Christen im ersten Jahrhundert*, S. B. Heidelberg, 1941–2, No. 2; W. Schweitzer: *Die Herrschaft Christi und der Staat im Neuen Testament*, 1949.

§ 61. *English:* O. D. Watkins: *A History of Penance*, 1920.

Non-English: H. Windisch: *Taufe und Sünde im ältesten Christentum*, 1909; S. Hoh: *Die kirchliche Busse im zweiten Jahrhundert*, 1932; B. Poschmann: *Paenitentia secunda: Die kirchliche Busse im ältesten Christentum*, 1940; P. Bonnard: "La discipline ecclésiastique selon le Nouveau Testament," in *Centenaire de la Faculté de theologie de l'église évangélique libre du Canton de Vaud*, 1947, pp. 115–135.

Bibliographical Note to the Epilogue.

The author, writing originally for persons of German tongue, was probably perfectly correct in ignoring non-German treatments of New Testament theology. It has been a singularly German branch of theology, but there have been several writers in English (as also in French and Dutch) who, stimulated by the German works, have seen the advantages of writing similar books in their own language. Their debt to German work is always great, but several of them are much more than mere imitations. A suggestive list, not meant to be exhaustive, of non-German works follows: J. J. v. Oosterzee: *De Theologie des Nieuwen Verbonds*, 1867 (English translation by M. J. Evans, 1870); E. Reuss: *Histoire de la Théologie Chrétienne du Siècle Apostolique*, 1852 and later; W. Alexander: *A System of Biblical Theology*, 1888; R. F. Weidner: *Biblical Theology of the New Testament*, 1891; W. F. Adeney: *The Theology of the New Testament*, 1894; G. B. Stevens: *The Theology of the New Testament*, 1899 and often reprinted, most recently 1947; E. H. van Leeuwen: *Prolegomena van bijbelsche godgeleerdheid*, 1890; the same: *Bijbelsche godgeleerdheit*, 1892:

BIBLIOGRAPHIES

G. G. Chavannes: *La religion dans la Bible II, le Nouveau Testament,* 1889; G. Fulliquet: *La pensée religieuse dans le Nouveau Testament,* 1893; W. Mackintosh: *The Natural History of the Christian Religion,* 1894; Orello Cone: *The Gospel and Its Earliest Interpretations, a study of the teaching of Jesus and its doctrinal transformation in the New Testament,* 1893; J. Bovon: *Théologie du Nouveau Testament,* 1893–4; D. F. Estes: *An Outline of New Testament Theology,* 1900; E. P. Gould: *The Biblical Theology of the New Testament,* 1900; H. C. Sheldon: *New Testament Theology,* 1911; A. Nairne: *The Faith of the New Testament* (Hulsean Lectures, 1919–20), 2nd ed., 1927; E. W. Parsons: *The Religion of the New Testament,* 1939; W. T. Conner: *The Faith of the New Testament,* 1940; E. F. Scott: *The Varieties of New Testament Religion,* 1947; F. C. Grant: *An Introduction to New Testament Thought,* 1950. If works on the theology of Paul or John or on separate theological concepts of the New Testament were added, the list would be much longer. (It should also be noted that several voluminous New Testament theologies written in the latter half of the nineteenth century were translated from German to English, among them theologies by C. F. Schmid, W. Beyschlag, B. Weiss, and also B. Weiss' *Religion of the New Testament.*)

Greek Index*

* Because of the purpose of this translation the Greek of the original has regularly been transliterated or translated; accordingly, the words in this index may occur in the text either in Greek or Roman type or in translation, but they should still be an aid in locating pertinent discussion.

[261]

GREEK INDEX

καινός, II, 205
καλεῖν, II, 160f.
καρδία, I, 220ff.
καταλλαγή, I, 285ff., 302
καυχᾶσθαι (καύχησις), I, 242f., 264, 267, 281; II, 197
κήρυγμα, I, 88f., 307
κόσμιος, II, 227
κόσμος, I, 229f., 235, 254–9; II, 15ff., 177, 186, 208f.
κρίνειν (κρίμα, κρίσις, κριτής), I, 75f., 215; II, 37–40, 156
κτίσις, I, 230
κύριος, I, 51f., 124–8; II, 36, 156
Λαός, I, 97; II, 164
λογίζεσθαι, I, 215f.
Λόγος, II, 64
Μακάριος, I, 72
μαρτυρία, II, 68f.
μάταιος, I, 104
μεριμνᾶν, I, 226, 241f.
μετάνοια, I, 73, 214, 317; II, 218
μονογενής, II, 85
μορφή, I, 192f.
Νήφειν, I, 76, 174
νόημα, I, 213
νόμιμα, II, 189
νόμος, I, 259–69
νόμος καινός, II, 164, 199, 206, 218
νοῦς, I, 211–16, 227
'Ομολογεῖν, I, 317f.; II, 136
ὄνυμα, I, 40, 125f., 133f., 137ff.
ὀργή (God's), I, 76, 288f.
ὅσιος, II, 170, 178, 213
Παράγγελμα, II, 191
παράδοσις, I, 64; II, 119ff.
παραθήκη, II, 119
παράκλητος, II, 88n.
παραλαμβάνειν, II, 119f.
παρουσία, I, 29; 11, 192
παρρησία, I, 323; II, 88, 167, 188
πεποιθέναι, I, 243, 264, 268, 323
περιπατεῖν, I, 338
πίστις, I, 89–91, 281, §§ 36–40; II, 70, 135f., 163, 164f., 167f., 174, 181f., 187, 189f., 197, 200, 211
πλάνη, I, 66; II, 128, 204

πνεῦμα, I, § 14, 165, 205–9, § 38 (esp. 333f.); II, 194, 198, 208
πρεσβύτεροι, I, 59; II, 101ff., 106
πρόνοια, I, 71
προστάγματα, II, 191, 223
Σάρξ, I, 199ff., 227, § 23–4, 334; II, 170, 177, 181, 186, 190, 194f., 198, 207
σατανᾶς, I, 258
σεμνός, II, 213, 226
σημεῖα, II, 44ff.
σκοπεῖν, I, 225
σκοτία (σκότος), I, 174f.; II, 15ff., 204
σοφία, I, 326; II, 128ff.
στοιχεῖα, I, 173, 257f.
συνείδησις, I, 71, 211, 216–20; II, 226
σφραγίς, I, 137
σχῆμα, I, 193
σῶμα, I, 165, § 17, 227
σῶμα Χριστοῦ, I, 94, 178, 310f.; II, 113, 151, 179
σωτήρ (σωτηρία, σωθῆναι), I, 78f.; II, 36, 156, 183
σωφροσύνη, II, 184, 226
Ταπεινοφροσύνη, I, 345; II, 182
Υἱοθεσία, I, 278
υἱὸς τ. ἀνθρώπου, I, 26, 29–31, 33f., 49, 52f., 78f.; II, 37, 156
ὑπομονή, II, 167, 174, 184
Φόβος, I, 243, 320f.; II, 213
φρονεῖν (φρόνημα), I, 214
φύσις, I, 71, 168; II, 23, 40, 169
φῶς, I, 173; II, 17ff., 192
φωτισμός, I, 143
Χαρά, I, 339f.; II, 83f.
χάρις, I, 268f., 281–5; II, 8, 75, 178, 181, 188, 198, 210f., 216
χάρισμα, I, 154f., 158f., 325; II, 8, 104, 198, 217
χρηστότης, I, 283; II, 226
χρῖσμα, II, 88
Χριστῷ, ἐν . . ., I, 311f., 327f.; II, 177, 183, 186n., 189, 193, 201
Ψυχή, I, 165f., § 18
ψυχικός, I, 166, 168, 192

New Testament Passages Discussed

(A selection of the more important)

NEW TESTAMENT PASSAGES DISCUSSED

Subject Index

ABRAHAM, I, 6, 36, 50, 95–7, 111f., 120, 194, 234, 237, 242, 253f., 265, 267, 280–2, 310, 315, 320, 323; II, 29, 163

Abstain, I, 104f.; II, 221, 224

Acknowledgment, of God, I, 213, 215, 229, 319; of Jesus as Lord, I, 315

Adam, I, 204, 227, 230, 246, 250ff., 258, 265, 289, 347; II, 149; first, I, 300; last, I, 178, 300, 302

Adamitic man, I, 173f., 178, 249, 251ff., 277, 300, 347

Adoption to sonship, I, 278, 297, 335

Advent of Christ, I, 29, 35, 43

Aeon(s), I, 173, 177; Adam-, I, 303; Christ-, I, 303; two, I, 5; new or old, I, 5, 172f., 256n., 278, 299f., 307f., 349; II, 208f.

Agape, I, 144, 150, 183, 262, 268, 291f., 345; II, 81f., 162, 165, 168, 178, 184, 221f.

Allegory, I, 111–18, 340; II, 143, 163

Altar, I, 149f.

Angels, I, 25, 110, 128f., 158, 170, 174, 176, 230, 255, 257f., 268; II, 149ff., 152, 154

Animism, I, 155, 157, 207

Anthropology, I, 71, 168, 174, 189, 191–268; II, 40

Antioch, I, 56, 61, 63f., 96, 188

Anxiety, I, 104, 226, 235, 240, 243, 247, 320

Apocalypticism, I, 4–6, 27, 35, 38, 47, 49f., 53, 74, 76, 79f., 173, 307, 346; II, 143

Apostasy, I, 170, 241, 250

Apostles, apostleship, I, 60, 62, 68, 77, 81, 114, 121, 125f., 133, 161, 163, 170f., 217, 222, 271, 308, 314, 318, 325, 340, 343, 350, 352; II, 105ff., 138, 140

Apostles' Creed, see *Symbolum Romanum*

Apostolic Council, I, 56, 61, 95, 108, 188

Areopagus address, I, 68, 71–3, 68, 77, 92

Ascension, I, 45, 123, 127, 176

Asceticism, I, 11, 102f., 107, 110, 152, 160, 166, 170, 182, 199, 202; II, 220f., 223

Atonement I, 46, 85, 285ff., 302; II, 53f.

Attis, I, 140, 148, 167, 299

Authority, I, 61, 137, 171, 180–2, 219f., 223, 289, 294, 309; of O.T., I, 16, 118; II, 138–42

Authorization (*exousia*), I, 181, 342–344

BAPTISM, I, 39f., 57, 74, 101, 107, 114, 116, 120–2, 126, 133–44, 153, 157–63, 167–9, 180, 293, 298f., 311–14, 333, 335, 337–9, 348; II, 160, 166, 236; of Jesus, I, 26, 131; of Jewish proselytes, I, 39f.; of John, I, 39f., 59, 138; vicarious, I, 141, 169, 312

Barnabas, I, 56, 61, 64, 95, 98, 101, 108f., 155, 188; Epistle of, I, 110f., 114; II, 143, 163–5

Barth, Karl, I, 274, 295

Baur, F. C., II, 244

Belief in God, I, 67f., 73, 89f., 120, 300, 317; II, 145

Between-ness, II, 162, 163, 168, 175, 180, 185, 191, 198, 199f.

Bishop, I, 116, 135, 149, 153, 310; II, 102, 108ff., 139, 141

Blood, I, 198, 233, 244, 249, 288, 295; of Christ, I, 46, 73, 84f., 103, 111f., 142f., 146–50; II, 54; of "God", I, 129

[268]

Humanity of Jesus, I, 80, 129, 131, 168f., 297; II, 41, 69

Hymns, I, 27, 125, 131, 175, 177, 298; II, 150, 153, 155

"I AM" (in John), II, 65

Idolatry, I, 65, 67, 72, 74, 98–100, 105, 110, 114, 119, 123, 217–19

Ignatius, I, 83, 129, 179f.; II, 9, 144, 153, 191–9

Ignorance, I, 66; II, 128, 204

Illumination, I, 143; II, 192

Image of God, I, 132, 167, 229

Immortality, I, 147, 152, 203, 313f., 345; II, 193

Imperative (—indicative), I, 101, 332f.; II, 79–82, 133, 168, 170, 173, 176, 180, 186, 189, 205

Incarnation, I, 129, 175, 293, 295, 298, 300, 304f.; II, § 46, 156, 193, 203

"In Christ," I, 312, 327f.; II, 177, 183, 186n., 189, 193, 201

JAMES, brother of Jesus, I, 52, 54, 59

James, epistle of, I, 64, 74, 84; II, 162f.

James, son of Zebedee, I, 59

Jerusalem, I, 21, 27, 37, 44f., 55–61, 94f., 188, 236, 294f., 308; creed of, I, 70; destruction of, I, 115

John, Gospel of, I, 15, 36, 131, 136, 173–8; II, §§ 41–50

John, son of Zebedee, I, 59

John the Baptist, I, 42, 83, 86, 159; II, 5

Joy, I, 156, 226f., 320, 339f.; II, 83

Judaism, I, 11–17, 22–5, 31–8, 42, 47, 50–3, 57, 63, 65, 69, 74, 77, 87, 89, 96, 99f., 105, 108, 132, 138, 151, 157, 168, 170f., 186, 196, 243, 252, 256, 260, 270, 278–80, 340; II, 27

Judaism, Hellenistic, I, 65–74, 95, 116, 118, 171, 187, 216, 254f.; II, 143, 187

Jude, Epistle of, II, 154, 169

Judge, eschatological, I, 27, 172; Christ as, I, 78, 321; God as, I, 78, 272, 288f., 295, 295, 321

Judgment, II, 37–40, 169, 173

Justice, I, 12, 113, 271, 285, 288

Justification by faith ("rightwising"; see also Righteousness), I, 75, 85, 120f., 136, 216, 225, 253, 263–6, 270–89, 316–19, 332, 335, 347f.; II, 75, 162f., 167, 170, 172, 182, 189, 197, 212f., 225

Justin Martyr, I, 29, 113ff., 127

KERYGMA, the, I, 3, Ch. II, III *passim*, 187, 307, 318f., 324; II, 239ff.

Kerygma Petri, I, 66–77, 107, 119

Kingdom (or Reign), of Christ, I, 76, 78, 87f., 138, 346; of God, I, 4–10, 19–22, 25, 28f., 34, 37, 39, 48, 54, 76, 78, 87f., 133, 142, 151, 189, 201, 233, 338f.

Knowing, knowledge, I, 67, 120, 161, 165, 180–3, 190, 209, 211f., 216–22, 228, 241, 245, 261–4, 307, 318, 325–7, 347; II, 73f., 128–35, 165, 179; of God, I, 117, 213, 229

Krisis, II, § 45

Kyrios, title of Jesus, see Lord

LAMB OF GOD, II, 173f.

Law (Torah), I, *passim*, esp. 11–22, 55–7, 109–21, 259–69; II, 28, 162

Laying on of hands, I, 134, 138; II, 99, 104

Life, I, 203–10, 227; II, 19, 159, 191f.

Life, eternal, I, 16, 157f. 162, 204, 262, 274, 288, 290, 334, 336; II, 191; in faith, I, 324–9

Light, I, 173; II, 17, 192

Liturgy, I, 36, 51, 69, 98, 123, 126–8, 133–5, 145–51

Logos, I, 129, 132, 178; II, 13, § 46, 146